FROM KNOWLEDGE MANAGEMENT TO STRATEGIC COMPETENCE

Assessing Technological, Market and Organisational Innovation

Third Edition

Series on Technology Management*

Series Editor: J. Tidd (Univ. of Sussex, UK) ISSN 0219-9823

Published

*For the complete list of titles in this series, please write to the Publisher.

SERIES ON TECHNOLOGY MANAGEMENT – VOL. 19

FROM KNOWLEDGE MANAGEMENT TO STRATEGIC COMPETENCE

Assessing Technological, Market and Organisational Innovation

Third Edition

editor

Joe Tidd

SPRU, University of Sussex, UK

Imperial College Press

ICP

Published by

Imperial College Press
57 Shelton Street
Covent Garden
London WC2H 9HE

Distributed by

World Scientific Publishing Co. Pte. Ltd.
5 Toh Tuck Link, Singapore 596224
USA office: 27 Warren Street, Suite 401-402, Hackensack, NJ 07601
UK office: 57 Shelton Street, Covent Garden, London WC2H 9HE

British Library Cataloguing-in-Publication Data
A catalogue record for this book is available from the British Library.

Series on Technology Management — Vol. 19
FROM KNOWLEDGE MANAGEMENT TO STRATEGIC COMPETENCE
Assessing Technological, Market and Organisational Innovation
(Third Edition)

Copyright © 2012 by Imperial College Press

ISBN-13 978-1-84816-883-1
ISBN-10 1-84816-883-7
ISBN-13 978-1-84816-884-8 (pbk)
ISBN-10 1-84816-884-5 (pbk)

Typeset by Stallion Press
Email: enquiries@stallionpress.com

Printed in Singapore by World Scientific Printers.

Preface to the Third Edition

Innovation is about creating, capturing and combining knowledge — creating new possibilities through combining different knowledge sets. These can be in the form of knowledge about what is technically possible or what particular configuration of this would meet an articulated or latent need. Such knowledge may already exist in our experience, based on something we have seen or done before. Or it could result from a process of search — research into technologies, markets, competitor actions and other environmental change. And it could be in explicit form, codified in such a way that others can access it, discuss it, transfer it, or it can be in tacit form, known about but not actually put into words or formulae (Bessant and Tidd, 2011; Tidd and Bessant, 2009). The central contribution of knowledge and competencies to organizational effectiveness has long been recognized, but is still not well understood (Keupp *et al.*, 2012). In her pioneering work, Edith Penrose began to explore the relationships between internal resources, external opportunities and long-term strategic success:

"The productive activities of such a firm are governed by what we shall call its 'productive opportunities', which comprise all of the productive possibilities that its 'entrepreneurs' see and can take advantage of. A theory of growth of firms is essentially an examination of the changing productive opportunity of firms …it is never the *resources* themselves that are 'inputs' in the production process, but only the *services* that the resources can render. The services yielded by resources are a function of the way in which they are used — exactly the same resource when used for different purposes or in different ways and in combination with different types or amounts of other resources provides a different service or set of services" (Penrose, 1959, pp. 25–31, emphasis in original).

There continues to be much interest in the business and academic communities in the concept of strategic competencies or core capabilities, that is, how organizations define and differentiate themselves. More recently, this movement has fragmented into a number of related fields with subtle differences in focus: knowledge management — concerned with how organizations identify, share and exploit their internal competencies, in particular the knowledge of individuals; organizational learning — on the relationship between individual and organizational knowledge and how organizations "unlearn" past competencies and acquire new competencies; strategic management — how competencies can be assessed, and how these contribute to performance; and innovation management — on how such competencies are translated into new processes, products, and services. The current fashion for open innovation does not contradict this focus on internal knowledge and competencies, as these are needed to identify, adapt and exploit external sources of innovation (Trott and Hartmann, 2009; Mowery, 2009).

We believe that this fragmentation and increasing specialization of academic research is counterproductive, and makes it more difficult to provide clear guidance for managers on how to identify, measure, build and exploit strategic competencies. This book attempts to re-establish the links between strategic competencies, knowledge management, organizational learning and innovation management, in an effort to establish a more coherent and integrated framework for future academic research and business practice. We adopt a practical, but rigorous, approach to the subject. Contributors include leading researchers and consultants from the field. We focus on the measurement, management and improvement of organizational, technological and market competencies and, where possible, identify the relationships with strategic, operational and financial performance. In this third edition, we have five new chapters which feature the latest research, and have updated the rest.

In Part I, we begin with a review of the relationships between strategic competencies, innovation management and diversification, and argue that we need to re-integrate these fields in order to better understand and manage organizations. Specifically, we need to be able to operationalize or measure competencies and knowledge before we can model learning and innovation. Richard Hall follows with a review of the resource-based view of the firm and breaks down strategic competencies into four component capabilities: regulatory, positional, functional and cultural. Regulatory capabilities include contracts, patents and licences. Positional capabilities include reputation, distribution and supply chains and external networks. Functional capabilities include employee and supplier know-how and skills in research and development (R&D), operations, marketing and finance. Cultural capabilities include the ability to work in teams, a tradition of customer service and the ability to manage change and innovation. In each case, he makes the distinction between tangible and intangible assets. Based on his own experience and a survey of firms, he argues that it is the intangible resources which contribute most. This provides a link between strategic competencies and knowledge management. Ellonen *et al.* study the development of capabilities over time, and show how different types of dynamic capabilities, sensing, seizing and reconfiguring, have an impact of the development of market and technological capabilities.

In Part II, Tony Clayton and Graham Turner describe the PIMS (Profit Impact of Market Strategy) approach to measuring and improving market-based competencies, and provide empirical evidence and case studies of the significance of brand development and maintenance. Ciaran Driver and I extend the analysis and develop a model to link measures of technological and market competencies with financial performance based on an analysis of 40 firms. We demonstrate that whilst there appears to be no significant relationship between innovation and profitability at the level of the firm, there is strong evidence that measures of technological and market innovation have a significant effect on both short-term financial measures — such as value-added — and longer-term measures of financial performance, such as the market to book value. David Tranfield and co-authors use an empirical study of four firms to link the fields of knowledge management and innovation. They develop a framework which comprises eight generic routines: search, capture, articulate, contextualize, apply, evaluate, support and re-innovate. This can be applied to external sources of knowledge, including customers and collaborative organizations.

In Part III, we examine the role and measurement of technological competencies. Pari Patel reviews the range of measures available and discusses their relative merits, including R&D spending, patents, product announcements and innovation surveys. He assesses the relationship between firm size and technological performance, as well as the impact of technological activities on firm performance. He concludes by presenting an analysis of the technological specialization and performance of a sample of 440 firms based on patent activity. Francis Narin continues the assessment of technological competencies by bibliometric (publication) and patent analysis, specifically by means of the Tech-Line®database of more than 1,000 leading firms, universities and agencies in 26 industry groups in 30 technology areas, over 10 years. For each organization, the assessment is based on nine technology indicators, including the number and quality of patents and technological and science strength. Donald Hislop completes this section, with a study of how communities of practice and innovation processes interact in the implementation of organization-wide technological process innovations such as ERP (Enterprise Resource Planning), based on seven case studies.

In Part IV, we focus on the assessment of internal and external organizational competencies. Brion *et al.* examine how organizational context influences innovation ambidexterity. Based on a dataset of 108 large firms, they show that competencies have a strong moderating effect. Firms combining exploration innovation and exploitation innovation adopt long-term practices that favour risk taking and creativity, and thereby build an organizational suited to innovation ambidexterity. Jonathan Sapsed develops the notion of "knowledge bases" which applies to complex, multi-technology companies. He uses this to explore the classic tension in organizations between the needs of functional specialization and project co-ordination. He examines attempts to re-organize in two high-technology firms, and concludes that firms should challenge simplistic prescriptions of organization design, and need to consider likely losses as well as the potential benefits. In the final chapter in this section, Teichert and Bouncken investigate the capabilities required to support supplier–customer integration and innovation. Analysis of a survey of 241 suppliers illustrates that there are two strategic types, and that two dynamic capabilities contribute to success, the planning capability and the innovation orientation.

In Part V, we explore how organizations can improve their existing capabilities and, where necessary, develop new competencies. Ahmed and Zairi review a range of performance measures which aim to promote improvement and innovation, and illustrate these with case studies.

John Bessant provides a practical guide to organizational learning by describing the organizational routines which support the process of continuous improvement: experimentation, experience, reflection and conceptualization. Throughout, there is a strong emphasis on formal, documented processes and measurement. Based on his research, he presents a reference model against which an organization can benchmark, as well as a developmental model to enable an organization to improve its performance. Finally, Michael Hopkins, Paul Nightingale and I develop and illustrate the notion of generative interaction which describes a series of mechanisms that produce a self-reinforcing relationship between capability-development, innovation and value-creation. However, we also observe the opposite dynamics of self-reinforcing degenerative interaction, which can produce a cycle of declining innovation and performance.

Joe Tidd
SPRU, University of Sussex
Brighton, UK
January 2012

Contents

Part I

STRATEGIC COMPETENCIES

Chapter 1

Dynamic Capability and Diversification

Javad Noori
Sharif University of Technology, Iran

Joe Tidd
SPRU, University of Sussex, UK

Mohammed R. Arasti
Sharif University of Technology, Iran

Introduction

Dynamic capabilities are central to innovation strategy (Bessant and Tidd, 2011; Keupp *et al.*, 2012), and yet, despite 20 years of development and many theoretical contributions, the conceptualization, operationalization, and application of the resource-based and dynamic capabilities views of strategic management remains problematic. For instance, there is no consensus definition of dynamic capabilities. There are various and occasionally contrary theories and explanations for diversification of firms (Cantwell *et al.*, 2004). Practitioners also face significant challenges in determining diversification strategy and practice. These challenges become more fundamental when we consider firms in different contexts, e.g. stage of firm's growth, firm size, characteristics of industry, development level of country, and corporate mission (Khanna and Palepu, 1997; Zhao, 2009). While resources are core elements in linking and co-ordinating strategy dimensions (Collis and Montgomery, 1998), there has been less research linking specific firm resources and capabilities with the ability to create and implement diversification strategies (Seppanen, 2009). In addition, there has been limited success in translating the concepts and research into management prescriptions and practice (Wijngaarde, 2008).

In this introductory chapter we have three primary aims. First, to review the related literature on resource-based, dynamic capabilities and diversification views, in order to better identify linkages and challenges. Secondly, to develop a conceptual framework that better integrates these three concepts, and therefore contributes towards operationalization, research, and practice. Finally, we test the utility of this framework by applying it to the case of a large multi-technology and multi-business industrial company which has undertaken apparently unrelated diversification over many decades. The chapter structure follows this logic: in the first section we propose a typology of resources and represent definitions and functions of dynamic capability. Then we review the literature on content and process dimensions of business diversification. The second section develops a new framework to help explain how technology-based business diversification, non-technological business diversification, and context influence business diversification. The final empirical section tests the proposed approach by applying it to the case of an industrial multi-business corporation.

Literature Review

The generic literature of corporate strategy is characterized by a diverse range of competing theories and alternative perspectives. Among these, four generic perspectives are dominant: industrial organization; game theory; resource-based view (RBV); and dynamic capabilities view (DCV) (Verburg *et al.*, 2006). Both industrial organization and game theory approaches assume technology and other resources are exogenous factors to be incorporated in order to gain competitive advantage through the deployment of generic strategies (Porter, 1980, 1985). In contrast, the RBV and DCV define resources as aspects that induce the development of the strategy of the firm. Resources play an important role within the recognition and definition of competencies and capabilities. The translation of technology into business is important and recognized as crucial within the strategy process (De Wit and Meyer, 2005), in particular within large, multi-business firms (Trott *et al.*, 2009). Consequently, we believe that RBV and DCV are the most appropriate approaches to investigate the corporate-level strategies like business diversification. We review the RBV and DCV literature and related work on business diversification in the two next sections.

RBV and DCV

The RBV proposes that competitive advantage is primarily driven by a firm's valuable, rare, inimitable, and non-substitutable resources (Barney, 2001, 2002). The underlying assumption is that resources are heterogeneous across organizations and that this heterogeneity can sustain competitiveness over time.

Penrose (1959) provided initial insights into the resource perspective of the firm. Wang and Ahmed (2007) note that the RBV was first proposed by Wernerfelt (1984) and subsequently popularized by Barney (1991). Many authors (e.g. Zollo and Winter, 2000; Eisenhardt and Martin, 2000; Winter, 2003) have since made significant contributions to its conceptual development. Although the RBV as a theoretical framework helps to explain how firms achieve competitive advantage and create value, it does not adequately detail how firms do that in the context of fast-changing environments (Lockett *et al.*, 2009). The value of resources will depend on context, and their change and adaptations often lag behind environmental changes (Teece *et al.*, 1997). In rapidly changing markets, a dominant focus on core resources may create rigidities that prevent firms from adapting their resources to the new competitive environment (Leonard-Barton, 1992).

As a result, the RBV has been refined to the DCV, in which capabilities augment the role of resource to "integrate, build and reconfigure internal and external competencies to address rapidly changing environments" (Teece *et al.*, 1997). From this perspective, firms must adapt, integrate, and reconfigure their resources and competencies continuously in response to changing market conditions. Whilst some scholars assert that the resource-based view includes dynamic capabilities (Furrer and Goussevskaia, 2008), the strategy literature generally considers dynamic capabilities as a complement to the RBV, but shares similar assumptions (Wang and Ahmed, 2007; Furrer *et al.*, 2008). Therefore, it is important to more clearly differentiate the concepts of resources and dynamic capabilities, and the relationship between them.

Resources are stocks of available factors that are *owned, controlled,* or *accessed on a preferential basis* by the firm (Amit and Schoemaker, 1993;

Collis, 1994; Helfat *et al.*, 2007). Resources can be in *having* (stock) or *doing* (flow) forms (Hall, 1992, 1993; Katkalo *et al.*, 2010). "Having" resources are both tangible — like location, material, building, inventory, machinery, and low-skill people — and less tangible — like patents, databases, licenses, brand, and copyright. These resources are normally available to most firms, tradable in the market, and exogenous. In contrast, "doing" resources are intangible — skill-based, firm specific, not tradable in market — and endogenous. Examples of "doing" resources are capabilities incorporated in organizational and managerial processes, like product development, technology development, and marketing.

Capabilities refer to the organization's potential for carrying out a specific activity or set of activities (Fernandez *et al.*, 2000; Galbreath, 2005). Collis (1994), while noting that it is difficult to categorize capabilities, presents three categories: abilities that help in performing *basic functional activities* of the firm; abilities that help in *dynamically improving the activities* of the firm; and abilities involving strategic insights that can help firms *recognize the intrinsic value* of their resources and develop novel strategies ahead of their competitors (Katkalo *et al.*, 2010). He also distinguishes between a *first category of capabilities*, which reflect an ability to perform the basic functional activities of the firm, and a *second category of capabilities*, which deal with the dynamic improvement to the activities of the firm. Zollo and Winter (2002) and Winter (2003) also differentiate between *operational (zero-order)* and *dynamic (first-order)* capabilities. Operational capabilities are geared towards the operational functioning of the firm, including both staff and line activities; these are *"how we earn a living now"* capabilities. Dynamic capabilities are dedicated to the modification of operational capabilities and lead, for example, to changes in the firm's products or production processes. This classification has increasingly been adopted in recent models of dynamic capabilities (e.g. Helfat and Peteraf, 2003; Zahra *et al.*, 2006).

Aggregation of resources gives another insight to resource classification. Assets are disaggregated and undifferentiated inputs to organization, while competencies and core competencies are more aggregated and leveraged types of resources. Core capabilities are also an aggregated and leveraged bundle of lower operational capabilities. For instance, system integration is a core capability that includes many operational capabilities, like project

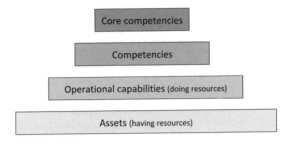

Fig. 1.   Resource base of the company, a hierarchical classification.

management, product and process development, marketing, and technology management (Praest, 1998; Blum, 2004; Ljungquist, 2007). Authors have proposed a schematic framework for resource classification (Fig. 1).

The dynamic capabilities view originates in spirit from Schumpeter's (1934) innovation-based competition where competitive advantage is based on the creative destruction of existing resources and novel recombination into new operational capabilities. These ideas were further developed in the literature, such as architectural innovation (Henderson and Clark, 1990), configuration competence, and combinative capabilities (Kogut and Zander, 1992). Extending these studies, Teece *et al.*'s (1990) working chapter is widely accepted as the first contribution developing explicitly the notion of *"dynamic capabilities"*. Despite being one of the most widely used and cited concepts, the central construct of dynamic capabilities is not well or universally defined. Teece *et al.*'s original definition as "the firm's ability to integrate, build, and reconfigure internal and external competencies to address rapidly changing environments" is rather broad and difficult to operationalize, so many authors have since offered their own definitions of dynamic capabilities (Table 1).

Some other scholars indicate the *functions* of dynamic capability without defining the DCV directly. In other words, they ask "what does dynamic capability do?" instead of "what is dynamic capability?" Different functional interpretations include:

- Inside-out capabilities, outside-in capabilities, and spanning capabilities (Day, 1994);
- reconfiguration processes, leveraging existing resources, learning, and creative integration (Ambrosini and Bowman, 2009);

Table 1.   Dynamic capabilities: Definitions and functions.

Study	Definition and functions
Teece *et al.*, 1990; working chapter.	The firm is somewhat richer than the standard resource-based view ... it is not only the bundle of resources that matter, but the mechanisms by which firms *learn* and *accumulate* new skills and capabilities, and the forces that limit the rate and direction of this process.
Teece and Pisano, 1994; first formal published chapter on DCV.	The subset of the competencies and capabilities that allow the firm to *create* new products and processes and *respond* to changing market circumstances.
Teece *et al.*, 1997.	The firm's ability to *integrate, build,* and *reconfigure* internal and external competencies to address rapidly changing environments.
Eisenhardt and Martin, 2000.	The firm's processes that *use* resources — specifically the processes to *integrate, reconfigure, gain,* and *release* resources — to *match* and even *create* market change; dynamic capabilities thus are the organizational and strategic routines by which firms *achieve new resource configurations* as markets emerge, collide, split, evolve, and die.
Teece, 2000.	The ability to *sense* and then *seize* opportunities quickly and proficiently.
Zollo and Winter, 2002.	A learned and stable pattern of collective activity through which the organization systematically *generates* and *modifies* its operating routines in pursuit of improved effectiveness.
Winter, 2003.	Those (capabilities) that operate to *extend, modify,* or *create* ordinary capabilities.
Zahra *et al.*, 2006	The abilities to *reconfigure* a firm's resources and routines in the manner envisioned and deemed appropriate by its principal decision maker(s).
Helfat *et al.*, 2007	The capacity of an organization to purposefully *create, extend,* or *modify* its resource base.
Wang and Ahmed, 2007.	A firm's behavioural orientation constantly to *integrate, reconfigure, renew,* and *recreate* its resources and capabilities and, most importantly, *upgrade* and *reconstruct* its core capabilities in response to the changing environment to attain and sustain competitive advantage.
Teece, 2007.	Dynamic capabilities can be disaggregated into the capacity (a) to *sense and shape* opportunities and threats, (b) to *seize* opportunities, and (c) to maintain competitiveness through *enhancing, combining, protecting,* and, when necessary, *reconfiguring* the business enterprise's intangible and tangible assets.
Lockett *et al.*, 2009.	The ability to continuously *adapt* and *reconfigure* a resource and capability base.
Pavlou and Sawy, 2011.	Capabilities that help units extend, modify, and reconfigure their existing operational capabilities into new ones that better match the changing environment.

- adaptive capability, absorptive capability, and innovative capability (Wang and Ahmed, 2007);
- de-linking and re-linking (Danneels, 2007);
- sensing and shaping opportunities and threats, seizing opportunities, and maintaining competitiveness through enhancing, combining, protecting, and, when necessary, reconfiguring the business enterprise's intangible and tangible assets (Teece, 2007);
- sensing, seizing, and transforming (Katkalo *et al.*, 2010);
- adaptation (Ellonen *et al.*, 2011);
- sensing, learning, co-ordinating, and integrating (Pavlou and Sawy, 2011).

For the purpose of this chapter we define dynamic capability as "the ability of the organization to continuously recognize, integrate, and leverage resources and connect them to the changing environment in order *to create value*".

This definition is similar to others but with some important differences. The first is that the definition should distinguish the DCV from other perspectives, so the dynamic feature is reflected by "... *continuously* ... *changing* ..." terms. By these terms we mean that dynamic capability needs to be ongoing, sensitive, and proactive to time and environment changes. This includes the emphasis on recognition to identify relevant resources and opportunities. The second distinction is the reference to *resources* instead of competencies and capabilities, which we consider as a more general term that includes assets, capabilities, and competencies (Table 2). The third aspect is *connection to environment*, without which resources cannot be translated to *create value*. Resources and capabilities are not an end in themselves, but a means to an end.

Business diversification

Corporate diversification consists of two levels: (i) *corporate diversification* that selects the mix of businesses, and (ii) *corporate management* that enhances the value of this mix (Goold *et al.*, 1994).

The content or know-what of business diversification starts by classi-fication and looking for "boundaries" of a business: that managers draw meaningful delineation lines in the environment, distinguishing one arena

Table 2.   Comparison of different resources.

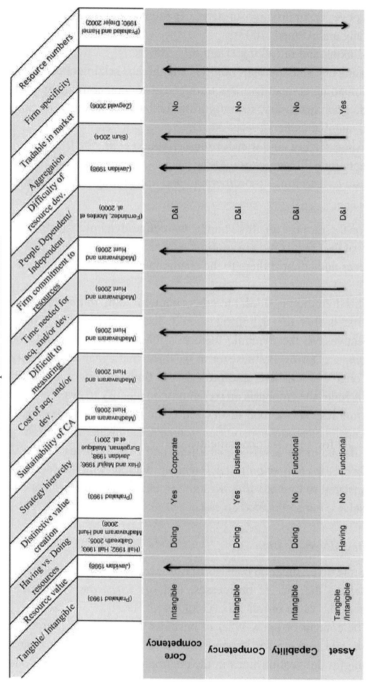

of business from another. Ideally, the environment would be made up of neatly compartmentalized businesses, with clear borders separating them. In reality, however, the situation is more complex. In order to delineate corporate businesses and clarify diversification, we need to identify and assess a range of different dimensions. These include industry, technology, value chain, product, service, market, and application. However, we can group these into two main components: supply component and demand component. The supply side emphasizes internal characteristics of the business such as inputs, processes, value chain, and products, whereas the demand side captures external features such as the market, product, and services. Product, as a connection point between supply side and demand side, is in both components. While supply side points to competencies of the business, demand side includes external and market features of the business. Therefore, we use competency and market as two main dimensions of each business (Fig. 2) (Lichtenthaler, 2005).

Competency and market sides match two main approaches in strategic management: RBV/DCV as inside-out or supply side, and positioning as outside-in or demand side approaches, respectively. We emphasize inside-out approaches that undertake competency or supply side, but consider market area too if market change affects competencies and activity systems considerably. These components indicate that changes in competency and/or market area steer the corporation to a new business area.

Based on the above classification of businesses, the following matrix is proposed for business diversification.

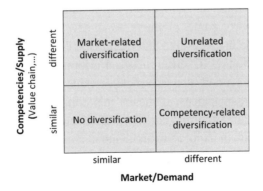

Fig. 2. The content of business diversification.

We define a business as "a group of competency-market related activities that create specific value for customers". This definition implies that:

- The main entity and the nature of business is activity, not sale, income, product, and so on. Therefore, each activity group potentially is a business.
- Grouping activities or determining relatedness is done in terms of business areas: competency and market. By changing the competency and/or market, the company diversifies its business area.
- Value creation is a cornerstone of the business concept. Each business should create a type of value to the customer. Value is not only in monetary terms, but also includes non-monetary types like social welfare, strategic values, job creation, power making, and technology upgrading. For instance, if a company enters a new group of activities that makes a sustainable and strategic advantage without short-term financial gains, it is assumed that this company diversifies to a new business area.
- Most significantly, we distinguish between "relatedness" in diversification and the "basis" of diversification. Relatedness reveals the linkages and commonalities among businesses (competency and market areas), whereas basis concepts (like resource-based and technology-based diversification) rationalize the why and how of diversification. In other words, while relatedness reveals the *content* of business diversification, basis explains the *process* of business diversification.
- Extensions of market without any organizational implications do not qualify for business diversification. For instance, if a car manufacturing company exports some products to a new market or establishes a production line in a new area that requires: (i) new product, process, and system technologies; (ii) different systems for production, logistics, after-sale, and finance; and also (iii) dictates value creation and competition under new circumstances, it means this company has diversified to a new business area (competency-related diversification). In contrast, if this type of growth happens in an identical situation to the home country products, processes, and systems, we assert that the company has not diversified to a new business area, even if it has extended its market in terms of marketing terminology.

There is extensive theoretical and empirical literature on the process of business diversification from various disciplines (Chiesa and Manzini, 1997; Forcadell, 2007). We can categorize this literature into two broad groups: (i) diversifications that are based on common resources and linkages or general commonalities between corporate businesses, and (ii) diversifications that are based on corporate resources as the whole or the corporate centre (parent). We refer to these processes as type 1 and 2 diversification, respectively.

For type 1, the rationale for diversification is based on the concept of "relatedness" between the different businesses of a diversified corporation. Certain types of relatedness can be identified, integrated, leveraged, and connected to environment. Relatedness includes the "traditional" approach to *operational linkages* (e.g. common areas of production lines, buyers, distribution channels, and equipments) and *market linkages* (e.g. complementary products and system solutions) as proposed by industrial economists. Another form of relatedness is by competence and technology, emphasized in the RBV and DCV. Type 2 business diversification is based on corporatelevel resources, like *market power* (e.g. cross subsidization and reciprocal buying arrangements); *generic and contact capabilities*; *dominant logic, cognitive, and entrepreneurship aspects of corporate management*; *brand, reputational, and positional advantage*; and *institutional power*. We can use these distinctions to propose a resource-based framework of business diversification.

A New Framework for Business Diversification

The main attributes of the two types of diversification processes are displayed in Table 3.

The driver of diversification is different in each case. Cross-business resources like operational linkages, market linkages, and technological competencies drive type 1. The resources of this category are mainly technological ones that point out the multi-tech nature of products and businesses. Technological competencies in type 1 are emphasized in literature and named technology-based or competence-based business diversification (TbBD and CbBD) (Chiesa and Manzini, 1997). In the TbBD process, the corporation creates a core competency by integrating

Table 3.   Characteristics of diversification in different processes.

Process of diversification	Div. logic	Driver resources for diversification	Driver resources	Direction of div. process	Emphasis on	Locus of driver resource	Tech. relatedness of diversified businesses
Type 1	Common resources among businesses	Resources like: operational linkages; market linkages; and technological competencies	Mainly technological resources (TbBD)	Inside-out	Competencies and supply side	Business units	Mainly related
Type 2	Specific resources of corporate or driver business	Resources like: market power; generic and contact capabilities; dominant logic, cognitive, and entrepreneurship aspects of corporate management; brand, reputational, and positional advantage; institutional power	Non-technological resources	Outside-in (market)	Market, environment and demand side	Mainly corporate centre and parent	Mainly unrelated
cRbBD	Type 1 + Type 2	Various resources		Both directions		Both businesses and corporate	Related/ Unrelated

and leveraging technology and other related "having" and "doing" resources and creates value by transforming into new businesses. In contrast, type 2 diversification is based on resources like market power, brand, and contact capabilities, which are non-technological resources. While many cases are pure type 1 or pure type 2, there are some examples that are driven by both processes simultaneously. We call this combined resource-based business diversification (cRbBD).

TbBD is the main form of type 1 category. In the TbBD process, identification of technological resources is the starting point, followed by the integration with complementary assets, capabilities, and competencies, pushing them to the core competency position capable of allowing the company to enter a new business area. This entry is from the industrial side of diversified business, either by process or product technologies. Technological resources are embodied in assets, capabilities, and competencies and are vital to this type of diversification process. Without these resources, the company cannot drive the dynamic capability from technology to business diversification.

However, some resources are non-technological and belong mainly to the corporation as a whole or the corporate parent. These resources typically drive type 2 business diversification. Examples are positional advantages, contact capabilities, brand, political and institutional power, dominant logic, market power, and reputational assets. Diversification based on these resources has a different story from TbBD. Corporations having dynamic capabilities are able to recognize non-technological competencies on one hand, and sense the opportunities of the environment on the other hand. Then they integrate and leverage these resources and connect them to the environment by entering a new business area. While there are a lot of pure type 1 and type 2 cases, there are also examples of diversification based on both technological/internal and non-technological/external resources. In the cRbBD process, both types of resource are critical and both parent company and related business unit participate actively in the diversification process.

A Case of Resource-based Business Diversification

This section applies the framework we have developed to the case of a large multi-technology and diversified business, Iran Khodro Company (IKCO).

IKCO was established on 19 March 1963, and is now Iran's largest industrial conglomerate and the largest auto producer in the Middle East and Africa. In 2009, IKCO had the highest level of sales (US$11.7 million), highest level of job creation (60,388 personnel), and second position in profitability (US$1.7 million). When production of the Hillman Hunter ceased in the UK in 1979, Peugeot Citroën (by then in control of Chrysler's former operations in Europe) began negotiations to sell the rights to the marque and the manufacturing plant to IKCO. The agreement was sealed in 1985 and the production line at Linwood, Scotland, was dismantled and shipped to Iran. As part of the deal, Peugeot Citroën also sold 65,000 engines to Iran. IKCO is famous in the domestic market with its first product, the so-called Paykan (1978 to 2005), a simple flagship passenger car. The company's product line is presently complemented by the Peugeot 405 model in a number of variants, and the 206, launched in 1990 and 2001, respectively. The former has local-parts integration close to 80%, while the 206 is exported by Peugeot in complete knock-down (CKD)-form.

IKCO has diversified away from its automotive beginning, and is now active in various businesses like oil, rail, power generation, banking, part manufacturing, construction and mining, after-sale, and repair. We consider here only four businesses for the purpose of testing our framework. Type 1 would include the first three businesses, and the banking business is type 2. All of these are unrelated businesses to IKCO's core business (car manufacturing). The businesses in type 1 include highly different resources for inputs, technological skills, hardware, value chain, production process, and products, compared to the automotive industry. Therefore, the similarity of these industries is very low. These businesses also have high dissimilarity on the market side, with different customers, competition level, environmental challenges, regulating rules, and political influences from the automotive market.

The type 2 category of business is the banking business of IKCO: BB. This business is completely different to the core automotive business in both areas of industry and market. Persian Bank Corporation is the owner of BB. The banking industry includes inputs, processes, products, technological services, physical resources, and hardware that have no similarity to automotive industry components. The market side also has this situation: features like customers, competition, business model, and

Table 4. Similarities of some business areas of IKCO to its main and original business area (automotive); 1–5.

| | | Business content | | Main business |
Row	Business name	Industry area	Market area	owner firm
1	OB (Oil Business)	2	1	TAM
2	RB (Rail Business)	3	1	TAM
3	PB (Power generating Business)	2	1	TAM
4	BB (Banking Business)	1	1	Persian Bank

KSFs are completely dissimilar to the core businesses. The comparison of these businesses' content on a scale of 1–5 is illustrated in Table 4.

Applying our framework to this case we can identify two primary resources that explain types 1 and 2 of diversification process. These resources are *industrialization* as a core competency, and *positional* resources of IKCO, respectively.

Industrialization is a core competency that has been accumulated, integrated, and leveraged from different competencies and assets, including skillful people, different types of engineering technologies, project management, organizational capabilities, and EPC capability. IKCO, in implementing the growth strategy from 76,000 to 1,000,000 units, established TAM Company in 1997 to provide and support process technologies and capabilities. IKCO appointed the TAM Company to be responsible for IKCO production capacity growth projects like assembly line, paint shop, robotic systems, logistic technologies, body in white, electrical, control, mechanical systems, press and die, maintenance and repair of production facilities, building construction, and utilities. By involvement in these projects, and based on knowledge and technology acquisition among the large internal and international network, TAM aggregated various assets and competencies and transformed them into a core competency under the dynamic capability framework. The main components of this core competency are mechanical, electric, and control technologies, general contract (GC), and electronic process control (EPC) management capabilities. This core competency developed mainly for automotive value chain industrialization, but has initiated other businesses in different industries such as oil and gas, rail, and power generation since 2004. These diversifications are mainly based on technological capability and

Table 5.   Technological basis of diversification.

Technology platform	Business						Power generation
	Automotive	Airplane	Motorcycle	Ship	Oil/gas	Railroad	
Electronics	△	△	△	△	△	△	△
ECU (Electronics, Software, Architec- ture,…)	△	△	△	△		△	
Engine (ECU, Solid mechanics, Fluid mechanics, Combus- tion,…)	△	△	△				
Automotive (Engine, Electronics, Mechanics, Suspension, Body,…)	△						

the inside-out approach. The main emphasis of these diversifications has been on internal aspects like competencies, industry, and supply, rather than external features like market and demand. The locus was in the TAM business unit rather than the IKCO Corporation as whole or parent. All three of the diversifications are related to the core business in terms of technology.

Technologies could be a source of a core competency at different levels. In other words, dynamic capability is able to generate different core competencies by starting from a different level in the technology trajectory. For instance, an automotive company could create core competencies of electronics, electronic control unit (ECU), engine, and automotive, named as platforms or generic technologies (Table 5). These platforms diversify the automotive company to various ranges of businesses, which means each degree of platform covers a varied scope of businesses. As Table 5 illustrates, basic technologies like electronics have more diversification capability than aggregated ones like engine and automotive platforms. For instance, electronic core competencies diversify the auto company to all exemplified industries, but the engine core competency does not diversify to an oil/gas and power generation business. Each platform needs its own sub-technologies. For the type 2 banking business, the main resource of IKCO is its positional advantage. IKCO is the biggest company in Iran, well known by and interesting to market players, investors, and government. This corporation has an influential position in the minds of the industrial, financial, and political players of Iran. The automotive value chain is very broad, ranging from parts-supply to after-sale and financial service to customers, and therefore provides many opportunities for diversification and growth. These are mainly non-technological and market-embedded resources that are able to initiate and drive new businesses. The banking business is based on these resources. In a similar situation to GM and GMAC in the USA, IKCO diversified to the banking business by establishing the Persian bank in 2001. This bank, as the first private bank of Iran, had first position in the banking sector and third position in the economic sector of Iran in 2010. The main aim of the Persian bank is to improve economic affairs by developing industrial activities, especially the car industry and related industries, by supplying facilities and expanding new finance tools, and also financially supporting construction, trading, and consumption industries, assets and capabilities, and to differ from other platforms.

Concluding Remarks

This study helps to integrate the theory of dynamic capabilities into the practice of business diversification. The definitions and framework we have developed and tested provide additional insights into the logic of apparently unrelated diversification. In particular, the distinction between type 1 and type 2 processes highlights the different sources and mechanisms for corporate and business-level diversification.

The main distinction between the two types of diversification helps to link the resource-based and dynamic capabilities view with the logics for diversification. While the main characteristic of type 1 is common resources among businesses (like operational linkages, market linkages, and technological competencies), type 2 diversification is based on specific resources of corporate and/or driver business (like market power, generic and contact capabilities, dominant logic, cognitive and entrepreneurship aspects of corporate management, brand, reputational and positional advantage, and institutional power).

The tautological nature of the concept of dynamic capabilities may be caused by the fact that it is frozen within theoretical firm-level derivations instead of a more operational and empirical grounding. This chapter attempts to help extend the conceptualization and operationalization of DCV, and to link this to business diversification. The framework we propose can be used to differentiate types of resources, and identify their contribution to the direction of diversification.

In this chapter we have applied our framework to help interpret the diversification pattern of a large multi-technology business over time. Whilst this illustrates the additional utility of the framework, further testing is necessary in a wider range of contexts. Qualitative studies may reveal more about the process of diversification, whereas quantitative research may identify the relationships between different types of resource and diversification strategies and paths.

Acknowledgements

The study would have been impossible without the support of the IKCO grant, the case study of IKCO group (including IKCO division, TAM, SAPCO, IKCO Diesel, ISACO, and IKIDO) and the close participation and involvement of managers and experts in interviews and discussions. The authors gratefully acknowledge the aforementioned people and are also grateful to two anonymous professors of SPRU.

Chapter 2

What are Strategic Competencies?

Richard Hall
University of Newcastle, UK

Introduction

Prior to becoming an academic, the author spent 14 years running a company manufacturing consumer products. For 12 years, the company was successful. Then it took two years to die. Whilst it was dying, it was perfectly obvious what was wrong; when it was successful, the management team did not ask, let alone answer, the question: "What are the sources of our success?" This experience was responsible for the intellectual curiosity regarding the sources of sustainable competitive advantage which has resulted in the research activity reported here.

The concept of strategic competencies, sometimes referred to as distinctive capabilities, has received much attention from academics and practitioners in the last 10 years, especially since the publication — in 1990 — of Prahalad and Hamel's seminal article, "The core competence of the corporation". This article suggested that the most critical task for management is to create new products which customers need, but have not yet imagined, and that they should do this by creating competencies which enable the new, unanticipated products to be conceived.

Suppliers have competencies and customers have needs. Products are, from time to time, the embodiment of the means by which suppliers' competencies fulfil customers' needs. This "inside out" perspective does not replace the previous "outside in" perspective which was concerned with products and markets; it complements it. This approach, which was triggered by the Prahalad and Hamel article, broadened the strategic manager's field of view to include corporate resources as well as markets, and the approach became known as the "resource-based view" of strategy. The essence of the resource-based approach can be captured in the following apocryphal tale:

> "A small British company in the 1970s decided that it was time to start exporting to Europe. The CEO called a meeting of his management team and asked if anyone could speak any language other than English. One manager said he could speak Spanish. 'Right', said the CEO, 'We will start exporting to Spain'."

The resource-based view is concerned essentially with identifying and building on strengths, preferably those which, for whatever reason, are unique to the firm.

One major consequence of the need to focus on competencies concerns organisational structure. An organisation which is structured around strategic business units (SBUs), each of which is product/market-focused, may be inappropriate because such an organisational structure could inhibit the development of the core competencies shared by all the SBUs. For example, if surface chemistry is a core competence common to all the divisions of Proctor & Gamble, it may be that the development of this core competence is hindered by a divisional structure based on toilet preparations, drugs, detergents and so forth. This is because each division will jealously guard the resources (competencies) which it should be sharing and developing with the other divisions. This train of thought leads us to the conclusion that companies ultimately compete with competencies, not with products.

Strategic competencies produce competitive advantage. Before we explore more fully the nature and characteristics of strategic competencies, it is necessary to examine the concept of competitive advantage.

Competitive Advantage

The early writers on business strategy suggested, not unreasonably, that any organisation which operates in a competitive environment needs a competitive advantage in order to survive and prosper.

For most organisations, the competitive environment exists in the "downstream" sales market. However, it can sometimes apply in the "upstream" supply market where, for example, an ambulance service may be in competition with a fire brigade for limited financial resources.

In his book *Competitive Advantage*, Michael Porter (1985) suggested that the product of a successful strategy was a competitive advantage which could be sustained in the marketplace. Porter suggested two generic types of competitive advantage: cost leadership and differentiation. The proposition that there are only two generic types of competitive advantage was widely accepted, and taught, for many years. It was held that companies had a basic choice: a strategy of cost leadership or a strategy of differentiation; any attempt to do both was not to be encouraged!

Cost leadership was not necessarily meant to result in selling price leadership, although it was assumed that in most cases the lowest cost producer would also be a low price seller. It was argued that the large volumes which usually go with low selling prices would result in a cost leadership company continually reinforcing its advantageous position by virtue of the learning curve effect (the more one does, the better one gets at doing it) and by virtue of its superior recovery of fixed costs. While there is strong evidence that companies with above average market shares do enjoy above average return on investment (Buzzell and Gale, 1987) the causal "trail" from low price to high market share to high return on investment is by no means established as a universal law; indeed, there are many examples of once dominant companies being overtaken by new entrants.

Differentiation was defined as offering a uniqueness in the marketplace with respect to features which were widely valued by customers. To be commercially advantageous, this uniqueness has to be rewarded with a premium on the selling price which exceeded the extra costs associated with producing the differentiation.

Porter suggested that it was dangerous to attempt to pursue both cost leadership and differentiation at the same time as this would result in the company being "stuck in the middle". This claim is now largely discounted as there are examples of companies which manage to differentiate their product offerings whilst at the same time selling at low prices. One example of such a company is the John Lewis Partnership (JLP), a chain of department stores in the United Kingdom. This company manages to differentiate the products it trades by the level of service it gives to its customers — the latter being due arguably to the profit-sharing arrangements made for all its employees/partners. As well as offering a differentiated product, JLP also sells at competitive prices. Indeed, it broadcasts its selling price policy with the slogan "Never knowingly undersold".

A more pragmatic view on the nature of competitive advantage was advanced by Coyne (1986) whose argument starts with the observation that any company which is making repeat sales in a competitive market must enjoy an advantage in the eyes of the customers who are making the repeat purchases! He went on to argue that for a *sustainable* competitive advantage to exist, three conditions must apply:

(i) Customers must perceive a consistent difference in important attributes between the producer's product/service and the attributes offered by competitors.

(ii) This difference is the direct consequence of a capability gap between the producer and its competitors.

(iii) Both the difference in important attributes and the capability gap can be expected to endure over time.

This approach echoes the statement made in the introduction to the effect that suppliers have capabilities and customers have needs. In Coyne's terms, customers recognise the attributes which will satisfy their needs and these attributes are the direct consequence of the supplier's capabilities. We are now getting closer to concepts which we can operationalise because it is now possible to ask the question, "What is the nature of the package of product/delivery system attributes which customers value?", and to go on to ask the question, "What is responsible for producing the valued attributes?". The product/delivery system attributes will include factors such as price, quality, specification and image. Selling price is one, albeit important, attribute in a package of attributes. It may be paramount if customers are constrained by the price they can afford to pay, or it may be subordinate to availability if demand exceeds supply. Coyne also points out that having a low cost base — and, in consequence, higher margins — only results in a competitive advantage in the marketplace if the extra margin is used to produce new valued attributes. If the margin is reflected in higher dividend payments to shareholders, then no competitive advantage results.

It is the application of resources, not their accumulation, which results in competitive advantage.

Coyne suggests that there are four — and only four — types of resource capability:

(i) *Regulatory*. The possession of legal entities, such as patents and trademarks.
(ii) *Positional*. The results of previous endeavour, such as reputation, trust and value chain configuration.
(iii) *Business systems*. The ability to do things well, such as consistent conformance to specification.
(iv) *Organisational characteristics*. This includes the ability to manage change.

This categorisation of resources has been included in the author's technique for analysing the role of intangible resources in business success which will be presented in this chapter.

Strategic Competencies

The essence of the resource-based view of strategy is neatly captured by Nooteboom (1996):

"... the firm is made up from a number of competences, based on resources, embodied in a configuration of various forms of capital (financial, human, social), which to a greater or lesser extent is idiosyncratic to the firm. It is such unique capabilities of firms that allow them a basis for profit."

Every firm is unique by virtue of its history, value chain configuration, organisation culture and so forth. The challenge is to make the firm's uniqueness the source of its sustainable competitive advantage. The factors which constitute a firm's uniqueness are "path dependent"; they will have taken time to acquire. Mole *et al.* (1996) express the point well:

"... strategic assets are built up over time and defy imitation because they have a strong tacit content and are socially complex. Their development is so tied to the history of the firm in terms of previous levels of learning, investment and development activity that these aspects of firm resources are non-tradable. Would-be imitators are thwarted by the difficulty of discovering and repeating the developmental process and by the considerable time lag involved in attempting to do so."

In describing strategic assets, Mole *et al.* use expressions such as "tacit" and "socially complex". These are concepts which are not usually subject to the scrutiny of accountants; they are intangible resources. In this chapter, tangible assets are identified as those which are normally represented on a balance sheet and intangible assets are those characteristics of a firm which usually cannot be represented on a balance sheet, but which are held to be the source of the firm's future earning capability. If, as is often the case, a firm's market capitalisation is a multiple of five, or even ten, times its balance sheet net worth, this means that the stock market's assessment of the value of the company places between four-fifths and nine-tenths of the value "off balance sheet". This is held to represent the company's future earning capability. The point is well expressed by Baxter (1984):

"A simple mind could hardly entertain the notion of intangible assets. In a child's tale, wealth is castles, land, flocks, gold — i.e., physical things. It is a long step forward to realise that the essence of wealth is the prospect of benefits, not their physical source."

From the foregoing, we can see that the important characteristics of strategic competencies are as follows:

(i) They are responsible for delivering a significant benefit to customers.
(ii) They are idiosyncratic to the firm.
(iii) They take time to acquire.
(iv) They are sustainable because they are difficult and time-consuming to imitate.
(v) They comprise *configurations* of resources.
(vi) They have a strong tacit content and are socially complex — they are the product of experiential learning.

This chapter will explore these characteristics and discuss how strategic competences may be identified, sustained, enhanced and leveraged.

"Find the Hero Inside Yourself"

This section will describe the technique for analysing intangible resources which the author has developed and validated. It is based on the identification and development of the strengths in the key product/delivery system attributes and the intangible resources which produce them.

The valued attributes

As Coyne has pointed out, any company which is making repeat sales in a competitive market has an advantage in the eyes of the customers who are making the repeat purchases. The nature of the advantage may be defined in terms of a package of product/delivery attributes. The identification of the key attributes and their relative weighting can be done by market research or by Delphi panels of relevant executives. Examples of product/delivery system attributes are shown in Table 1.

It may be necessary to identify different rankings for different categories of customers, such as new versus long-standing customers and retailers versus end users. In carrying out this analysis of attributes, it is appropriate to seek consensus between the relevant executives with respect to questions such as:

(i)   Can executives agree on an importance weighting for each attribute?
(ii) Can executives agree on a benchmark score for each attribute compared with the competition?
(iii) Can executives agree on the *sustainability* of the advantage represented by each attribute?

The degree of congruence, or dissonance, in executives' perceptions of these issues can in itself be illuminating. In addition to identifying the current strengths in the marketplace, it is also appropriate at this stage to identify known deficiencies in the product offering.

In the research carried out to date, the firms which dealt directly with end users tended to emphasise availability — buses must run to time, retail

Table 1.   Typical product/delivery system attributes which define sales advantage.

Image. What is the image of the product range? Is it important?

Price. Is a low selling price a key buying criterion?

User-friendliness. Is it important for the product to be user-friendly?

Availability. Is product range availability crucial?

Rapid response to enquiry. Is it important to produce designs, quotations and so forth very quickly?

Quick response to customer demand. Will sales be lost to the competition if they respond more quickly than you?

Width of product range. Is it important to offer a wide range of products and/or services to customers?

New product to market time. How important is the product development time?

Quality — the product's fitness for purpose. Does the product, or service, deliver exactly the benefits which the customers want?

Quality — the consistent achievement of defined specification. Is constant conformance to specifications vital?

Safety. Is safety in use a major concern?

Regulatory requirements. Does meeting regulatory requirements earlier/better than the competition give a competitive advantage?

Degree of innovation. Is it important for the product or service to represent "state of the art"?

Ability to vary product specification. Is it important to produce product or service modifications easily and quickly?

Ability to vary product valume. Is important to be able to increase, or decrease, production volume easily?

Customer service. Is the quality of the overall service which customers receive a key to winning business?

Pre- and after-sales service. Is the supply of advice, spares and so forth a key aspect of winning business?

---

outlets must be in the right location and stock the products which customers expect to find, firms engaged in manufacturing tended to emphasise quality. Is the product "fit for purpose", and do the products consistently conform to specification?

The intangible resources which produce the valued attributes

While it is possible for a valued product/delivery system attribute to be the result of a tangible asset, such as a building or a specialist manufacturing capability, the majority of the executives participating in the research have to date identified intangible resources, such as product reputation, employee know-how and so forth as the factors most often responsible for producing the attributes which are valued by customers.

The resources which produce product/delivery system attributes may be placed in a framework of capabilities derived from Coyne's work. This framework places resources into four categories as shown below:

(i) *The regulatory capability.* Resources which are legal entities:

    (a) Tangible, on balance sheet, assets.

    (b) Intangible, off balance sheet, assets, such as patents, licences, trademarks, contracts and protectable data.

(ii) *The positional capability.* Resources which are not legal entities and are the result of previous endeavour, that is, with a high path dependency:

    (a) Reputation of company.

    (b) Reputation of product.

    (c) Corporate networks.

    (d) Personal networks.

    (e) Unprotectable data.

    (f) Distribution network.

    (g) Supply chain network.

    (h) Formal and informal operating systems.

    (i) Processes.

(iii) *The functional capability.* This comprises resources which are either individual skills and know-how or team skills and know-how, within the company, at the suppliers or distributors:

    (a) Employee know-how and skills in operations, finance, marketing and R&D.

    (b) Supplier know-how.

    (c) Distributor know-how.

    (d) Professional advisors' expertise.

(iv) *The cultural capability.* This comprises resources which are the characteristics of the organisation:

    (a) Perception of quality standards.

    (b) Tradition of customer service.

    (c) Ability to manage change.

(d) Ability to innovate.
(e) Teamworking ability.
(f) Ability to develop staff, suppliers and distributors.
(g) Automatic response mechanisms.

The identification of the intangibles responsible for each key product attribute results in a summary, such as that shown in Table 2.

The resources which occur frequently in the body of the matrix are those which, either by themselves, or in combination with others, are the company's strategic competencies.

Development scenarios

Having identified the key intangible resources, it is appropriate to examine development scenarios in terms of protection, sustenance, enhancement and leverage. Some of the results of the empirical work which has been carried out using this approach by Hall (1992, 1993b) are summarised in the next section.

Table 2.   An example of the matrix of attributes and resources.

Key product/ delivery attributes	The resources which produce, or do not produce, the key attributes:			
	Regulatory capability	Positional capability	Functional capability	Cultural capability
Strengths				
1. e.g. availability		Value chain configuration	Forecasting skills	
2. e.g. quality				High perception of quality
3. e.g. specification	Patent "abc"		Technology "xyz"	
etc.				
Weaknesses				
1.				
2.				
Summary of the key resources				

The Results of Empirical Work on the Role of Intangible Assets

A national survey into the contribution which intangible assets make to business success

Ninety-five CEOs answered the question, "What contribution does each of the listed factors make to the success of the business?" The six most important factors are shown below, the first five being intangible assets:

Rank	Intangible asset
1	Company reputation
2	Product reputation
3	Employee know-how
4	Organisational culture
5	Personal networks
6	Specialist physical resources

The ranking was independent of sector and company performance. The value in this finding is not that successful companies rate "reputation" as being important while unsuccessful companies do not; the value is in the wide acceptance of the important contribution which "off balance sheet items" make to corporate success.

The section of the questionnaire relating to employee know-how contained a sub-section regarding the most important area of employee know-how. The ranking of each area of employee know-how, analysed by sector, is shown in Table 3.

It should be stressed that the question relates to the most important area of employee know-how, *not* the most important function. It is possible that this ranking reflects the tacit knowledge content needed for practitioners to be effective in the different areas. For example, "Operations" may have been ranked as an important area of employee know-how by executives in four of the six sectors because its high tacit knowledge content takes a considerable time to acquire and is difficult for competitors to replicate.

Table 3.   Ranking of the "Most important area of employee know-how".

	Operations	Sales, and marketing	Technology	Finance	Others
Manufacturing consumer products	Second	First	Third	Fourth	Fourth
Manufacturing industrial products	First	Third	Second	Fourth	Fourth
Retailing	Third	First	Second	Third	Fifth
Other trading	First	Second	Fourth	Second	Fourth
Services	First	Fourth	Second	Fourth	Third
Diversified	First	Second	Third	Fourth	Fifth

The results of six case studies using product attributes and the four capabilities framework

The most important product/delivery system attributes quoted by the six case study companies are shown below.

Company	Most important attribute
Motor Manufacturer	Quality (Fitness for purpose and conformance to specification)
Packaged Food Manufacturer	Quality
Outdoor Clothing	Quality
Retail Baker	Availability (outlet location)
Bus Company	Availability (routes)
Supermarket Chain	Availability (outlet location)

Quality was identified as the most important attribute by the manufacturing companies, whereas availability was the most important attribute for those companies dealing directly with the public.

The key intangible resources identified in the case studies were similar to those identified in the national survey:

(i)   In the *Cultural Capability*: Perception of high quality standards, ability to manage change

(ii) In the *Functional Capability*: Eleven different areas of employee know-how

(iii) In the *Positional Capability*: Reputation

(iv) The *Regulatory Capability*: Was not held to be of great importance.

When executives have identified the key intangible assets, it is pertinent to ask questions concerning *protection, sustenance, enhancement* and *leverage*. Examples of such questions are found in Table 4.

Examples of the analysis of product/delivery system attributes, intangible resources and development scenarios are given in Appendix 1. These examples relate to classroom work carried out on the specialist UK car manufacturer, The Morgan Car Co. Ltd.

An advantage of using the "four capability framework" is the emphasis it gives to the importance of *positional capability*, an importance which other strategic analysis techniques may not emphasise sufficiently.

Table 4.   Issues with respect to the development of intangible resources.

With respect to protection:

(i) Do all concerned recognise value of this intangible resource to the company?

(ii) Can the resource be protected in law?

With respect to sustainability:

(i) How long did it take to acquire this resource? Is it unique because of all that has happened in creating it?

(ii) How durable is the resource? Will it decline with time?

(iii) How easily may the resource be lost?

(iv) How easily and quickly can others identify and imitate the resource?

(v) Can others easily "buy" the resource?

(vi) Can others easily "grow" the resource?

(vii) How appropriable is the resource? Can it "walk away"?

(viii) Is the resource vulnerable to substitution?

With respect to enhancement:

(i) Is the "stock" of this resource increasing?

(ii) How can we ensure that the "stock" of this resource *continues* to increase?

With respect to exploitation:

(i) Are we making the best use of this resource?

(ii) How else could it be used?

(iii) Is the scope for *synergy* identified and exploited?

(iv) Are we aware of the key linkages which exist between the resources?

The benefit which participating executives have reported from the use of this approach to the analysis of intangible resources is the acquisition of a new perspective and language that enable them to codify the tacit knowledge which they have of their companies. In particular, executives have welcomed the, sometimes new, emphasis placed on issues such as:

(i) How can the key resource of reputation be protected, enhanced and leveraged?

(ii) How can management ensure that every employee is disposed to be both a promoter and custodian of the reputation of the company which employs him/her?

(iii) What are the key areas of employee know-how? Can they be codified? How long do they take to acquire?

(iv) Is the business organised so that working and learning are the same?

Every turn of the business cycle should result in an increase in the "stocks" of intangibles, such as employee know-how and reputation, because the intangibles account for the bulk of the worth of most companies.

The Knowledge-Based View of Strategy

In the light of the views presented above, the reader will not be surprised to learn that the "resource-based view" of strategy is beginning to develop into the "knowledge-based view" of strategy. The essence of this new perspective is described by Grant (1997):

> "If individuals must specialise in knowledge acquisition and if producing goods and service requires the application of many types of knowledge, production must be organised so as to assemble these many types of knowledge while preserving specialisation by individuals. The firm is an institution which exists to specialise in developing specialised expertise, while establishing mechanisms through which individuals co-ordinate to integrate their different knowledge bases in the transformation of inputs into outputs."

A model which helps our understanding of the issues concerning the knowledge-based view of strategy is shown in Fig. 1. This model, and much

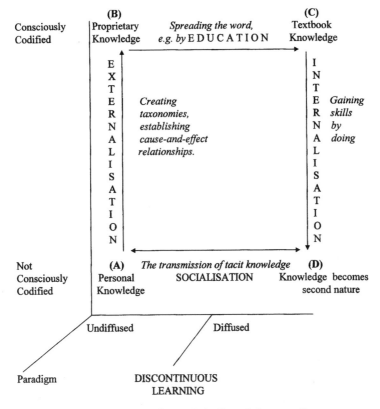

Fig. 1. The learning cycle in "knowledge space".

of the recent work on knowledge management, come from Boisot (1995) and Nonaka (1994).

The characteristics of the model of knowledge space are as follows:

(i) *Regions A and D*. These comprise tacit knowledge. Tacit knowledge is not codified; it is concerned with knowing *what* things work. It is characterised by confusion with respect to cause and effect and, consequently, it is usually difficult to communicate other than by time-consuming observation, imitation and shared experience.

(ii) *Regions B and C*. These comprise explicit knowledge. Explicit knowledge is concerned with knowing *why* things work. It is concerned with the creation of taxonomies and the establishment of cause and effect relationships. The codification of the knowledge means that it is more easily communicated than tacit knowledge and, for this reason, it is usually desirable to create explicit knowledge by *externalising* the tacit knowledge.

The codification axis is described in this paper as "*Consciously* Codified" and "*Not Consciously* Codified" rather than simply "*Codified*" and "*Uncodified*". This is because once knowledge has been codified, it cannot lose its codification. Instead, the complete learning cycle results in a practitioner ceasing to rely consciously on the codification of the knowledge. This is because, for the expert, the knowledge has become second nature. It is possible to achieve expert status by the transfer of tacit knowledge only, such as a child gaining verbal fluency in its first language. Alternatively, expert status can be achieved by the acquisition, initially, of explicit knowledge — such as an English child learning French grammar at school — followed by a process of *learning by doing*, or *internalisation*, during which the reliance on the codification becomes less and less. There are, therefore, two types of tacit knowledge: tacit knowledge which has never been codified; and tacit knowledge which is the internalised explicit knowledge of the expert who no longer needs to refer to the codification because the application of the knowledge has become second nature.

The diffusion axis may represent the transfer of knowledge from one person to another, from one to many, or from many to one; the diffusion may be to a team, a department, or from a society to an individual. An example of the latter transfer is when an individual joins a new company; (s)he is not given a manual which codifies the organisation's culture — its diffused tacit knowledge — but the individual will usually have little difficulty in assimilating the culture.

The dynamics of the learning cycle are described below:

(a) *Externalisation*. Nonaka describes "externalisation" as usually involving the use of metaphors to articulate individual perspectives and release trapped tacit knowledge. This is the stuff of social science research!

(b) *Education*. The codified nature of the knowledge which is being diffused enables this process to involve many participants at large distances.

(c) *Internalisation.* Nonaka describes "internalisation" as representing the gradual loss of the need for the codification of the knowledge. It is evidenced by the learning curve phenomenon and may be described as "learning to *do things better*". It is the "*single loop learning*" described by Argyris and Schon (1978).

(d) *Socialisation.* Nonaka suggests that tacit knowledge is transferred by a process of "socialisation" which usually involves shared experiences and the creation of trust.

(iii) *Discontinuous learning.* It is about "learning to *do better things*". It results in a change in mindset, a paradigm shift.

It is possible to relate the four types of capabilities described earlier (regulatory, positional, functional and cultural) to the model of knowledge space. This is because each capability has different types of knowledge associated with it. The identification of the differing natures of these knowledge bases is crucial if we are to manage the capabilities effectively.

The regions of the knowledge space illustrated in Fig. 1 relate to the four types of capability as shown in Fig. 2.

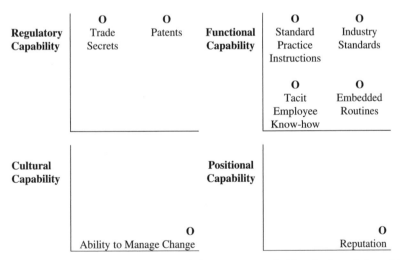

Fig. 2. Example of the regions of knowledge space occupied by the knowledge which underpins the four capabilities.

Continuous and discontinuous learning

Prahalad and Hamel (1996) have advanced the proposition that operational efficiency, by itself, is not enough to win sustainable competitive advantage on the grounds that operational efficiency is relatively easy to replicate. They suggest that operational efficiency, like quality, is a hygiene factor, and that discontinuous learning which produces fundamentally new ways of doing things is the key to future success. This is because fundamentally new operations *are* difficult to replicate.

Continuous learning may involve four of the stages described in the learning cycle: externalisation, education, internalisation and socialisation. Discontinuous learning is concerned with learning to do better things; it may be "triggered" by major threats or opportunities. In view of the fact that one man's step change may be another man's incremental change, there is no clear divide between continuous and discontinuous learning. For the purposes of this chapter, we will assume that discontinuous learning involves fundamental change and will require significant *unlearning*. This unlearning is difficult, for as Sir Francis Bacon (1620) wrote:

> "The human understanding, when it has once adopted an opinion, draws all things else to support and agree with it. And though there be a great number and weight of instances to be found on the other side, yet it either neglects and despises, or else by some distinction sets aside and rejects, in order that by this great and pernicious predetermination, the authority of its former conclusion may remain inviolate."

Stacey (1993) recognises the fact that human organisations are complex non-linear dynamic systems with both positive and negative feedback loops. He suggests that such *self-adaptive systems*, like most eco-systems, are at their most flexible when they exist in a state of bounded instability where positive, as well as negative, feedback operates. He argues that the formal organisation, by definition, cannot be self-adaptive and that it is usually the informal (self-adaptive) organisation which produces discontinuous learning. He argues that by nature and training, most managers strive for predictability and stability by practising negative feedback in order to eliminate variances from the desired norm. A consequence of this is that the lead indicators of required change may be damped out. He describes two styles of management:

> "Ordinary management is practised when most of the managers in an organization share the same mental models or paradigm. Cognitive feedback loops then operate in a negative feedback manner so that shared mental models are not questioned. Ordinary management is about rational processes to secure harmony, fit or convergence to a configuration, and it proceeds in an incremental manner."

> "Extraordinary management involves questioning and shattering paradigms, and then creating new ones. It is a process which depends critically upon contradiction and tension. Extraordinary management, then, is the use of intuitive, political, group learning modes of decision-making and self-organizing forms of control in open-ended change situations. It is the form of management that managers must use if they are to change strategic direction and innovate."

It seems, from this argument, that where discontinuous learning is required, confrontation and conflict are not only likely, but they are also desirable. It seems that we need to practise "ordinary (command and control) management" in order to "sweat the assets" — to achieve the operational efficiency which is hygiene. However, we also need to practise "extraordinary management" in order to facilitate discontinuous learning. Are the two management styles mutually exclusive?

Conclusion

This chapter has reported research which suggests that the sources of corporate success are the intangible, off balance sheet resources, such as employee know-how and reputation, and it has been argued that companies should try to organise their affairs so that every turn of the business cycle results in the "stocks" of the intangible resources increasing.

The research has suggested that the most important intangible resources are company reputation, product reputation, employee know-how, organisational culture and personal networks. In view of the nature of these resources, it is not surprising that the management of knowledge is currently receiving increasing attention.

The management of knowledge involves an understanding of the different types of learning, particularly the dichotomy between continuous and discontinuous learning. The former is needed for operational efficiency, the latter for fundamental change. Is it possible to organise one's corporate affairs so that the formal organisation sweats the assets whilst the self-adaptive informal organisation produces the fundamental changes which will be required to create new strategic competencies?

Appendix 1

The Morgan Car Company analysis

	The Morgan attributes (%) importance weighting
1. Specification — High performance	20
2. "User" statement — Image	20
3. "Family" feeling — Morgan car clubs	20
4. Conformance to specification — Reliability	15
5. Value for sterling pound — Low depreciation	15
6. Appearance	10
TOTAL	100

The competitive advantage	
	Comparison with competitor
A. Positive Attributes	
A1. Specification	+
A2. "User" statement	+
A3. "Family" feeling	++
A4. Conformance to specification	+
A5. Value for sterling pound	++
A6. Appearance	+
B. Negative Attributes	
B1. Availability	−

Worse than competitor
− Much worse than competitor
+ Better than competitor
++ Much better than competitor

The sustainability of the advantage

	Competition's ability to replicate		
	Easy	Medium difficulty	Difficult
1. Specification			✓
2. "User" statement		✓	
3. "Family" feeling			✓
4. Conformance to specification	✓		
5. Value for sterling pound			✓
6. Appearance	✓		

The intangible resources related to the key product/delivery system attributes

Key product attributes	Regulatory resources	Positional resources	Functional resources	Cultural resources
1. Specification			Design capability	
2. User statement	"Morgan" TM	Reputation		
3. Family feeling		Clubs		
4. Conformance to Specification			Craftsmanship	Perception of quality
5. Value for sterling pound		Overhead structure		
6. Appearance			Design capability and craftsmanship	

Development scenarios

Actions/key intangibles	Protecting	Sustaining	Enhancing	Leveraging
1. The trademark	Worldwide registration			Licence in California
2. Reputation		Damage limitation plans	Promote by word of mouth	
3. Product development	Succession?	Succession?		
4. Craftsmanship		Recruitment	Train in just-in-time (JIT), etc.	
5. Perception of quality		Be careful with organisational culture		

Chapter 3

The Role of Dynamic Capabilities in Developing Innovation-related Capabilities[1]

Hanna-Kaisa Ellonen, Ari Jantunen and Olli Kuivalainen
Lappeenranta University of Technology, Finland

Introduction

Firms face the challenge of keeping up with changing market needs, especially in fast-moving operating environments. They have to continuously improve their existing processes and products, and develop new products that match market requirements. In this they have to reconfigure their asset base by creating new combinations from existing and new resources. Especially in situations where a technological discontinuity occurs, there is a need for speedy capability reconfiguration or substitution (Lavie, 2006). To be able to overcome such external shocks, new capabilities are needed (Zollo and Winter, 2002; Teece, 2007). It is, therefore, crucial to understand how such capabilities develop.

The current literature recognizes the hierarchical nature of company capabilities, and distinguishes between first-order operational capabilities and second- or higher-order capabilities that are needed for changing operational routines (e.g. Zollo and Winter, 2002; Winter, 2003; Helfat and Peteraf, 2003; Ambrosini *et al.*, 2009; Ambrosini and Bowman, 2009). Operational capabilities, such as market or technological capabilities, are

---

[1] An earlier version of this chapter was published in the *International Journal of Innovation Management*, 2011, **15**(3), 459–478.

essential to the daily operations of the firm (see, e.g. Collis, 1994; Danneels, 2002; Cepada and Vera, 2007), whereas dynamic capabilities come into play in processes of organizational renewal. According to the dynamic capability view (Teece *et al.*, 1997), dynamic capabilities define firms' ability to develop their asset base and build new operational-level capabilities.

In the dynamic capabilities literature several authors (Verona and Ravasi, 2003; Wang and Ahmed, 2007; Teece, 2007; Ambrosini *et al.*, 2009) have categorized different types of dynamic capabilities at a theoretical level, but only a few have tried to operationalize these capabilities and open up the actual practices that form dynamic capabilities. Also, the relationship between dynamic capabilities and operational level capabilities has been widely covered in conceptual terms (e.g. Zollo and Winter, 2002; Winter, 2003; Helfat and Peteraf, 2003; Ambrosini *et al.*, 2009; Ambrosini and Bowman, 2009). However, this underlying assumption has not been studied in empirical settings, and the actual role of dynamic capabilities has not been uncovered. Newey and Zahra's (2009) study is a notable exception in that it establishes some linkages between product-portfolio planning (dynamic capability) and product development (operational capability). However, given the somewhat idiosyncratic nature of capabilities, Newey and Zahra called for more exploration of the relationship between the dynamic type and the development of operational capabilities.

The purpose of this study is to explore the role of dynamic capabilities in the development of innovation-related operational capabilities. We aim to conceptualize and illustrate the connections between different types of dynamic capabilities (sensing, seizing, and reconfiguring), and the development of technological and market capabilities. Our research includes a single case study from the publishing industry, which has been strongly affected by the emergence of the Internet and digitalization of the media. Hence, new capabilities are needed in this industry for companies to remain competitive and meaningful to their customers. By building on a data set of interviews and secondary data, we analyze the development and interrelations of the focal publisher's capabilities over a time period of five years, and are thus provided with a relevant and interesting example of the role of dynamic capabilities in the development of innovation-related capabilities.

The rest of this chapter is organized as follows. The next section gives the theoretical background of the study and discusses different types of capabilities and their development. Thereafter, we present our research strategy, methods, and data, and then we report the findings of our empirical study. We conclude with a discussion of the theoretical and practical implications.

Theoretical Background

Innovation-related operational capabilities

Operational capabilities are the first-level capabilities needed for the day-to-day running of the firm (see, e.g. Collis, 1994; Danneels, 2002; Cepada and Vera, 2007). According to Helfat and Peteraf (2003, p. 999), an operational capability "... generally involves performing an activity, such as manufacturing a particular product, using a collection of routines to execute and co-ordinate the variety of tasks required to perform the activity".

In the innovation context, market and technological capabilities are considered seminal given that product innovations require simultaneous consideration of both markets and technologies (e.g. Dougherty, 1992; Danneels, 2002). There is broad agreement in innovation literature that linkages between key components such as technology development and R&D and creation of products and services driven by changing consumer needs will produce successful innovations (Berkhout *et al.*, 2010). Hence, we will focus on these two types of innovation-related operational capabilities in this study.

Market capabilities are needed in order to serve both current and potential future customers and could be considered key antecedents of competitiveness and superior performance. According to many authors, these capabilities are exercised through specific market-related processes (Guenzie and Troilo, 2006) focusing on product/service development (see, e.g. Dutta *et al.*, 1999; Newey and Zahra, 2009), pricing (Dutta *et al.*, 2003), market-information management (e.g. Day, 1994), marketing planning (Morgan *et al.*, 2003) and channel bonding (i.e. the ability to build relationships with channel members, cf. Day, 1994). For the purposes of this chapter, we focus on four main components of market capabilities: first, in order to understand customer needs and actions it is important to be able to collect and process customer knowledge from both new and existing customers. Secondly, the firm needs to able to satisfy customer needs by offering suitable product features and operations. Thirdly, we focus on the customer relationship, meaning the ability to identify and serve customer groups and build customer loyalty. Finally, customer communication implies the ability to communicate to and with customers through appropriate channels.

Technological capabilities, in turn, generally constitute tangible and intangible technically related resources, processes, and knowledge such as engineering and manufacturing know-how, efficient manufacturing processes, production facilities, new product development, and quality-control procedures geared to quality products, related managerial and organizational skills, and the ability to forecast technological change in the industry (Abernathy and Clark, 1985; Danneels, 2002, 2007; Tseng, 2005; Song *et al.*, 2008). Increasing efficiency in the various R&D and manufacturing processes will reduce costs and improve consistency in delivery and, consequently, competitiveness (Day, 1994). In this chapter we focus on three components of technological capabilities: the first is the ability to design and manufacture online products with certain features. The second refers to production systems and know-how, which here means the ability to carry out everyday processes related to updating and maintaining the functionality of online products. Finally, managerial skills refer to the capability to set up processes related to everyday work and product development.

Development of operational capabilities

The development of capabilities happens over time and is strongly path-dependent (e.g. Penrose, 1959; Nelson and Winter, 1982). Most often, crucial idiosyncratic assets such as intangible resources and capabilities are built internally rather than bought from the markets (Dierickx and Cool, 1989; Hall, 1992, 1993; Collis, 1994; Teece, 2007; Katkalo *et al.*, 2010). Consequently, much of the development of operational capabilities is incremental and occurs through learning-by-doing and routinization of the experience (e.g. Zollo and Winter, 2003; Newey and Zahra, 2009; see also Tranfield *et al.*, 2003).

Although extant research on organizational learning focuses mostly on "learning-by-doing", Helfat and Peteraf (2003, p. 1002) suggest that improvements in the function of the certain capability "... derive from a complex set of factors that include learning-by-doing of individual team members and of the team whole, deliberate attempts at process improvement and problem-solving, as well as investment over time". They suggest that capabilities have life-cycles with stages such as introduction, growth, maturity, and decline. Eventually, in the maturity phase, the development of the capability may end or a firm may renew, redeploy, or make recombinations of the original capability and consequently, capability transformation occurs. Lavie (2006) suggests that there are three main mechanisms through which capabilities are reconfigured: evolution (development in an evolutionary manner), transformation (old capabilities are reconfigured), and substitution (the new substitute the old).

Capability evolution relates to incremental learning and modifying existing routines (Lavie, 2006). The learning source in most cases is the internal environment, or in some cases the existing value network of the firm. The evolution of capabilities is strongly path-dependent rather than determined by the nature of technological change (Lavie, 2006). Helfat and Peteraf (2003) use the term "capability renewal" to describe modifications of a capability leading to a new development stage.

According to Lavie (2006), *capability transformation* involves the acquisition, disbandment, and modification of routines. Nevertheless, the transformed capabilities still serve the same function as the original ones, and there is a certain degree of carry-over of existing routines. The transformation mechanism involves learning from both internal and external sources (Lavie, 2006). Helfat and Raubitschek (2000) use the term "step function learning" to describe the rather similar situation involving fundamental changes to core or integrative knowledge.

Capability substitution is the most radical type in Lavie's classification in that at least some of the old capabilities become obsolete. The practice is advocated in competence enhancing/destroying frameworks (Abernathy and Clark, 1985; Tushman and Anderson, 1986; Anderson and Tushman, 1990; Danneels, 2002, 2007), and typically follows an exogenous shock that turns the company's operating capabilities into core rigidities (Newey and Zahra, 2009). Collis (1994) sees the risk of substitution being especially high for market leaders as competitors normally would pursue substitution strategy. Complex capabilities incorporating a large number of routines are more likely to be substituted because it may be difficult or ineffective to reconfigure them fully (Lavie, 2006).

It is interesting to note that while capability development literature categorizes different development mechanisms, it does not explicate how these processes get started or are maintained. Hence, we turn our attention to dynamic capabilities.

The role of dynamic capabilities in developing operational capabilities

Dynamic capabilities could be considered higher-order organizational capabilities that facilitate learning about new domains, create new asset combinations, and build new capabilities in order to match market (perceptible and latent) needs (Collis, 1994; Teece *et al.*, 1997; Winter, 2003; Wang and Ahmed, 2007; Helfat *et al.*, 2007; Danneels, 2008; Ambrosini *et al.*, 2009; Newey and Zahra, 2009). Helfat *et al.* (2007, p. 4) define dynamic capabilities as "the capacity of an organization to purposefully create, extend, or modify its resource base".

A common perception in many conceptualizations is that there are three types of dynamic capabilities: those needed to take in external knowledge, those needed to link the innovativeness to products and markets, and those needed to align the firm's resources and capabilities (e.g. Verona and Ravasi, 2003; Wang and Ahmed, 2007; Teece, 2007; see also Barreto, 2010). For the purposes of this chapter we adopt Teece's (2007) categorization and distinguish between sensing, seizing, and reconfiguring capabilities (for an empirical illustration see Ellonen *et al.*, 2009).

Sensing capabilities denote the firm's activities in scanning and monitoring changes in operating environments and identifying new opportunities. They comprise processes and practices such as R&D, customer-need identification, systematic ways of tapping technological developments and innovations in the market, and through complementors and suppliers. *Seizing* capabilities are needed in the design of product architecture and business models or brand management. They also include decision-making practices concerning new ventures, partners, and choice of distribution channel. *Reconfiguring* capabilities are used in asset "orchestration", i.e. activities such as the redeployment of existing assets, the management of complementary assets, and reengineering processes. Structures, practices, and processes included in reconfiguring capabilities include knowledge management, resource-base reconfiguration, and asset co-specialization (internally and with external partners). In our view, leadership practices promoting commitment and new ways of allocating resources, such as incentives, also belong to the set of the firm's reconfiguration capabilities.

To sum up the research setting of this study: we assume that, driven by the technological change in the operating environment, incremental development occurs both at the operational and dynamic capabilities levels. A firm's market and technological capabilities affect its innovation outcomes in the next phase. In line with the dynamic capability view, we also assume there will be interactive mechanisms linking dynamic capabilities with the development of operational capabilities (marked with dark arrows in Fig. 1). The purpose of this study is to conceptualize and illustrate the connections between different types of dynamic capabilities (sensing, seizing, and reconfiguring) and the development of technological and market capabilities. Figure 1 illustrates the research setting.

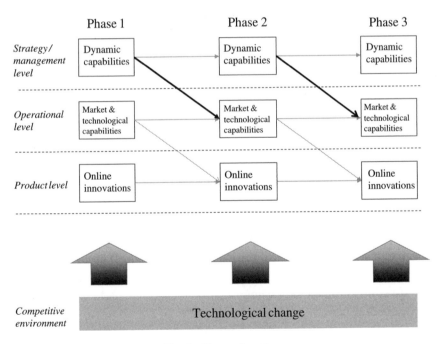

Fig. 1.   Research setting.

Research Design and Methods

Given our objective to explore the relationship between dynamic capabilities and the development of innovation-related operational capabilities, we followed Lavie's (2006) and Ambrosini and Bowman's (2009) suggestions and conducted a case-based qualitative analysis of the development of the capabilities of a single firm. A single case study was chosen to provide a detailed, context-dependent understanding of capability development (Yin, 2009).

Our case is a leading Scandinavian newspaper publisher which has made substantial investments in online product development since 2005. We decided to focus on the online innovation projects of the publisher, since online development has required new practices and routines to be developed in the organization. Hence, our case represents a critical case study (Yin, 2009) allowing us to explore the assumptions of prior theory.

Data collection

Our primary data-collection method was the semi-structured interview. We conducted 14 interviews within the case company and its main internal partners (shared technology and online sales departments of the larger media group). We interviewed people at both the top-management (four) and operational (ten) level. All the informants had been actively involved in at least one of the online innovations during the previous five years. In other words, we chose information-rich cases (cf. Patton, 2002) as our informants. The interviews were tape-recorded, with the permission of the interviewees, and transcribed. They typically lasted 60–90 minutes.

The interviews focused on the particular online innovation(s) in which the interviewees had been involved, the aim being to obtain an understanding of the actual processes deployed and actions taken in developing the innovations, the lessons learnt during the process, and how the increased knowledge was deployed in other activities later. They were informal and narrative in nature, the aim being to tap into authentic and contextualized experiences (Eriksson and Kovalainen, 2008).

However, in order to minimize interviewee hindsight bias and the limitations of memory recall, we followed Golden's (1992) suggestions to complement the interview data with secondary sources, such as annual reports, press releases, and published newspaper articles covering the online-related actions of the case firm (see also Van de Ven and Poole, 2005; Lavie, 2006). This resulted in an additional dataset of over 200 pages of text.

Data analysis

We conducted the analyses in five consecutive phases, which are summarized in Table 1. As Laamanen and Wallin (2009) point out, capabilities are seldom context-independent. We therefore started by drawing up a case history in order to clarify the context of the phenomena in question.

Table 1. Phases of case analysis (adapted from Laamanen and Wallin, 2009).

Analytical goal	Analytical process used and the outcome	Implications for conceptual development
Describe the pattern of case evolution.	Producing a time line of the evolution of the case firm.	Understanding the context of actions.
Identify the different types of capabilities.	Thematic analysis. Coding of different types of capabilities according to initial capability templates.	Operationalization and illustration of dynamic and operational capabilities in practice.
Build the time line of events and actions.	Arranging the identified capabilities on time lines.	Dynamic capabilities and operational capabilities develop over time.
Uncover the linkages between dynamic and operational capabilities.	Inductive coding of the linkages between dynamic capabilities and operational capabilities into the time line (six examples are illustrated in Fig. 2).	Dynamic capabilities would seem to be linked with operational capabilities, and the linkage would seem to result in operational capability development.
Examine the nature of the linkages between dynamic and operational capabilities.	Categorizing of the identified linkages.	Dynamic capabilities would seem to spark off capability-development mechanisms (transformation and substitution).

We then analyzed the data by means of thematical analysis in order to identify and categorize the dynamic and operational capabilities. We adopted Teece's (2007) classification (sensing, seizing, and reconfiguring) as the coding frame for dynamic capabilities. We used the components of market and technology capabilities presented earlier as the coding template for operational capabilities.

The third phase of the analysis focused on the time line and sequences of the accounts and events. As the interviews focused on particular innovation projects, we could pinpoint the time when certain events happened or certain practices started. The aim in the fourth phase was to expose the interrelationships between dynamic capabilities and operational capability development. The information gleaned from the first two rounds of analysis enabled us to develop simple box arrow diagrams showing how certain dynamic capabilities seemed to be linked with operational capabilities and their development. Finally, we focused our attention on the linkages we had identified and compared them with Lavie's (2006) categorization.

In order to maximize the reliability of the study we prepared a case study protocol to support data collection (e.g. Yin, 2009). Also, to increase the validity of the study, multiple sources of evidence were used, and all authors cross-checked the analysis and the interpretation of the results (e.g. Yin, 2009).

Results

Our case firm has focused strongly on online development since 2005. Three successive phases between 2005 and 2009 can be distinguished: at the beginning of phase 1 in 2005 the company invested heavily in online operations, mostly related to the print product, and started developing internal practices and routines for the management of the new online projects. The next phase, from late 2006 to 2007, saw the launch of the first online innovation that was truly independent of the print product, and several product-development-oriented key people were recruited. Several successive independent online innovations were launched during the third phase from 2008 to early 2009, and the number of online staff grew up until spring 2009.

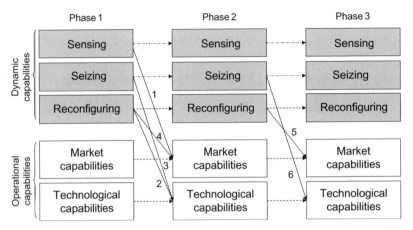

Fig. 2. The development of and relationships between dynamic and operational capabilities.

Based on our analysis, we noted some interconnections between dynamic and operational capabilities. Let us discuss this notion in more detail by describing the six examples depicted in Fig. 2.

Example 1

During phase 1 the company employed a systematic and purposeful practice of sending many of its key people to conferences and seminars abroad to follow the general development in the industry. Also, they visited international benchmark competitors in order to get new ideas and learn from their experiences.

> "We used to visit — and still do to some extent — our international competitors .... The good thing about these visits is that people also share the lessons they learn about what went wrong and what not to do."

These practices represent sensing capabilities, and in particular, capabilities related to following the general technological developments in the industry. However, while the company was primarily searching for new ideas and insights, these practices resulted also in a large external industry expert network.

Later it became evident that the external networks they had built in phase 1 could provide important complementary knowledge regarding customer needs. Their contacts provided them with information on customer behavior in their respective markets, and new types of online products developed for different target groups. Thus, via the external networks, the company acquired new customer knowledge and was able to develop their market capabilities in that area by integrating that knowledge into their internal processes.

> "We have many international contacts who send us links and tip us about the developments in the world ... there is always somebody who remembers to send you an email and check 'Have you seen this? Would this work for you?' "

Their sensing capabilities in phase 1 thus seemed to support the modification and acquirement of new market capabilities (knowledge of new customer needs and customer solutions) in phase 2.

Example 2

At the beginning of phase 1, the case company was having difficulties with motivating their staff to work with online projects. To overcome this problem, the company managers were active in promoting commitment to online development through their own example: they wrote personal blogs describing their experiences with online media and made a company-wide roadshow to all departments presenting the online projects and their importance for the company. Senior managers put special emphasis on publicly rewarding successful online projects and smaller-scale online initiatives. Staff commitment was also promoted by implementing an incentive system that rewarded online development activities. A responsive attitude towards online projects was also implemented as a criterion for promotions and special bonuses. These leadership practices fostered new ways of allocating resources, and thus represent reconfiguring capabilities.

> "For many years now we have had the ability to adopt online activities and online innovations as evaluation criteria in our incentive systems. That's how we try to encourage them to make an effort and try."

"The management level has been really great in encouraging and supporting online work, especially our editors-in-chief."

"As a director, I find it extremely important that I support the online development and try my best to have as many people involved and interested in that."

It seems that the leadership practices had an effect on the commitment of staff and the allocation of resources in the company. By phase 2 more and more individuals and departments actually took responsibility for the daily updates and modifications of the online innovations. There were also more print people involved in the larger online projects planning the daily production of the respective services. Thus, it was evident that technological capabilities, especially related to production, did evolve over time as new practices were employed.

"In most of our news rooms... they also publish online material while working with the print newspaper... it's not only the online people."

"We have adopted a new system whereby the journalists rotate in different sections and everybody has to work with online news, too... people have become used to it and can manage it."

Thus, it would seem that these reconfiguring capabilities related to leadership practices supported the modification and acquirement of new technological capabilities (production).

Example 3

In 2005, the case company implemented a formal three-level committee structure for approving and monitoring online development projects. Clear procedures for the evaluation of potential and ongoing projects were set for different stages of the projects and for different committees. For example, each project idea would be presented using a standard business plan template that enabled comparison of different projects. These practices refined their decision-making protocols and hence represent seizing capabilities.

"Now we have a structured and formal method for running projects and making decisions there. That has worked really well..."

"I think we really need this level of systematization in the decision-making process... with online projects you tend to lose sight of the real costs of the projects. This system supports discussion and prioritizing, and people do not take it personally if their ideas are not taken further."

The implementation of new decision-making structures led to a clear improvement in the management and co-ordination of individual development projects. The business side of all new projects was better prepared. Individual project managers became more efficient and professional in monitoring the projects and co-ordinating actions between different internal departments, internal technological partners, and external partners. All in all, their technological capabilities, particularly in the area of project management, were modified and some new practices acquired.

"We have learned a lot about the internal process, how to work with projects like this... how to sell the ideas to different departments and to managers, and still remain friends with everybody."

As we see it, the seizing capabilities focusing on decision-making protocols in phase 1 helped to modify project-management-related technological capabilities in phase 2.

Example 4

The key people had gained experience in several online projects. They took a practice of sharing some of the best practices and lessons learnt amongst them. This type of knowledge-sharing between projects represents reconfiguring capabilities.

One such lesson was that company staff should actively engage in online discussions with their customers in order to promote loyalty and customer input in product development. The following exemplifies one of the lessons learned during the experimentation phase in 2005–2006.

"We know by experience that even a single comment written by a journalist, maybe 'sorry', or 'I'll think about this when I write my next story', will change the nature and quality of the discussion."

The lessons were passed on to the next projects in phase 2. This resulted in the development of market capabilities as they adopted their existing forms of customer communication to suit the online context and initiated new practices when communicating with customers.

> "We sent a personal email to all registered users ... and you notice that it's a way to create loyal visitors, those who are more committed to our service and are eager to react and help when it's down or something."

> "So I have this software that I'd like to test ... I post a message to our blog asking 'has anyone tested this yet?' Soon a couple of people have answered my post and written a report. That is like awesome. ... Then I write an article on the software and mention their names and thank them ... After that these guys will be in your network forever and you will have independent experts at your disposal."

Thus, the reconfiguring capabilities focusing on knowledge management helped to modify existing and acquire new customer-communication-related market capabilities during phase 2.

Example 5

In phase 2 the company decided to invest in web-analytics software. It licensed the software and recruited dedicated and trained experts. Hence, they reallocated their resources, which is an example of reconfiguring capabilities.

> "Completely new positions have been opened ... for example I was involved in the recruitment process of an analytics expert who will monitor everything we do online ... it has been great to have that sort of new expertise in house!"

When they gained experience with the software and the analysis it provided, they realized its value in providing new information on customer behaviour that they had not had an access to before. Based on this information, they were able to redesign some of their products and services and currently use it as the basis for their development plans.

> "In late 2008 we launched the first version of a new service and then kept analyzing customer behavior and iteratively developed it further. We kept drawing statistics from the analytics software and noted that there were applications that our customers did not find but those who did were loyal to it ... so we changed the service and were able to increase the number of visitors and even noted that the loyalty trend still continued."

> "The data we get from the analytics is used monthly to make decisions regarding the types of services we will produce."

> "Every week we get a detailed summary of all our services. We use that report as the basis of future development and prioritizing."

The reallocation of resources had led to the implementation of new routines and practices for obtaining and following real-time knowledge of online customer behavior, and using that knowledge as the basis of their development projects. Hence, the resource-reconfiguring capabilities developed in phase 2 helped to acquire new market capabilities, especially in terms of acquiring new types of customer knowledge, in phase 3.

Example 6

It was realized in phase 2 that online innovations need to be developed iteratively in order to meet customer needs and remain competitive. However, the existing IT systems and external partners were "big-scale", i.e. expensive and relatively inflexible. As a result, the company partnered with new, smaller partners who could help them to launch and iteratively improve new services inexpensively and flexibly through the use of open software, for example. It thereby manifested seizing capabilities in the area of managing platforms.

> "A big company is so used to selecting large and well-known partners, but that's so expensive and time-consuming ... one of the platforms we chose was clearly a wrong choice, for example. It

was so expensive and difficult to work with, and it was almost impossible to get the necessary knowledge and skills."

The new partnerships resulted in new types of services and a new, quicker way of designing and producing online innovations:

"Now the first reaction is no longer, 'hey we have this system that costs half a million. Let's buy this and solve our problems' ... now

Table 2. The linkage between dynamic capabilities and operational capability development.

Example	Dynamic capability	Capability-development mechanism	Outcome of the capability development
1	Sensing: building the partner and industry contact network	Capability transformation	Market capabilities modified and acquired: complementary knowledge of new customer needs and customer solutions
2	Reconfiguring: leadership and incentives foster commitment	Capability transformation	Technological capabilities modified and acquired: new production process, as more people and departments participate in the production
3	Seizing: refinement of the decision-making protocols	Capability transformation	Technological capabilities modified and acquired: project management more efficient
4	Reconfiguring: knowledge sharing between different projects	Capability transformation	Market capabilities modified and acquired: new customer-communication channels and practices employed
5	Reconfiguring: investment in new resources (web analytics software and experts)	Capability substitution	New market capabilities acquired: routines for obtaining real-time knowledge of online customer behavior
6	Seizing: new partnerships and platforms	Capability substitution	New technological capabilities acquired: flexible and inexpensive systems developed with new partners

we have a number of small partners we chose for each project.... Now we're able to flexibly design and produce new applications online very quickly, and develop the service based on customer feedback and behavior."

"When developing our new iPhone applications, we managed to get a great new partner. They were actually very dedicated to making the best possible service and were willing to redesign the service after the first attempt that we were not happy about ... our previous partners were not willing to do that."

Therefore, the seizing capabilities in the area of managing platforms in phase 2 led to the acquisition of new technological capabilities (both design and production capabilities) in phase 3.

A common element in all the examples presented above is the role of dynamic capabilities sparking off capability development, i.e. a manifestation of dynamic capabilities seems to be linked with the development of market or technical capabilities. Based on these examples, this notion seems to be applicable to all three types of dynamic capabilities (sensing, seizing, and reconfiguring) and to two categories of capability-development mechanisms (transformation and substitution). Table 2 summarizes the examples.

Discussion and Conclusions

In this study we explored the role of dynamic capabilities in the development of innovation-related operational capabilities. We conceptualized and illustrated the connections between different types of dynamic capabilities (sensing, seizing, and reconfiguring) and the development of technological and market capabilities. The study makes a notable contribution given the scarcity of empirical investigation of dynamic capabilities. This study provides empirical support for the underlying assumption of the role dynamic capabilities in modifying operational capabilities. We noted how dynamic capabilities started off two different capability mechanisms, namely transformation and substitution, which go beyond incremental development.

Based on the results of the present study it seems that all types of dynamic capabilities are linked with innovation-related operational capability development. Thus, it is not only the reconfiguring capabilities that, by definition, act to modify the resource-base, but also capabilities in sensing and seizing can foster the development on market and technological capabilities. The examples presented earlier illustrate how sensing and seizing capabilities may, indeed, indirectly result in the development of operational capabilities, while their initial purpose was to capture external knowledge and make innovative ideas into reality. This notion complements Bruni and Verona's (2009) finding on how market knowledge has sometimes been used to reorganize the product development process.

We noted how dynamic capabilities started off two different types of capability mechanisms, namely transformation and substitution. The mechanisms stem from the work by Lavie (2006; see also Helfat and Peteraf, 2003) and characterize how new capabilities are acquired to perform the same functions as prior capabilities (transformation) or new capabilities make the existing capabilities obsolete (substitution). The notion of new capabilities enhancing or destroying existing capabilities was already introduced by Abernathy and Clark in 1985, and similar frameworks have more recently been used by, e.g. Danneels (2002, 2007). However, the role of dynamic capabilities in the development process has not been addressed in these studies. Thus, the present study bridges the gap between capability development research and dynamic capabilities research by explicating the role of dynamic capabilities in the capability development process.

Based on the findings of this study, we suggest that dynamic capabilities enable, channel, and foster the development of market and technological capabilities towards new strategic goals. It is worth noting that operational capabilities do evolve over time also without explicit development activities as knowledge accumulates through learning-by-doing and routinization of key activities. Hence, learning, change, and adaptation do not necessarily need the intervention of dynamic capabilities (see Helfat and Raubitschek, 2000; Helfat and Peteraf, 2003). However, the function of dynamic capabilities is to take the lead in the development and steer the evolutionary path into new territories beyond the scope of incremental evolution (see also

Pandza and Thorpe, 2009). As the results imply, dynamic capabilities start more radical development mechanisms (transformation and substitution) than mere evolution (see Lavie, 2006). Correspondingly, the presented examples are in line with the notion that dynamic capabilities' role is to change a company's capabilities or resource base in an *intentional* and *deliberate* manner (see, e.g. Ambrosini and Bowman, 2009) and, in practice, they govern the rate of change of the ordinary first-order capabilities (see, e.g. Teece, 2007; Winter, 2003). For example, ability to seize new business models and opportunities by possessing dynamic capabilities related to investment and partnering processes made it possible for the case company to reconfigure operational capabilities rapidly (see Example 6). In practice, they were able to develop online platforms fast to serve customers better and stay competitive.

Dynamic capabilities are related to the question: what are the sources of company-level competitive advantage over time (Teece, 2007)? Dynamic capabilities literature focuses on the capacity of the organization as a source of competitive advantage and shares many similar assumptions with a resource-based view of the firm (see, e.g. Penrose, 1959): it is unique resources and capabilities which should form the basis for a company's strategy and how it competes. According to the dynamic capabilities framework the focus is more on change, however; there is a need to change, i.e. continuously create, extend, and upgrade the company's assets or capabilities to be able to stay competitive (Teece, 2007). Many changes in the company-level over time involve decisions by corporate managers (Adner and Helfat, 2003) and deployment of dynamic capabilities requires high levels of time and energy from committed managers (Ambrosini and Bowman, 2009; see also Lavie, 2006). This means that dynamic capabilities are closely linked to strategic decision-making of the top management. In many cases, they facilitate managers' decision-making. The examples presented in this study also illustrate how purposeful strategic decisions at the top-management level (see also Narayanan *et al.*, 2009), such as changing the decision-making structures, introducing new incentive systems, and managing new platforms, had such a dramatic effect on the development of innovation-related operational capabilities that it is unlikely to have taken place without the impact of dynamic capabilities. There need to be processes which facilitate efficient development of first-order capabilities in the way the case company was able to develop them: one example was an internal process which made managers lead the utilization of blogs and other online tools, and which eventually led to new production innovations (see Example 2).

Whilst presenting the actual example discussed above we suggested that some leadership practices can be seen to belong to the set of the company's reconfiguration capabilities — but it is also important to point out that management itself can be seen as a critical determinant of how dynamic capabilities are deployed in a company (Adner and Helfat, 2003; Teece, 2007; Ambrosini and Bowman, 2009). Adner and Helfat (2003) even make a distinction between dynamic managerial capabilities (where the unit of analysis is a manager) and more general dynamic capabilities (where the unit of analysis is an organization). Clearly the companies would benefit if best practices (i.e. tacit knowledge) of the managers could be leveraged to the company level — and a company would be able to build and possess processes which would become dynamic capabilities, and which, in turn, would help strategic decision-making, which would then foster the development or reconfiguration of the operational capabilities.

Based on our experience we also believe that what managers should pay attention to is the fact that seemingly structural changes in the firm's internal operations (e.g. incentive systems, decision-making protocols, organizational responsibilities) have an impact on the capabilities needed for innovation activities, and can indeed foster their development. Additionally, as our study shows, practices related to getting new ideas and actions, and related to linking new ideas with current business, may also have a significant impact on the development of market and technological capabilities needed in new product development. Consequently, managers should pay attention to all kinds of capabilities, both dynamic and operational, and consider their relationships carefully, as it is the interplay of these capabilities which provides the competitive advantage and superior performance. There is a warning, also, as some dynamic capabilities may create a renewal but not value, and in this case a company would not be doing "right things" and, hence, long-term competitive advantage would not be gained (Helfat *et al.*, 2007).

Finally, the shortcomings of the study should also be acknowledged. Given that the study builds on a single case and selected six examples, the results may have idiosyncratic features, and future research could use a comparative setting (see Langley, 1999) in order to increase the generalizability of the results. Furthermore, the longitudinal aspect builds on retrospective accounts, which carry their own limitations. However, the study represents an attempt to take seriously the challenge of operationalizing dynamic capabilities, and their relationship with basic-level capabilities.

Part II

MARKET COMPETENCIES

Chapter 4

Brands, Innovation and Growth: The Role of Brands in Innovation and Growth for Consumer Businesses

Tony Clayton
Office for National Statistics, UK

Graham Turner
Strategic Planning Institute, USA

Benchmarking Business Performance

For over 20 years, a programme of business measurement and comparison has been in operation, capturing data on the markets, operations and performance of thousands of businesses, in companies across all sectors of the economy. If invented today, this work would carry a name including the word "benchmarking". It is called PIMS, which stands for Profit Impact of Market Strategy. Its purpose is to quantify and compare for client companies the key differences between successful and unsuccessful businesses, and to advise them what aspects of "winners'" behaviour and marketing strategy are likely to pay off in the long run.

PIMS was originally born at General Electric (GE). The company developed, by the early 1970s, a consistent framework for measuring and comparing business units and understanding the differences between those which were consistently profitable and growing, and those which were not. In 1973, GE decided to move this framework outside its own markets and involve many other North American companies. PIMS was created as an independent organisation to hold confidential information under secure conditions from a range of companies, and to develop the measurement and applications approaches for quantitative comparison.

The framework used in PIMS comparisons has evolved and expanded over time, with key components added as new research is completed. Over 200 variables are captured and tracked in constituent parts of PIMS, with the most extensive range of experience still focused in the core areas of competitive position, market attractiveness, cost structure and productivity. The key measures used for comparison are summarised in Table 1.

The early research results from PIMS, based on the original measurement parameters covering competitive position, market attractiveness and productivity, made a significant impact on business planning concepts and practice. Evidence generated on links between non-financial measures

Table 1.   Examples of PIMS "profit driving" measures.

Measures of:	Example
Competitive Position	
• Scale	Share of target or "served" market
• Relative scale	Relative share = business share/share of top three competitors
• Relative quality	Weighted preference score versus major competitors
• Relative value	Preference score set against relative price positioning
• Innovation investment	R&D spend as a percentage of sales
• Innovation output	Percentage of revenue from products/services under three years old
Market Attractiveness	
• Customer price sensitivity	Importance of product to buyer budget
• Customer buying power	Amount negotiated in one contract/transaction
• Customer Complexity	Number of key customers, customer communication cost
• Seller power	Share of top four sellers into the market
Productivity	
• Investment intensity	Net assets as a percentage of business value added per annum
• Capital flexibility	Gross fixed assets as a percentage of value added
• Labour productivity	Value added per employee
Human/organisation capital	
• Culture	Measured attitude to problem resolution
• Training/time management	Balance of top management time on tasks
IT capital	
• Strategic fit	Balance between IT spending and strategic goals
• Change investment	Percentage of IT investment in change related projects

and financial results shaped a generation of thinking. The importance of quality, share and customer value for business unit profits, and the damage caused by fixed capital intensity, are covered in a range of PIMS publications (Buzzell and Gale, 1987).

Benchmarks for Growth

PIMS' early focus on the determinants of profit margins or return on assets as performance measures quickly broadened to include the drivers of growth. Benchmarking profit and growth plans became the core of work for contributing companies.

In 1994, the Industry Directorate of the European Union (EU) approached PIMS, on the recommendation of its clients, to advise on the key determinants of business growth. The study they commissioned was designed to test the relative importance of "intangible" business measures, alongside "hard" measures such as costs and productivity. It looked at the role of such business measures — quality, innovation, intellectual property and marketing investment — in driving growth, value added, employment and profits. We chose these indicators because they measure:

(i) The ability to compete for customers preferences.
(ii) The ability to create value and jobs.
(iii) The ability to compete in markets for capital — an essential for growth.

Our findings were no surprise to companies that had worked with PIMS. But they were sufficiently different to be published in the Commission's Panorama of EU Industry (EU, 1996). The three main findings — all proven from the businesses we observed — were that:

(i) "Intangibles" are not necessarily difficult to measure and they are powerful growth drivers for individual businesses.
(ii) Innovation and intellectual property are the key determinants of growth in competitive markets.
(iii) Quality, innovation and intellectual property are more effective as creators of wealth and jobs than investment in fixed assets.

The 1997 EU "Competitiveness" White Paper accepted this PIMS evidence on the key role of intangibles, including quality, innovation and intellectual property, in driving business and employment growth.

Do Brands Help Growth?

The earlier work outlined above, although highlighting the importance of intellectual property, did not say anything specific about brands. Brands represent an important part of intellectual property for businesses, sometimes more than the technical know-how behind product or service advantage.

The European Brands Association, therefore, commissioned the research described below to examine behaviour and performance in branded consumer markets. The purpose of the study is to test whether the competitive forces that drive individual businesses are the same as those which create consumer value and economic growth, and if brands play a measurable part in turning new product ideas into growth.

Scope of the Study

We look at how branded fast-moving consumer goods (FMCG) businesses grow by:

(i) Winning market share in the battle against competitors for customer preference.
(ii) Creating additional value added — their contribution to growing the economy.
(iii) Achieving return on capital employed (ROCE) above the cost of capital so that they can compete for investment capital — essential for any business wanting to grow.

We also look at job creation, which is closely related to business growth.

Evidence comes from over 200 businesses in the PIMS database, mainly in the EU and NAFTA, which are clearly FMCG operations. Each is tracked in detail over a minimum of four years on financial and non-financial measures. Most are branded, but the sample contains some businesses which are "unbranded" or which do not support their brands, and these provide some interesting comparisons. The conclusions we show from this data have been separately tested on both sides of the Atlantic, and over time.

The Role of Brands

The economic case for branding is dynamic. A brand should be a means of communication to facilitate innovation and to help realise benefits from R&D investment. There are at least two ways in which this can happen:

(i) Known brands can help consumers recognise trusted suppliers in changing markets, that is, brands aid the process of consumer choice.
(ii) Brands can help producers gain trust for new approaches to meet consumer needs thus providing access to market for innovation.

If this case is real, we should expect to see the processes of choice work more responsively in branded markets. Branded businesses should be sensitive to "value for money" pressures and are more likely to compete through innovation.

What the Evidence Shows

The data shows that branding in FMCG markets does boost competitive innovation. Branding is associated with more dynamic response by producers to consumer needs and competitive activity. Branded businesses do invest more in innovation, strongly associated with business and employment growth. Successful brands must deliver improving value to consumers through innovation — otherwise, they cease to prosper.

Earlier PIMS work showed that quality, innovation and intellectual property drive business and employment growth in the wider economy. We can now show that the links from investment in innovation, quality and value to business growth are stronger for branded consumer products than for other sectors.

Competitiveness and Growth

We begin with an analysis of the ability of a business to grow "relative market share", defined as share of the target market divided by the sum of shares of its top three competitors.

In the branded FMCG sector, more than any other, the drivers of business growth are dynamic; to win the competitive battle for market share,

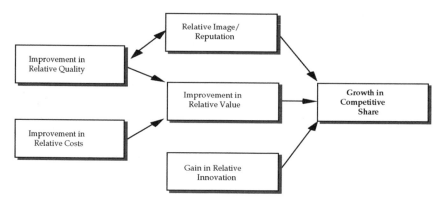

Fig. 1.   The key growth drives.

businesses must be able to:

(i) Offer improving quality and increasing value for money to consumers.
(ii) Move faster and more successfully than competitors on innovation.
(iii) Sustain a strong market reputation.

Just "being good" isn't enough (Fig. 1).

In the charts which follow, we show the impact of value, innovation and reputation on share change versus competitors for branded FMCG businesses. To do so, we must first establish and allow for the starting share position of a business — since for very high share operations, there is nowhere to go but down!

Improving value for money is an important way for high share businesses to limit share loss and for low share businesses to grow (Fig. 2). A business can boost its value position either by improving the relative quality of the offer or by reducing the relative price. When it comes to sustaining growth, "intangible" quality is a more powerful driver than price.

Innovation advantage is essential for businesses with high shares to maintain their position. Again, simply maintaining high rates of new product introductions isn't enough; what matters is increasing success in innovation versus the competition (Fig. 3).

Reputation, or brand image, can give a huge boost to the share prospects of small share businesses (Fig. 4). Reputation is a key enabler for share growth; without it, businesses are less likely to get new products tested in

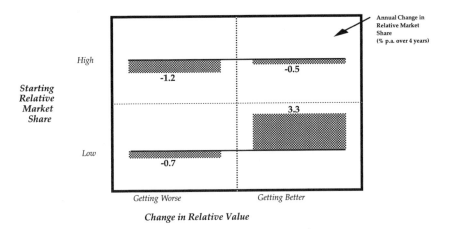

Fig. 2.   Better value for money helps share retention or growth.
Source: PIMS branded FMCG database.

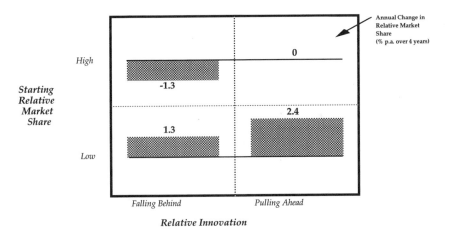

Fig. 3.   Staying ahead on innovation helps drive share gain.
Source: PIMS branded FMCG database.

their markets or quality/value improvements appreciated. At the same time, failure to maintain a strong brand reputation by a market leader can bring rapid erosion of share position. There is little chance of a "quiet life" for high share branded produces — if their competitions innovate or match them on image, they can lose customers quickly.

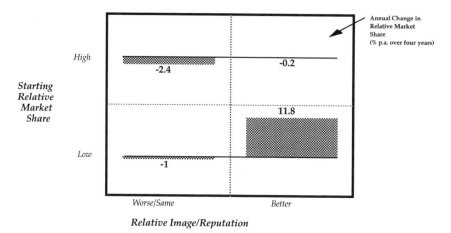

Fig. 4.   Superior reputation helps market share.
Source: PIMS branded FMCG database.

For each of these key relationships, we can track the driving forces of growth back to investment in product and process R&D, to advertising and promotion, and to key capabilities in intellectual property, speed to market and service to distribution channels. These linkages are:

(i) R&D and intellectual property investment in consumer businesses boost successful product innovation and, thus, relative quality.
(ii) Process innovation reduces competitive costs and improves value to consumers.
(iii) Innovation, good service to retailers and investment in commercial communication enhance brand image and company reputation.

The entire set of relationships combines to present a dynamic mode of competitive growth more explicit and powerful than in other types of business. It is a model (Fig. 5) which responds rapidly to changes in consumer requirements and gives branded businesses a major incentive to invest in new products to meet them. Each of the relationships in this model can be demonstrated in multi-variate regression and by simple statistical relationships.

Evidence on value added growth shows a very similar set of relationships (Fig. 6). Innovation, the ability to deliver superior quality products and services and to reduce costs are the key drivers of real value added growth at

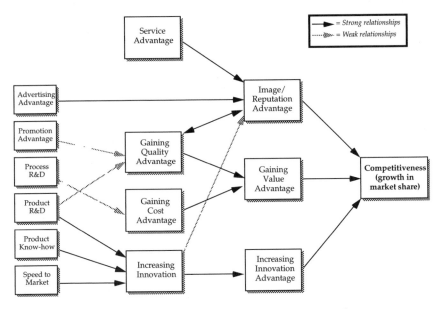

Fig. 5.   From intangible investment to business growth.

Source: PIMS branded FMCG database.

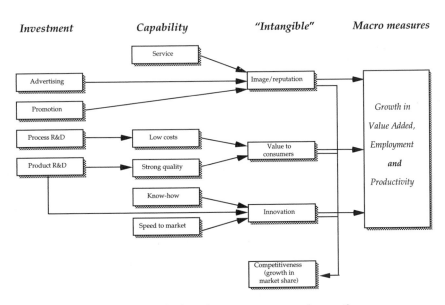

Fig. 6.   From business investment to economic growth.

Source: PIMS branded FMCG database.

the business level. Not only do businesses which win on these factors gain a bigger share of their markets, they also make the biggest contribution to the growth of the economy. And, as we shall see later, innovative branded businesses grow employment and, at the same time, achieve the highest level of productivity.

Brands and Innovation

Not surprisingly, given this set of relationships, branded businesses undertake more innovation in the consumer products sector than unbranded producers (Fig. 7). They spend more on product and process R&D as a percentage of their sales revenue. New products, defined as the percentage of products with significantly new characteristics introduced in the last three years, also represent a much higher proportion of their sales.

For jobs, after stripping out the impact of market growth (clearly a strong driver of employment creation), innovation matters a great deal. Innovative branded businesses in growing markets are where new jobs are created faster. This is because meeting new consumer needs creates new employment opppportunities (Fig. 8). Of course, some of this growth is at the expense of other firms, but the message for European businesses competing in a global context is that successful innovation is the key to growth.

But what about the costs and benefits of innovation to business profits? Evidence shows that strong brands are an essential part of sustainable innovation. Preferred brands help manufacturers to invest in innovation

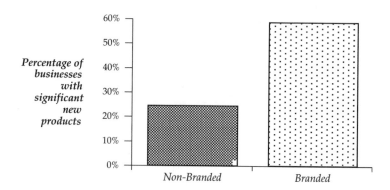

Fig. 7. The majority of branded businesses innovate.

Source: PIMS branded FMCG database.

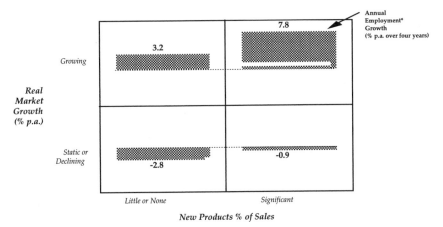

Fig. 8.   Innovation is linked to new jobs.

Source: PIMS branded FMCG database.

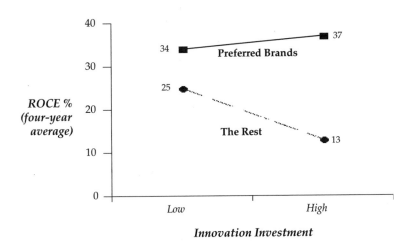

Fig. 9.   Preferred brands make innovation profitable.

Source: PIMS branded FMCG database.

successfully and profitably; without brand preference, the costs of innovation are substantially higher (Fig. 9). Innovation is, in turn, essential to
keep strong brand positions ahead of the competition — without it, they fall
behind.

Competition, Innovation and Growth

This research on fast-moving consumer goods is mirrored by work we have done elsewhere on durables markets. This is further evidence that branded consumer businesses have a strong profit incentive to innovate behind good brand positions to keep their offering to consumers fresh and ahead of competition. Competitive forces raise the pressure for innovation and they increase the rewards for "doing it right". There is a virtuous circle of incentives that should encourage EU branded businesses to compete in global markets through innovation.

If the economic case for branding set out at the start of this chapter is real, we would expect to see branded businesses achieving a significantly better "return" on innovation. If we do the "accounting" in terms of value added, we find that branded FMCG businesses show a strong correlation between R&D and business value added (Fig. 10). Looking at the relationship between R&D spending and value creation per employee, typically an extra Euro of R&D spending in this sector is associated with an extra 2–2.5 Euros in value added. In the rest of the economy, the ratio is typically 1:1.3. This suggests

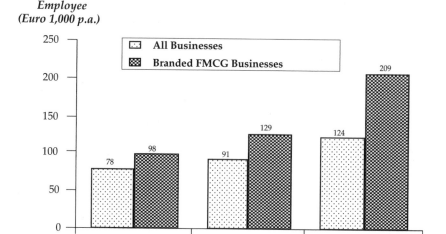

Fig. 10.   Brands boost value from R&D.

Source: PIMS database.

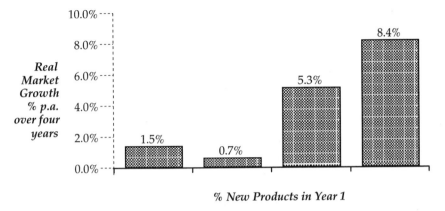

% New Products in Year 1

Fig. 11. Innovation is strongly associated with market growth.

Source: PIMS branded FMCG database.

that branding does increase the effectiveness of businesses in creating value from R&D investment.

These business level incentives help explain the higher innovation in branded markets. And, at the "macro" level, we can also show a strong relationship between innovation and market growth (Fig. 11). It is not possible, from data on individual businesses, to "prove" the direction of the relationship between innovation and market growth. However, it is clear that the markets where our observed businesses have little or no new product revenue are those which do not grow.

Conclusions

PIMS evidence shows that the ability of branded consumer businesses to win the battle for consumer preference is best explained by three interrelated factors:

(i) The abiliy to improve value to consumers through better products and more competitive price.

(ii) The ability to get new products to market faster and more effectively than competitors.

(iii) A sustained advantage in consumer and trade reputation, without which it is unlikely that value advantage will be seen by consumers or that innnovation will reach the market.

We have also examined FMCG producers who focus on unbranded or "unsupported" products. They are much less innovative and invest less effort in key drivers of growth.

The evidence, from real businesses operating in real markets, shows that:

(i) Branding is essential for innovation and growth in consumer markets in competitive economies.

(ii) Successful brands deliver ever improving value to consumers through innovation and quality improvement; if they fail in this, they fail to grow.

(iii) Policies on competition and intellectual property should take as much account of branding in "everyday" products (where the bulk of this evidence comes from) as they do in the more conspicuous "hi-tech" areas of the economy, where much of the debate on intellectual property protection has focused.

Our results show that branding helps producers to innovate and consumers to choose. The economic case for brands stands up; the importance of marketing communication in promoting innovation and growth is proven.

Implications for Policy and for Management

Partly as a result of this study, EU policy-makers have increased efforts to make the single market in commercial communication a reality. European firms suffer the disadvantage in that while they can move products around the single market, the marketing to support them is still seriously limited by national regulations. Restrictions on promotional offers in Italy and bans on advertising toys in Greece are examples.

American companies — in addition to their advantage of a having a single language for their domestic market — suffer fewer restraints on marketing and the use of brands. This helps to explain why US businesses have historically been better able to capitalise on quality advantages in their markets and have been more innovative. It is not always appreciated by policy-markets that the commercial communication costs associated with innovation can be greater than the costs of technical development. Therefore, restraints which push up marketing costs can stifle new product launches. Europe needs more than a single market in physical products to compete on equal terms in innovation markets.

There are lessons, too, for branded business managers. A brand is not, as some have suggested, a device to "tax" consumers. Successful brands justify themselves through innovation and improving value to consumers. If they fail in this, leaving themselves with nothing to communicate, they die. PIMS evidence shows that branding sharpens the operation of competitive forces. Any brand owner who ignores this does so at his or her own peril.

Chapter 5

Technological and Market Competencies and Financial Performance

Joe Tidd
SPRU, University of Sussex, UK

Ciaran Driver
Imperial College Business School, UK

Introduction

In this chapter, we summarise and review the range of technological, market and organisational measures of innovation discussed in this book and elsewhere, and examine the relationship between these measures and financial performance. The chapter consists of three sections. First, we review the range of technological, market and organisational measures of innovation discussed in this book and elsewhere. Secondly, we examine a range of financial measures of performance, as well as the relationship between these and our measures of innovation. Finally, we develop a simple — but, we believe, comprehensive — model of innovation based on selected indicators of innovation at 40 companies in the United Kingdom (UK), representing all key sectors, and identify the relationships between different measures of innovation and the financial performance of these companies.

Measures of Innovation

The aim of this section is to identify a range of measures of technological, organisational and market which can be used to construct an innovation scoreboard. By definition, the study of innovation is multi-disciplinary.

However, to date, most studies have been conducted within a single, narrow discipline, principally economics. Therefore, the literature review presented here is broad and covers relevant research in the economics, finance and strategic management literatures. We focus on measures based on data in the public domain, rather than survey data, as these are more readily accessible and comparable across different companies, sectors and nations. For a recent review of survey-based studies, see Smith (1992) or Crepon and Mairesse (1993).

The most established, and still the most commonly used, indicators of innovation are technology-based, including capital expenditure, expenditure on research and development and patent activity. The respective strengths and weaknesses of technological indicators, such as expenditure on research and development and patent, are well documented (see, for example, Chapters 6 and 7). These indicators have the advantage that definitions are relatively consistent and data is collected on a routine basis. However, previous research suggests that such indicators may be more reliable indicators at the national and sectoral levels than at the firm level. The review that follows identifies the advantages and drawbacks of different technology-based indicators of innovations.

Innovation can be viewed as a set of outputs responding to inputs, that is, the so-called "linear" model. Although this view does not command unanimous support — and we will point to some limitations — it is convenient to use this framework and there is no obvious alternative. R&D expenditure or R&D capital stock is usually taken as an input. Data is available on expenditure, but we generally have little idea what depreciation rate to use to construct capital stock estimates. Hence, we can let the capital stock be represented by a weighted sum of previous R&D expenditures, where the weights can either be estimated or imposed. There is a further problem as to whether we should deflate the R&D expenditures. If we do, we are trying to deal with a technical or production relationship. If we do not, we are simply looking at relationships in monetary terms.

As for the outputs, this is often taken as deflated production (assuming that the R&D figures are deflated), usually adjusted first to take account of other inputs such as labour, fixed capital or materials. However, as we will discuss later, some studies look at profitability instead — perhaps because of the restrictive assumptions needed for production function estimation. Other possible output measures are patents, innovation counts and the diffusion of innovations. Griliches (1990) reviews the use of patent statistics as indicators of innovation. He makes the important observation that the standard of novelty and utility for granting patents is not very high, and that it varies greatly over time and across different countries. Archibugi (1992) provides a comprehensive list of the advantages and disadvantages of patent statistics as indicators of innovative activity. The main advantages of patents are:

(i) Patents represent the output of the inventive process, specifically those inventions which are expected to have an economic benefit.

(ii) Obtaining patent protection is time consuming and expensive. Hence, applications are only likely to be made for those developments which are expected to provide benefits in excess of these costs.

(iii) Patents can be broken down by technical fields, thus providing information on both the rate and direction of innovation.

(iv) Patent statistics are available in large numbers and over very long time series.

The main disadvantages of patents as indicators of innovation are:

(i) Not all inventions are patented. Firms may choose to protect their discoveries by other means, such as through secrecy. It has been estimated that firms apply for patents for 66% to 87% of patentable inventions.

(ii) Not all innovations are technically patentable — for example, software development.

(iii) The propensity to patent varies considerably across different sectors and firms. For example, there is a high propensity to patent in the pharmaceutical industry, but a low propensity in fast-moving consumer goods.

(iv) Firms have a different propensity to patent in each national market, according to the attractiveness of markets.

(v) A large proportion of patents are never exploited, or are applied for simply to block other developments. It has been estimated that between 40% to 60% of all patents issued are used.

In order to determine whether patents measure anything of relevance, it is necessary to look for correlations with other indicators, such as R&D expenditure, productivity growth, profitability or the stock market value of the firm. For example, there is quite a strong relationship between R&D and the number of patents at the cross-sectional level, across firms and industries. However, at the level of the firm, the relationship is much weaker over time. More promising are econometric studies of the relationship between patents and financial performance. An example is the use of patent numbers as a proxy for "intangible" capital in stock market value of firm regressions.

Econometric techniques can be used to assess the impact of innovation inputs, specifically, the expenditure on research and development, and on some measure of performance, typically productivity or patents. The work of Griliches (1984) and Stoneman (1990) suggests that product R&D is significantly less productive than process R&D according to the estimates. Studies by Geroski (1991, 1994) use the usual production function framework, but include significant innovations (Science and Technology Policy Research Unit (SPRU) databank) categorised by the producer sector and the user sector at three-digit standard industrial classification (SIC) level. The greatest significance was found for innovations used (nearly four times as much as for innovations developed). A further breakdown showed that innovations used originating in the engineering industries had the strongest effect. The study noted that the productivity increases took 1–15 years to be fully effected. The fit between inputs (R&D) and outputs (patents) improves the broader categorisation used in the study. At the national level, patents and R&D are correlated and, also, to some extent at the sectoral level. As Pavitt (1988) notes, however, the extent of unexplained variation is high at the level of cross-company analysis (see also Silberston, 1989) which gives a ranking of patents and R&D by activity heading using the UK standard industrial classification. It is clear from his figures that the correlation is far from perfect. Furthermore, he suggests that important patents are likely to be located in high R&D industries.

Part of the difficulty in obtaining stable relationships between patents and R&D lies in the fact that firms have different propensities to patent their discoveries. This partly reflects the ease of protecting the gains from innovation in other ways, such as secrecy and first-mover advantages. Furthermore, the effectiveness of patents may vary across industries as Levin et al. (1987) have shown. R&D statistics also display industry-specific bias with some sectors classifying their development work as design or production (Pavitt and Patel, 1988). The fact that weaker relationships between outputs and inputs are observed at the firm level, rather than at the industry level, suggests that there is a lot of variability in the productivity of technological inputs, and that there may be some point in studying the particular conditions under which the inputs are used most effectively. The most likely explanatory factors are scale, technological opportunity and management (Hay and Morris, 1991).

The evidence on scale is mixed. There are two linked hypotheses — that the size of the R&D effort counts, and that the size of the firm makes R&D more effective, say, because of economies of scope between projects (Cohen and Levin, 1989). Studies suggest that the scale of R&D effort is important only in chemicals (Hay and Morris, 1991) and pharmaceuticals (Jensen, 1987). Firm size is a more difficult issue to study because the interpretation of R&D and patents differs between class sizes of firms. A study by Blundell *et al.* (1993) compared over 600 manufacturing firms between 1972 and 1982 in the UK, matched to the SPRU database of significant technical innovations. It suggested that large firms tend to innovate more because they have a higher incentive to do so: a doubling of market share from the mean of 2.5% will increase the probability of innovation in the next period by 0.6%. This result is qualified by noting that less competitive firms (higher concentration and lower import ratios) innovate less.

Technological opportunity at the industry level is surveyed by Levin *et al.* (1987) in the context of their study of appropriability. Technological opportunity also exists at the firm level via the spillover effects from other firms (Jaffe, 1986). Geroski (1994) reaches similar conclusions. The classic study of the managerial efficiency of R&D inputs is project SAPPHO, best summarised in Freeman (1982). Not surprisingly, commitment to the project by senior management and good communications are crucial to success. Chusil (1978) shows that growth markets are less favourable to overspending than stable or contracting markets.

A major problem with measuring inputs and outputs is: how do we take account of the "spillover" of innovation benefits or information to other firms or industries? For example, if we are looking at a particular sector's industrial output or productivity in relation to its R&D spending, how do we take account of spillover from other sectors or non-industry R&D? (Mansfield, 1984).The question really relates to the appropriate level of investigation — is it the company/or industry/or entire economy?

Freeman (1982) discusses the question of spillover, arguing that the appropriate connection to make is not so much company R&D and productivity as industry R&D and productivity. For example, the whole electronics industry benefited from Bell's work on semiconductors, and only a small part was recovered by Bell in the form of licensing or sales. There may also be a different kind of spillover internal to the firm. Some products fail, but their R&D is still useful. For example, the large sums spent by IBM on the (failed) Stretch computer in the 1960s (only a few were sold) led to the successful 360 series.

Geroski (1991) notes that the spillover from innovations between closely related sectors is not as great as previous research has suggested with regard to R&D spending (Jaffe, 1986). Rather, there is spillover between producers and users. This is presumably because the innovation itself is too firm-specific to show much spillover effect, whereas the information shared with R&D spillover is less firm-specific. Although firms are increasingly drawing upon external sources of innovation, few have yet to systematically scan outside their own sector (Tidd and Trewhella, 1997). A particular form of spillover occurs when the economy, as a whole, benefits more from an innovation than is appropriated as profits. A difference, then, occurs between the private rate of return and the social rate of return (Mansfield, 1990).

The limitations of R&D and patents, as surrogates for innovation, have led to more recent studies turning to less robust but market-based measures, such as new product announcements and innovation counts. Jensen (1987) related the number of new chemical entities discovered in the US pharmaceutical industry to constant price R&D and other variables. A non-linear (convex) relationship with R&D was discovered and there was some indication that when R&D was interacted with sales in a large firm, it was more effective. The study by Devinney (1993) reports the strength of the relationship from patents to innovations in order to judge whether patents can be used as an innovation indicator. Innovation is measured by a count of citations in the *Wall Street Journal*. The results are striking in that at the four-digit industry level, there is a strong relationship. This disappears when the firm level data is analysed. Indeed, the best predictor of a firm innovation is the patent intensity of the industry it is in.

The collection and analysis of innovations in the "product news" columns of trade journals has three advantages over company surveys.

First, data can be collected without contacting companies. This reduces the resources required and places no additional burden on industry. Secondly, data can be collected relatively cheaply by scanning trade journals and databases. Thirdly, the data set can be extended into the past to allow comparisons over time. The main drawback of this approach is that it fails to capture process innovations. Few, if any, firms choose to make public announcements of their process innovations. However, official statistics focus on factor productivity — labour and capital. Hence, this may not be a major shortcoming.

The use of product announcements to measure innovation first took place in the US in the early 1980s (Edwards and Gordon, 1984). This pioneering study, commissioned by the US Small Business Administration, developed a database of product announcements in 100 technology, engineering and trade journals. Firms were classified by size and the four-digit SIC code. The innovations were then classified according to a four-point scale of significance.

A subsequent study analysed innovations announced in all major US publications in the year 1982 (Acs and Audretsch, 1988), but more recent studies have restricted the scope to leading financial publications such as the *Wall Street Journal* (Chaney et al., 1992). These studies indicate that innovation tends to be concentrated in larger firms, in less concentrated industries and is strongly affected by joint investment in advertising and R&D. At the industry level, patent intensity and new product announcements are strongly related, with 60% of the variance in the new product sample being explained by patent intensity. However, at the level of the firm, the relationship is very weak, and only 2% of the variance of individual firm level new product activity appears to be explained by patenting activity (Devinney, 1993). As use of the absolute number of patents or new products would introduce bias towards large firms, the measures used were a proportion of total patents and a proportion of new product total announcements. What also stands out from Table 1 is that firms introducing new products tend to be large and R&D and advertising-intensive.

A growing body of research on product announcements emerged in the 1990s. Various studies in the US, the Netherlands, Austria, Ireland and the UK have refined and validated the methodology. Most recently, the use of product announcements as an indicator of innovation has been the subject

Table 1. Patenting versus non-patenting firms.

	Patenting Firms		Non-Patenting Firms	
	No New Products	New Products	No New Products	New Products
Assets ($ millions)	882	3,328	1,705	3, 960
Advertising/sales (%)	1.0	2.9	1.4	4.2
R&D/assets (%)	2.3	4.8	2.1	6.3
Debt/market value (%)	39.2	33.5	43.4	29.2
Return on assets (%)	6.6	6.0	5.9	0.0
New products (number)	0.0	4.5	0.0	1.8
Patents (number)	156	592	0	0

Source: Derived from Devinney, 1993.

of a number of studies in the UK. The Technology Policy Unit at Aston has examined the relationship between the expenditure of R&D, patents and new product announcements in the pharmaceutical industry (Steward, 1994). A study by UMIST (Coombs *et al.*, 1994) applied a similar methodology to the Dutch study. The researchers examined product announcements in 35 trade and industry journals over a period of three months in 1993. The unit of analysis was the product announcement rather than the firm. The study identified almost 1,000 product announcements originating from a similar number of companies.

The Dutch study (Kleinknecht and Reijnen, 1993) is of particular interest because it developed a detailed scheme of classification which has been adopted by many subsequent studies. The research, supported by the Ministry of Economic Affairs, examined all product announcements in the 1989 volumes of 36 trade and industry journals. Data was collected on each of the following:

   (i) The identity of the firm and the four-digit SIC code.
  (ii) The product name and a brief description of the innovation.
 (iii) The degree of complexity of the innovation (see below).
 (iv) The type of innovation (see below).
  (v) The properties of the innovation (see below).
 (vi) The origin of the innovation.
(vii) The main market of the innovation.

The study distinguishes three levels of complexity:

(i) *High.* A system consisting of a larger number of components, often from different disciplines, such as a new car or aircraft.

(ii) *Medium.* A unit consisting of a smaller number of components, such as a new machine tool.

(iii) *Low.* A single innovation, such as an improved component.

In addition, the research distinguishes five types of innovation:

(i) A *completely new* or decisively changed product or service, such as a mountain bike or electronic banking.

(ii) A *modestly improved* product or service, such as a more energy-efficient machine or improved safety protection of credit cards.

(iii) A new or improved *accessory* product or service, such as a safer child's seat for a car or improved life assurance connected to a mortgage.

(iv) A product or service *differentiation*, such as new packaging.

(v) A *process* innovation.

It is important to note that in this scheme of classification, the complexity and the type of innovation are independent of each other. A highly complex product may only be a modest improvement or, conversely, a product of low complexity can be totally new. The distinction made between incremental innovation and product differentiation is also important. The test used involves checking a product announcement against a list of 14 innovation properties, such as greater efficiency, longer life and easier maintenance. If a product announcement does not satisfy any of the properties listed, it is classified as a product or service differentiation.

Significantly, the EUROSTAT pilot questionnaire for the EC innovation survey specifically excludes product or service differentiation. However, research suggests that more than a quarter of all innovations are product or service differentiation (Coombs *et al.*, 1994). Other studies also indicate that product differentiation is one of the main drivers of profitability (Luchs, 1990). Therefore, the inclusion of product and service differentiation is a significant benefit of using product announcements as indicators of innovation. There are a number of additional reasons for choosing this methodology:

(i) It is a useful measure of innovation output and allows comparison with more conventional input indicators, such as R&D and patents.
(ii) It provides a direct measure of product differentiation, which is not captured by other indicators.
(iii) It can be aggregated to compare the performance of different firm sizes, sectors and regions.
(iv) It provides a direct measure of the flow of innovations into the UK.
(v) By adopting a common methodology, it allows direct comparison with similar databases overseas.
(vi) It identifies new product and service development for subsequent in-depth case studies.

Measures of Innovation and Financial Performance

Many traditional accounting and financial indicators concentrate on short-term measures of profitability and, therefore, may undervalue innovation. However, measures based on value added, market to book value and price to earnings multiple may be better indicators of innovation. A recent study of accounting practice suggests that traditional financial performance measures, such as return on capital employed, earnings per share and cash flow projections, are being replaced by performance indicators based on the highest level of the firm, such as strategic benchmarking or, at the very detailed level, activity-based costing (CIMA, 1993). Rappaport (1986) lays down some "fundamental criteria" which measures of financial performance should attain:

(i) *Valid.* Consistent with basic economic theory of value.
(ii) *Verifiable.* Calculated unambiguously from readily available data.
(iii) *Controllable.* The person being measured must be able to control performance.
(iv) *Global.* Applicable everywhere.
(v) *Communicable.* Easily explained.

The most common measures of stock market performance are earnings per share (EPS) and the price to earnings (P/E) multiple. In particular, it is commonly assumed that provided a company achieves a satisfactory growth in its EPS, the market value of its shares will increase. However, an increase or decrease in earnings may not result in a corresponding increase or decrease in shareholder value. This is because, first, earnings do not take into account the level of financial and business risk. Secondly, earnings do not include the capital and fixed investment needed to achieve the anticipated growth. Thirdly, the time value of money is ignored.

For these reasons, return on investment (ROI) has become a more popular measure of financial performance. The assumption is that if the ROI is greater than the cost of capital, shareholder value will be increased. However, in practice, this is highly misleading as ROI is an accrual accounting-based measure, whereas the cost of capital is the economic return demanded by shareholders. ROI tends to overstate the economic or discounted cashflow (DCF) return for a number of reasons: capitalisation policy; depreciation policy; and the lag between investment outlays and subsequent cash flows. As a result, ROI tends to understate the economic rate of return during the early stage of an investment, and overstate rates at later stages as the undepreciated assets base decreases. Unfortunately, the effects are rarely self-correcting. A further objection to the use of ROI to evaluate performance is that it ignores the residual value of the business after the period in question. Clearly, the true change in shareholder value must take into account the present value of future cashflows and the residual value of the business.

Rappaport (1986) proposes a practical means of assessing changes in shareholder value. He identifies a number of value drivers: sales growth rate, operating profit margin, working capital investment, fixed capital investment, forecast duration, cost of capital and rate of tax. These factors can be used to calculate the present value of forecast cashflows. However, for most businesses, the cashflow over the next five or ten years represents only a small proportion of the change in value. In most cases, the residual value of the business is the largest proportion of the change in value. This is particularly so where a business attempts to increase market share by increasing expenditure on production capacity, new product development and marketing. Typically, such businesses may experience negative cashflows for several years, but may enhance value in the long run.

Therefore, the estimate of the residual value of a business is critical. However, there is no agreed method of calculating residual value and, to a large extent, it depends on the assumptions made for the forecast period. One commonly used method is based on perpetuity value. The perpetuity method assumes that after the forecast period, the business will earn, on average, the cost of capital on new investments. In other words, after the forecast period, the business will invest in strategies which will, on average, have a zero net present value. This assumption can be justified by the behaviour of most competitive markets. If a company is able to earn returns above the cost of capital, it will eventually attract competitors who will, in turn, drive down return to the minimum acceptable or cost of capital rate.

There are a number of alternative methods of estimating residual values, such as those based on the market to book (M/B) value or price to earnings (P/E) multiple. Using the M/B ratio, the residual can be estimated by multiplying the book value of equity by the projected M/B ratio at the end of the forecast period. However, the book value is affected by earnings calculations rather than actual earnings and, in practice, it is difficult to forecast future M/B ratios. Similar objections exist for using P/E multiples. The residual value can be estimated by multiplying the earnings at the end of the forecast period by the forecast P/E. However, in practice, average P/E multiples vary significantly over time, making them difficult to forecast. Conceptually, use of either M/B and P/E is unsatisfactory because both use accounting data to estimate the residual value, whereas the present value of cashflows is used for the forecast period.

A practical implication of shareholder value analysis is the concept of a threshold margin. This is defined as the minimum operating profit margin a business must achieve in order to maintain shareholder value. In other words, it represents the operating profit margin at which the business earns exactly its cost of capital. The threshold margin can be expressed either as the margin required on incremental sales or the margin required on total sales.

The view frequently taken is that the stock exchange consistently undervalues shares of the firms which spend on R&D because expensed (as opposed to capitalised) R&D reduces earnings per share in the year of expenditure — one of the two major performance criteria used by analysts. The fact that analysts use fundamentals such as EPS was confirmed by Arnold and Moizer (1984). Some industrialists believe that this approach systematically undervalues long-term research and development and capital expenditure. This is because, first, discounting reduces the value of expected future revenue. Secondly, it is difficult to value the future options which research and development may create. The fact that there is a weak correlation between company valuations, in terms of the price to earnings, and expenditure on R&D suggests that the problem of undervaluation is industry-specific, if it exists at all. The problem appears to have more to do with a lack of communication between industry and its investors.

The financial community relies heavily on various financial ratios and scoring methods to evaluate company performance. Both Altman (1971) and Taffler (1991) have used ratios to help create an index to predict corporate failure, although the third seminal author (Argenti, 1976) prefers a taxonomy of events/factors to a multi-variate approach. Altman (1983), in the US, and Taffler (1982), in the UK, have used multiple discriminant analysis to identify what factors differentiate financially successful companies from those which fail. Multiple discriminant analysis involves attributing weights to each variable such that the distribution of scores for each group has the least overlap. The reliability of these models has proven to be high, being able to predict company failure with 95% accuracy.

However, such indices are difficult for managers to interpret. Therefore, we prefer specific financial ratios which have some relation to long-term performance. For example, Kay (1993) places great emphasis on the value added by a firm as a measure of corporate performance. He argues that there can be no long-term rationale for a firm which does not add value. There is no agreed definition of value added, but essentially it is simply the difference between the market value of outputs and the cost of inputs. This contrasts with operating profit, which is the difference between the value of output and the value of material and labour inputs. The assessment of value added must also take into account the cost of capital inputs — depreciation and a provision for a reasonable return on the capital invested. The simplest definition of value added is turnover less depreciation and bought in materials and services. This definition has the advantage that it is simple to calculate and interpret; it enables comparison to be made between companies with very different activities and cannot be manipulated to the same extent as accounting profit.

Walker (1979) uses a R&D/value added ratio as a proxy for innovation output in his study. In his justification for the measure, he points out that identical R&D expenditures in different industries do not necessarily indicate identical innovation activity. He also argues that R&D thresholds will be different for different industries, some being far more capital-intensive than others. Budworth (1993) proposes a related but more complex ratio. He develops an "innovation ratio" based on the ratio of cash outlay to cash return, as well as the ratio of development time to market life of specific development projects. The idea is that when, or if, a company with a portfolio of different products reaches steady state, the innovation ratio will be equivalent to the ratio of innovation spending to value added. On this basis, it is possible to calculate an innovation ratio for specific sectors and companies. For example, Budworth calculates the ratio for the UK mechanical engineering sectors to be around 14%. As the value added for that sector is some 50% of turnover, this suggests that at least 7% of revenue should be devoted to innovation in order to sustain intangible assets. Conceptually, this ratio is similar to the depreciation charge for tangible assets.

Peters and Waterman's (1982) bestseller, *In Search of Excellence*, provides a good example of the application of financial ratios to company evaluation. The authors use average return on equity, return on capital and return on sales as measures of success. Perhaps more promising, they also use the average ratio of market value to book value as a measure of the long-term innovative potential of a company. The reasoning behind this is that the difference between the two methods of company valuation represents the contribution of future earnings above and beyond the tangible assets. This element of "goodwill" can be substantial and may be a useful proxy for innovativeness. It may be possible to disaggregate this into components, such as the value of brands, levels of staff training, R&D and other intellectual assets.

Geroski (1994) shows that the profit margin of innovators — using matched data from the SPRU database and company accounts — is higher than non-innovators, controlling for other influences. However, the effect was rather small, suggesting that benefits may have been captured by users. Innovating firms are also more protected from cyclical downturns. Scherer and Ravenscraft (1982) looked at the relationship between profitability and lagged indicators of capital input, marketing expenses and R&D. The main conclusion was a rate of return to R&D of about 33% with an average lag of about five years. Process R&D had four times the rate of return as product R&D, but was more risky with a more variable return.

The impact of R&D on the stock market is more difficult to judge as one needs a prior position on the efficiency, or otherwise, of financial markets before setting up a testable hypothesis. Some key papers are Pakes (1985), who observed a significant (though noisy) effect, and Hall (1993a). The latter paper raises an important worry about whether stock market valuations of innovation are consistent. The valuation of R&D capital collapsed from a value of unity to a quarter over the 1980s, a result that is robust to measurement and specification tests. The market valuation of R&D does not appear to be affected significantly by accounting policy. The revenues accruing to any particular project might be many years removed from the time of the development costs. This has led firms on to capitalise their expenditures until the revenue arrives. Surveys suggest that analysts, as a whole, are able to "see through" this kind of capitalisation and, in consequence, do not treat such companies any differently from those which write off the expense. The same research suggests that analysts even prefer R&D spending to increasing the productive base of the firm through asset acquisition. Countering the view that analysts are short-sighted is the fact that analysts in the UK graded the importance of R&D information with a 2.32 on a scale of seven (with one as the "best"), making it the fourth most important, with product development coming in third at 2.36 (Pike *et al.*, 1993).

The use of stock market value as an output indicator has a major advantage over other financial measures. Other indicators, such as profits or return on investment, are likely to reflect the effect of innovation only slowly. In contrast, developments which cause the market to re-evaluate the future output of the firm should be recorded immediately. The simplest market value model assumes that the market value of the firm is proportional to its physical, or tangible, capital and intangible capital. This can be written as

$$V = q(A + gK) = qA(1 + gK/A),$$

where V is the market value of the firm, A is the current replacement cost of its tangible assets, K is its level of intangible assets, g is its relative shadow price, and q is the current premium or discount of market value over the replacement cost of tangible assets. The contribution of innovation to the value of the firm, net of expected dividend and investment policy, can be written as the sum of three components:

$$qV = w + n + u,$$

where q is the rate of return on stock holding, V is the total market value of the firm's assets, w corresponds to the change in the firm's R&D position arising from news associated with current patent applications, n reflects a re-valuation of past patents and u reflects all other sources of fluctuations in the value of the firm.

Research suggests a significant, independent effect of patents on the market value of firms, beyond the R&D expenditure, but fluctuations in patents account for only around 1% of the total fluctuations in market value. Griliches *et al.* (1991) examined the relationship between patents and the market value of the firm and found that with the exception of the pharmaceutical industry, changes in market value due to changes in the patent rate were not significant. Product announcements may be a more generic indicator of product innovation. A benefit of using product announcements as a measure of market innovation is that it lends itself to an event-study methodology to link product announcements with the market value of a firm. This is an extension of the rational expectations/efficient market assumptions of financial economics, that is, the share prices in an efficient stock market will instantaneously reflect all available information on the firm. For example, a study (Chaney *et al.*, 1991) of more than 1,000 product announcements in the *Wall Street Journal* found that these had a positive effect on the share price of the originating firm. The impact of the announcement on share price will depend on two factors: first, an assessment of the probability of success of the new product; secondly, an evaluation of the level of future earnings from the product.

The study found that firms introducing new products accrue around 0.75% excess market return over three days, beginning one day before the formal announcement. The average value of each new product announcement was found to be $26 million (in 1972 dollars). Of course, the precise

Table 2. Firms making new product announcements versus non-announcers.

	Total Expenditure ($m)	
	Firms Announcing New Products	Firms Not Announcing New Products
Asset	532.57	95.84
Sales	2119.68	467.88
Advertising	45.58	6.39
R&D	56.50	11.55
Capital exp.	178.77	32.24
P/E	x15.82	x7.95

Source: Derived from Chaney *et al.*, 1991.

return and value of each product announcement depends on the industry sectors: the highest returns were found to be in food, printing, chemicals and pharmaceuticals, computers, photographic equipment and durable goods. Excess returns due to new product announcements suggest that past and current accounting data have little predictive value. However, the P/E ratio may be a better predictor. The study found that the average P/E ratio of the firms making new product announcements was almost twice that of the firms which made no new product announcements (Table 2). This implies that the stock market is valuing the long-term stream of future earnings generated by the innovative firms at a much higher rate than the non-innovators.

So far, little attempt has been made to relate innovation to company performance. The PIMS (Profit Impact of Market Strategy) database attempts to do this. PIMS was established in 1972. Since then, some 3,000 business units representing 450 companies have contributed data. For each business unit PIMS collects data on market conditions, competitive position and financial and operating performance. The measure of performance used in each case is profit as a percentage of sales (that is, profit margin or return on sales — ROS) and profit as a percentage of investment (return on investment — ROI). Of the two measures, ROI is superior to ROS as it relates results to the resources used to achieve them. By analysing such data using multiple regression, PIMS attempts to identify common patterns of relationships between different factors. The factors listed in Table 3 explain about 40% of the difference in performance between businesses. A more

Table 3.   Measures of strategy dimensions and impact on performance.

Strategy Dimension	Measure	Impact on ROI/ROS
Competitive position	Market share	Positive
Product policy	Relative quality	Positive
	New products % sales	Negative
Marketing	Marketing as % sales	Negative
Investment	Plant % sales	Negative
	Newness of plant	Positive
	Labour productivity	Positive
	Inventory %sales	Negative
Vertical integration	Value added % sales	Positive
Research & development	R&D as % of sales	Negative

Source: Derived from Buzzell and Gale, 1987.

complete statistical model, which includes market and other conditions, can explain over 70% of the difference.

The product life cycle model suggests several measures of market characteristics:

(i)   The age of products, that is, how long ago the products were developed.
(ii) The stage in the life cycle, that is, introduction, growth, maturity or decline.
(iii) The real rate of growth of the market, that is, excluding price inflation.

Generally, profitability declines as the market evolves over time for a number of reasons. First, product and service differentiation tend to be reduced. Secondly, competition tends to shift to price and rates of return fall. Thirdly, at least in the manufacturing and production sectors, capital intensity tends to increase, driving returns down even further. More specifically, the real rate of market growth is associated with profitability. At the extremes, a real annual rate of growth of 10% or more has a ROI four points higher than markets declining at rates of 5% or more. High rates of market growth are associated with:

(i)   High gross margins.
(ii) High marketing costs.
(iii) Rising productivity.
(iv) Rising value added per employee.

(v) Rising investment.

(vi) Low or negative case flow.

Market differentiation measures the degree to which all competitors differ from one another across a market. Therefore, market differentiation is related to market segmentation and is a measure of market attractiveness. Customers in different market segments will value different product attributes. The joint effect of relative quality and market differentiation is significant. Markets in which there is little differentiation and no significant difference in the relative quality of competitors are characterised by low returns. High relative quality is a strong predictor of high profitability in any market conditions. Nevertheless, a niche business may achieve high returns in a market with high differentiation without high relative quality. A combination of both high market differentiation and high perceived relative quality yields very high ROI, typically in excess of 30%.

The importance of market share varies with industry. Intuition would suggest that share would be most important in capital-intensive manufacturing and production industries, where economies of scale are required. However, PIMS suggests that market share has a much stronger impact on profitability in innovative sectors, that is, those industries characterised by high R&D and/or marketing expenditure. For the R&D and marketing-intensive businesses, the ROI of the market leader is on average 26% points higher than the average small share business. In the manufacturing-intensive businesses, the corresponding difference is only 12 points. This suggests that scale effects are more important in R&D and marketing than in manufacturing.

It appears that the same factors which affect short-term ROI have a similar effect on long-term value enhancement. However, there are some important differences between factors which affect performance over the short- and long-term. These factors are rate of new product introduction, R&D expenditure and marketing expenditure. All three factors are central to innovation and long-term performance, but may depress performance in the short run. As shown earlier, high rates of product introduction and high expenditure on R&D and marketing all reduce ROI in the short run. However, all three factors are positively related to the long-term value enhancement of the business.

Towards a Synthesis of Measures

There are three difficulties in constructing a model of the effects of innovation on the financial performance of the firm.

First, at the firm level, the relationships between inputs and outputs is much weaker than at the industry level. The weakness in the relationship may be caused simply by the random unpredictability of innovation. If this were the case, then firms spending more on inputs could be said to be more innovative in a probabilistic sense even if they did not actually innovate strongly. However, if firms differ in their technological opportunities, it may not make sense for one firm to innovate more than another — it would mean a misallocation of resources. Even if spillover was believed to be particularly strong so that innovation was likely to be sub-optimal in general, it would not be clear, without looking at the specifics of a firm, whether it was over- or under-investing in R&D. Any comparison must, therefore, be across homogenous firms and this may be difficult to arrange.

Secondly, the reporting behaviour of firms may change in respect of any variable that is monitored to be used in an index of innovation. This reflects the so-called "Goodhart" law phenomenon whereby monetary indicators devised by the government became subverted as behaviour changed in response to measurement.

Thirdly, an objective of the indicators may be to influence financial markets and lending behaviour. However, these markets at present give a lot of attention to the management and efficiency of technological inputs which are assessed almost entirely by track record. It is not clear that any index of innovation activity is likely to supplant this. Furthermore, financial markets will concern themselves only with the gain appropriable by the firm itself.

As noted earlier, it is convenient to conceptualise innovation as a set of outputs responding to inputs — the linear model. We fully appreciate the limitations of this model from both a theoretical and an empirical perspective (see, e.g. Tidd and Bessant, 2009), but it allows technological, market and financial indicators to be incorporated in the scoreboard. To help assess the relative perceived importance of the various measures available, we consulted 25 organisations and, where possible, at the level of the chief executive or other person responsible for assessing the company's performance. The scope of consultation was sufficiently broad to include all the relevant communities: industry, finance, media and academia. We found that there was general support for better measures of innovation and its contribution to financial performance. Managers frequently linked innovation with the broader issue of competitiveness, which they associated with a range of non-price factors, such as product quality and product differentiation. Therefore, few of the practitioners we consulted were interested in improved measures of technological inputs, such as R&D expenditure, capital expenditure or patent activity. Rather, there is a demand for measures of the *efficiency* and *effectiveness* of the innovation process: efficiency in the sense of how well companies translate technological and commercial inputs into new products, processes and services; effectiveness in the sense of how successful such innovations are in the market and their contribution to financial performance.

We have chosen to use expenditure on research and development and capital investment as indicators of technological innovation and inputs into the innovation process. The ratio of research and development to sales is a proxy for product innovation, and the ratio of capital expenditure to sales is a proxy for process innovation. Despite their limitations, both measures are well understood by both academics and managers. Data on patents have not been included in the trial scoreboard, but may feature in the final version. Research suggests a significant independent effect of patents on the market value of firms, beyond the R&D expenditure, but fluctuations in patents account for only around 1% of the total fluctuations in market value. In addition, there is the practical problem that data on UK patents are not as accessible as data on US patent activity.

Product announcements made in trade and industry journals are included to provide a better indicator of innovation outputs at the firm level. As noted earlier, this approach has three advantages over company surveys. First, data can be collected without contacting companies. This reduces the resources required and places no additional burden on industry. Secondly, data can be collected relatively cheaply by scanning trade journals and databases. Thirdly, the data set can be extended into the past to allow comparisons over time. The main drawback of this approach is that it fails to capture process innovations as few firms choose to make public announcements of their process innovations. However, the scoreboard does include data on capital expenditure, which may act as a proxy for investment in process innovation.

Clearly, it is not sufficient to simply count new product announcements. It is necessary to classify and weight the raw data to get a better idea of the relative importance of the innovations. In this pilot study, we were not able to adopt the method of classification proposed by Kleinknecht and Reijnen (1993) and used by Coombs *et al.* (1994) and others. For the purpose of the feasibility study product announcements were extracted from the Predicasts *F&S Index* database of 1,000 journals. However, in most cases, the database does not abstract sufficient information to classify the innovation by type and complexity. Future work will be based on more detailed product announcements received direct from the companies.

To give an idea of the potential of product announcement data, we interrogated the Predicasts *F&S Index plus Text* database. This commercial database contains abstracts compiled from 1,000 trade and industry journals worldwide. More importantly, it allows analysis by company, country, product and event. Products are classified down to a seven-digit level. For example,

36	Electrical & electronic equipment
365	Consumer electronics
3651	Audio & TV equipment
36511	Radios
365111	Household radios
3651111	Table radios

Events include market information, people, resources, management procedures and products and processes. Events are identified by a single-digit code, and sub-classes by two digits:

3	Products & processes
30	Products dictionaries
31	Science & research
32	Manufacturing processes
33	Products design & development
34	Product specification
35	Product

For the purpose of the trial scoreboard, event code 33 — product design & development — was used to identify product announcements. The initial search revealed more than 20,000 entries in the year examined. By restricting the search to the 15 sample companies, the number of citations were reduced to a manageable level. The raw data were checked for errors and duplications, which reduced the total number of recorded new product announcements to 228. In most cases, the database provided an abstract of the original article, but these were found to be insufficient to determine the type and complexity of the innovation.

The trial innovation scoreboard also includes three financial indicators of innovation: value added, price to earnings multiple and the ratio of market to book value. We included value added because of the emphasis managers and management texts place on it as a key measure of corporate performance (Kay, 1993). In addition, intuitively we would expect some relationship between innovation and value added. We chose the price to earnings multiple because it remains one of the most common measures of stock market performance. It also reflects future potential rather than past performance. The other financial indicator included is the market to book value. The average ratio of market to book value would appear to be some measure of the long-term innovative potential of a company. The reasoning behind this is that the difference between the two methods of company valuation represents the contribution of future earnings above and beyond the tangible assets. This element of "goodwill" can be substantial and may be a useful proxy for innovativeness. The trial scoreboard shown in Table 4 includes indicators of technological, market and financial performance for 40 companies, representing five different sectors. The companies were chosen to provide a range of R&D intensity in each of the five sectors. Analysis of the data confirms the findings of previous research, but it also reveals relationships which warrant further study.

The data confirm that expenditure on research and development, as a proportion of sales, has a significant positive effect on value added (regression not shown) and the number of new product announcements made (Table 5). This suggests that research and development activities contribute both to increasing the number of new products introduced as well as their value. The use of sales revenue as a proxy for firm size indicates that the number of new product announcements made may also be a function of

Table 4. An innovation scoreboard.

	R&D/ Sales[1]	Capex/ Sales[2]	R&D/ Value Added[2]	Value Added[2]/ Sales	New Prod Count[3]	R&D mil/ New Prod[3]	Sales mil/ New Prod[3]	Price/ Earnings[2]	Market/ Book[2]
1. Chemical									
Chem. A	5.4	6.8	39.6	15.8	63	10.3	191	24.8	1.2
Chem. B	2.9	10.9	6.8	38.4	7	11.6	462	15.9	2.4
Chem. C	1.9	5.6	6.2	30.7	12	3.1	171	12.2	3.4
Chem. D	2.8	6.9	36.6	34.8	2	18.9	971	21.5	3.9
Chem. E	1.2	16.4	3.7	42.3	1	7.2	254	20.3	5.5
Chem. F	1.7	4.6	5.7	29.4	2	3.0	261	19.1	2.9
Chem. G	1.6	10.0	5.3	28.7	1	5.2	328	16.4	1.7
Chem. H	2.2	3.4	6.2	34.9	0	n.a	n.a	11.9	5.4
2. Electrical									
Elec. A	7.2	3.5	17.6	42.2	55	7.6	102	17.2	2.7
Elec. B	4.2	3.8	13.4	42.7	10	7.6	127	11.5	1.3
Elec. C	0.7	10.2	1.8	28.2	23	1.1	194	23.4	5.5
Elec. D	3.2	2.9	5.2	61.0	3	4.4	139	25.1	4.4
Elec. E	5.0	4.6	13.7	35.9	2	6.2	126	60.6	4.8
Elec. F	8.7	2.9	14.1	47.8	3	3.4	40	14.7	9.4
Elec. G	3.4	7.2	6.3	53.4	0	n.a	n.a	23.7	6.8
Elec. H	7.8	3.3	20.3	39.8	3	2.7	34	21.6	2.9
3. Engineering									
Eng. A	5.7	4.4	8.0	51.2	0	n.a	n.a	20.2	5.0
Eng. B	3.4	4.1	7.1	48.0	8	4.9	144	28.2	6.6
Eng. C	1.1	5.4	57.1	39.7	10	9.3	977	21.3	6.6
Eng. D	3.3	3.6	9.8	34.1	2	12.0	360	n.a	3.2
Eng. E	1.8	5.5	5.8	30.8	2	10.1	570	31.9	3.1
Eng. F	1.2	3.2	2.9	42.3	1	12.8	1035	19.8	2.3
Eng. G	1.8	5.9	4.1	43.2	0	n.a	n.a	19.2	3.6
Eng. H	1.2	1.5	3.8	30.8	13	0.8	73	n.a	1.4
4. Food and drink									
Food A	0.9	4.5	8.3	22.6	18	25.6	1372	16.5	1.0
Food B	0.6	5.2	2.1	30.1	3	5.9	934	22.4	1.8
Food C	0.4	5.7	1.2	29.4	5	2.4	674	18.3	1.9
Food D	0.4	3.3	1.7	25.6	0	n.a	n.a	n.a	2.0
Food E	0.4	1.5	3.3	12.1	1	13.4	3395	35.7	2.6
Food F	0.2	2.3	1.2	20.5	0	n.a	n.a	12.8	n.a
Food G	0.2	1.7	2.3	9.9	0	n.a	n.a	14.2	n.a
Food H	1.2		n.a		0	n.a	n.a	n.a	2.1

(Continued)

Table 4. (*Continued*)

	R&D/ Sales[1]	R&D/ Capex/ Sales[2]	R&D/ Value Added[2]	Value Added[2]/ Sales	New Prod Count[3]	R&D mil/ New Prod[3]	Sales mil/ New Prod[3]	Price/ Earnings[2]	Market/ Book[2]
5. Services									
Service A	n.a	12.8	n.a	58.3	2	n.a	161	n.a	1.5
Service B	n.a	9.7	n.a	50.9	9	n.a	625	38.1	1.8
Service C	n.a	n.a	n.a	11.1	3	n.a	2928	24.0	2.4
Service D	n.a	n.a	n.a	24.3	8	n.a	1348	n.a	2.0
Service E	n.a	n.a	n.a	39.3	7	n.a	853	19.6	2.6
Service F	n.a	n.a	n.a	n.a	2	n.a	252	n.a	n.a
Service G	n.a	n.a	n.a	4.1	1	n.a	2818	31.2	n.a
Service H	n.a	n.a	n.a	33.5	2	n.a	1145	n.a	2.1

[1] From 1993 UK R&D Scoreboard.
[2] Derived from Datastream and accounts.
[3] Derived from Predicasts database.
Source: Tidd *et al.*, 1996.

the size of the firm. This finding is consistent with the work of Devinney (1993) and Chaney *et al.* (1991). Absolute expenditure on research and development also has a significant positive effect on the number of new product announcements (third column in Table 5). The introduction of a term to represent the interaction of research and development with sales indicates diminishing efficiency with firm size (fourth column). In short, larger firms make more product announcements, but not in proportion to their size. This is consistent with the findings of Jensen's (1987) study of new chemical entities in the pharmaceutical industry. The inclusion of industry dummy variables had no significant effect. This is something of a surprise given the importance of technological opportunity, but firm size may proxy to the industry effect.

Table 6 explores the relationship between various inputs and market to book value. Three variants on the relationship are reported, with the highest R^2 obtained for the specification in the third column. First, the data confirm that research and development, as a percentage of sales, has a significant positive effect on the market to book value. This supports the findings of previous work (Sciteb/CBI, 1991). The results suggest that the financial

Table 5.   Regression analysis of new product announcements.

Dependent Variable: Number of New Product Announcements

	(1)	(2)	(3)
Intercept	−7.33	−3.54	1.50
	(−1.33)	(−0.99)	(1.38)
Sales	0.002***	0.002***	—
	(3.59)	(3.63)	
R&D/Sales	2.72***	2.60***	—
	(2.82)	(2.80)	
Capex/Sales	0.65	—	—
		(0.93)	
R&D	—	—	0.00131***
			(7.53)
R&D* Sales	—	—	−0.0000003*
			(−1.91)
N^1	32	32	32
R^2	0.40	0.39	0.87
Mean	8.06	7.81	7.81
S.E. of regression	12.02	11.78	5.51

*$p < 0.10$
**$p < 0.05$
***$p < 0.01$
[1]The number of observations were reduced as data on R&D expenditure were not available for all firms.
Source: Tidd *et al.*, 1996.

markets do value expenditure on research and development. The coefficient of about 0.3 on R&D/Sales may be used to estimate an elasticity of the dependent variable at the mean value of R&D/Sales of 2.9. A 1% rise in R&D/Sales would translate into a 0.08% rise in the market to book value. This suggests that the market may somewhat undervalue R&D expenditure, but a larger sample would be needed to confirm this result. Secondly, the use of the ratio of new product announcements to absolute R&D as a proxy for research efficiency indicates that the efficiency of research also has a significant positive effect on the market to book value. This suggests that the market values the past *efficiency* of research and development (that is, track record), as well as the *expenditure* on research and development. Clearly,

Table 6. Regression analysis of market to book value.

	Dependent Variable: Market/Book Value		
	(1)	(2)	(3)
Intercept	2.04	2.54	3.10
	(2.13)	(4.38)	(5.12)
R&D/sales	0.33*	0.33**	0.29*
	(1.97)	(2.13)	(1.92)
Capex/sales	0.12	—	—
	(1.02)		
New prod/R&D	—	10.91*	9.35*
		(1.88)	(1.70)
Sales	—	—	−0.001**
			(2.12)
N^1	29	29	29
R^2	0.14	0.21	0.33
Mean	3.63	3.63	3.63
S.E. of regression	1.97	1.88	1.76

$^*p < 0.10$
$^{**}p < 0.05$
$^{***}p < 0.01$
[1] The number of observations were reduced due to the absence of data on expenditure on R&D and capital expenditure.
Source: Tidd *et al.*, 1996.

this analysis does not take into account the time lag between research and product launch. Nevertheless, product announcements may be a useful indicator of research productivity in those cases where research expenditure is relatively stable, such as the automotive and chemical industries, or where product development cycles are short, such as the electronics and food industries. In other cases, the effect of lags would need to be incorporated.

Conclusions

In this chapter, we presented the results of a study on the feasibility of developing an innovation scoreboard to measure and track the performance of companies based on data in the public domain. The statistical relationships identified suggest that there is sufficient empirical support to develop such an innovation scoreboard. However, two aspects demand further development.

First, a more detailed model of the drivers of innovation in different circumstances must be developed. At present, the effect of factors such as the size of the firm, sector and market structure are ill understood. Our analysis confirms that both expenditure on research and development and the number of new product announcements increase with firm size. However, there appears to be diminishing returns to scale. Previous research suggests that the sector has a significant effect on the firm, but the fact that weaker relationships between outputs and inputs are observed at the firm level, rather than at the industry level, suggests that there is a lot of variability in the productivity of technological inputs, and that there may be some point in studying the particular conditions under which the inputs are used most effectively. Research suggests at least three explanatory sets of reasons: scale, technological opportunity and management. Scale has received a disproportionate amount of attention in the literature, although more recent studies have begun to examine technological opportunity (Geroski, 1994). However, there is still a need to unravel the effect of *technological* opportunity, essentially a supply-side factor, and *market* opportunity, essentially a demand-side factor. In addition, the effect of different organisational structures and processes needs to be incorporated into our model.

Secondly, the quality of data on new product and service announcements must be improved. A number of problems remain with the use of data on product announcements. The first and most fundamental shortcoming is that product announcements do not capture process or organisational innovations. It is difficult, if not impossible, to capture such innovations using data in the public domain. The collection of primary data from firms, as used by PIMS (Buzzell and Gale, 1987) and other benchmarking methodologies, would appear to be the only option. Moreover, although analysis of product announcements does not capture all forms of innovation, we hope we have demonstrated that it represents an important addition to the existing indicators of innovation, such as R&D and patents. Of particular benefit is the ability to capture product differentiation and service innovations.

The more practical problem is the collection of sufficient data to ensure that all product announcements are captured. For example, there are more than 4,000 specialist trade and industry publications in the UK. For the purpose of the feasibility study, product announcements were extracted from the Predicasts *F&S Index* database of 1,000 journals. However, in most cases, existing commercial databases do not abstract sufficient information to classify the innovation by type and complexity. More robust sources of data will be necessary for the innovation scoreboard. Thus, it may be necessary to restrict the search to selected journals and a representative sample of UK companies. However, the quantity of data is likely to present less of a problem than the quality. Specifically, the editorial policy of the specialist press is likely to be influenced by factors other than the technical merit of an innovation, such as advertising revenue or company sponsorship. For these reasons, it may be preferable to short-circuit the specialist publications and, instead, receive announcement direct from companies. Therefore we are currently developing a database of product announcements made by UK companies based on their press releases. Combined with data on research and development, patents and financial performance, this should provide further insights into the links between innovation and firm performance.

Chapter 6

Knowledge Management Routines for Innovation Projects: Developing a Hierarchical Process Model[1]

David Tranfield
Cranfield University, UK

Malcolm Young
Cranfield University, UK

David Partington
Cranfield University, UK

John Bessant
University of Exeter, UK

Jonathan Sapsed
CENTRIM, University of Brighton, UK

Background — Innovation and Strategic Advantage

Innovation is widely recognised as a core renewal process within organisations. Unless managers continuously look for ways to change or at least improve offerings (product/service innovation) or create and deliver those offerings (process innovation), organisations risk becoming increasingly vulnerable to hostile and turbulent environments (Bowen, 1994). For this

[1]This chapter results from EPSRC Grant GR/M72869, "Teamworking for Knowledge Management: building capabilities in complex environments", D.R. Tranfield, J. Bessant, D. Partington. First published as a paper "Knowledge Management Routines for Innovation projects: Developing an Hierarchical Model", *International Journal of Innovation Management*, 2003, **7**(1), 27–50.

reason growing attention has been paid to the challenge of innovation management in trying to understand the generic and firm-specific issues surrounding the problem of dealing with this challenge (Tidd and Bessant, 2009). A number of issues related to this have emerged from previous research:

- Organisations need to be prepared for innovation — that is, to be capable of picking up signals about change threats and opportunities in internal and external environments, remain receptive to those signals as triggers for change, and be capable of processing their information content (Christenson, 1997; Utterback, 1994).

- Managers need to share an understanding of the nature of innovation, and in particular the way it operates as a process. Moving from a loosely articulated possible response, to trigger signals, through to an implemented and diffused innovation requires the creation of structures and procedures and the disposition of scarce resources within a series of time-based stages (Freeman, 1982; Van de Ven *et al.*, 1989; Rothwell, 1992).

- Organisations need to develop a strategic portfolio of innovation projects, covering the spectrum from incremental "do what we do better" improvements through to more radical "do different" options across both product and process innovation fields. These must be matched with the existing internal and accessible resources which the organisation can deploy (Tushman and O'Reilly, 1996; Day and Schoemaker, 2000; Hamel, 2000; Leifer, 2000).

- Central to this strategic process is the question of knowledge, particularly in terms of technologies, products, markets, etc. and the ways in which organisations can mobilise this knowledge (held in tacit as well as codified form) to create advantage through innovation (Nonaka, 1991; Leonard-Barton, 1995).

From these perspectives a key management task is one of enabling and managing the knowledge creation and deployment processes associated with innovation. This development of "dynamic capability" has been highlighted by a number of writers who see the challenge as being more than the simple accumulation of technological competence. In their studies, Teece and Pisano suggested that firms demonstrating sustained competitive advantage exhibited "timely responsiveness and rapid product innovation, coupled with the management capability to effectively co-ordinate and redeploy internal and external competencies" (Teece and Pisano, 1994). A central feature of this model is its dynamic nature. Overall, the argument is that there is a need to create and deploy different responses to meet differing environmental challenges. The model also places emphasis on the conscious role which can be played in shaping and configuring the organisation and its competencies to meet these challenges; what Teece *et al.* term "managerial capability".

In other words, what distinguishes a firm and gives it competitive advantage is not so much its size or position, nor its depth of knowledge (competence) but, rather, its ability to respond and lead in the continually shifting environment described above. In the dynamic capability model three factors determine the strategic nature of the firm: its position, path and processes. Position refers to the current endowment of technology plus other assets such as relationships with key customers or suppliers, in other words, what many writers call the "core competence", which must, in turn, be supported by the firm's specific "strategic architecture" (Kay, 1993; Prahalad and Hamel, 1994; Bogner *et al.*, 1999). Technological competence of this kind can be built in many ways, ranging from internal R&D (learning by experimenting) through to transferring technology, which emphasises acquiring solutions developed elsewhere and learning through a process of using. Such competence is firm specific, or, often in the case of large firms, division-specific (Brown, 1998), because it results from a cumulative learning process and cannot easily be replicated through acquisition.

The second element — path — refers to the strategic direction which a firm chooses to follow. Again this is firm-specific but is also shaped by the prior experience and activity of the firm, the so-called technological trajectory (Dosi, 1982). This path-dependent view argues that whilst history matters strongly in influencing the future search for new strategic opportunity, it also opens the firm up to the risk of doing "more of the same". In such cases "core competencies" become "core rigidities" and constrain the firm from seeing and taking on new strategic directions (Leonard-Barton, 1992). This explanation is advanced by Christensen (1997) for the otherwise paradoxical observation that many highly successful firms fail in trying to move into new technological fields. Thus, a key capability here is to see, and if necessary reframe, the emerging patterns of technological opportunity and environmental demand, and to follow or switch trajectories (Pavitt, 1990).

"Processes" are essentially concerned with the particular ways in which an individual organisation has learned to behave, and include the routines which characterise the "culture" of the organisation (Schein, 1984). How the firm searches for opportunities, how it hears and processes the signals from the environment about threats and opportunities, how it mobilises creativity and innovative behaviour amongst its employees and how it manages the learning and knowledge accumulation activities, are all activities made up of organisational routines. They may become embodied in particular structures or procedures, but underpinning them is a set of organisational behaviour patterns which are highly firm-specific. They constitute the firm's problem-solving capability in dealing with the puzzles outlined above, and have strategic value because they are difficult to replicate. Routines of this kind evolve over time and cannot simply be copied (Nelson, 1991).

Our interest in this chapter is to identify and understand how knowledge is managed to drive innovation within a variety of organisations and across a range of projects. In this sense, our aim was to investigate and understand those knowledge processes on which dynamic capability depended. Specifically, this chapter reports on the development of a process model of innovation constructed from a synthesis of innovation literature from which we derived the overall conceptual framework, and knowledge management routines resulting from our fieldwork conducted across a variety of sectors.

The "D-R-N" Process Model of Innovation

Models of innovation take a number of forms, each of which is helpful in highlighting particular aspects and enabling better understanding and practice (Abernathy and Utterback, 1978; Van de Ven, 1986; Angle and Van de Ven, 1989; Rothwell, 1992; Jelinek and Litterer, 1994; Utterback, 1994; Dodgson and Rothwell, 1995; Bellon and Wittington, 1996; Pavitt, 2000; Tidd and Bessant, 2009). For our purposes in this chapter we are interested in looking at innovation as a staged process within the firm. In dealing with the challenge of renewing products/processes, our research has identified three distinct phases of activity from the literature which we have termed discovery, realisation and nurture.

Discovery emphasises the need to scan and search environments (internal and external) and to pick up and process signals about potential innovation. These could be needs of various kinds, opportunities arising from research activities, regulative pressures, or the behaviour of competitors. In total, they represent the bundle of stimuli to which the organisation must respond if it is to survive and grow (Millett and Honton, 1991; Coombs *et al.*, 1992; de Gues, 1996; Tidd and Bessant, 2009).

The realisation phase is concerned with issues surrounding how the organisation can successfully implement the innovation, growing it from an idea through various stages of development to final launch as a new product or service in the external market place, or a new process or method within the organisation. Realisation requires selecting from this set of potential triggers for innovation those activities to which the organisation will commit resources. Even the best-resourced organisation cannot do everything, so the challenge lies in resources activities which offer the best chance of developing a competitive edge (Adler, 1989; Dodgson, 1993; Roussel *et al.*, 1991; Ford, 1996; Cooper, 1994; Tidd and Bessant, 2009).

Nurturing results from the organisation having chosen an option. Here, organisations need to provide resources, developing (either by creating through R&D or acquiring through technology transfer) the means for exploration. This might be a simple matter of buying off-the-shelf or exploiting the results of research already carried out, or it might require extensive search to find the right resources. It involves not only codified knowledge formally embodied in technology, but also tacit knowledge in the surrounding social linkage which is needed to make the innovation work. The nurture phase involves maintaining and supporting the innovation through various improvements and also reflecting upon previous phases and reviewing experiences of success and failure in order to learn about how to manage the process better and capture relevant knowledge from the experience. This learning creates the conditions for beginning the cycle again, a pattern which Rothwell and Gardiner (1984) term "re-innovation". Activities in this phase include learning through diffusion, and user-involvement in the innovation, as well as other learning effects (Arrow, 1962; Rosenberg, 1982; Rogers, 1984; von Hippel, 1988; Herstatt and von Hippel, 1992; Moore, 1999).

In different ways, organisations build structures and procedures to enable progress through these phases, and there is enormous contingent variation depending on factors like firm size, sector, market, etc. Prescriptions for structuring the process abound, for example, in the area of product innovation management, Booz *et al.* (1982). Many variations exist on this theme, for example, Cooper's (1994) work suggests a slightly extended view with "gates" between stages which permit management of the risks in the process. Similar models have been advanced for managing process innovation (Davenport, 1992).

Of course, in practice this apparently straightforward linear process rarely emerges. Most innovation is messier, involving false starts, recycling between stages, dead ends and jumps out of sequence, etc. Various authors have tried different metaphors, for example, seeing the process as a railway journey with the option of stopping at different stations, going into sidings or even, at times, going backwards, but most agree that there is still some sequence to the basic process (Van de Ven *et al.*, 1989).

Research Methodology

Unit of analysis — the organisational routine

Levitt and March describe routines as involving established sequences of actions for undertaking tasks enshrined in a mixture of technologies, formal procedures or strategies and informal conventions or habits. Importantly, routines are seen as evolving in the light of experience that works. They become the mechanisms that "transmit the lessons of history" (Levitt and March, 1988). In this sense, routines have an existence independent of particular personnel. New members of the organisation learn them on arrival, and most routines survive the departure of individual organisational members. Routines have been argued to represent "effortful accomplishments", the more formal and codified aspects of organisational life, and also "automatic responses", the more uncodified or taken-as-given aspects (Pentland and Rueter, 1994). It has also been postulated that these routines have within them cognitive, behavioural and structural aspects (Tranfield and Smith, 1998) which are constantly being adapted and interpreted such that formal policy may not always reflect the current nature of the routine, as Augsdorfer points out in the case of 3M (Augsdorfer, 1996). Our purpose, therefore, was to identify and understand the various aspects of knowledge management activity prevalent in the innovation projects of the collaborating organisations, and by synthesising organisational practices across cases, investigate the possibility of developing a set of "generic routines" which might inform the theoretically derived D-R-N process model.

Approach

We adopted an inductive approach to the research programme, which we believed would be most likely to surface appropriate data. At the core of our approach we placed the fundamental principle that the key characteristics of an organisation would be revealed by identifying how managers and others allocate their scarce attention (March, 1998). We further surmised that within these characteristics we would discover their priority knowledge needs. These needs would initiate management action to find knowledge sources which would satisfy the needs. However, those same characteristics would also represent (internal) knowledge sources to meet other needs. Viewed holistically then, management action would scan both internal and external knowledge sources to satisfy knowledge needs (see Fig. 1). Finally, we made the fundamental assumption that the key knowledge management routines and practices within an organisation would be revealed by the way in which informants described their actions.

Sample

We engaged in a programme of research which included a total of 11 dissimilar organisations across 9 sectors: health, food packaging, whisky

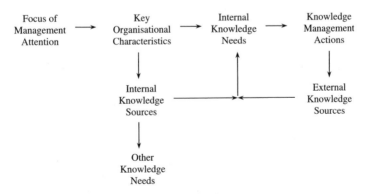

Fig. 1. Sequential model of management attention and knowledge management action.

distillation and bottling, highway maintenance, software development, simulation, advanced electronics and aerospace. Our aim was to surface as large a spectrum of idiosyncratic activities as possible, then to make comparisons across sectors, to discover whether or not "generic routines" existed and, if so, to identify their nature and characteristics.

The innovations chosen for investigation were defined by four categories bounded by the dimensions incremental-radical and product-process. Thus, we investigated examples of radical product, radical process, incremental product and incremental process innovations. Because of the difficulties of definition, we chose not to differentiate between goods and service in the category of "product". In each of the four cases below, generic routines are exemplified by actual practices signified by specific activities. Each case ends with examples of broader contextual enabling and blocking activity which the informants saw as significant.

Data collection

Working towards what Partington (2000) refers to as a "grounded theory of management action", and following the methodology of Glaser and Strauss (1967), we used as the prime data source in-depth open-ended interviews with key managers and operators in the collaborating organisations, supplemented by archival data in the form of written procedures, etc. and observation of operations. In all, data was collected from 123 interviews from all levels in the organisation. Interviews were of variable length but with a mean of approximately 1.5 hours. Where possible, interviews were tape recorded and transcribed for analysis. Where this was not possible or inappropriate, extensive field notes were made immediately after the interview. These were validated by respondents and also transcribed in order to become part of the final data set. We eschewed any attempt to render a fundamentally new definition of knowledge at the outset but, following the grounded theory concept, we chose to derive our final notion of knowledge mainly from our informants. During the fieldwork, therefore, we chose to operate by the simple minimalist explication of knowledge as *the capacity to act in a context*. In the event, our data also agreed with the many explications of knowledge in common parlance which connote the ability to make decisions and to act on those decisions, both having contextual significance.

Validating the data

We started from the fundamental principle that the key characteristics of an organisation would be revealed by identifying how managers and others allocate their scarce attention (March, 1998). Our view was that these characteristics would be revealed by how respondents described their work. We surmised that collecting data in this way would reveal temporally significant knowledge needs. We used detailed analysis of in-depth open-ended interviews with key managers and operators in a broad cross-sector collaborator group, supplemented by theoretical archival and observational data. Throughout, by continually feeding-back our results and emerging theory to our collaborators both individually and in open workshops, we were able to achieve a high level of consensual validity (Gouldner, 1970). This practitioner-based approach allowed us to identify firm-specific knowledge management activities which, on closer examination, camouflaged more generic groupings of routines which exhibited clear, cross-sector resonance.

Case 1: Radical Product Innovation — Computer-based Training Solutions

Innovation narrative

Organisation A (Org A) is a provider of customised simulators and training solutions to military and civilian markets. These high value, complex products require the integration of various engineering disciplines: software, electrical, electronic and mechanical, as well as specialist knowledge of the applications such as image generation, or user-end knowledge such as the behaviour of artillery in the field. The workflow is project-based and the firm has adopted a functional matrix organisation for familiar product lines, but deploys cross-functional project teams where applications are novel and more project management is required. Org A, therefore, has built up capabilities in new product areas different from their customary business. In the 1990s civil aviation companies ceased the practice of flying actual aeroplanes in the "type conversion" of their pilots. There was a considerable cost advantage in the use of flight simulators when compared with real flight training. Concurrently, lesser devices were being developed to fulfil some training requirements. In particular, microcomputer-based training

(CBT) was proving to be an effective and low-cost alternative to high-end customised simulators.

The trend towards PC-based solutions had lowered barriers to entry in the simulation and training industry, meaning that Org A faced competition from new entrants exploiting the relatively small investments needed for PC-based CBT. Increasingly, the lower cost solutions were proving attractive to military customers. Key individuals in the company believed that its people needed to move from a position of thinking that they provided simulators which were large, high-cost pieces of equipment, to a position where they provided solutions to training needs, involving whatever technologies were appropriate. This change of mindset has progressed to the extent that it is characterised here as a radical product innovation. The company now has a qualitatively different competence to support new product offerings that are of themselves quite different from its traditional products.

High-level phase (Theoretically informed)	Generic routine (Synthesised from data)	Organisational activities (Empirically derived)
Discovery	Search	Establish trends through regular customer contact. Scan published information sources. Attend academic and industrial conferences. Specify responsibilities to staff.
	Capture	Incorporate trends and other data in working paper.
	Articulate	Circulate working paper to provoke discussion. Present ideas to key actors.
Realisation	Contextualise	Connect idea to invitation to tender for large MOD contract. Demonstrate need for change of mindset. Demonstrate primary computer-based training (CBT) as solution to nature, scale and cost structure.
	Apply	Make customer training need analysis (TNA) a core contracting procedure. Match technology to need parsimoniously.
Nurture	Evaluate	Monitor customer satisfaction.
	Support	Recruit TNA specialists and educational psychologist to exploit novelty and diversification opportunities.
	Re-innovate	Create training needs and courseware department. Contribute to industrial standardisation.

Enabling activities

The relatively small size of the customer base means that close relationships are maintained through regular face-to-face contact and through formal visits. Such regularity of contact and familiarity with the customer is helpful to become aware of and apprehend new thinking about customer requirements. The company champions of CBT were helped in their cause by the fact that the company had produced prior work that, they argued, was a form of CBT package. Champions could point to such work as effective CBT of the type they were advocating. The area seemed less of a "brave new world" given these previous developments. The recruitment of an experienced technology champion from outside the company was seen as more efficacious than an insider in mobilising people to think seriously about the emerging trends. Other recruits were from backgrounds that were new and fresh to the company and bore no preconceptions. This was seen as a key complement to the body of industry specialists already in the firm.

Blocking activities

The overarching hindrance to this innovation was the culture of the industry and the company. Traditionally ITTs specified simulator equipment and technology, containing no guidance as to training needs. The company had therefore adopted this mindset over time, and it was difficult to change. The champions of CBT also had to challenge the idea that the existing software engineers in the firm could develop the CBT applications. In the early stages there was no general appreciation of the qualitatively different nature of what was proposed. Existing quality assurance procedures were inconsistent with the new training needs analysis procedure and this required some time and effort to co-ordinate and implement.

Case 2: Radical Process Innovation — Reorganisation of Psychiatric Services

Innovation narrative

Organisation B (Org B) is a psychiatric unit within the NHS renowned for its innovative approach to issues of old-age psychiatry, which usually means patients over 60 years of age. Specifically, the condition "dementia" is usually age related and indeed most evident in ages over 60. Services are therefore generally optimised for delivery to this age group. However, through continuous review of both parochial and more general information, Org B identified an unsatisfied need for the provision of dementia related services to an emerging population of patients well under the age of 60, including some in their teens.

This led to the development of a range of in-patient, out-patient, community care and "drop-in" services which could span this enlarged age range by bringing expertise in dealing with old age dementia, the results of leading edge research and a highly innovative style to bear. This initiative currently stands as unique in the field of the provision of dementia services.

High-level phase (Theoretically informed)	Generic routine (Synthesised from data)	Organisational activities (Empirically derived)
Discovery	Search	Track and share clinical experiences across departments. Scan professional information sources. Liaise with research facility.
	Capture	Make sense of information flow. Isolate inadequacies. Identify emerging realities.
	Articulate	Explore options in open forum. Challenge orthodoxy.
Realisation	Contextualise	Focus on demand not supply. Make community care the primary delivery mechanism. Prioritise work by need not departmental specialism. Compare needs of old and young.
	Apply	Reorganise social workers (ASW) and community psychiatric nurse (CPN) as integrated teams. Establish common resource pool. Appoint head of service. Make in-patient, out-patient and community care a continuum. Provide a "drop-in" facility.
Nurture	Evaluate	Establish a "research forum". Share experiences in open forum.
	Support	Co-locate staff. Amalgamate care report media. Provide professional and personal counselling across team.
	Re-innovate	Appoint knowledge and practice leaders in differentiated but complementary fields.

Enabling activities

The key enabler was a charismatic, maverick tendency in the lead clinician (consultant) and the willingness to develop service "out of the gaze" of the formal organisation. This has led to the development of open internal communications with high levels of informality. There is broad visionary sweep and a willingness to challenge health service orthodoxy.

Blocking activity

This unit works within an unharmonised Department of Health and Department of Social Security milieu. These departmental frictions (differentiated budgets, staff conditions, statutory requirements, etc.) coupled with hierarchical, command and control orthodoxy and an element of need blindness at high levels makes progress laborious.

Case 3: Incremental Product Innovation — Use of Global Positioning System

Innovation narrative

Organisation C (Org C) is a wholly-owned subsidiary of a major construction group with a large in-house labour force. Org C provides road maintenance and management services to the Highways Agency and to several local authorities in the south and west of England. The company employs around 800 production staff and 200 support staff.

Road maintenance contracts are renewable, typically over a four-year term. Contracting practice in the sector has moved beyond pure short-term price considerations. There is a new and important emphasis on partnering with local authority clients and the provision of "best value". Technological and administrative innovations which support these aims present significant opportunities to demonstrate efficiency gains and other advantages to clients which their rivals in the contract renewal process cannot match. Innovations thus enable Org C to work towards continuity and a longer term prospect. A notable recent example of the innovative use of technology for mutual benefit is HiMaSSS (Highway Maintenance Satellite Support System). HiMaSSS is a vehicle-mounted system which uses differential Global Positioning System (GPS) technology interfaced with a communication link via mobile telephony. The system provides detailed, accurate records of the location and condition of client assets including street lighting, gullies and manholes, at the same time allowing geographical and temporal monitoring of road maintenance vehicles, and reducing paperwork.

HiMaSSS is an interesting case since it can be interpreted as both a product and a process innovation. It constituted a process innovation since it changed the ways in which the company operated in this particular task area, but it was also a product innovation since it involved adapting and reconfiguring an existing product on the market to suit a specific set of conditions for the firm.

High-level phase (Theoretically informed)	Generic routine (Synthesised from data)	Organisational activities (Empirically derived)
Discovery	Search	Manage and facilitate exchange of ideas through cross-functional forums. Gain access to people known to think in different ways.
	Capture	Remain open to the genesis of new ideas. Develop ideas for presentation. Showcase ideas at divisional innovation forums.
	Articulate	Appoint champion to identify short- and long-term advantages of proposed innovation.
Realisation	Contextualise	Investigate and develop ideas in specific context. Prototype application in advance of formal launch.
	Apply	Develop operational model from prototype application. Launch initiative on limited geographical scale. Deploy initiative across operations.
Nurture	Evaluate	Reflect self-critically on process and application. Identify lessons learned. Identify modifications.
	Support	Encourage and publicise innovative applications.
	Re-innovate	Identify additional applications. Encourage alternative suggestions.

Enabling activities

Org C had an understanding client, sympathetic to the fact that doing things differently might need some initial investment.

Blocking activities

There is a local government direct labour organisation tradition with no incentive to innovate, exacerbated by the pressure of day-to-day work and the difficulty in finding energetic champions within the business.

Case 4: Incremental Process Innovation — Work Breakdown Structure

Innovation narrative

Organisation D (Org D) is a supplier of high-end technology screen displays and structures for a wide range of visualisation applications. These include corporate presentation and broadcasting, training devices such as simulators and a growing range of applications in virtual reality, which involve visualisation in education and engineering, as well as in entertainment. The firm is organised around three core cross-functional teams that specialise in specific product lines. Although this promotes a degree of standardisation, the workflow is project-based and involves considerable customisation for each client. The firm has been growing at a steady rate of around 20% for 10 years and is entering a stage of consolidation and maturity, as distinct from its early period as an entrepreneurial start-up.

Managers thought that the firm needed more structure and control over its work processes. In its early days as a technology-centred start-up, there was little rigour and transparency in the projects. Project and team managers planned in different ways with no standard framework for comparison of data. As a result, there was little understanding of where excess costs were incurred on projects and where efficiency gains were available. As part of a drive to improve profitability, the company decided to develop and implement a work breakdown structure to apply across the organisation. The resulting structure is now used on every bid and on every project. This enables consistent booking to projects and measurable information on each part of the business process. The company knows the real cost structures of projects and this is reflected in much more accurate bids.

High-level phase (Theoretically informed)	Generic routine (Synthesised from data)	Organisational activities (Empirically derived)
Discovery	Search	Appoint development manager (DM) with specific search responsibilities.
		Develop product architecture to focus search.
	Capture	Match information to product architecture.
		Embody in work breakdown structure (WBS).
	Articulate	Publicise emerging WBS and iterate through formal and informal feedback.
Realisation	Contextualise	Pilot WBS in a specific project and adjust as necessary.
	Apply	Launch WBS.
		Establish (progressively) as standard procedure for all projects.
Nurture	Evaluate	Monitor (DM) use of WBS and amend as necessary.
	Support	Link WBS to enterprise resource planning (ERP).
	Re-innovate	Link to WBS and ERP through management information system (MIS).
		Encourage alternative applications.

Enabling activities

The protracted period of consultation enabled broad involvement and agreement with the aims of the WBS. It ensured that all interested parties were compliant and contributing to the structure. This improved its accuracy and utility in projects. Another enabler was introducing the WBS concurrently with a project management software package; the adoption of each supported the other.

Blocking activities

The culture of Org D was primarily technology and engineering-centred, as opposed to project management and processes-centred. People were not used to collecting data, or booking time and resources in all their activities. It is still taking time to implement the WBS comprehensively to operate as a matter of routine. A source of conflict in the process was the level of detail stipulated in the WBS, the concern of the PMDM and Directorate was that the level should be high enough to apply across all product teams, otherwise the benefits would be lost. Criticism was constructive throughout the process of developing the innovation. However, this was insisted on in the consultation process.

Discussion

Synthesising a process approach to managing knowledge for innovation

Achieving synthesis from the diverse data sets represented by the empirical data from the projects posed a challenge, for it is always problematic to generalise findings from a series of projects which are unique. Indeed, the organisations involved are unlikely to carry through such innovations again and therefore even within the confines of any of our collaborating partners, the opportunity to identify, articulate and codify specific behaviours remains limited. In order to ensure confidence in the generality of our findings, synthesis of data from our fieldwork required, therefore, an explicit and replicable methodology based on a transparent set of assumptions and philosophy. Here we were helped considerably by taking an action perspective on research synthesis.

In line with Pentland and Rueter's (1994) notion of "grammars of action", we made a detailed analysis of the reported data to isolate significant verbs (e.g. seek, select, shape, envision, advocate, champion, redefine) and the context within which they were expressed. In this way we were able to identify the organisational activities to which they referred. Where one verb could be used generically to cover a range of reported activities we referred to this as "a generic routine". Hence, we created "natural groupings" of verbs, labelling them appropriately and arriving at synthesis through harmonisation of the lists of verbs. Finally, we identified whether, where and how the labelled groupings of "generic routines" aligned with the D-R-N framework. The identification of "generic routines" made the link between the theoretically informed high-level process model and the empirical data on idiosyncratic activity in the cases. As we will describe, what emerged were eight "generic routines", based on the knowledge management activities in the cases. These "generic routines" were labelled search, capture, articulate, contextualise, apply, evaluate, support and re-innovate (SCACAESR — see Fig. 2).

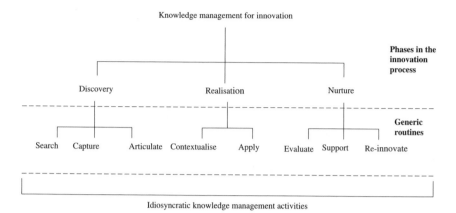

Fig. 2.   Hierarchical process model of knowledge management for innovation.

Definitions and descriptions of generic routines can be seen in Fig. 3, together with examples of specific knowledge management activities from the research data.

The innovation cases provided a ready and rich source of examples. As the four empirical examples given above indicate, organisations develop and enact a suite of superficially idiosyncratic routines and practices most relevant to the needs of their projects, retaining and developing those which confer advantage and discarding those which lack efficacy. These successful innovations were highly performative, based on the timely sharing (knowledge flows), rather than the secured custody (knowledge stocks) of organisational knowledge. However, even from this small sample, the idiosyncratic knowledge management activities exhibit common themes and purposes inherent in which lies the potential for them to be grouped into more generic categories. When taken together with the remainder of the empirical data (which yielded a further 24 case examples), this phenomenon became progressively more apparent. By detailed analysis of the data for each case, collapsing actions and practices into routines in the manner indicated in the example cases, we were able to identify generic routines which organisations enact, to a greater or lesser extent and with greater or lesser effectiveness, in managing organisational knowledge.

These generic routines represent a class which captures the fundamental essence of a spectrum of activity camouflaged by the superficial idiosyncrasy of particular projects and programmes. Such a taxonomy of processes

Phase in the innovation process	Generic routines	Description	Examples of detailed knowledge management activities
Discovery	Search	The passive and active means by which potential knowledge sources are scanned for items of interest.	Active environmental scanning (technological, market, social, political, etc.). Active future scanning Experiment – R&D, etc.
	Capture	The means by which knowledge search outcomes are internalised within the organisation.	Picking up relevant signals and communicating them within and across the organisation to relevant players.
	Articulate	The means by which captured knowledge is given clear expression.	Concept definition – what might we do? Strategic and operational planning cycles – from outline feasibility to detailed operational plan.
Realisation	Contextualise	The means by which articulated knowledge is placed in particular organisational contexts.	Resource planning and procurement – inside and outside the organisation. Prototyping and other concept refining activities. Early mobilisation across functions – design for manufacture, assembly, quality, etc.
	Apply	The means by which contextualised knowledge is applied to organisational challenges.	Project team mobilisation. Project planning cycles. Project implementation and modification – "cycles of mutual adaptation" in technological, market, organisational domains. Launch preparation and execution.
Nurture	Evaluate	The means by which the efficacy of knowledge applications is assessed.	Post-project review. Market/user feedback. Learning by using/ making/ etc.
	Support	The means by which knowledge applications are sustained over time.	Feedback collection. Incremental problem-solving and debugging.
	Re-innovate	The means by which knowledge and experience are re-applied elsewhere within the organisation.	Pick up relevant signals to repeat the cycle. Mobilise momentum for new cycle.

Fig. 3. Hierarchical process model linking innovation phase to knowledge management activities.

represents a synthesis across the range of projects studied, for it is by using these "generic mechanisms" that innovation and improvement is delivered rather than by the projects themselves (Pawson, 2001).

There was evidence to suggest that there was sequential significance at both the phase (D-R-N) and routine (SCACAESR) levels. However, within each level were discrete, essential elements to be addressed. The relationship between these elements could be interpreted as thematic, in the musical sense of prominence or recurrence, and only contingently sequential (Scholes, 1974). It can therefore be more important to understand in which thematic category current activity is located, rather than being prescriptive about strict temporal sequence. Indeed, all informants agreed that they frequently iterated between the generic routines, without the need continually to re-initiate the process *in toto*, while driving innovations. This echoes the findings of Van de Ven *et al.* (1989) in their analysis of a wide range of innovation cases.

Knowledge management — a description and definition

Taken together, the outcomes of this research indicate that knowledge management is the process by which the capacity to act is facilitated or enhanced. By extension from our fundamental principle of the focus of management attention and action, this is achieved by the matching of knowledge sources to knowledge needs. This suggests that knowledge management is a performative competence which, for the most part, privileges the flow and sharing of knowledge over the custodial role of storage and security. In turn, knowledge and knowledge management are value rated by their contextual efficacy. Given these insights we can now propose a new description of knowledge management, that is:

> *The process by which the capacity to act is facilitated or enhanced, matching knowledge sources to knowledge needs, using performative competencies which privilege the flow and sharing of knowledge over simple custody, and which is value rated by its contextual efficacy.*

Conclusions — Implications for Theory and Practice

In addition to this synthesised description, we believe that we have established a link between the theoretically-informed phases of knowledge management and the organisationally idiosyncratic knowledge management activities which can be represented by the hierarchical process model shown in Fig. 3. This hierarchical process model has a number of implications for both theory and practice.

From a practitioner perspective it offers a conceptual framework for knowledge management in innovation, a map of the territory rather than a prescriptive route. It offers managers a framework within which they can initially locate, and then subsequently monitor, their innovation activity. Secondly, it enables managers to audit their knowledge management processes, either off-line as a review of past procedures or online during a current innovation, to assess the presence or absence of routines, to exploit those at which they are adept and to improve on those at which they are less so. Thirdly, this synthesis and generic model is both theoretically and empirically grounded in evidence from widely dissimilar organisations. It therefore provides a basis for cross-sector transfer of learning and practice. It can, for example, be used to identify and develop communities of practice in similar knowledge management contexts which may transcend superficial organisational and project dissimilarities.

Finally, our work has implications for the understanding of the theory of innovation, particularly in project-based environments. For example, in mass production environments generic operational routines are relatively easy to identify and understand since there is sufficient repetition to enable learning and improvement. But work on project-based innovation, for example in complex systems, suggests that although each project may be unique, many projects share similar characteristics and can also be mapped on to a generic process model of the kind developed in this chapter (Rush *et al.*, 1997). As mass production environments seek to use projects to "customise" to gain advantages of serviceability and tailoring, and "stranger" or "one-off" production environments try to ensure knowledge transfer, so project environments become increasingly popular forms of organisation. Developing a deeper understanding of such forms, therefore, has become a key academic task. Our work contributes by arguing the case for thinking in terms of routines which can be adapted, developed and crafted locally, but which are grounded in the repetition of common generic patterns. Investigating and understanding the form and nature of such patterns is required if we are to understand both the efficacy of project-based environments and the nature of innovation itself.

Part III

TECHNOLOGICAL COMPETENCIES

Chapter 7

Indicators of Innovation Performance

*Pari Patel**

SPRU, University of Sussex, UK

Introduction

The purpose of this chapter is to review the considerable progress that has been made over the last 40 years in the measurement and understanding of the activities that generate innovation and technical change at the level of the firm. These are the activities concerned with producing knowledge, skills and experience necessary to create new products, processes and services which are now widely recognised as key factors both in economic growth and welfare at the national level and in competitive performance at the firm level.

Since the beginning of the 1960s there has been continued improvement in empirical understanding of the sources and patterns of innovation and technical change, especially at the level of industrial sector and country. This reflects in large part the marked increase in resources devoted to the measurement of innovative activities arising out of two very practical concerns. The first was the growing demand, mainly from scientists, corporate managers and governments, for more reliable information on science, technology and innovation activities to which an increasing proportion of public, corporate and national resources were being allocated, often with the expressed intention of gaining competitive advantage. The

---

*In preparing this chapter, the author has benefited greatly from comments by Keith Pavitt.

second development has been in information technology, as a result of which major new possibilities for analysing scientific and technological activities are continuing to emerge.

The progress in the range, accuracy and availability of firm-level measures has mainly been the result of a mixture of public and private initiatives. The New York Stock Exchange made the public disclosure of R&D expenditures mandatory for quoted companies in the mid 1970s. In the 1980s, *Business Week* began publishing an R&D scoreboard for the 600 largest US companies each year, and in the 1990s the same magazine began publishing comparisons of company patenting (*Business Week*, 1993). Similarly, in 1991 the UK *Financial Times* first published an annual R&D scoreboard for British companies, including data for 300 of the world's largest R&D spenders. Since then, company-level R&D scoreboards have been published by the UK government[1] and the European Commission.[2]

The initiatives by the US Patent Office at the beginning of the 1980s to computerise and disseminate information from patent records have also had a major impact on firm-level analysis of innovation performance. At the same time, private organisations became a major source of information and analysis on patenting activities: see, in particular, the work of Narin and his colleagues (1987) at *Computer Horizons Inc.* in the USA. More recently, an increasing number of studies on firm-level innovative activities have been based on data gathered from innovation surveys. Since the mid-1990s these surveys have been conducted by all EU countries every two to three years.

The plan of this chapter is as follows. First, we discuss the main measures used together with their main strengths and weaknesses. Next we review the state of our knowledge resulting from firm-level studies based on these data, grouped around three sets of issues:

- Impact of innovative activities on corporate performance.
- Relationship between firm size and innovation performance.
- Analyses of the nature and characteristics of firm-level technological competencies.

---

[1] For the 2010 edition see http:/www.innovation.gov.uk/rd_scoreboard/.
[2] For the 2011 edition see http://iri.jrc.ec.europa.eu/research/scoreboard_2011.htm.

Finally, we highlight the conclusions and point to questions that remain unanswered as yet.

The Major Measures of Innovation Activity

Table 1 lists the main measures of innovative activities used in the various studies, their main strengths and weaknesses and an indication of possible levels of comparison. The main message from the table and the discussion below is that in common with measures of most other important economic and social activities, there is not (and never will be) a single perfect or best measure of innovation.[3] Some indicators work well for certain classes of firm (e.g. R&D for big chemical and pharmaceutical firms). Others work well for certain fields of technology (e.g. patents for biotechnology). Yet others for certain types of innovation outputs (e.g. product announcements for product innovations).

Research and Development (R&D)

The widely used R&D indicator is better at measuring technological activities in the science-based classes of technology (chemicals and electronics) than in the production-based and information-based classes (mechanical and software). As Freeman (1982) and Mowery and Rosenberg (1989) have pointed out, R&D activities grew in importance as sources of innovation and technological change following the growing contribution of professionalised science (particularly chemistry and physics) to industrial technology, and the spread of R&D as a separate functional form, especially in a growing number of large firms. R&D has the following important limitations as a measure of inputs to innovation activities:

First, it underestimates technological activities related to production, because much technical change in production technologies takes place in and around the design, building and operation of complex capital goods and production systems. In such circumstances, innovation is generated in

---

[3]For the most widely used indicator (GDP) there is very little consensus on how to measure output in service sectors which form a major part of the economy in most leading industrial countries.

Table 1.   Strengths and weaknesses of measures of innovative activities.

Measure	Strengths	Weaknesses	Possible levels of comparison			
			Country	Industry	Tech field	Firm
Research & Development (R&D) Activities	Regular and recognised data on main source of technology.	Lacks detail (technical fields). Strongly underestimates small firms, design, production engineering and software.	✓	✓	×	✓
Patents	Regular detailed and long-term data. Compensates for weaknesses of R&D statistics.	Uneven propensity to patent. Misses software (but now patentable in USA).	✓	✓	✓	✓
Significant innovations	Direct measure of output.	Measure of significance. Cost of collection. Misses incremental changes.	×	✓	×	✓
Innovation surveys	Direct measure of output. Comprehensive coverage.	Variable definition of innovation. Cost.	✓	✓	×	×
Product announcements	Close to commercialisation.	Misses in-house process innovations, and incremental product improvements. Possible manipulation by marketing and public relations.	?	✓	×	✓
Technical employees	Measures tacit knowledge.	Lack of homogeneity of qualifications.	×	✓	✓	✓
Expert judgements	Direct use of expertise.	Finding independent experts. Judgements beyond expertise.	?	✓	✓	✓

✓ = Yes × = No ? = Maybe

design offices and production engineering departments as well as in R&D laboratories.

The second limitation of R&D statistics is that they capture only very imperfectly innovative activities in small firms, where such activities often do not have a separate functional and accounting identity (Kleinknecht, 1987). Nearly all manufacturing firms with more than 10,000 employees have R&D laboratories. Most with fewer than 1,000 employees do not (Pavitt *et al.*, 1989).

Thirdly, R&D activities underestimate the development of (mainly software) technology related to information processing, in part because a proportion of such technology is developed outside R&D in systems departments; and in part because a growing proportion is developed by firms in the service sector, where the coverage of official R&D surveys is typically very weak.

Finally, the main practical difficulty with using R&D expenditure as a measure of firm-level competencies is that it cannot be classified according to areas of technology (or fields of knowledge) such as biotechnology or nanotechnology.

Patenting activity

Since they are a record of invention, many economists treat patents as an intermediate output of R&D activities. Whilst this assumption has its potential uses, it also leads to puzzles and anomalies. Thus, the most sophisticated econometric analyses have detected no time-lag between R&D "inputs" and patenting "outputs" at the level of the firm (Pakes and Griliches, 1984; Hall *et al.*, 1986). This raises the question of when patenting occurs in the R&D sequence — a subject on which we have precious little direct empirical information. If it typically takes place early in the innovation process, it will be a poor measure of the output of development activities.

The main advantages of patent data are that they reflect corporate capacity to generate change and improvement, they are available at a detailed level of technology over long periods of time, are comprehensive in the sense of covering small as well as large firms and they are used by practitioners themselves.[4] However, the main drawbacks of patent statistics are as follows:

First, there are major inter-sectoral differences in the relative importance of patenting in achieving its prime objective, namely, acting as a barrier to imitation. Thus, studies show patenting to be relatively unimportant in automobiles but very important in pharmaceuticals (Arundel *et al.*, 1995; Levin *et al.*, 1987; Bertin and Wyatt, 1988). Moreover, patents do not fully measure technological activities in software, since copyright law is often used instead as the main means of protection against imitation (see Barton, 1993; Samuelson, 1993). Given this inter-sectoral variety in the propensity to patent the results of R&D, patent statistics are most reliable when normalised by sectoral totals.

Secondly, there are major differences amongst countries in procedures and criteria for granting patents. For this reason, comparisons are most reliable when using international patenting, or patenting in one country. Historically, US patent statistics have been used in a large number of studies. This reflects the early efforts made by USPTO to disseminate patent information and the strong incentives for firms to get patent protection for world class technology in the world's largest market (see Bertin and Wyatt, 1988). More recent studies have made use of data from the European Patent Office (especially the PATSTAT database).

There is a further criticism of patenting as an indicator of technological activities, which we think is not justified. We are not convinced that it is a drawback that patents differ greatly in their economic value (Schankerman and Pakes, 1986). The same is true of R&D projects (Freeman, 1982), and for the same reasons. Technological activities involve cumulative learning under uncertainty. There are therefore bound to be failures, major successes and follow-up improvements, all of which are interdependent. We would therefore expect similar and large variations in the distribution of the value of both R&D and patenting across all firms and countries.

---

[4]See: Aspden, H. (Director of European Patent Operations, IBM) (1983) "Patent Statistics as a Measure of Technological Vitality", *World Patent Information*, **5**, 170–173; Narin, F., Noma, E. and Perry, R. (1987) "Patents as Indicators of Corporate Technological Strength", *Research Policy*, **16**, 143–155; *Business Week* "The Global Patent Race picks up Speed", 9 August 1993: 49–54.

Direct measurement of innovation

There are three different ways in which analysts have attempted to measure directly the inputs and outputs of the innovative activities:

First, they have attempted to measure directly the output of innovations through the identification of significant innovations and their sources (Freeman, 1971; Kleinman, 1975; Feinman and Fuentevilla, 1976; Townsend *et al.*, 1981). The main contribution of this tradition of analysis has been to identify important sources of innovation not satisfactorily captured by the R&D and patenting measures: in particular, the important contribution of small firms, suppliers and customers. Again, the relative importance of the various sources of innovation has been shown to vary systematically amongst sectors (Pavitt, 1984; Cesaratto and Mangano, 1993). The main disadvantage of this approach is that if undertaken comprehensively, it is labour-intensive, and therefore costly and time-consuming. It also poses difficult conceptual and practical problems regarding how to classify the varying degrees of innovation, from the incremental, through the significant to the epoch-making.

Secondly, analysts have collected and analysed new product announcements in trade journals as a measure of innovation output (Acs and Audretsch, 1990; Kleinknecht and Bain, 1993; Coombs *et al.*, 1996; Santarelli and Piergiovanni, 1996; Tidd *et al.*, 1996). The main advantages of this approach have been that it provides a direct indicator of products that are close to commercialisation, and the data can be collected relatively cheaply without contacting the company. Moreover, these data can be combined with other firm-level measures such as R&D and patenting to expand the range of possible analyses that can be undertaken. The main drawback is that this method does not capture process innovations. In addition, for most purposes the new product announcements need to be classified or weighted in some way to gauge their importance, a task which requires considerable technical expertise. The main contribution of this approach has been to show that small and medium sized firms account for a much higher share of technological activities than that shown by their share of total R&D (Acs and Audretsch, 1990; Kleinknecht and Bain, 1993).

Thirdly, are the large scale firm-level surveys undertaken in a number of EU countries to gather information about the inputs and outputs of innovative activities (see OECD, 1992, 1996). These surveys provide a direct measure of the output of all the innovative activity within a firm: proportion of total sales due to the introduction of new products. More importantly, they measure the total costs of innovation, including not just R&D, but design, testing, production engineering, start-up investment and marketing. They are comprehensive in coverage, including firms from all size classes and innovating as well as non-innovating firms. These surveys also include information on relative importance of both different sources of innovation and different collaboration partners. The major drawback of this approach is that it relies on the subjective assessment by a firm as to its own level of innovative activities and the costs associated with them. This is most clearly illustrated by Calvert *et al.* (1996), who show that Spanish firms, on average, report a higher level of sales in new products across all industries compared to French firms. A review of the major achievements of this approach can be found in Smith (2005). We discuss later the new possibilities opened up by these firm-level innovation surveys for analysing the relationship between innovation and economic performance. Here it is worth mentioning that these data have been used to analyse the determinants of innovation status, for example, between innovative and non-innovative firms and between firms engaged in different types of innovation (product, process, organisational). Studies have also examined the relationship between innovation performance and a range of innovation process variables such as internal versus external sourcing of knowledge, different types of collaborative strategies and different types of innovation (see Mairesse and Mohnen, 2010).

Technical employees

Finally, another indirect measure used more recently is based on detailed statistics of the educational background of employees with higher educational qualifications in engineering and science. For example, using systematic data collected by the Swedish Association of Graduate Engineers, Jacobsson *et al.* (1996; and Jacobsson and Oskarsson, 1995) have examined the fields of technological competencies of Swedish firms. The main advantages of this approach are that it captures tacit knowledge which, by definition, does not result in patents or publications, and it also captures "non-R&D" activities within large firms and the activities of small firms. The main conceptual problem is the assumption that there is a one-to-one correspondence between categories of scientists and engineers and categories of technological competencies. While this may hold for some cases, e.g. chemical engineers, it may not hold for others, such as physicists, who may be employed in solving a variety of different problems within a firm.

The main contribution of this approach has been to show that the level of technological diversity within firms is greater when using educational data than that shown when using patent data (Jacobsson *et al.*, 1996). In particular, educational data are much better at capturing the multi-disciplinary character of technological activities. However, the main drawback at a practical level is that such systematic information on the educational background of employees does not exist for other countries, especially those with a larger volume of scientists and engineers.

Indicators of Innovation Performance: What We Know

In this section we review some of the major firm-level studies which have used the indicators discussed above. The purpose is to highlight the methodology used and the main results rather than an attempt to present comprehensive coverage of all the studies. In particular, we group our review around three sets of issues:

- Impact of innovation activities on firm performance.
- Relationship between firm size and innovation performance.
- Analysing the nature and characteristics of firm-level technological competencies.

The majority of the studies addressing the first two sets of issues are based on R&D data, with occasional use of patent data and that from innovation surveys as additional information. Data on new product announcements have also been linked to firm performance by Tidd *et al.* (1996) and to firm size by Acs and Audretsch (1990), Kleinknecht and Reijnen (1993), Coombs *et al.* (1996) and Santarelli and Piergiovanni (1996). The third issue above is mainly analysed using patent statistics and technical employees.

Impact of innovation activities on firm performance

The studies concerned with measuring the impact of innovation activities on some measure of firm performance were pioneered in the late 1970s and early 1980s by the group of scholars associated with Zvi Griliches[5] at the National Bureau of Economic Research (NBER) in the USA in the 1980s. Amongst these, the majority are concerned with an econometric estimation of a production function (or cost function) using a measure of R&D capital stock as one of the independent variables, a smaller number are concerned with analysing the relationship between R&D and patenting and the stock market value of the firm. A small number of studies have examined the relationship between *ex post* profitability and technology. The main conclusion to be drawn from reviewing these studies is that although innovation activities make a positive contribution to firm performance it is very difficult to be precise about the magnitude of this contribution given the large element of "noise" in the data.

Production function approach

This approach consists of estimating a regression equation where the dependent variable is some measure of output, either sales[6] or value added. Independent variables are: labour (number of employees), measure of physical capital (plant and equipment) and a measure of "knowledge" capital, i.e. a capital stock measure based on R&D expenditures. In some studies this becomes a regression of labour productivity (sales or value added divided by employees) on physical and R&D capital divided by employees. In yet others the relationship being tested is between the rate of growth of total factor productivity and R&D intensity. The aim of most of these studies is to arrive at a single estimate of the magnitude of the contribution of R&D to some measure of performance.

A thorough review of firm-level studies based on this approach is contained in Hall *et al.* (2010). The majority of these are based on US firms, and a smaller number on French and Japanese firms. There are a

---

[5] See Pakes and Griliches (1984) for a compilation of some of the early studies.

[6] If using sales as the dependent variable then some measure of materials needs to be included in the list of independent variables.

number of measurement problems involved in the estimations based on the production function approach such as:

- A correct specification should have value added as the dependent variable. However, if sales are used instead then materials need to be included in the list of independent variables. Usually such data are not available (e.g. for US firms). Moreover, another serious measurement problem in the time-series dimension is the lack of appropriate price indices to deflate sales or value added.
- Construction of R&D capital stock by means of the "perpetual inventory" method requires (a) a long enough history of R&D expenditures, (b) appropriate R&D deflators and (c) some idea about a rate of depreciation. In practice, each of these presents major measurement problems. These are avoided in some studies by using a specification that relates "total factor productivity" growth[7] directly to R&D intensity with the coefficient on the latter interpreted as a rate of return to R&D.
- There needs to be a correction for double counting in the measures for capital and labour as they will include R&D equipment and R&D employees. Failure to correct for this will result in an underestimation of the contribution of R&D.
- Given the discussion above of the inter-sectoral variability in R&D as a source of technology, the analysis needs to be sectorally based, which is the case in only some of the studies.

The main results of the studies reviewed in Hall *et al.* (2010) can be summarised as follows:

Cross-section studies show that the elasticity of R&D capital with respect to some measure of output is between 0.01 and 0.20 (i.e. a 1% increase in R&D capital stock increases sales or value added by between 0.01% and 0.20%) and statistically highly significant. Those studies that report sectoral results, such as Mairesse and Griliches (1984), show that the elasticity for the so-called science-based sectors is substantially

---

[7]However, as Mairesse and Sassenou (1991) point out, such estimations are beset with problems of measurement and interpretation. For example, the construction of total factor productivity assumes that data on the share of labour and capital in total output is readily available.

greater than the average. However, the problem with some of the studies is that the reported estimates may be biased due to the omission of variables characterising firms or industries and such biases may result in an overestimation of the value of the elasticity of R&D capital. Thus, in studies such as Mairesse and Cueno (1985), the value of the R&D elasticity reduces from 0.16 to 0.10 with the inclusion of industry specific variables.

A number of studies use panel data (cross-sections over time) to include the influence of firm-specific characteristics by introducing firm-specific dummy variables, or equivalently use deviations of the variables from their individual firm means. It turns out that such regressions using time-series data produce estimates of the elasticity of R&D capital which are much lower in magnitude (and in some cases close to zero) than the ones discussed above, and are also mostly statistically insignificant.

Finally, another interesting "stylised fact" emerges from the work by Hall (1993b) and Mairesse and Hall (1996). By comparing their more recent estimates based on data for French and American firms for the 1980s to their earlier estimates based on data for the 1970s for the same countries, they show that the contribution of R&D to productivity has fallen in the 1980s compared to the 1960s and 1970s: from around 0.10–0.15 to 0.02. For US firms, Hall (1993b) shows that in this period (1970 to 1990) US firms as a whole increased the proportion of sales devoted to R&D. At the same time the relative cost of R&D funds to these firms became lower with the introduction of R&D tax credit, and there was increasing willingness on the part of US investors to buy "technology" stocks.

Market value approach

This approach is based on the idea that the extent to which technological activities create "intangible capital" for the firm which, in turn, generates future income and profits, should show up in the valuation of the firms by the stock market. There are two types of studies based on this approach: the first examines the effect of changes in a firm's R&D or patenting on its stock market rate of return over time[8] (see Griliches

---

[8] A variant on this is to examine the impact of public announcements on R&D expenditures on the change in market value of the firm (see Chan *et al.*, 1990).

et al.,1991; Pakes, 1985), and the second examines the relationship between market value and the value of all the other assets that belong to the firms, including a measure of R&D capital stock (see Hall, 1993a, 1993b).

The first set of studies use time series analysis to examine the dynamic relationship between patents, R&D expenditures and the stock market rate of return (measured as one period rate of return to holding a share of the firm). The idea is to examine how "unpredictable" changes in R&D and patenting are related to changes in the rate of return of firms. Thus Pakes (1985) uses data for 120 US firms over a period of 8 years (1968–85) to show that although there is a strong correlation between these 3 variables, very little of the variation in the stock market rate of return (only about 5%) has to do with the variations in the technology variables. Griliches *et al.* (1991), using a much larger sample of US firms (340 firms over the period 1973–80) and similar methodology, come to very similar conclusions. In particular, they emphasise that annual fluctuations in the number of patents account for a very small proportion of the variation in the market value of firms.

The second set of studies begin by specifying a "value function" of the firm which is the sum of "physical" capital (mainly plant and equipment) and all the "intangible" assets that are valued by the market but are not included in the measured capital of the firm. The latter includes R&D capital (as defined above) as well as other factors such as brand name and reputation which are, in principal, not measured. The main problem in such analyses is that they are *inferring* the market's valuation of R&D capital not really *measuring* it. Thus, any explanatory variable that is left out of the regression but affects firms' valuation and is correlated with R&D will have its effects imputed to R&D.

Two major studies based on this approach are by Hall (1993a, 1993b) and use data on US firms from the 1960s to 1990. The dependent variable is the ratio of total market value (defined as debt plus equity) to the book value of physical assets (plant and equipment). The main independent variable is the R&D capital stock (as defined above) as a proportion of the value of physical assets. Other variables included in some specifications are cash flow (as a measure of market power or profitability) and advertising expenditures.

In the cross-section dimension, the coefficient on the R&D variable is large and highly significant and explains a fair amount of variance in market value (Hall, 1993a). However, the most significant result of the two Hall studies is that estimating this coefficient in successive panels from 1970 to 1990 shows that its value declined very steeply in the 1980s: from around 1 in 1982 to 0.2 in 1990. This decline in the aggregate stock market value of R&D assets relative to ordinary capital stock is composed of two contrasting movements: an increase in the value of ordinary capital and a very steep decline in the absolute value of R&D assets. There are also major differences amongst industrial sectors: electrical-electronics (including computing) and instruments have seen the steepest decline, but in chemicals this relative valuation of R&D assets has risen and in pharmaceuticals it has remained high throughout. The implication of these results is that there has been a very high rate of obsolescence in technology-related assets in the US electronics and instrument industries, probably as a result of rapid technological change.

More recently, a promising new avenue for future work has been opened up through a pilot study undertaken by Tidd *et al.* (1996). For a sample of 40 UK companies, they link data on new product announcements and R&D expenditures to firm performance, as measured by market to book value. Both the technology variables have a positive and statistically significant effect on the ratio of market to book value.

Relationship between technology and profitability

A small number of studies have used regression techniques to measure the impact of technology on *ex post* profitability. For example, Geroski *et al.* (1993) use matched data from company accounts and the SPRU innovation survey to examine this relationship for UK firms.[9] The dependent variable used is net profits before tax and interest payments as a proportion of sales and the list of independent variables includes the number of innovations introduced as well as a number of industry specific variables. They show that the number of innovations produced by a firm has a positive and statistically significant effect on its profitability but the effect is small. There are substantial "permanent" differences between the profitability

---

[9]They gather data for 721 large publicly quoted UK firms for the period 1972–83, 117 of whom introduced at least one innovation.

of innovating and non-innovating firms which are not closely tied to the timing of the introduction of specific innovations. Profit margins of innovating firms are less sensitive to cyclical downturns than those of non-innovators.

Innovation and economic performance using firm-level survey data

A promising new avenue for firm-level analysis combines the data from innovation surveys discussed above with other firm-specific information from national databases. Such an approach opens up a whole new range of possibilities for examining the relationship between innovation and economic performance. It also overcomes one of the major drawbacks of the studies discussed above, namely the simultaneous nature of the relationship between innovation and economic performance.

Studies based on this approach (see Klomp and Van Leeuwen, 2001; Loof and Heshmati, 2002; OECD, 2009) employ multiple measures for both innovation performance and economic performance. In terms of the former they use:

- Innovation intensity based on total innovation costs.
- R&D intensity.
- Sales in new products.
- Measures based on investment expenditures.

In terms of economic performance, the measures included were:

- Sales per employee.
- Exports per employee.
- Growth rates of sales, totals assets and employment.
- Operating profit ratio.
- Return on investment.

In general, these studies confirm that innovation has a positive effect on firm performance.

Firm size and innovation performance

Considerable progress has been made in the past 20 years in the conceptualisation of the relations between firm size and market structure on the one hand, and innovation performance on the other. In particular, it has become more widely accepted that both are jointly determined by the degrees of technological opportunity and appropriability (Dasgupta and Stiglitz, 1980; Nelson and Winter, 1982). These vary widely amongst sectors, and explain most of the variance amongst them in market structure and the size distribution of innovating firms (Levin *et al.*, 1985; Geroski and Pomroy, 1990). Amongst other things, this has exposed the difficulty of isolating the influence of firm size and market structure on technological activities in cross-sectoral comparisons, where technological conditions vary greatly amongst industrial sectors.

At the same time, the past 20 years have shown that empirical results on the relationship between firm size and technology intensity are sensitive to the sample of firms, and to the measure used for technological activities. In the 1960s, an r-shaped relationship was established between technology intensity and size in large US firms, when using patenting as the indicator of technological activities (Scherer, 1965): i.e. patent intensity increases more than proportionately in smaller firms and less than proportionately in the largest ones. In the 1970s, systematic data on large US firms' R&D expenditures showed a linear relationship between technology intensity and size (Soete, 1979). In the 1980s, a U-shaped relationship was found in UK firms covering all size categories, between size and technology intensity measured as numbers of significant innovations divided by employment (Pavitt *et al.*, 1987): i.e. innovations per employee are highest in the smallest and the largest firms.[10] Our own more recent work using R&D and patent statistics for large (Fortune 500) firms showed a linear relation between firm size and the volume of technological activity (Patel and Pavitt, 1992).

At a more descriptive level, patent statistics also show that the relative importance in technological activities of firms in different size categories varies across product groups and technological fields (Patel and

---

[10]However, this may be partly a measurement error as some of the innovating units in this database were regarded as independent entities when in fact they were a part of large firms (see Tether *et al.*, 1997).

Pavitt, 1991). In broad terms, large firms predominate in R&D intensive sectors (chemicals, electrical-electronic, transport equipment), whilst small firms predominate in capital goods (machinery, processes, instruments and metal products).

Measuring and mapping technological competencies

The basic premise of the studies concerned with mapping and measuring firm-specific technological competencies is that they are major factors in explaining why firms are different, how they change over time and whether or not they are capable of remaining competitive. There are two ways in which such competencies have been measured. The first uses patents granted in different technical fields for a given firm (Granstrand *et al.*, 1997; Patel and Pavitt, 1997; Prencipe, 1997), and the second uses the different fields of educational qualifications of scientists and engineers employed by a firm (Jacobsson and Oskarsson, 1995; Jacobsson *et al.*, 1996). Most of the studies reviewed below are based on patent data and have focused on the activities of large firms.

One of the main objectives of the research based on this approach is the measurement and analysis of the spread of firm-level technological competencies across different fields of technology (or technology diversification). Some analysts have explored the relationships between technology diversification and product diversification, growth of sales and R&D (Oskarsson, 1993; Gambardella and Torrisi, 1998). Others have examined the extent to which firms are related to each other (both within the same industry and across different industries) in "technology space" in order to measure research "spillovers" (Jaffe, 1989). Narin *et al.* (1987) have used these data for corporate and competitor analysis.

Characteristics of technological competencies

This section highlights our own systematic study of the technological activities of 440 of the world's largest firms classified according to one of 16 product groups (Granstrand *et al.*, 1997; Patel and Pavitt, 1997) and based on their US patenting activities broken down into 34 technical fields. This shows that technological competencies have the following characteristics:

(i) They are typically *multi-field* with substantial proportion of activities outside what would appear to be the core fields. For example:

elect./electronic firms	= ~34% outside broad elect./ electronic fields,	of which ~20% in machinery;
chemical firms	= ~33% outside broad chemical fields,	of which ~16% in machinery;
automobile firms	= ~70% outside broad transport fields,	of which ~46% in machinery.

Thus, firms in all sectors are active in machinery technologies, where they often do not have a distinctive technological advantage, and where smaller firms are particularly active.

(ii) The range of technological competencies is broader than the range of products, as shown in Table 2, which compares the number of firms

Table 2.   Number of active large firms in selected principal products, and in closely related technologies, 1985–90.

Principal product	No. of firms (out of 440)	Technological field (out of 34)	No. of active* firms (out of 440)
Computers.	17	Calculators and computers, etc.	151
Electrical & electronic	56	Semiconductors	94
Instruments	21	Instruments and controls	288
Chemicals	66	Organic chemicals	190
Pharmaceuticals	25	Drugs and bioengineering	114
Mining and petroleum	31	Chemical processes	304
		Apparatus for chemical, food, etc.	234
Non-electrical machinery	58	General non-electrical industrial equipment	246
		Non-electrical specialised industrial equipment	241
		Metallurgical and metal working equipment	225
Automobiles	35	Road vehicles and engines	77
Aerospace	18	Aircraft	28

*With five or more patents granted 1985–90.

with their principal activity in selected product groups with the number of firms active in their corresponding distinctive technologies. In all cases, the latter is considerably larger than the former.

(iii) Thus, each firm has a measurable *profile* of competencies, with varying levels of commitment and competitive advantage in a range of technological fields. In general, firms' technological profiles are *highly stable* over time, reflecting the localised and cumulative nature of technological learning. Fewer than 10% of the 440 firms have no significant correlation between their profiles in 1969–74 and in 1985–90.

(iv) The technological fields where firms have been acquiring an in-house capability most vigorously since the early 1970s — computers, biotechnology and pharmaceuticals and materials — are also those where firms have increased most vigorously their external alliances for technological exchanges and joint developments.

(v) Large firms' technological profiles are *highly differentiated*, according to the products that they make. First, firms have significantly different profiles of technological competence to most others: only 15% (of the 440 firms) are similar. Secondly, in all sectors, firms have a higher probability of finding others with similar technological profiles *within* their sector than *outside* their sector: from twice as high for machinery firms, to more than ten times as high for pharmaceutical firms. Thirdly, the frequency of technological proximity between firms in different industrial sectors is not evenly spread or random, but reveals three distinct groupings:

(a) chemicals, pharmaceuticals and mining and petroleum sectors;

(b) machinery and vehicles; and

(c) electrical and computers.

These results:

- *Confirm* the importance of *path dependency* in the accumulation of firm-specific technological competencies.
- *Confirm* the importance in technology strategy of integration (or "fusion") of different fields of technological competence.
- *Challenge* much of the current conventional wisdom about technology strategies in large firms. In particular, they show the following:
  - Large firms are heavily constrained in their choices about technology strategy.

- External alliances in technology are a complement to internal competence-building, and not a substitute for it. In technology strategy, "make or buy" is not a feasible choice set.
- Radical technological breakthroughs are very unlikely to destroy all — or even the majority — of technological competencies in large firms. Indeed, they are more likely to augment the range of competencies that firms develop.
- In many sectors (particularly transportation), large firms do not focus their technological activities only on their "distinctive core competence", but also on technological linkages in their supply chain.
- Notions of "focus", normally applied to production and marketing strategy, do not necessarily apply to technology strategy.

Technology and product diversification and corporate performance

A number of recent studies have explored the relationship between technology diversification, product diversification and corporate performance. Gambardella and Torrisi (1998) use data on new subsidiaries, acquisitions, collaborative agreements and patents for 32 of the largest US and European firms in electronics to show that, in the 1980s and early 1990s, many firms focused on fewer businesses but not on fewer technical areas. They also show that corporate performance is positively associated with technological diversification as well as with greater focus in business operations.

Using data on sales, R&D and patenting for 57 large firms based in Europe, Japan and the US, Oskarsson (1993) shows that in the 1980s there was a general increase in technology diversification within the sample even in firms where product diversification decreased. Moreover, technology diversification is a significant variable in explaining the growth of corporate sales and corporate R&D.

Geographic spread of technological competencies within firms

Analysts have also examined the nature and extent of the geographic spread of technological activities within large firms using data on patenting[11] (Cantwell, 1992, 1995; Patel and Pavitt, 1991; Patel, 1995, 1996, 2011; Patel and Vega, 1998, 1999). The main "stylised facts" to emerge from comparisons of more than 500 large firms based in Europe, Japan and the US are as follows:

(i) Large firms continue to perform a high proportion of their technological activities in their home[12] countries although there are some differences amongst them, mainly according to nationalities, with Japanese firms continuing to concentrate their activities in Japan and European firms locating more technology outside their home countries.

(ii) A very high share of European firms are technologically active outside their home countries. However, in terms of volume, foreign sources account for a small share of overall technology creation amongst the EU firms.

(iii) The degree of internationalisation of technology varies greatly according to the nationality of EU firms and according to their main industry of activity. In relation to the first, there is some evidence that this is a reflection of country size, as companies based in some of the smaller countries, such as Belgium, Sweden, Austria, Finland and Switzerland have the highest share of technological activity in foreign countries. At the same time, firms with their headquarters in large countries like Germany and Italy have much smaller shares outside the home country. A large majority of EU firms have small scale activities outside their home country.

(iv) There is a considerable variance across industries in terms of foreign sourcing of technological knowledge. EU firms in four industries appear to be amongst the most globalised when we consider the geographic spread of their knowledge creation: mining and petroleum, chemicals, ICT and pharmaceuticals.

(v) According to Cantwell (1992), there is a statistically strong relationship between the share of large firms' technological activities

---

[11] They use the country of residence of the inventor of a patent as a proxy measure for where the technological activity was performed.

[12] Country in which their headquarters is located.

performed outside their home country and their share of foreign production.

(vi) The proportion of firms' technological activities performed abroad *decreases* with the technology intensity of the industry and the firm (Patel, 1995, 1996). Thus, the industries with the most internationalised firms are food and drink, building materials and mining and petroleum, and the least internationalised are aircraft, instruments and automobiles.

(vii) Analysing the activities of the most internationalised large firms, Patel and Vega (1998) show that in a large majority of cases these firms tend to locate their technology abroad in their core areas where they are strong at home and where the location has complementary strengths. In a small minority of cases, firms go abroad in their areas of weakness at home to exploit the technological advantage of the host country.

These results suggest that adapting products and processes and materials to suit foreign markets and providing technical support to off-shore manufacturing plants is a major factor in the internationalisation of corporate technology. They are also consistent with the notion that firms are increasingly engaging in small scale activities to monitor and scan new technological developments in centres of excellence in foreign countries within their areas of existing strength. However, there is very little evidence to suggest that firms routinely go abroad to compensate for their weakness at home.

Conclusions

The above review shows the considerable progress that has been made over the past 40 years in the measurement and understanding of the activities that generate innovation and technical change at the firm level. In particular, the greatly improved coverage, range and accuracy of technology indicators have:

- Shown that although R&D statistics are important, they are not always a satisfactory measure for all those activities at the firm level directed towards knowledge accumulation and technical change.
- Enabled more detailed and meaningful analyses of technological competencies within firms, especially in terms of their spread across technical

fields and geographic space, the results of which have important implications for the management of technology.

• Resolved some of the controversies surrounding the relationship between firm size and market structure, on the one hand, and technological performance, on the other.

There remain unresolved issues concerned with establishing a robust relationship between technology and economic performance at the firm level. While cross-section studies show that there is a statistically significant relationship, this becomes less robust over time and within specific industrial sectors. This points to the need for: (a) more firm-specific data both on technological and on financial performance over longer periods of time, and (b) a wider set of approaches than those based on just the production function and market value function.

Finally, in the future our understanding of the nature and economic impact of innovation and technical change will be greatly improved by studies which are based on the combined use of the range of publicly available measures such as R&D expenditures, patents, innovation surveys, new product announcements and technical qualifications of employees. At the same time, the new possibilities opened up by information from the new innovation surveys will become increasingly more important.

Chapter 8

Assessing Technological Competencies

Francis Narin
CHI Research Inc, USA

General Introduction

The forecast of a company's probability of success is enormously complicated and depends on many financial, managerial and technological variables. In the financial realm, the analyst has a wide variety of quantitative financial indicators available to aid in the analysis. Until recently, however, the managerial and technological inputs to the models have been based on less objective, but more qualitative, data. The new Tech-Line® Technology Indicators system created by CHI Research is designed to address the technology part of the problem. It seeks to bring the quantitative indicators of company technological strength "out of the black box and onto the spreadsheets" and into the models.

Technological knowledge and innovation are central forces driving modern, high-tech companies. The quantitative indicators of company technological strengths will allow securities analysts, investment professionals and economists to explicitly include company technology strengths in their analyses.

The data in the first online Tech-Line® covers 1,139 companies (including top universities, agencies and organisations) in 26 industry groups and 30 technology areas over 10 years with 9 technology indicators. This yielded approximately 4,000,000 data elements for analysing company performance.

Before the advent of technology indicators, analysts assessed the technological strengths of companies from R&D budgets, announcements by management, interviews with R&D managers, new products and other important, but qualitative, information. Occasionally, patent analysis was used as an input, especially by the economists. Otherwise, it was of not much use to the financial community because the data were of a low quality and inaccessible. Specifically, three major problems have restricted the production of this kind of indicator in the past: identification of company patents, allocation into usable categories, and identification of quality in the patent portfolio.

Tech-Line addresses all three problems. To produce Tech-Line®, CHI developed techniques which unify more than 19,000 variant names and subsidiaries of the 1,139 top patenting companies, regroup the patents into 30 technology areas and 26 industry groups familiar to analysts, and use advanced patent citation indicators to provide measures of the quality of the patents within each technology areas for each company in each year.

All these ideas will be discussed in greater detail in subsequent sections of this chapter. For the moment, upon acceptance of the idea that company patents are correctly identified, that the technology areas make sense and that citation analysis identifies quality in the patent portfolios, the following are a sample of questions which can be addressed with this kind of patent portfolio data:

(i) Which companies have the highest impact patents in semi-conductors?

(ii) In a mergers and acquisitions (M&A) situation, which of the companies has the most valuable patent portfolio?

(iii) How concentrated is a company's R&D across different technology categories?

(iv) How much do patent portfolio properties add to the prediction of stock market prices? (Fig. 1 indicates that this may be quite a significant factor.)

(v) Which smaller companies have leading edge technology portfolios in biotechnology?

(vi) How similar are the technological profiles of the major pharmaceutical companies?

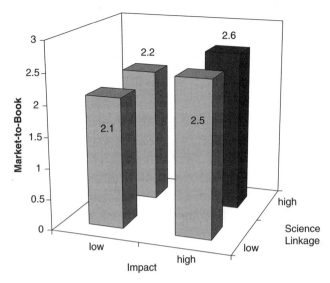

Fig. 1. Chemicals: median portfolio market to book (M/B) ratio based on classifying firms by patent impact and science linkage in the previous three years averaged over six prediction periods.

(vii) How completely has Monsanto shifted its research emphasis into agriculture?

(viii) Would the merger of Glaxo-Wellcome and SmithKline Beecham have been a good one from the point of view of the technological leadership at Glaxo-Wellcome?

Tech-Line data can answer these and many other questions about the relationship of technology to economic and financial performance.

The next section of this chapter discusses the basic ideas behind the database and its application. This is followed by a review of the key research literature behind the database. The last section then defines and discusses each of the indicators used in Tech-Line. Detailed documents on all aspects of these technology indicators are available at www.chiresearch.com.

Technical Introduction

Tech-Line provides a series of quantitative indicators of company techno-logical strengths based on patent portfolio analysis. All these indicators (and many more specialised ones) have been used internally by CHI

Research, Inc. in its consulting practice, tracking the world's technology for industrial and public clients. However, these have not been made widely available to the financial, investment and economics communities before because of the difficulties in obtaining unified, clean company data to work with, technology definition and differentiation between run-of-the-mill and important patents.

Company identification and reassignments

Company identification requires a massive process of consolidation of company names. The 1,139 Tech-Line companies — where "companies" include some major research laboratories, government agencies, universities and other entities patenting in the United States (US) — exist in the US patent system under more than 19,000 different assignee names. For example, the patents of Bayer include patents from more than 150 different assignee names under which Bayer and its subsidiaries have patented in the US. The 1,139 Tech-Line companies include 460 US companies, 565 non-US companies, 66 universities, 30 government agencies and 18 research institutes. Together, they account for about 63% of all US patents.

In addition to company identification, hundreds of thousands of patents originally assigned to one company have been reassigned as a result of property or asset sales, mergers and acquisitions, various changes in corporate structure and so forth; those reassigned patents are assigned to their current corporate owners.

Technology categorisations

Classification problems have also bedevilled the use of patent data in strategic and financial analysis. The most obvious way to partition patents is by patent classification — the assignment of a patent by patent examiners. However, hundreds of major classes and many tens of thousands of sub-classes, covering all forms of technology, are used by the US Patent Office. Moreover, these classifications are invention-art-based, rather than application-specific. Hence, for example, a classification describing a blade for a rotating bladed member might cover both a desk fan and a jet engine. Thus, devising a way to partition patents by classification requires a high degree of knowledge and experience.

Tech-Line partitions patents based on the International Patent Classification (IPC) system, which has a somewhat more industrial orientation than US patent classifications. The 30 technology areas in Tech-Line (Table 1) are based on the first given IPC on each patent. (There can be more than one IPC assigned, but the first is usually considered to be the main classification.) These categories should go a long way towards meeting the general needs of the non-technical community for patent data in categories which make sense from a corporate viewpoint.

Identifying important patents

The third major problem is the identification of important patents from the many tens of thousands of patents issued each year. For this, we use techniques developed from patent citation analysis to characterise a company's overall patent portfolio and within each of the 30 technology areas.

The basic idea of patent citation analysis is that highly cited patents — patents that are listed as "references cited" on many later patents — are generally of much greater importance than patents which are never cited, or are cited only a few times. The reason for this is that a patent which contains an important new invention — or major advance — can set off a stream of follow-on inventions, all of which may cite the original, important invention upon which they are building.

The key indicators used in Tech-Line, summarised below, are:

(i) *Number of patents.* Indicating company technology activity, it is a count of Type 1 (regular, utility) patents issued in the US patent system from 1987 to the present.

(ii) *Cites per patent.* Indicating the impact of a company's patents, this indicator is based on cited year; for example, all 1990 company patents as cited in subsequent years.

(iii) *Current impact index (CII).* A fundamental indicator of patent portfolio quality, it is the number of times the company's previous five years of patents, in a technology area, were cited from the current year, divided by the average citations received by all US patents in that technology area from the current year. Expected = 1.0.

Table 1. Patent growth and concentration indicators for all Tech-Line® companies, 1993–1997.

Technology area	Number of patents 1993–1997	Patent growth percentage in area	Percentage of company patents in area
1. Agriculture	4,542	6	1.3
2. Oil and gas	4,604	−19	1.3
3. Power generation and distribution	4,730	0	1.3
4. Food and tobacco	2,641	−18	0.8
5. Textiles and apparel	4,165	5	1.2
6. Wood and paper	2,035	8	0.6
7. Chemicals	40,828	4	11.6
8. Pharmaceuticals	12,610	23	3.6
9. Biotechnology	6,113	89	1.7
10. Medical equipment	8,348	43	2.4
11. Medical electronics	3,769	73	1.1
12. Plastics, polymers and rubber	20,117	2	5.7
13. Glass, clay and cement	2,880	−16	0.8
14. Primary metals	1,913	−15	0.5
15. Fabricated metals	4,879	1	1.4
16. Industrial machinery and tools	14,426	−4	4.1
17. Industrial process equipment	9,488	−2	2.7
18. Office equipment and cameras	22,076	23	6.3
19. Heating and ventilation	2,211	22	0.6
20. Miscellaneous machinery	11,250	−5	3.2
21. Computers and peripherals	37,078	81	10.6
22. Telecommunications	33,350	44	9.5
23. Semiconductors and electronics	26,740	39	7.6
24. Measuring and control equipment	16,333	0	4.7
25. Electrical appliances and computer	17,132	12	4.9
26. Motor vehicles and parts	13,169	0	3.8
27. Aerospace and parts	1,996	−6	0.6
28. Other transport	2,518	−4	0.7
29. Miscellaneous manufacturing	15,477	2	4.4
99. Other	3,530	1	1
All	350,948	16	100

(iv) *Technology strength (TS)*. Indicating patent portfolio strength, it is the number of patents multiplied by the current impact index, that is, patent portfolio size inflated or deflated by patent quality.

(v) *Technology cycle time (TCT)*. Indicating the speed of invention, it is the median age, in years, of the US patent references cited on the front page of the company's patents.

(vi) *Science linkage (SL)*. Indicating how leading edge the company's technology is, it is the average number of science papers referenced on the front page of the company's patents.

(vii) *Science strength (SS)*. Indicating how much the company uses science in building its patent portfolio, it is the number of patents multiplied by science linkage, that is, patent portfolio size inflated or deflated by the extent of science linkage. This is a count of the total number of science links in the company patent portfolio.

Research Background

In this section, we will review the evidence that indicators of company technological strength, based on patent portfolio analysis, provide a valid way of assessing the quality and value of a company's patented technology. We will do this by first reviewing the background research in science and patent citation analysis, as well as in economics. All these studies point to the conclusion that citation analysis provides significant measures of quality when assessing portfolios of publications or patents. In addition, there is emerging evidence that patent portfolio analysis, including citation indicators of the impact of the holdings in those portfolios, are indicative of — and in some cases predictive of — company technological, economic and stock market success.

Figure 1, for example, from some preliminary and ongoing research at New York University, indicated that companies which have highly science-linked and highly cited patents may have substantially higher stock market/book ratios than companies with less highly science-linked and less highly cited patents.

The main thrust of this section is that in both the scientific and technological realms, there is compelling evidence that high citation — to research papers in the scientific literature and to issued US patents in the technological literature — is associated with the importance of the scientific or technological discoveries being cited. Since this association is a statistical one, it does not guarantee that every highly cited paper or patent is of importance, or that a paper or patent that is not highly cited is not of importance. It does argue, however, that a company with a portfolio of highly cited and science-linked patents is more likely to be technologically successful than one that does not have such a portfolio.

Just having a strong intellectual property portfolio does not, of course, guarantee a company's success. Many additional factors do affect the ability of a company to move from quality patents to quality products, or even to high profits. The decade of troubles at IBM, for example, is certainly illustrative of this, since IBM has always had very high quality and highly cited research in its laboratories.

The key studies discussed in this section were selected to capture the parallel growth of the three disciplines behind Tech-Line: science citation analysis, patent citation analysis, and closely related economic and policy analysis. Each of those studies has an additional bibliography, from which the reader can get to literally hundreds of papers which provide the relevant background.

Science citation analysis

The origins of large-scale citation analysis are traced to the work of Eugene Garfield, who first proposed the *Science Citation Index* in the 1950s as a tool to increase the power of scientists to retrieve prior scientific papers (Garfield, 1955). Garfield also pointed out that in evaluating science, it is important to trace the impact that a given paper has had. This is because all scientific work builds on earlier scientific work. For a scientist to be able to fully understand the impact his own work is having, he should have a tabulation of its citation impact and all the later papers that cite it.

In the early 1960s, Garfield created the *Science Citation Index*, which has since grown to a major resource for science covering more than 4,000 scientific journals, more than half a million papers, and more than five million citations annually.

Although Garfield and his colleagues were well aware of the potential use of citation data in measuring the impact of individual papers, the widespread acceptance of science citation data in evaluation is associated with the creation, by the National Science Foundation, of the first *Science Indicators* report in 1972. Narin and his colleagues at CHI Research (then called Computer Horizons, Inc.) utilised the *Science Citation Index* data for *Science Indicators* and created both national and international scientific performance indicators. They used counts of publications and, most importantly, counts of how frequently those publications were cited to create the first major indicators of national scientific performance used in that report.

The large-scale use of publication and citation techniques has continued in the subsequent *Science Indicators* reports issued every two years since the 1972 report. For example, the *Science and Engineering Indicators 1998* report contained many tables and graphs based on this kind of bibliometric data.

As part of the general development of *Science Indicators* techniques, CHI, under contract with the National Science Foundation, produced a monograph entitled *Evaluative Bibliometrics* (Narin, 1976), which reviewed the state-of-the-art of citation analysis techniques, and, in particular, their application to the evaluation of the performance of scientific institutions. In Chapter Five of *Evaluative Bibliometrics*, 24 different validation studies were summarised, all of which support the idea that high citation in the scientific literature is associated with positive peer opinions of the importance of scientific papers, with peer rankings of research institutions, and with other independent indicators of quality and the impact of sets of research papers.

One of the most fascinating and telling demonstrations of the importance of very high citation is the publication of a series of papers related to the bibliometric characteristics of Nobel laureates in science. In an early paper discussing the quality of research and Nobel prizes, Inhaber noted: "The quality of the work of Nobel laureates in physics, as measured by citations, is an order of magnitude higher than that of other scientists" (Inhaber and Przednowek, 1976, 34).

Garfield himself has written on this extensively and has published a relatively comprehensive table illustrating the very high citations received by papers of Nobel laureates. Specifically, he looked at 125 Nobel laureates in the fields of chemistry, physics, physiology and medicine. He found that 80% had published what he calls citation classics, that is, papers in the most cited 1,000 articles in the *SCI* between 1961–1982, or papers that are cited more than 300 times. This corresponds roughly to the top 4/10,000 of all published scientific papers (Garfield, 1986).

The area of citation analysis continues to be a vibrant one, with a steady stream of papers applying these techniques to the evaluations of groups of scientists, research departments, institutions and nations. This work is particularly active in Europe, with major bibliometrics research and education programmes in all the major European countries. The journal *Scientometrics*, edited in Hungary, is devoted almost entirely to this field, and is an important resource for anyone looking to update themselves on the many applications of citation analysis in science. Finally, in April 1998, Ron Kostoff placed an extensive monograph on various metrics of science on the Internet. This monograph may be accessed directly at http://www.dtic.mil/dtic/kostoff/index.html. Kostoff's monograph is self-contained and extensive, and contains more than 5,000 references to earlier works.

The early validation techniques covered the full range of studies still being used in research evaluation. They covered the correlations between the publication and citation measures of national, institutional, research group and individual performance, and external rankings. At the national level, for example, an early policy analysis by Derek de Solla Price showed that nations publish research papers roughly in proportion to their gross domestic product (GDP); that is, in proportion to their economic size, and not to their population or land area or anything else (Price, 1969). Much later, CHI showed that this also carries over into technology, and that other nations' inventors patent in the US patent system in general proportion to their national economic size as measured by the GDP (Narin, 1991).

At the institutional level, citation techniques have been applied extensively to the ranking of university departments. This had been done systematically in the US in a series of reports in which relatively large numbers of senior academics ranked major university departments. In a paper published in 1978, and reprinted in 1980, CHI showed that not only do these peer rankings of universities correlate well with publication rankings, but that the correlations are always increased substantially when citation data is included. That is, the rankings of university departments based on a combination of the number of papers and how frequently they are cited are much more highly correlated with peer rankings than those based on publication counts alone (Anderson *et al.*, 1978).

Basics of patent citation analysis

When a US patent is granted, it typically contains eight or nine "References Cited — US patents" on its front page, two references cited to foreign patents, and one to two non-patent references cited. These references link the just-issued patent to the earlier cited prior art and limit the claims of the just-issued patent. They point out where the essential and related art already exists, and delineate the property rights of the invention as determined by the US Patent and Trademark Office.

The "references cited" on US patents are a fundamental requirement of patent law. When a US patent is issued, it has to satisfy three general criteria: it must be useful, novel and not obvious. The novelty requirement is the primary factor which leads to the references that appear on the front page of the patent, since it is the responsibility of the patent applicant and his attorney — and of the patent examiner — to identify, through the various references cited therein, all of the important prior art upon which the issued patent improves. These references are chosen and/or screened by the patent examiner, who is "not called upon to cite all references that are available, but only the best" (Patent and Trademark Office, 1995).

When this referencing pattern is turned around, and all of the subsequent citations to a given patent are tabulated, one obtains the fundamental information used in patent citation analysis, namely, a count of how often a given patent is cited in later patents. These distributions tend to be very skewed: there are large numbers of patents that are cited only a few times, and only a small number of patents cited more than ten times. For example, for patents issued in 1988 — and cited in the next seven years — half the patents are cited two or fewer times, 75% are cited five or fewer times, and only 1% of the patents are cited 24 or more times. Overall, after ten or more years, the average cites/patent is around six.

As was the case with science citation analysis, there is, of course, no official standard by which the importance of a patent may be judged except, perhaps, for the Federal Court's designation of "pioneering patents".

Therefore, most studies of citation frequency and patent importance are based upon the opinions of knowledgeable scientists or engineers, or correlations with non-patent measures. However, in the case of pioneering patents, we have a direct legal indicator of patent importance and, as will be shown in a moment, pioneering patents are cited, on average, six or more times as frequently as average patents issued at the same time.

The first paper of which we are aware that looked at patent citations as a way of finding important patents was an early study carried out by Reisner (1965) at IBM, who experimented with the use of citation analysis to find key patents. By tracing the references from one patent to another, Reisner found 43 of 60 patents she was looking for.

Computerised citation data covering all US patents first became available in 1975. In the following year, in the Sixth Technology Assessment and Forecast report, the Patent and Trademark Office tabulated the patents which were most highly cited and suggested that "the number of times a patent document is cited may be a measure of its technological significance" (Patent and Trademark Office, 6th Report, 1976).

In 1978, Ellis, Hepburn and Oppenheim in the UK experimented with citation networks, tracing from patents to identify key discoveries and turning points.

The first relatively formal study of patent citation analysis was carried out by CHI Research under the sponsorship of the National Science Foundation (Carpenter *et al.*, 1981). At the time the study was proposed, in the late 1970s, the Science Indicators Unit at the National Science Foundation was considering whether to add technology indicators, based on patent citations, to the stable of science literature indicators which were then being used in the *Science Indicators* reports. NSF commissioned CHI to do a study to see whether patents associated with important discoveries were more highly cited than average patents.

A set of 100 important patents and a set of 102 control patents were selected. The former was obtained by identifying a key patent underlying a product which had received the IR-100 award, which was established by the journal *Industrial Research & Development*. This award "honors the 100 most significant new technical products — and the innovators responsible for them — developed during the year" (*Industrial Research & Development*, **13**, 3, December 1980).

Patents related to the 1969 and 1970 awards were used in order to ensure that there was sufficient time for the patents to be cited to their full potential. The results of that study are summarised in the following tabulation:

	IR-100	Control
Total patents	100	102
Total cites	494	208
Cites/patent	4.94	2.04
Patents cited > 10 times	17	4

Clearly, the IR-100 patents are much more highly cited. This difference is due to the presence of highly cited patents in the IR-100 set.

Following this study, patent citation indicators were added to the *Science Indicators* report (by then called *Science and Engineering Indicators*) and their use has expanded over the subsequent years.

Another formal validation study, carried out by Carpenter and his colleagues at CHI in 1983, tested whether the citations from issued US patents could be used to measure the science dependence and foreign dependence of patented technologies. Rankings based on the number of citations per patent to the scientific literature and foreign-origin material were compared to peer rankings of the science and foreign dependence of the patents. Overall, a high degree of agreement was found between the expert opinions on the science and foreign dependence, as well as corresponding bibliometric rankings. For example, the eight technologies judged most science-dependent by experts averaged 0.92 cites per patent to scientific journal papers. Meanwhile, the eight technologies judged least science-dependent had only 0.05 references per patent to journal papers.

Another citation validation study was carried out by students at the Worcester Polytech Institute and the US Patent and Trademark Office. The abstract of that report succinctly summarises its contents:

"This report, prepared for the United States Patent & Trademark Office, analyses the importance of patents frequently cited by patent examiners. Information regarding the commercial and technical significance of the 419 most highly cited patents from 1975 and 1980 was obtained through a survey of patent attorneys and patent examiners. The characteristics of an important patent were determined through the survey. The results were found to support the hypothesis that highly cited patents are important." (Worcester Polytech, 1988).

A quite formal validation study of patent citation importance within an industrial context was carried out by CHI Research in co-operation with Eastman Kodak Laboratories. Kodak was interested in the possibility of using patent citation data in an analysis of their own and some of their competitor's technology, and had desired to independently validate whether, within an industrial laboratory, high patent citation was associated with knowledgeable peer assessment of the importance of the patents. In that study, a collection of nearly 100 Kodak patents in their core area of Silver Halide Technology were divided into sets of 16 each. The sets were then given to senior laboratory staff for evaluation. Every patent was evaluated by three or four different people. As a result, the rankings of the patents could be cross-tabulated. The Kodak evaluators were senior intellectual property staff, the senior laboratory management and senior laboratory scientists. In the case of scientists, the patents they were given to rank were screened to make sure that they did not rank their own patents. Each person was asked to rank the patents based on how much each has changed the state-of-the-art in the field of the invention.

The results of that study were very well summarised in Fig. 2. It shows, quite clearly, that whether a patent is cited one, two or three times does not seem to make much difference in the peer ranking, but that patents cited more than five times, that is, relatively highly cited patents, were ranked far more highly by the Kodak staff. This finding is statistically significant, especially for group 8, the most highly cited patents. Of the 15 respondents in the study, eight gave group 8 patents the highest average rating. Using the binomial model, the probability of this is 0.0002 (Albert *et al.*, 1991).

The most recent evidence for the importance of highly cited patents comes from within the Patent Office itself: from the strong associations between citation frequency and Patent Office recognition, and in the extremely high citation to pioneering patents.

CHI has looked at the citation frequency of three different categories of patents: patents listed in the National Inventor's Hall of Fame; patents of Historical Significance in a list prepared by the US Department of

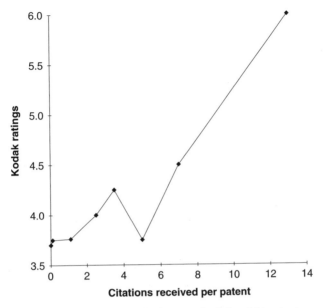

Fig. 2. Average rating versus average citations received for eight patent groups: Kodak highly cited patents are much more highly rated.

Commerce for the US bicentennial; and patents that had been adjudged as pioneering patents by the Federal District Court.

A summary of this data is shown in Fig. 3, which plots citation indices for the three sets of patents: Pioneering, Hall of Fame and Historically Significant. Because the patents are distributed over a relatively long period of time, we divided the number of times each patent was cited by the expected number of times patents issued in the same year have been cited, counting citations in our database from 1971 through March of 1995. The results were striking. Pioneering patents are cited almost seven times as often as expected; Hall of Fame patents are cited more than six times as often as expected; and Historically Significant, almost 2.5 times as often as expected! And, in fact, of all the patents looked at, only one was cited fewer times than expected. This is certainly a very direct validation of the idea that important patents tend to be cited much more heavily than on average.

A paper, still in publication by F.M. Scherer of Harvard and colleagues in Europe and at CHI, has looked at a sample of US and German patented

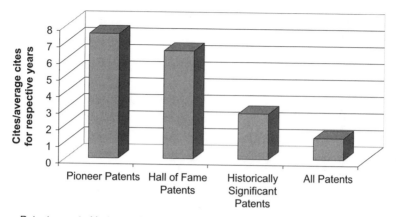

Patents granted between 1960 and 1995. Citations from 1971 to March 1995.

Fig. 3.   Very high citation indices are found for selected patents.

inventions on which profitability information — the private value of the patents — was obtained (Harhoff *et al.*, 1998). They considered only patents for which all the fees had been paid to keep the patents in force in Germany for the full 18 years of the patents, and then queried the owners of those patents as to the asset value of the patent — by essentially asking: what is the smallest amount which they would have been willing to sell this patent to an independent third party for in 1980? In the German patent system, the two patents in the highest value category were much more highly cited than the others; in the US patent system, the patent citation frequency of the patents with an estimated value of US$20 million or more were substantially more highly cited than those with lesser estimated values.

Economic and policy analysis

In this section, we review a few studies which support the idea that there is a positive relationship between important technological advances and economic outcomes. This is the so-called "linear model" of innovation: the idea that invention and innovations originate in basic and applied research before progressing into technological and economic benefit. This simple linear model has been supplanted by much more complex views of the process with many feedback loops, but the origins of technical knowledge in basic research still lie at the core of this process (Turney, 1991).

It is also, of course, widely accepted today that research makes an important contribution to economic growth. In his statement on technology for America's economic growth, President Bill Clinton stated that

"Scientific advances are the well-spring of technical innovations. The benefits are seen in economic growth, improved healthcare and many other areas." (Clinton and Gore, 1993).

A recent paper of ours discussed quite extensively the increasing linkage between US technology and public science, and has demonstrated that the underlying citation by patents to research papers, used in Tech-Line as science linkage, has increased dramatically over the last decade (Narin *et al.*, 1998).

As far back as the late 1960s, systematic efforts were underway to trace the linkage between research and economically important innovations. A key study done then was the TRACES study (Technology in Retrospect and Critical Events in Science) performed under NSF's sponsorship at IIT Research Institute (Narin, 1969). It looked at five economically important innovations, including magnetic ferrites, video-recording and the contraceptive pill, and traced back to their origins in applied and basic research.

The key advance embedded in TRACES was the semi-quantitative approach. Although citation analysis was not utilised — partially because citation data was essentially inaccessible then — there was an attempt to classify, count and identify the key events leading up to the innovations.

By the early 1980s, it was possible to obtain reasonably large-scale patent data and Griliches and his colleagues at Harvard, as well as the National Bureau of Economic Research (NBER), began a long series of quantitative studies looking at the economic importance of patents. In a 1981 paper, Griliches found a significant relationship between the market value of the firms and its "intangible" capital. It was provided by past R&D expenditures and the number of patents (Griliches, 1981).

A particularly interesting paper in this sequence, by Ariel Pakes in 1985, "On patents, R&D and the stock market rate of return", found that an unanticipated patent is associated with an increase in firm value of US$865,000.

In 1990, Griliches comprehensively surveyed the use of patent statistics as economic indicators (Griliches, 1990).

Those studies, and most of the economic studies up to recent time, were very aggregate. They were based on corporate identifications that were either not unified at all or not nearly as refined as those that are now available on Tech-Line, and without the augmentation that citation analysis adds.

In 1987, Narin and his colleagues studied a group of 18 US pharmaceutical companies and showed that the number of patents they obtained, and especially whether the companies had highly cited patents, were both correlated with the peer opinions of the companies and with ncreases in pharmaceutical company sales and profits (Narin *et al.*, 1987). That study showed quite clearly that highly cited patents tended to occur around economically important inventions such as Tagamet for SmithKline, and that these important technological events lead, in that industry, to increases in company sales and profits. In fact, the Tagamet patents that were highly cited in the 1980s are still the underpinnings of SmithKline Beecham today.

A somewhat different approach, with the same results, was taken in a study by Trajtenberg (1990) with the marvellous title "A penny for your quotes" ("quotes" is the European term often used for citations). Trajtenberg analysed patent citation patterns associated with advances in CAT scanners and showed a close association between citation-based patent indices and independent measures of the social value of innovations for computed tomography scanners. Of particular significance is his finding that "the weighting scheme appears to be non-linear (increasing) in the number of citations, implying that the information content of citations rises at the margin" (p. 172). This directly supports the idea that highly cited patents are of particular technical importance.

In a broader study, Franko, at the University of Massachusetts, showed that the US and UK losses in global markets between 1960 and 1986 may have been caused by a lack of investment in technology when compared to their Japanese and continental European competitors. According to him,

> "The proportion of corporate sales revenues allocated to commercially oriented R&D emerges as a, perhaps the, principal indicator

of subsequent sales growth performance relative to competition over 5–10 year periods. Insofar as many US and UK firms have lost global market share relative to Asian and European competitors over the past two decades, a significant contributory factor would appear to have been negligence on the part of many US and UK firms of investment in technology as a factor determining strategic, competitive advance." (Franko, 1989)

An interesting observation is that the superior technological performance of the US in the mid to late 1990s is associated with an increasing US inventor share of US patents, back up to over 5% of the patents granted in the US.

In a beautifully-written general article in *Scientific America*, Rosenberg and Birdzel at Stanford put forth the thesis that the linkage of knowledge and technology, as well as the freedom to absorb and use it in industry, was the fundamental driving force behind the economic rise of the West. Specifically,

"Close links between the growth of scientific knowledge and the rise of technology have permitted the market economies of the Western nations to achieve unprecedented prosperity." (Rosenberg and Birdzel, 1991)

A few years later, *Business Week* published the two Patent Scoreboards using CHI Research data to rank major companies across ten different industries (Coy and Carey, 1993; Buderi *et al.*, 1992). These Patent Scoreboards were two of the first times when these ideas were introduced directly to the business community. Hence, analysts could look at the relationship between the business performance of companies and their technological strengths.

There is also a growing awareness of the value of intellectual capital — of which patents are a major component. This is reflected in an article in *Fortune*, "Your company's most valuable asset: Intellectual capital", by Stewart (1994), which asserted that the modern company is really driven by knowledge, and not by bricks and structures.

The economists associated with the NBER are now using patent citation techniques in a wide variety of ways to study the following: the spillovers of research from company to company and from university to company; the characteristics of successful companies; and, in general, the acceptance of the notion that patent citation is equivalent, in the statistical sense, to high impact technology. A paper by Jaffe *et al.*, (1993) provides a linkage to this literature.

Interest is also rapidly growing in finding ways of valuing corporate intangibles for financial purposes. The intangibles research project, headed by Professor Baruch Lev at The Stern School of Business in New York University, is addressing the accounting treatment of corporate investment and intangibles such as R&D franchise and brand development. In particular, a study by Professor Lev showed that the accounting rule, which allows an acquiring company to set a value for the "in process" research and development assets and write off that amount immediately, significantly allows the acquirers to avoid future charges to earnings from goodwill. Thus, this tends to provide companies with a boost to their future earnings (Deng and Lev, 1998).

In a work that is still underway, Bronwyn Hall and her colleagues at the NBER are looking at market value and patent citations by using a new database that has been assembled by NBER for research purposes. Their research, while still preliminary, is quite advanced in its mathematical techniques and is being used to estimate how much citations to patents contribute to such indicators as the market value of a company. They found that "citation weighted patents do better, especially in the earlier years when the citation measure is more complete", and that "an increase of one citation per patent is associated with a 3–4% increase in market value at the firm level" (Hall *et al.*, 1998).

Finally, a relevant and important preliminary study by Professor Lev and his student, Zhen Deng, assisted by CHI, looked at the relationship between Tech-Line variables and various financial indicators, including R&D budgets and stock market performance (Deng *et al.*, 1998). In particular, they found that companies whose patents had above average current impact indices (CIIs) and science linkage indicators (SLs) tended to have significantly higher market to book ratios and stock market returns, both contemporaneously and for a number of years into the future (Fig. 1). This finding is one of the key evidence that indicators of corporate technological performance, based on patents and patent citations, may provide significant new tools to securities and financial analysts.

Indicator Definitions

This chapter will cover, in some detail, the specific indicators used in Tech-Line, as well as the many decisions and unifications that must be undertaken to create a usable technology indicators database.

We will begin with the choice of patents to include and the identification of the company (assignee) which owns the patent currently before proceeding to the most basic indicator: the cites per patent received by a patent from subsequently issued patents. We will then define the current impact index, a synchronous citation indicator which characterises the quality of a company's patents in the last five years, and then on to technology cycle time, which characterises the rapidity with which companies invent, and finally, science linkage, which shows whether a company's patents are linked to scientific research. The latter is a strong indicator of leading edge position across a wide range of science-based advanced technologies. A few composite indicators constructed from these basic ones will also be defined.

Number of patents

The number of patents indicates company technology activity. It is a count of a company's Type 1 (regular, utility) patents issued in the US patent system from 1987 to the present.

For its patent counts, Tech-Line considers only regular (Type I) US utility patents. Other categories of US patents, such as plant patents, design patents, reissues, continuations and so forth, are not counted in order to maintain the focus of the database on the key category of patents which contributes to corporate technological strengths.

Company name unification

When a US patent is issued, it is issued to the inventor and, if the inventor works for a company, the rights to the patent are normally assigned to the company. The latter is then identified as the assignee of that patent.

The first problem is that companies obtain their patents under many different names: companies may patent under divisional names; subsidiaries may obtain patents in their own names; companies' names may change over time; and so forth. CHI has gone through a massive unification of these various assignee names for the 1,100 companies covered in Tech-Line, which are constructed by combining more than 19,000 different original assignee names in a major attempt to identify correctly the company to which patents are assigned in the first place. For example, the following shows a few names under which patents assigned to Hitachi were filed, and which have been unified in Tech-Line:

Step 1. Typographical unification

Step 2. Company unification

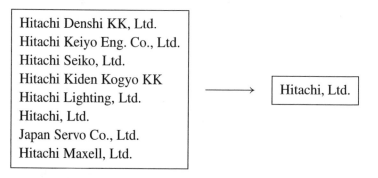

Company restatement

The second problem related to the assignment of a patent to a company is mergers, acquisitions and divestitures, which CHI has attempted to take into account by restating all companies as at the end of 1997.

More specifically, insofar as we can tell which patents belong to a subsidiary or part of a divested or acquired company, these patents are moved with a merger/acquisition. For example, the patents of SmithKline Beecham not only include those under its name, but also those that were originally filed under SmithKline and French Laboratories, Beckman Instruments, Beecham, and so forth. This process is carried out by scanning a number of resources, but is by no means perfect, especially for the smaller companies. Hence, the corporate identification in Tech-Line, while better and more up-to-date than any database of which we are aware of, is certainly not perfect.

Reassignments

Another major attribute of the Tech-Line database is that we have attempted to account for the major reassignments of patents. When a merger and acquisition takes place, or a major area of technology is sold, it sometimes happens that a reassignment of patents is registered in the Patent Office from the original assignee to a new assignee. This reassignment is captured in a complex, as well as extremely difficult to process, database produced by the Patent Office. CHI has processed this database and moved, via reassignment, hundreds of thousands of patents from the original assignees to their new assignees, including the many patents moved across Tech-Line companies. Some of the reassignments are not very important from a company strength's viewpoint, such as from one part of a company or one version of a company's name to another, while others are indicative of the genuine transfer of intellectual property from one company to another. As well as we could, the reassignments — which were recorded by the Patent Office — affecting the Tech-Line companies have been accounted for and the reassigned patents are, within Tech-Line, assigned to their current owners.

Restatement limitation

It is very important to mention, however, that companies do not, by any means, always reassign their patents, even when major divestitures and acquisitions occur. For example, the old patents of AT&T were not reassigned to Lucent by registration of the reassignment at the USPTO. However, there is a public record in SEC documents of which patents went to Lucent and NCR from AT&T; we have made use of those public filings to assign to Lucent the great majority of the patents which were originally assigned to AT&T. In cases where patents were not explicitly reassigned, and we have not found any public record of them, the patents stayed with the original company. For example, Imation, which was split off from 3M, and is now beginning to patent vigorously under its name, does not appear to have been reassigned any 3M patents. Therefore, it does not yet have enough patents to be included as a Tech-Line company.

Choice of companies

The online Tech-Line database was built upon earlier CD-ROM versions of Tech-Line. The criteria for selecting companies in those earlier times were relatively large numbers of patents in the late 1980s and early 1990s, with each edition of Tech-Line adding to it companies that had newly emerged as major patenters. However, the earlier versions broke the data down into broad sets of chemical, electrical and pharmaceutical companies, and the coverage was not even across other areas. Thus, while most of the top 1,100 patenting companies are covered in Tech-Line, there may be a few companies with recent rapid increases in patenting which we have missed. We will attempt to get any that should be covered in future releases of Tech-Line, which may also be expanded to cover smaller companies.

The lists of all the companies covered in Tech-Line are given on the CHI homepage at www.chiresearch.com. The coverage is global; approximately one-half of all US patents are foreign-invented. This is reflected in the Tech-Line company proportions. More specifically, the first edition of Tech-Line in July 1998 covers the following:

(i) 48% are US organisations.
(ii) 52% are foreign organisations.

Specifically:

  (i) 355 US parent companies.
 (ii) 105 US subsidiaries.
(iii) 469 non-US parent companies.
 (iv) 96 non-US subsidiaries.
  (v) 30 government agencies (10 from US).
 (vi) 18 research institutes (13 from US).
(vii) 66 universities (64 from US).

Patent growth percentage and percentage of company patents according to area

Two indicators are based directly on the number and growth rate of patents. These are patent growth percentage in area and percentage of company patents in area. Patent growth percentage in area, from one period to the next, is just the number of patents in the current period less the number of patents in the previous period and divided by the number of patents in the previous period expressed as a percentage. The percentage of company patents in area is, just as it says, 100 times the number of patents in the area divided by the total number of patents for the company. Both are illustrated for all Tech-Line companies in the first edition of Tech-Line online in Table 1.

Note that the largest area is chemicals with 11.6% of all patents followed by computers and peripherals at 10.6%. It is also apparent that the high-tech areas expand the fastest. The most rapidly growing area over the five-year period is biotechnology: with a growth rate of 89%. It is followed by computers and peripherals (80%) and medical electronics (73%).

Still growing at a rapid rate, but down from the top three, are medical equipment (43%), telecommunications (43%) and semiconductors and electronic components (38%). In addition, three other areas are growing faster than the patent system: pharmaceuticals (23%), office equipment and cameras (23%), and heating and ventilation (22%). The overall Tech-Line growth rate was 16%. The areas which seem to be shrinking in patenting most rapidly are oil and gas (19%), food and tobacco (18%), glass, clay and cement (16%) and primary metals (15%). Real differences exist, in the rates of growth of patenting within different areas. As mentioned before, it is important that comparisons be made within technology areas.

Cites per patent

Cite per patent indicates the impact of a company's patents. It is a count of the citations received by a company's patents from the front pages of subsequent patents. For example, the cites per patent in 1990 report the number of times a company's patents were mentioned.

In patent citation analysis, high citation counts are often associated with important inventions, which are fundamental to future inventions. Companies with highly cited patents may be more advanced than their competitors, as they will have more valuable patent portfolios. After six years, the average US patent is cited about five times.

When comparing cites per patent, one must be careful to do so within a given technology area and within a specific year. The next section will discuss variations in citations in different technology areas.

The reason that comparisons can only be made within a specific year is because citations accumulate over time. For the first online edition of Tech-Line, the cite count per patent were those received by a particular patent from all US patents issued through June 1998. The result is that a US patent

Table 2.   Cites per patent received by all
Tech-Line® patents.

Year	Cites per patent
1988	6.6
1989	5.9
1990	5.4
1991	4.8
1992	4.2
1993	3.4
1994	2.6
1995	1.6
1996	0.8
1997	0.1

Note: Citations counts through 16 June
1998 for US patents.

issued in 1990 will have more than seven years of citation, whereas a patent
issued in 1992 will have only five years of citations. This is illustrated in
Table 2, which shows the number of cites for each patent in Tech-Line in
all technology areas between 1988 and 1997.

Current impact index (CII)

The current impact index (CII) indicates patent quality of the patent
portfolio. It is the number of times a company's patents in the last five
years have been cited during the current year, relative to the entire patent
database. A value of 1.0 represents the average citation frequency; a value
of 2.0 represents twice the average citation frequency; and 0.25 represents
25% of the average citation frequency within the technology.

The key characteristic of CII is that it is a synchronous indicator: it
looks back to the last five years. As a result, it moves alongside financial
indicators and is sensitive to a company's current technology. For example,
10- or 15 year-old patents that are highly cited will not affect the CII, except
those that the company has issued within the last five years. Essentially, the
CII is the sum of the citation ratios for each of the company's patents in the
last five years and cited by all patents during the current year. The following
illustrates the computation of the CII for a hypothetical company, ABC:

Number of patents issued in year.

	1986	1987	1988	1989	1990
World	71,662	72,860	81,954	76,542	95,530
ABC	104	250	125	180	285

Number of citations from 1991 to year.

	1986	1987	1988	1989	1990
World	35,321	36,854	50,765	40,970	52,635
ABC	62	130	65	102	165

Average cites per patent from 1991 to year.

	1986	1987	1988	1989	1990
World	0.49	0.51	0.62	0.53	0.55
ABC	0.60	0.52	0.52	0.57	0.58

For each of the last five years, we form a citation ratio, which is the ratio of average cites to ABC's patents divided by the average cites for all patents. For example, for each of the five years included in the table above, we obtain the following citation ratios:

ABC's citation ratios (ratio to world).

1986	1987	1988	1989	1990
1.22	1.02	0.83	1.07	1.05

The final step in calculating the CII is the sum of these ratios, which is weighted by the number of patents the company has in each of the previous five years. The following illustrates this:

$$CII = \frac{1.22 \times 104 + 1.02 \times 250 + 0.83 \times 125 + 1.07 \times 180 + 1.05 \times 285}{104 + 250 + 125 + 180 + 285}$$

$$= 1.03$$

The current impact index is a citing year indicator. It gives you the impact or quality of the company's patents based on citing from the current year backwards. This is the reverse of the standard cites per patent indicator. The latter is based on the year cited and the sum of all the citations received in subsequent years.

For the entire patent system, the expected CII is 1.0. This means that a company whose patents have a CII of 1.5 has patents which are cited 50% more than expected during the current year in the last five years.

Since the CII only takes into account the last five years, one of its important characteristics is that when a company begins to run out of bright, new, inventions, its CII will begin to fall relatively quickly. This gives the analyst a stronger picture of what is likely to happen to a company's technology in the near future. However, in some industries, such as the pharmaceutical industry, there is a long time lag between patents and products, this should, perhaps, be factored into the analysis.

However, the essence of all citation indicators is to capture the fundamental technological strengths and capability of a company, and not to identify exactly which products or discoveries are going to be commercially important. There is too much uncertainty in technology to do it with any kind of general indicator. To borrow a sports metaphor, it is virtually impossible to know which player on a team will score. However, by analysing the talents in both teams, you can greatly improve your prediction of which team will win.

The basic premise behind technology indicators is that they are a necessary, but not sufficient, condition for company success. While it is not sufficient for a company to have a strong, creative technological and inventive capability, it is necessary if it wishes to become competitive in any of the technology-driven fields. A company either has to have or develop that technology in-house. Alternatively, it can license it in. Otherwise, it will be at a grave disadvantage.

Table 3 shows the five-year CII, by technology area, compared against the entire patent system for all the Tech-Line companies combined.

Again, there are substantial differences in technologies. The highest CII is found for medical equipment (2.38) while the lowest, in agriculture, is only 0.64, thus roughly indicating that the former is almost four times as highly cited as the latter.

Table 3. Current impact index by technology area for all Tech-Line® Companies, 1993–1997.

Technology area	Current impact index
1. Agriculture	0.64
2. Oil and gas	0.84
3. Power generation and distribution	0.90
4. Food and tobacco	0.91
5. Textiles and apparel	0.79
6. Wood and paper	0.99
7. Chemicals	0.79
8. Pharmaceuticals	0.79
9. Biotechnology	0.68
10. Medical equipment	2.38
11. Medical electronics	1.77
12. Plastics, polymers and rubber	0.77
13. Glass, clay and cement	0.78
14. Primary metals	0.59
15. Fabricated metals	0.82
16. Industrial machinery and tools	0.77
17. Industrial process equipment	0.89
18. Office equipment and cameras	1.22
19. Heating and ventilation	0.95
20. Miscellaneous machinery	0.86
21. Computers and peripherals	1.88
22. Telecommunications	1.65
23. Semiconductors and electronic	1.35
24. Measuring and control equipment	1.02
25. Electrical appliances and computer	1.01
26. Motor vehicles and parts	1.33
27. Aerospace and parts	0.68
28. Other transport	0.70
29. Miscellaneous manufacturing	0.88
99. Other	1.06
All	1.14

A second important observation of the table is that the value for "All" is 1.14 and not 1.00. The reason for this is that CII is calculated against the entire US patent system, whereas the Tech-Line companies only account for 63% of US patents. The fact that this number is substantially higher than 1.0 indicates, just as one would expect, that the major companies covered in Tech-Line have patents which are more highly cited than the entire patent system. In fact, patents owned by individual inventors and not assigned to companies in the US system are cited much less frequently than those assigned to companies.

Technology strength (TS)

Technology strength indicates the strength of the patent portfolio. It is the number of patents multiplied by CII, that is, the patent portfolio size is either inflated or deflated by patent quality.

We have tried, using the technology strength indicator, to capture both the size of the company's technological activity through the number of patents, as well as quality through the CII. There is, we must admit, a slight inconsistency in the way technological strength is defined, in that the number of patents refers to those in the current year while the CII citation indicator is based on cites of the company's patents in the last five years. The implicit assumption of technology strength is that the company's newly issued patents will have a similar impact and quality as its other recent patents.

Technology cycle time (TCT)

Technology cycle time indicates the speed of innovation. It is the median age, in years, of US patent references cited on the front page of the company's patents.

Fast-moving technologies, such as electronics, have a life cycle that is as short as three to four years. Slow-moving technologies, such as ship and boat building, may have a technology life cycle that is as long as 15 years or more. Companies with a shorter life cycle than their competitors in a given technology area may be advancing more quickly from previous technology to current technology.

Technology cycle time captures some elements of the rapidity with which a company is inventing, since it measures, in essence, the time between the previous patent and the current patent. As mentioned earlier, it varies substantially from one technology area to another (Table 4). Technology cycle time also varies from country to country. For example, Japanese inventions patented in the US tend to have a much shorter technology cycle time than their American counterparts, which in turn, have

Table 4. Technology cycle time by technology area for all Tech-Line® companies, 1993–1997.

Technology area	Technology cycle time (1993–1997), in years
1. Agriculture	10.2
2. Oil and gas	11.9
3. Power generation and distribution	9.0
4. Food and tobacco	11.9
5. Textiles and apparel	12.9
6. Wood and paper	12.3
7. Chemicals	9.0
8. Pharmaceuticals	8.1
9. Biotechnology	7.7
10. Medical equipment	8.3
11. Medical electronics	6.7
12. Plastics, polymers and rubber	10.2
13. Glass, clay and cement	10.1
14. Primary metals	10.3
15. Fabricated metals	10.1
16. Industrial machinery and tools	10.7
17. Industrial process equipment	11.1
18. Office equipment and cameras	6.7
19. Heating and ventilation	10.4
20. Miscellaneous machinery	12.3
21. Computers and peripherals	5.8
22. Telecommunications	5.7
23. Semiconductors and electronic	6.0
24. Measuring and control equipment	7.7
25. Electrical appliances and computer	8.3
26. Motor vehicles and parts	7.1
27. Aerospace and parts	13.2
28. Other transport	11.1
29. Miscellaneous manufacturing	10.1
99. Other	9.7
All	8.0

a shorter life cycle than European inventions. This difference is particularly noticeable in technologies such as electronics. We interpret this as a sign that the Japanese companies are innovating very rapidly, and possibly making incremental but rapid changes in their technology and products, whereas the European companies tend to innovate at a much slower pace, particularly in electronics. The US companies straddle somewhere between the two.

Table 5.   Technology cycle time illustration.

Patent: 05200004
Application date: 16 December 1991
Issue date: 6 April 1993
Title: Permanent Magnet

	Year	Patent number	Age
References to	1957	2810640	36
US Patents	1966	3241930	27
	1988	4722869	5
	1988	4770718	5
	1990	4925741	3
	1991	5043025	2

Another interesting aspect of technology cycle time is that it can be used, alongside the rate of increase in patents, to identify areas in which a company is intensively active. This is because if a company is increasing its patenting and is at the forefront of a technological area, it will tend to have a short technology cycle time. We found that companies which are relatively slow in their inventive cycles tend to be very fast in one area, which is often the area in which they are known to be technology leaders.

As with many of the other indicators, the computation of TCT is not totally straightforward. For one, we use the median, rather than the average, age of the cited references. This is because there are, very often, one or two classic references in a patent. If we were to use the average, these one or two references would distort the data. The actual computation is illustrated in Table 5, where we show the six US patent references given in US patent 5200004.

Next to the patent and the year, which is normally given in the reference, is the age of each of the references from the point of view of the patent issued in 1993. The problem is: what is the median since it falls between two patents, each of which appears to be of five years of age?

In order to approximate this, we make the assumption that when there are multiple references to the same age (in years), they are evenly distributed throughout the year. The technology cycle time, computed for that patent, would then be 5.5 years.

Science linkage

Science linkage (Ω) indicates how leading edge the company's technology is. It is the average number of scientific papers referenced on the front page of the company's patents.

High science linkage indicates that a company is building its technology based on advances in science. Companies at the forefront of a technology tend to have higher science linkage than their competitors. This type of citation is growing rapidly, averaging roughly one per patent: drug and medicine patents often have five or more; leading edge biotechnology patents, 15 or more; and Genentech's patents, 25 or more.

Science linkage is a particularly interesting indicator and one that has received a lot of coverage in the press. This is because CHI's research has shown that some 75% of all scientific references cited on the front pages of US patents had their origins in public science; that is, they were based on research done at universities, government laboratories, various non-profit research institutions and so forth (Narin *et al.*, 1998). Thus, we established quantitative evidence as a major role for fundamental, mainstream basic research in support of leading edge industrial technology. This work has been reported in a number of papers, including *The New York Times* (Broad, 1997), and elsewhere.

The construction of the basic data for the science linkage indicator is rather complex and tedious. This is because we differentiate between scientific references — which are included — and other non-patent literature references — which are excluded. When a US patent is issued, in the category known as "other references cited", there is a great variety of materials, including publications that are clearly scientific and those that are not. For example, there are thousands of references to technology disclosure bulletins which we exclude from our science linkage calculations.

In order to make that distinction, we have, by combining computer matching, manual verification and correction, processed more than two million non-patent references since 1983. Currently, we are processing close to 14,000 per week. This means that there are currently more than 14,000 non-patent references per week on the front pages of US patents. Figure 4 illustrates how this choice is made. The particular patent, 5200001, for a permanent magnet, contains seven non-patent references. Of these seven, we considered five to be scientific references, that is, published scientific papers

Patent: 05200001

Application date: 29 November 1990

Issue date: 6 April 1993

Title: Permanent magnet

References to non-patent literature:

Science   1: M. Endoh, *et al.* (1987) Magnetic properties and Thermal
                 stabilities of Ga substituted Nd-Fe-Co-B Magnets. *IEEE
                 Trans. on Magnetics*, 23(5), 2290.

Science   2: X. Shen, *et al.* (1987) The effect of molybdenum on the
                 magnetic properties of the Nd-Fe-Co-B system. *J. Appl. Phys.*
                 61(8), 3433.

Non-science   3: Liu Guozeng, *et al.* (1989) Effect of Mo addition on the
                 magnetic properties and thermal stability of sintered (Prnd)-
                 Fe-Co-Al-B Magnet. Paper distributed at Kyoto, Japan, in
                 May 1989.

Science   4: W. Rodewald & P. Schrey (1989) Structural and magnetic
                 properties of sintered Nd14.4Fe67.0-Xc011.8Moxb6.8 magnets
                 IEEE Transactions of Magnetics, 25(5), 3770–3772.

Non-Science   5: *Patent Abstracts of Japan* (1988) 12(82), and Jp-A-62
                 (1987) 218543 (Seiko).

Science   6: A. Maocai, *et al.* (1985) Effects of additive elements of
                 magnetic properties of sintered Nd-B-Fe magnet. *Proceedings
                 of the Eighth International Workshop of Rare Earth Magnets*,
                 pp. 541–552.

Science   7: S. Hirosawa, *et al.* (1990) High coercivity Nd-Fe-B type
                 permanent magnets with less dysprosium. *IEEE Transactions
                 on Magnetics*, 26(5), 1960–1962.

Fig. 4.   Science reference illustration.

and papers presented at formal scientific meetings. We do not consider the third reference a scientific one since it refers to a manuscript which may or may not have been distributed at a scientific meeting. As for the fifth reference, which alludes to the Patent Abstracts of Japan, it is almost certainly not a scientific paper.

In highly science-dependent fields such as biotechnology, the great majority of non-patent references are, in fact, scientific references. However, in many other fields, including some areas of electronics and those in the mechanical fields, most of the non-patent references are not scientific references. This differentiation is likely to be important since it seems that the linkage to science is the driving force behind many important areas in technology.

The fact that science linkage varies widely from one technology to another is depicted in Table 6. It lists the average science linkage measures for the five years, 1993 to 1997, for all Tech-Line companies in each of the 30 technology areas.

Quite clearly, there is a wide range of science linkage with biotechnology which, at 14.4, is almost twice that of the next highest area, pharmaceuticals, which is 7.3. Interestingly enough, the third highest area is agriculture. This is almost certainly due to the biotechnology revolution and the many advances in plant and animal genetics which are revolutionising agricultural technology. The fourth most science-linked area is chemicals. Undoubtedly, this is due to the fact that chemistry is a science and some biologically active agents are classified as chemicals rather than pharmaceuticals. Finally, the fifth area is medical electronics.

The areas which are the least science-linked are those which one would expect — miscellaneous machinery, motor vehicles and parts, and other transport — each of which have an average of less than one-tenth of scientific references per patent.

Science strength

Science strength (SS) indicates how much the company uses science to build its patent portfolio. It is the number of patents multiplied by science linkage, that is the size of the patent portfolio being inflated or deflated by the extent of science linkage. This is a count of the total number of science links in the company's patent portfolio.

Table 6.   Science linkage by technology area for all Tech-Line companies, 1993–1997.

Technology area	Science linkage (science references/patent)
1. Agriculture	3.3
2. Oil and gas	0.8
3. Power generation and distribution	0.7
4. Food and tobacco	1.3
5. Textiles and apparel	0.3
6. Wood and paper	0.9
7. Chemicals	2.7
8. Pharmaceuticals	7.3
9. Biotechnology	14.4
10. Medical equipment	1.1
11. Medical electronics	2.2
12. Plastics, polymers and rubber	0.9
13. Glass, clay and cement	1.0
14. Primary metals	0.9
15. Fabricated metals	0.7
16. Industrial machinery and tools	0.2
17. Industrial process equipment	0.7
18. Office equipment and cameras	0.4
19. Heating and ventilation	0.2
20. Miscellaneous machinery	0.1
21. Computers and peripherals	1.0
22. Telecommunications	0.8
23. Semiconductors and electronic	1.3
24. Measuring and control equipment	0.9
25. Electrical appliances and computer	0.4
26. Motor vehicles and parts	0.1
27. Aerospace and parts	0.3
28. Other transport	0.1
29. Miscellaneous manufacturing	0.6
99. Other	0.9
All	1.5

Conclusions

Taken together, the combination of unified patent counts and indicators of technology quality in Tech-Line® should go far towards providing analysts with new and detailed insights into company technological strengths and the prospects for future company success.

Chapter 9

The Complex Relations Between Communities of Practice and the Implementation of Technological Innovations[1]

Donald Hislop
Loughborough University, UK

Introduction

One of the benefits of the current growth of interest in the subject of knowledge and learning in organizations is that this work has produced a number of concepts which may significantly improve the understanding of a wide range of organizational processes. Lave and Wenger's (1991) "community of practice" idea represents one of the potentially most useful of these concepts, and is arguably the most enduring element of their theory of situated learning (Contu and Willmott, 2000, p. 272; Fox, 2000, p. 853). Its importance is indicated by the extensive way it has been used in the burgeoning knowledge literature (Baumard, 1999; Brown and Duguid, 1991, 1998; Arthur, 1998; Fox, 2000; Hildreth *et al.*, 2000; Liedtka, 1999; McDermott, 1999; Pan and Scarbrough, 1999; Raelin, 1997).

This chapter applies the "communities of practice" concept to analyze the implementation of IT-based process innovations in a number of case studies, and suggests that it has the ability to provide fresh insights into the dynamics of innovation processes. The socio-technical perspective

---

[1]This chapter first appeared as a paper in the *International Journal of Innovation Management*, 2003, **7**(2), 163–188.

conceptualizes the implementation of technological innovations as involving the blending and synthesis of new knowledge and artefacts with existing organizational practices, artefacts and knowledge (Clark and Staunton, 1989; McLoughlin, 1999). Thus, if, as the communities of practice literature suggests, organizational communities of practice both shape the structure of the organizational knowledge base, and represent important reservoirs of organizational knowledge, they have the potential to play an important role in the implementation of technological innovations.

The chapter considers how organizational communities of practice (CoPs), and innovation processes mutually impinge on each other. Thus, the chapter considers both how communities of practice affect innovation processes, as well as how the implementation of change affects organizational communities of practice. Specifically, this involves examining a number of questions, including: how did the existing CoPs shape the distribution of relevant knowledge? How did the sense of identity possessed by members of CoPs impact on the sharing of knowledge within and between existing CoPs during the change process? Did the CoPs facilitate or inhibit the sharing and utilization of relevant knowledge during the innovation processes? What effect did the changes examined have on the knowledge/practices of existing CoPs? What effect did the changes examined have on the population size/character of existing CoPs?

The chapter has two primary objectives, to empirically and theoretically examine the links between innovation processes and communities of practice. The empirical objective is addressed through utilising case study evidence from a number of companies. The data used is drawn from longitudinal, qualitative studies of comparable innovations in seven case study companies. While the companies examined are from a range of countries and sectors of activity, the focal innovation in each organization was similar: all the case companies researched were attempting to implement IT-based, multi-site, cross-functional management information systems.

The theoretical objective is achieved by reflecting on what the empirical data presented says about the way innovation processes and communities of practice are linked, and the general way that the community of practice concept requires modification and re-conceptualization to make it a more useful analytical tool. This is important, as while the terminology of "communities of practice" has been become widely used, it still remains a relatively poorly developed concept. Issues which arguably need to be more effectively addressed include taking greater account of the difficulties involved in sharing knowledge between different communities of practice and more fully taking account of the potential negative aspects of communities of practice. Such analyses are required as too much contemporary writing on communities of practice focuses narrowly on their benefits and advantages (e.g. Brown and Duguid, 1991; McDermott, 1999).

The next section more fully conceptualizes both innovation processes and communities of practice. Following this, the chapter briefly describes the organizational context of the seven case study companies, as well as the type of innovation projects they were undertaking. This section of the chapter also contains empirical evidence on the extent to which communities of practice existed in the case companies. The following section, which represents the empirical core of the chapter, describes the empirical evidence on the inter-relationship between the organizational CoPs outlined and the innovation processes being carried out. The main body of the chapter then closes by discussing the theoretical implications of the data presented.

Theorization on Communities of Practice and Innovation Processes

The communities of practice concept is based on two central premises: the activity-based nature of knowledge/knowing, and the group-based character of organizational activity. The development of an activity-based view of knowing in organizations, what Cook and Brown refer to as an "epistemology of practice" (1999), has been developed to overcome what are regarded as the limitations of traditionally static, objectified views of knowledge (Blackler, 1995; Brown and Duguid, 1991; Clark, 2000, Chapter 13; Tsoukas and Vladimirou, 2000). While traditional, static views of knowledge are based on a dichotomy between thinking and doing, in stark contrast, the activity-based perspective suggests that this represents a false separation. Thus, thinking and doing are fused in knowledgeable activity, the development and use of embodied knowledge in undertaking specific activities/tasks. Secondly, these organizational activities are typically social/communal activities (Gherardi *et al.*, 1998; Hayes and Walsham, 2000; Lave and Wenger, 1991; McDermott, 1999; Raelin, 1997). Barnes

(1977, p. 2) provides a concise summary of this idea in the following quote,

> "knowledge is not produced by passively perceiving individuals, but by interacting social groups engaged in particular activities. And it is evaluated communally and not by isolated, individual judgments."

Fox (2000, p. 854), and Contu and Willmott (2000, p. 272) reinforce this when they define communities of practice, as, respectively, a group of people involved in a shared practice, and a community which reproduces its knowledge ability through common, collective practice. Thus, activity is embedded in the particular social–occupational–functional groups that people work within. Knowing and working are, therefore, ultimately social processes involving an ongoing interaction among individuals working within the same context, or addressing similar issues. For example, Arthur (1998, pp. 131–2), in a study of film production, showed that for apprentice technicians processes of learning by watching were crucial. Also, Brown and Duguid (1991), drawing heavily on Orr's (1990) study of photocopy repair engineers, also showed how knowing was an ongoing development process, based in engaging with day-to-day, practical tasks.

Based on such insights, Baumard defines a community of practice as a "community of practitioners within which situational learning develops ...", which results in the community developing "... a system of relationships between people, activities and the world" (1999, pp. 209–10). Communities of practice thus typically possess three primary characteristics. First, participants in a community possess a stock of common, shared knowledge. Secondly, communities typically also develop shared values and attitudes. Finally, and equally importantly, participants/members of communities also possess a sense of collective/group identity (Brown and Duguid, 2001).

The relationship between communities of practice, and the implementation of innovations is potentially of great interest for a number of reasons. First, the communities of practice which exist in organizations are likely to influence the implementation process. The socio-technical perspective considers the implementation of technological innovations as involving the mutual adaptation of the technological system being implemented, and the organizational context within which they are being introduced

(Badham *et al.*, 1997; Bryman, 2000, p. 470; Fleck, 1997; McLoughlin, 1999; Scarbrough and Corbett, 1992; Leonard-Barton, 1995; Orlikowski, 1992). From this perspective, the integration of knowledge represents a key element of these processes, typically involving the customization of "new" knowledge and artefacts and their integration with existing organizational structures, practices and knowledge (which will themselves require some level of customization) (Barley, 1986; Hislop *et al.*, 1997; McCabe, 1996; Harris, 1997). Thus, if communities of practice both shape the distribution of knowledge in organizations, and are important reservoirs of knowledge, the specific character of an organization's communities of practice may significantly influence the dynamics of technological implementation processes. Dougherty (2001), for example, suggests that one of the defining characteristics of successful innovating organizations is their effective cultivation, use and support for organizational communities of practice.

Another reason for examining the relationship between innovation processes and communities of practice is that the relationship between them is likely to be two way, and not simply unidirectional. Thus, not only will an organization's communities of practice influence the nature of innovation processes, but the changes being implemented may also have implications for the communities. Lave and Wenger (1991, pp. 113–117) suggest that there are likely to be tensions and contradictions within any community of practice between continuity and change, i.e. between the sharing and utilization of existing practices/knowledge, and the evolution, development and ongoing modification of these practices. The implementation of technological innovations, such as those examined thus far, represent a potential discontinuity impinging upon the practices, knowledge and norms of existing communities of practice.

Finally, the community of practice concept can also supplement and enrich our understanding of the dynamics of innovation processes through providing a new analytical concept with which to more fully understand behavior during the implementation of innovations. Thus, for example, while issues such as the dynamics of inter-functional and business unit relations are well developed in the mainstream innovation literature, the community of practice concept provides a potentially useful extra dimension with which to characterize and explain these dynamics.

Organizational Context: Organization-wide Innovations, Fragmented Knowledge and Multiple Communities of Practice

This section of the chapter describes the character of the organizations and innovations which are examined, outlining their cross-functional, multi-site character, and concludes by outlining the range and types of community of practice which are affected by, and involved in, the change projects examined. The data presented is from seven detailed longitudinal case studies, all of which were implementing similar, standardized, cross-functional, multi-site information management systems. Each company was visited at least twice (typically there were three to four visits per company), with visits occurring over a time period of between 12 and 18 months. The focus of the research was on the progress and dynamics of the implementation projects described, with the longitudinal nature of the research allowing each implementation project to be followed over a number of stages. The source of data in each of the companies was semi-structured interviews with a range of project and general management representatives. Table 1 lists the general characteristics of the case companies, the innovations examined and the number of sites involved in the changes.

One issue worth briefly commenting on is the organizational context to the focal innovations. In all seven companies, the stated managerial objectives from their innovation projects were extremely similar and were concerned with the closely inter-related objectives of improving co-ordination levels (between sites, functions, business units), and/or developing greater levels of standardization (see Table 2). This issue will be returned to later, as it had quite significant implications for many organizational CoPs.

From the research conducted, a number of general conclusions can be drawn regarding the communities of practice which existed in the case companies. One of the most striking common features across all seven companies was the fragmented nature of their knowledge bases. To some extent this was related to their multi-site, multi-divisional character. However, in relation to the focus of this chapter, one of the most important consequences of this fragmentation was that each organization possessed a large number of separate and distinct communities of practice. Further, because the innovations examined were organization-wide in scope this meant that

Table 1. Organization and innovation characteristics.

Company	Company details	Innovation type	International project	Number of sites involved in innovation project
UK-Cast	UK-based international specialist in castings and injection mouldings.	ERP System (Enterprise Resource Planning)	Yes	12
UK-Pharm	Specialist international pharmaceuticals corporation.	ERP System	Yes	4
UK-Pen-Gem	UK pension and life assurance company.	Sales Automation Tool	No	60
UK-Pen-Swin	UK pension and life assurance company.	Telephone Service Centre	No	10+
France-Connect	French mechanical connectors.	ERP System	No	6
Neth-Bank	Dutch-based international bank.	Intranet	Yes	100+
Swed-Truck	Swedish-based international fork lift truck company.	ERP System	Yes	11 divisions (20+ sites)

in each of the case companies significant numbers of communities both possessed organizational knowledge of relevance to the innovations being implemented, and were also affected by the changes that were occurring.

Finally, not only did the case companies all contain large numbers of distinct communities of practice, there were also a number of different and distinctive types of community. The most typical focuses for these communities were business units and functions. This was largely because within these organizations work activities tended to be sub-divided and separated along these lines. Thus, any individual, or group of individuals, had

Table 2.   Objectives of change.

Company	Change type	Stated managerial objectives of change
UK-Cast	ERP System	♦ Standardization of operating practices/IT systems. ♦ Improve cross-business co-operation.
UK-Pharm	ERP System	♦ Improve efficiency of manufacturing practices. ♦ Improve cross-functional co-ordination. ♦ Improve inter-business co-ordination of manufacturing.
UK-Pen-Gem	Sales Automation Tool	♦ Automation and standardization of sales support processes. ♦ Improve co-ordination between sales offices and corporate centre.
UK-Pen-Swin	Telephone Service Centre	♦ Improve customer service and business retention. ♦ Improve co-ordination of assurance and pensions business.
France-Connect	ERP System	♦ Improve/Introduce co-ordination across sites/businesses. ♦ Improve cross-functional communications.
Neth-Bank	Intranet	♦ Create a "networked bank". ♦ Improve co-operation across business units.
Swed-Truck	ERP System	♦ Standardization of business processes/IT systems in Europe.

responsibility for, and involvement with, a specific range of work activities. These groups of individuals can be referred to as communities of practice, as they possessed, to differing degrees, all three of the characteristics of such communities outlined above (some common knowledge/practices, a shared sense of identity and some element of common, work related values). Table 3 provides a brief summary of the characteristics of the main communities of practice in the case companies which were relevant to the innovation processes examined.

Table 3.   Communities of practice.

Company	Common identity	Common knowledge	Share values	Origin
UK-Cast	Business unit	Localized, specific business knowledge (products, markets, etc.).	Autonomy of business unit is positive (provides flexibility to respond to particular market/customer demands).	Corporate centre acted as holding company. History of relatively strict autonomy for BUs.
UK-Pharm	Business unit & function	Localized, specific business knowledge & specialized functional knowledge.	Business — localized autonomy is good. Function — collegiality within functions, but inter-functional antagonism and rivalry for status.	Historical culture of functional and site/business isolation. Sites focused on particular product lines. Lack of co-ordination between sites.
UK-Pen-Gem	Business unit & function	Localized, specific business knowledge & specialized functional knowledge.	Business — localized autonomy is positive. Function — collegiality within functions, but specialized nature of knowledge makes inter-functional interaction difficult.	Strong historic culture of sales function autonomy. Also, dominant historical culture of product/business "silos" which operated in isolation.
UK-Pen-Swin	Business unit & function	Localized, specific business knowledge & specialized functional knowledge.	Business — localised autonomy is positive. Function — collegiality within functions, but specialized nature of knowledge makes inter-functional interaction difficult.	Dominant historical culture of product/business "silos" which operated in isolation from each other. Isolation and independence of IT, administration and sales.

(*Continued*)

Table 3. (Continued)

Company	Common identity	Common knowledge	Share values	Origin
France-Connect	Function & geographic site	Specific functional knowledge.	Collegiality within functions, but inter-functional antagonism and rivalry for status.	Dominant historical culture of functional isolation. Functional isolation reinforced by geographic separation of main functions (production, sales, IT).
Neth-Bank	Business unit & occupation	Localized, specific business knowledge & technical, occupational knowledge.	Business — localized autonomy is positive. Occupation (IT) — sense of collegiality and commitment to help and share knowledge.	Dominant, historic culture of business unit autonomy. Antagonistic, competitive relations between BUs.
Swed-Truck	Business unit	Localized, specific business knowledge.	Autonomy of business unit is positive.	Historic culture of business unit autonomy. Limited interaction between BUs.

These characteristics can be more fully illustrated by describing one of the cases in detail. In the case of Swed-Truck, which sold, rented and serviced fork lift trucks, work was organized into small, discrete business units, which had responsibility for all business within specific geographic regions (typically nationally focused). Within this structure, there was, in general, little need for interaction between business units, and they operated as virtual stand-alone businesses. The structuring of work within Swed-Truck had historically been managed like this, and had, to some extent, become institutionalized.

While each of the national business units in principle sold the same range of products and services, in reality they had significant autonomy over how they did this. This was not only because the nature of the market and character of customers varied significantly for each business, but that management in each business unit offered different levels of service and support to their customers. This resulted in the development of separate and somewhat specialized knowledge communities, which only had knowledge of their own customers and working practices. The autonomy of the business units was such that the evolution and development of their working practices, the upgrading of their IT systems, etc., was done purely on the basis of local considerations, and issues of corporate-wide compatibility were never considered. Thus, discrete and specific knowledge communities developed, with staff in each business unit possessing substantial amounts of specialized knowledge relevant to their own localized working practices and customer demands, which had limited transferability and relevance in other business units.

The implementation of a corporate-wide information management system into this context had a number of implications for these local business-unit-focused communities of practice, as will be seen. Primarily, the introduction of greater levels of standardization somewhat impinged on the autonomy of the communities over how they worked. Ultimately, the greater level of interaction between and knowledge sharing amongst local communities that the changes required, to some extent threatened the local communities through (attempting) to create a larger, organization-wide community. Thus, the technological innovation being implemented by Swed-Truck had quite significant implications for its traditional, business-unit-focused communities of practice.

Relations Between Communities of Practice and Innovation Processes

This section of the chapter presents the main empirical evidence from the organizations/innovation processes examined. The richness of the qualitative data that was collected means that, within the space available in a chapter, it is impossible to fully do justice to it. Thus, to address these specific episodes/aspects, some of the case studies are presented to illustrate the diversity of ways in which the communities of practice and innovation processes interacted. This section is therefore structured thematically. A summary table (see Table 4) also draws these findings together. Finally, where other published data exists on the case companies, references are given, as they provide more detailed analyses of some of the case companies.

As illustrated in the previous section, the broad, typically organization-wide scope of the innovation processes examined, combined with the fragmented nature of (all) the organizational knowledge bases meant that a diverse range of different communities of practice were involved. In fact, this arguably represents one of the defining characteristics of the innovation processes examined. These innovation processes thus required the co-ordination and management of personnel with significantly different knowledge bases, experiences, values and identities. As will be seen, this was an important aspect of these innovation processes, as one of the main ways in which the communities of practice affected them was through the character of the interaction *between* different communities.

The innovation processes examined provided evidence that the existence of communities of practice can act to either inhibit or facilitate the utilisation and sharing of knowledge. Therefore, while the existence of the communities of practice identified undoubtedly had a significant impact on the innovation processes examined, their overall effect was somewhat ambiguous. The rest of this section describes different episodes which illustrate key aspects of the relationship between the innovation processes examined and the organizational communities of practice involved in or affected by these processes.

Ambiguous effects: Neth-Bank

The ambiguity referred to is well illustrated by the case of Neth-Bank, where communities of practice both inhibited and facilitated processes of

Table 4. Effects of Community of Practice on innovation processes.

Company	Community type	Effect of CoPs on innovation process
UK-Cast	Business	Need to involve staff from range of business unit communities with knowledge of their processes/systems.
		Strength of identity to BUs produced resistance to change. Change seen as threatening BU autonomy.
UK-Pharm	Functional and geographic	Antagonistic functional communities inhibited co-operation. Need to involve staff from range of business unit communities with knowledge of their processes/systems.
		Production function/community highly resistant to change — seen as challenging their power.
		Site-based identity overcome through careful selection and training.
UK-Pen-Gem	Functional and business	Staff from sales function/community not involved in project development.
UK-Pen-Swin	Functional and business	Need to involve staff from product area communities with knowledge of their processes/systems.
		No significant resistance to change.
France-Connect	Functional and geographic	Antagonistic functional communities inhibited co-operation.
		Cross-functional nature of innovation required involvement of staff from all functions.
		Strong resistance to change from sales function — seen as challenging their power/autonomy.
Neth-Bank	Occupational and business	Need to involve staff from range of business unit communities with knowledge of their processes/systems.
		Management staff from BUs resistant to development of global intranet — seen as undermining their autonomy.
		Cross-BU co-operation of some IT staff supported intranet development.
Swed-Truck	Business	Need to involve staff from range of business unit communities with knowledge of their processes/systems.
		Negligible resistance to change.

knowledge sharing in its attempts to develop a corporate-wide intranet system. As with all the other case companies, Neth-Bank had a strong historical culture of business autonomy. It had historically been structured into distinct and separate business units, which operated with complete autonomy from each other. This, therefore, influenced the development of distinct communities of practice within these business units, whose staff typically had little or no knowledge of the work carried out in other business units. Further, relations between these communities were typically antagonistic and competitive, rather than supportive (Newell *et al.*, 2000; Swan *et al.*, 1999).

The innovation that was studied within Neth-Bank, the development of its global intranet, was an attempt to overcome this, and develop a more co-operative culture. However, without exception, the various intranet (sub-)projects that were developed were significantly inhibited by the reluctance of staff from different business units to collaborate and share knowledge with each other. The character of these business communities proved to be one of the major factors inhibiting the development of their global intranet, which required them to work together collectively to effectively implement it. In fact, what occurred in Neth-Bank was that each business unit developed its own separate and distinctive intranet system. Thus, ironically, an innovation whose intention was to improve inter-business unit collaboration in the end had the effect of reinforcing rather than reducing business unit boundaries.

At the same time within Neth-Bank, however, another type of community of practice existed, a professional community of practice focused around their IT activities. While IT staff within Neth-Bank typically had a business unit focus, being employed by, and working within specific business units, there was evidence that a significant number of IT personnel also possessed a sense of identity as being part of an organization-wide IT community, which to some extent transcended their narrower business unit identities. In contrast to the narrowly focused business unit communities, many IT staff who were part of this community had a positive, supportive impact on the development of the intranet. This was visible through the informal sharing of knowledge amongst IT staff across business units, with business unit boundaries appearing not to inhibit these processes. These processes of knowledge sharing arguably supported the development of the global intranet through facilitating the dissemination of relevant and important specialist knowledge. However, these communities were limited by the fact that they were typically partial, and highly localized, being based on the personal, informal networks of different IT staff. Therefore, their impact on the intranet projects was limited, and they weren't able to counterbalance the knowledge hoarding of the business communities.

Inhibiting knowledge sharing: clashes between functional communities

In two of the companies, UK-Pharm, and France-Connect, their communities of practice had a uniformly negative influence on their innovation projects. In both companies there had been a historical culture of autonomy and isolation between the main functions involved in and affected by the innovations examined (sales, manufacturing and IT in both cases). As with Neth-Bank's business units, relations between them had typically been competitive and antagonistic. Further, in both cases these functional groups could be described as communities of practice as they had developed their own specific specialist knowledge and values and had a coherent sense of identity. In both companies these characteristics of their functional communities of practice significantly inhibited the progress of the innovation processes examined, as they failed to effectively work together and share relevant knowledge as was necessary for the success of the innovations. As a consequence, in both cases, not only were the implementation timetables extensively delayed, but the overall functionality of the innovations were also significantly compromised.

These cases are also of interest due to the way that the attitudes and behaviors of the functional communities of practice were shaped by the effect that the innovations processes had on them. The lack of co-operation and participation by the different communities of practice in both companies was due as much to the perception that they would be adversely affected by the innovations being implemented, as by any antagonism between the communities. In these companies, different communities developed a perception that they would lose autonomy and power from the implementation of an organization-wide information management system. These communities treasured their historical autonomy, and interpreted the proposed changes as being about reducing, attacking or undermining it through the development of (as they saw it) more standardized and centrally-controlled working practices. Thus, in these two cases the two-way nature of the relationship between innovation processes and communities of practice was clearly evident.

Local community loyalties: resistance and transcendence

In UK-Cast and Swed-Truck, communities of practice were typically organized around business units rather than functions. Further, while the innovations in both cases could be interpreted as reducing and undermining the historical autonomy of these communities, the communities of practice in these companies reacted quite differently to the changes that were being implemented. While in both companies the innovations being implemented witnessed a move from highly autonomous and locally determined practices towards more constrained local autonomy and the use of more standardized practices, in Swed-Bank these changes were embraced, while in UK-Cast they were challenged.

In the case of Swed-Truck, whose innovation process was one of the most successful of the seven companies examined, the project management methods used played a significant role in encouraging staff from business communities of practice to transcend their traditionally localized senses of identity and embrace and support the changes being implemented (Hislop, 1999; Swan *et al.*, 1999). In the development phase of their innovation project, a cross-business unit project team was utilized. Further, the project team were able to create a sense of involvement and participation among local staff during the roll-out phase, as they were allowed to have an important role in local customization activities. These project management methods had the effect of creating support for, and active involvement in, the innovation process in Swed-Bank by staff from all but one business unit, and their project was deemed a success internally.[2]

---

[2]The only resistance of any significance in Swed-Truck's case was by one local business unit. Interviewees were extremely divided about the source of this resistance. In the end their resistance was overcome by a combination of carrot and stick methods, where some of their concerns were deemed legitimate and addressed, while others were challenged, rejected and ignored.

These generally positive attitudes to change by Swed-Truck business communities contrasted starkly with the more generally negative reaction of staff in UK-Cast to an innovation with similar objectives. In UK-Cast the localized, business-unit-focused communities of practice were resistant to UK-Cast's proposed changes as they were interpreted as being against the interests of the local business unit communities. In this innovation process, a them-versus-us dynamic emerged between the corporate centre ("them"), who were interpreted as imposing change which would significantly increase levels of central control, and the local business units ("us") who the local communities interpreted as being the losers, through the dilution of their highly treasured autonomy. Thus, the innovation was seen to threaten existing and traditional communities of practice, which produced a negative reaction to the changes that corporate management in UK-Cast were attempting to implement.

The general findings, outlining the inter-relationship between the communities of practice and innovation processes, are detailed in Table 4.

Discussion

This section of the chapter draws together the dominant themes and issues which emerge from the empirical data just examined, and links back to the theoretical issues touched on at the start of the chapter. Before doing this, it is necessary to acknowledge the limitations of the empirical data utilized. First, the case study-based nature of the research, and the anecdotal nature of the evidence presented, limits the generalizibility of the conclusions. Thus, further research is necessary to evaluate the generalizibility of the findings presented. For example, the research specifically examined innovations with organization-wide implications, thus, further research could be done into different types of innovation, which may involve and affect different ranges and types of communities in different ways.

After some general issues have been discussed regarding the nature of organizational activity and knowledge, the discussion will examine three focal themes in detail: the two-way nature of the relationship between innovation processes and communities of practice; the (significant) difficulties involved in sharing knowledge between different communities of practice; and the potentially negative aspects of communities of practice.

The empirical evidence presented reinforced and supported the suggestions made earlier in the chapter concerning both how knowledge/knowing in organizations is deeply embedded in practice/activity and, further, how such organizational practice is typically collective in nature (Barnes, 1977; Brown and Duguid, 1998; McDermott, 1999). Thus, the different communities of practice in each organization developed their specialized and localized knowledge through the autonomy they had to structure, organize and carry out the (collective) tasks and activities they deemed necessary to meet the specific needs of their particular customers and market conditions. Thus, the communities examined developed specialized knowledge both as a consequence of the autonomy they had, as well as the specificity of their customer/market conditions. Therefore, the communities of practice identified did provide an important social mechanism through which knowing and understanding developed, and further, they also represented important reservoirs of knowledge within the case companies.

The empirical evidence presented also reinforced arguments concerning the diffused, fragmented and highly differentiated nature of organizational knowledge (D.N. Clark, 2000, pp. 255–257; Fox, 2000), and that organizations can be usefully conceived as distributed knowledge systems (Blackler *et al.*, 2000; Grant, 1996b; Tsoukas, 1996). All of the case companies examined contained large numbers of separate and distinct communities of practice, with their own specialist knowledge bases. Therefore, they need to be viewed as a "community-of-communities" (Brown and Duguid, 1991, p. 53), making one of the general tasks of management to be to co-ordinate these diverse communities (Brown and Duguid, 2001; Cohen and Levinthal, 1990; Kogut and Zander, 1992).

Relations between communities of practice and innovation processes

In general terms, the data presented reinforces the mutuality of the relationship between innovation processes and communities of practice, thus, not only did the communities of practice affect the dynamics of the innovation processes researched, but the innovation processes have some quite significant consequences for the organizational communities of practice.

One of the most significant ways in which the communities of practice affected the innovation processes examined was through the way they influenced attitudes and behavior of their members/participants. This was visible in two main ways. Firstly, the sense of identity workers had as being part of a community, combined with their interpretation of how their community was being affected by the innovations examined, significantly shaped their general attitude to the innovations. Thus, in Swed-Truck the business unit communities supported the changes being implemented, as did the IT-based occupational community in Neth-Bank. Equally, the negative reaction of UK-Cast's business unit communities, and UK-Pharm and France-Connect's functional communities, to their innovations could equally be explained in this way. These findings are also reinforced by another study which showed how scientific communities of practice in a UK research organization resisted moves towards commercialization as they interpreted this change as being fundamentally in contrast with the values of their community, which was related to developing scientific knowledge as an end in itself, rather than the commercial exploitation of scientific knowledge (Breu and Hemingway, 2002).

Secondly, the sense of identity that the workers in the case companies had in specific communities of practice also significantly shaped with whom they were willing to share knowledge. Thus, the antagonistic and competitive nature of relations between Neth-Bank's business unit communities, and UK-Pharm and France-Connect's functional communities of practice, shaped their reluctance to share knowledge important to the innovations being implemented with each other.

The impact of these attitudes and behaviors on the innovation processes examined was significant, and crucially affected their degree of success. Thus, the relative success of Swed-Truck's innovation and the relative failure of Neth-Bank's, UK-Pharm's and France-Connect's innovations were, to a significant extent, shaped by the willingness or reluctance of relevant communities to share their knowledge with each other. This, therefore, reinforces the socio-technical perspective on innovation processes (embodied most clearly in the work of Leonard-Barton, 1995; McLoughlin, 1999; Orlikowski, 1992), which considers the blending and integration of artefacts and knowledge as being a fundamental component of all technological innovation processes.

The type of innovations examined, which have impact and relevance for a range of different CoPs, can be referred to as boundary objects (Brown and Duguid, 1998). Boundary objects, which can be physical, symbolic or linguistic, can be utilized to develop relations between the communities they impact on, through providing a common focus (Gherardi and Nicolini, 2002). The relative success of Swed-Truck and UK-Pen-Swin's implementations is arguably because the project management methods examined emphasized and utilized this aspect of these innovations. This resulted in community members learning that the different communities had more in common than had historically been understood to be the case, with this realization creating an element of willingness among people to participate in inter-community collaboration.

The innovation processes examined also had significant consequences for the organizational communities of practice, which, as illustrated, to some extent shaped their reaction and attitudes towards the innovations. The innovations examined were regarded by community members as presenting a potentially significant threat to the existence and viability of their traditional communities of practice. This was because these innovations potentially undermined the three core elements of these communities: their knowledge, identity and values.

The implementation of an organization-wide information management system was regarded as threatening the values of independence and autonomy, which most communities treasured (see Table 3). This was because such systems, requiring a greater level of standardization than had been historically traditional (see Table 2), were felt to reduce the ability of divisions to respond independently to the specific needs of their markets and customers. Secondly, and relatedly, these innovations were perceived as threatening the common knowledge base of these autonomous communities through devaluing and making redundant the specific knowledge they possessed, and replacing it with more standardized knowledge and working practices developed at a corporate level. Thus, the ability and need to develop local knowledge was regarded as being reduced. Finally, these innovations were also perceived to threaten and weaken the sense of identity possessed by community members. This sense of identity existed and was sustained because these communities had the ability to develop an independent body of common knowledge, shaped by the value of having local autonomy. Thus, by potentially undermining the values and knowledge of these communities, the innovations examined were also perceived as weakening the bonds which created a coherent and independent sense of identity.

Thus, overall, the relationship between the implementation of innovations and CoPs can be seen as two-way: not only do organizational CoPs affect the dynamics of innovation processes, but these innovation processes will impact on and affect the organizational CoPs. Separating cause from effect in such a relationship is thus likely to be difficult. This relationship is summarized in Fig. 1.

These findings reinforce the idea that communities of practice are dynamic rather than static, and that they evolve over time (Fox, 2000). Lave and Wenger (1991) suggested that there are likely to be tensions between continuity and change, as new practices or changes in the constitution of communities may threaten or undermine existing practices and social relations. Such tensions are likely to occur on an ongoing basis, as members of communities grow old and their skills and competencies change; and through changes in the membership of communities, as some members of a community leave and new ones join. What the research data presented suggests is that if new organizational innovations introduce a significant discontinuity in working practices, then the conflict and tensions this produces may well result in organizational communities of practice not supporting these innovations.

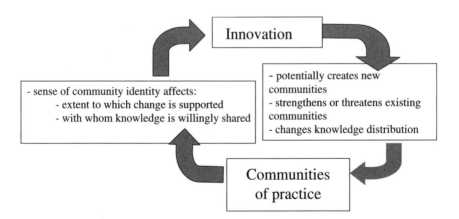

Fig. 1. Innovations and communities of practice.

The (not insignificant) difficulties of knowledge sharing between communities

One of the starkest findings from the research data presented was that the sharing of knowledge between different communities of practice was by no means straightforward. Thus, in Neth-Bank and UK-Cast there were problems in sharing knowledge between their business-focused communities of practice, and in UK-Pen-Gem, UK-Pharm and France-Connect there were problems in knowledge sharing between their functional communities of practice. In fact, the research data suggests that there are a number of significant difficulties to such processes.

Acknowledging and examining the differences of sharing knowledge within and between communities, and the potential difficulties involved in sharing knowledge across communities, need to be addressed as they are issues which are neglected in much of the literature on this subject (e.g. Brown and Duguid, 1991; Arthur, 1998; McDermott, 1999). Arguably, this is because much of the communities of practice literature focuses narrowly on the dynamics of knowledge sharing within communities.

As has been well illustrated by the majority of the communities of practice literature, the existence of communities of practice facilitates the sharing of knowledge within a community, due to both the sense of collective identity, and the existence of a significant common knowledge base. However, the sharing of knowledge between communities is much more complex, difficult and problematic, due to the lack of both these elements. Thus, the dynamics of knowledge sharing within and between communities of practice are likely to be qualitatively different (Brown and Duguid, 1998).

Taking the issue of divergent identities first, the existence of different identities between different communities of practice arguably complicates the knowledge sharing process through the perceived or actual different interests between communities and the potential for conflict this creates. This was visible in the majority of the case companies, and, as illustrated earlier, one factor inhibiting knowledge sharing between the communities examined was the perception that there were significant differences of interest. These findings are not unique to the case companies examined, as other research has shown that actual or perceived differences of interest have actively inhibited processes of knowledge sharing (Ciborra and Patriotta,

1998; Hayes and Walsham, 2000; Lazega, 1992; Storey and Barnett, 2000). In general terms, the communities of practice literature tends to play down or neglect issues of power, politics and conflict. However, this represents a general weakness of much of the contemporary literature on organizational knowledge (Hayes and Walsham, 2000; Blackler, 1995; Swan and Scarbrough, 2001).

The other factor which arguably complicates the sharing of knowledge between communities of practice, is the distinctiveness of their knowledge bases, and the lack of common knowledge which may exist. Further, not only is the knowledge of these communities different, but their knowledge bases may be based on qualitatively different assumptions and interpretative frameworks (Tsoukas, 1996; Becker, 2001). Brown and Duguid (2001) referred to these as "epistemic differences", which significantly increase the difficulty not just of sharing knowledge between communities, but understanding the knowledge of another community and the assumptions it is based on in the first place. Thus, the limited degree of common knowledge which can exist between different communities is likely to inhibit and complicate the sharing of knowledge.

Thus, paradoxically, the features which make communities of practice effective vehicles for communication and knowledge sharing within a community — a shared common knowledge base and a sense of collective community identity — may inhibit knowledge sharing across communities (Alvesson, 2000). For the type of cross-functional, multi-site innovation examined in this chapter, which typically involved staff from a range of communities having to work together, this issue was extremely pertinent, as the innovation processes examined involved and required a substantial amount of knowledge sharing between communities.

The potential and unexplored dark side of communities of practice

While the period since the late 1990s witnessed an enormous growth of interest in the concept of communities of practice, the vast majority of the writing on the topic has been saturated in an almost suffocating optimism. Thus, communities of practice have been variously argued to underpin levels of organizational innovativeness (Amidon, 1998; Brown and Duguid, 1991; Dougherty, 2001; Liedtka, 1999; Mitsuru, 1999), support and encourage organizational, individual and group learning (Arthur, 1998; Iles, 1994; Lave and Wenger, 1991; Raelin, 1997), and facilitate processes of knowledge sharing (Brown and Duguid, 1998; Hildreth *et al.*, 2000; McDermott, 1999; Ward, 2000). Connecting to the issue examined in the previous section, this bias may be a consequence of the fact that the communities of practice literature has typically focused rather narrowly on intra-community dynamics and knowledge sharing, rather than on inter-community dynamics. Arguably, however, through emphasizing the positive aspects to communities of practice, this work has tended to neglect or overlook any potential negative consequences to them.

For the community of practice concept to be a useful analytical tool for understanding organizational processes and innovation dynamics, a more balanced perspective is needed which accounts for both the potential benefits and disadvantages of communities of practice. The data presented in this chapter, for example, suggests that communities of practice are just as likely to resist as to support innovation processes, and that they have the potential to inhibit as much as facilitate knowledge sharing. Breu and Hemingway (2002) also show how communities of practice do not necessarily support innovations that are not deemed to be compatible with community interests.

Other work also suggests further ways in which communities of practice may have a dark side. Alvesson (2000), Baumard (1999, p. 211) and Brown and Duguid (2001) all suggest that if communities of practice have a particularly strong sense of identity this may create a sense of exclusion and isolation which may inhibit communication or collaboration with the wider organization. Leonard and Sensiper (1998), and Starbuck and Milliken (1998) also suggested that a potential negative aspect to any closed working group was the way they could blinker thinking, which can result in the exclusion or sidelining of relevant ideas.

Conclusion

As outlined earlier, the twin objectives of the chapter were to, first, provide empirical evidence on whether and how communities of practice influenced the appropriation of innovations in a number of case study organizations, and, secondly, contribute to theory on innovation processes through utilizing the community of practice concept. In general, the "communities of practice" concept proved useful and relevant for understanding the dynamics of the innovation processes examined. Not only were a wide range of communities of practice identified in all seven case companies, but they were also found to exert a significant influence in the innovation processes examined. Thus, it is suggested that the communities of practice concept represents a potentially useful analytical tool for understanding the dynamics of innovation processes and knowledge sharing practices more generally.

The data presented showed that for all of the case companies examined, organizational knowledge tended to be specialized, fragmented and highly diffused across sites, functions and business units. Further, this knowledge tended to be concentrated in specific communities of practice, with each community having responsibility for and conducting a particular range of organizational tasks. This, therefore, reinforced Brown and Duguid's (1991) vision of an organization as constituting a "community of communities". One of the major effects of this on the innovation processes examined was that they typically involved the collaboration of a wide range of different communities of practice.

Sharing and utilizing knowledge between different communities of practice, which is an issue not adequately addressed in the large majority of the academic literature on the subject, was found to be a non-trivial issue. First, the narrow specialist nature of knowledge which can develop within communities may create problems of communication and understanding with individuals not in possession of this specialist knowledge, particularly as the knowledge of specialist communities may be based on very different assumptions and interpretative frameworks (Becker, 2001). Secondly, the sense of identity that individuals can invest in communities may act to inhibit the communication or sharing of their knowledge with individuals outside of the community of practice, particularly if there is a perception that the interests of different communities may be in conflict (Storey and Barnett, 2000).

While the majority of the communities of practice literature has typically emphasized their positive effects on knowledge sharing, the data presented here suggests that they had a more ambiguous impact. Thus, while there was evidence that communities facilitated the sharing of knowledge in some circumstances, in others they actively inhibited it. Thus, while the communities of practice concept is useful in understanding and explaining the dynamics of innovation processes, such an analysis should be open to the possible negative aspects, to avoid the blinkered focus on their advantages which occurs when the concept is reified.

Part IV

ORGANISATIONAL COMPETENCIES

Chapter 10

Managing Competences to Enhance the Effect of Organizational Context on Innovation[1]

Sebastien Brion, Caroline Mothe and Maréva Sabatier

IREGE, University of Savoie, France

Introduction

Recent work has advocated the superiority of ambidexterity (He and Wong, 2004; Jansen *et al.*, 2005; O'Reilly and Tushman, 2004). However, research into the concept of ambidexterity is still in its infancy and has, until now, concentrated on showing that firms that use only one hand show lower performance than those that use both hands.[2] To the best of our knowledge, no studies have examined how firms can simultaneously combine exploitation and exploration strategies to achieve superior innovation, which is a prerequisite for sustained performance (He and Wong, 2004). This observation led us to look at the antecedents of innovation ambidexterity.

Since March's pioneering article (1991), the conceptual distinction between exploration and exploitation has been widely used in a number of fields outside organizational learning, including innovation management (e.g. Cheng and Van de Ven, 1996; He and Wong, 2004; Jansen *et al.*, 2005; O'Reilly and Tushman, 2004; Smith and Tushman, 2005). A consensus seems to emerge that firms should develop the capacity to explore new technological paths while continuing to exploit their existing competences

---

[1] An earlier version of this chapter was published in the *International Journal of Innovation Management*, 2010, **14**(2), 151–178.

[2] We thank an anonymous reviewer for suggesting this idea.

(e.g. Levinthal and March, 1993; March, 1991; O'Reilly and Tushman, 2004; Tushman and O'Reilly, 1996). An appropriate balance between these two activities is seen as necessary for a firm to be both competitive in mature markets — where costs, efficiency and incremental innovation are essential — and innovative in terms of product development for emerging markets — where experimentation and flexibility are needed (Tushman and O'Reilly, 1996). The capacity to simultaneously pursue these two contradictory objectives (Smith and Tushman, 2005) is called ambidexterity.

Previous research has resulted in a number of conflicting perspectives on how to simultaneously separate and integrate exploration and exploitation activities. It has been shown that firms need to combine contradictory management practices in order to create an organizational context that is favorable to ambidexterity (Ghoshal and Bartlett, 1994; Gibson and Birkinshaw, 2004). In line with Ghoshal and Bartlett (1994), organizational context is viewed as being created and renewed by management; therefore, it is highly dependent on managerial actions and practices. However, questions remain about the nature of the organizational context managers should develop in order to encourage ambidexterity for innovation, and about the antecedents of combining exploration and exploitation innovation activities. The present research is an attempt to fill this gap. It also analyses the moderating effect of competences (Gilsing and Nooteboom, 2006), thereby following Mom *et al.*'s (2007) recommendation to look at the impact managers have on innovation through the actions they take and the competences they try to develop.

As well as defining ambidexterity and innovation, the following section outlines the theoretical background to our research and advances hypotheses on the effect of organizational context on innovation ambidexterity, and on the moderating role of competences. After providing details of the sample set, data collection method and measures, we present our empirical findings. This is followed by a discussion of the results and suggestions for further research.

Literature Review and Hypotheses

Ambidexterity and innovation

The present research focuses on exploitation and exploration activities that are intended to promote innovation. In line with He and Wong (2004), we define exploration innovation in terms of activities aimed at entering new product-market domains, whereas exploitation innovation is considered to encompass activities aimed at improving an existing product-market position. Exploration usually generates radical (or discontinuous) innovation; exploitation tends to produce more incremental innovation (O'Reilly and Tushman, 2004; Tushman and Anderson, 1986). We provide a brief review of the difficulties and tensions involved in combining exploration and exploitation activities, and show how the literature solves these difficulties in terms of structure and/or organizational context.

Finding the right balance between exploration and exploitation activities is not easy, but it is essential for a firm's survival (March, 1991). The question of whether these activities are antithetical or complementary has not yet been resolved. It is difficult to imagine how an organization can combine efficiency in managing current activities and efficacy in experimentation and risk management, as they are based on different competences and organizational capabilities (Christensen and Overdorf, 2000; Benner and Tushman, 2003). The imperatives of short-term survival through the effective employment of current assets and capabilities, and of long-term success through the development of new capabilities have even been viewed as paradoxical (Gilsing and Nooteboom, 2006). However, dealing with these contradictions — that is to say, being "ambidextrous" — is likely to improve performance.

Research into ambidexterity has therefore tried to analyze how exploration and exploitation should be combined. There is still no consensus, and different ways of achieving ambidexterity have emerged, especially in terms of organizational structure (Duncan, 1976; O'Reilly and Tushman, 2004) and/or the creation of a specific organizational context (Gibson and Birkinshaw, 2004). "Structural" ambidexterity can be viewed in terms of R&D organization (Duncan, 1976; Benner and Tushman, 2003; Argyres and Silverman, 2004; Tirpak *et al.*, 2006) or in terms of the separation of exploration and exploitation activities (O'Reilly and Tushman, 2004). However, developing an appropriate organizational structure is not the only way of achieving ambidexterity. Gibson and Birkinshaw (2004) argue that ambidexterity might best be achieved through individuals, thereby challenging traditional and ingrained ideas about the difficulties human beings have in devoting their time and energy to paradoxical objectives, such as the trade-off between efficiency and flexibility (Adler *et al.*, 1999).

Gibson and Birkinshaw (2004) define "contextual ambidexterity" as the individual behavioral capacity to demonstrate both alignment and adaptability. This type of ambidexterity depends on the systems, incentives and processes that shape individual behaviors in an organization, and these features define the organizational context (Ghoshal and Bartlett, 1994). Hence, the organizational context, which is created through tangible and concrete managerial actions, emphasizes the role of managers in strategic processes — a theme that has led to much debate between researchers who view management as primordial and those who assign it a lesser role (Burgelman, 1983).

The present research examines the relationship between organizational context and innovation, focusing on innovation ambidexterity. First, we identify the main dimensions of a firm's organizational context as an antecedent of innovation ambidexterity. Secondly, we analyze the moderating role of the different types of competence.

Organizational context as an antecedent of innovation ambidexterity

Organizational context has been defined as "the systems, processes, and beliefs that shape individual-level behaviours in an organization" (Gibson and Birkinshaw, 2004, p. 212). In line with previous research, we focused on general managers (Barnard, 1938; Ghoshal and Bartlett, 1994) and on the systems and incentives they implement in order to operate ambidextrously. General managers are required to achieve a pragmatic balance between fundamentally different requirements (Burgelman, 1983). As competition and complexity intensify, managers no longer face a simple choice between favoring routine processes that ensure efficient exploitation, and introducing non-routine processes and exploration tasks that favor innovation; rather, they are required to implement management practices and create the context needed to allow the simultaneous pursuit of both objectives (Volberda, 1996). Flexibility requires task autonomy, variety and creativity, whereas efficiency requires formal rules, hierarchical controls and high levels of standardization, formalization and specialization (Adler *et al.*, 1999). Mechanisms for managing the conflict between efficiency and flexibility are dependent for their success on the broader organizational context (Adler *et al.*, 1999), which is largely created by the firm's management team.

Since the pioneering work of Barnard (1938), there has been a long history of research into how managers can create contexts that enhance organizational performance (e.g. Chandler, 1962; Porter, 1991; Rumelt *et al.*, 1991). Although the strategic management literature of the 1980s and 1990s did not highlight the link between performance and management, recent organizational research (e.g. Ghoshal and Bartlett, 1994; Gibson and Birkinshaw, 2004; Smith and Tushman, 2005) has tended to rebuild this bridge, arguing that management plays a leading role in developing rules, characteristics and tools, and, more generally speaking, the organizational context. Hamel (2009) recently stressed the importance of this argument when he asked: "How in an age of rapid change do you create organizations that are as adaptable and resilient as they are focused and efficient?" (p. 92). This question highlights the dilemma and contradictions of the managerial task, which should go "beyond today's bureaucracy-infused management practices" (p. 92).

The present research was designed to further our understanding of how management can create an organizational context in which it is possible to pursue flexibility and the search for new knowledge, while simultaneously promoting efficiency and the use of existing knowledge (Levinthal and March, 1993). Believing that "traditional control systems ensure high levels of compliance but do so at the expense of employee creativity, entrepreneurship, and engagement", Hamel (2009, p. 93) encourages firms to overcome the "discipline-versus-innovation trade-off". Organizational leaders must deal with this trade-off and overcome potential problems caused by contradictory organizational alignments (Ghoshal and Bartlett, 1994; Smith and Tushman, 2005; O'Reilly and Tushman, 2007):

"Although these trade-offs can never entirely be eliminated, the most successful organizations reconcile them to a large degree, and in so doing enhance their long-term competitiveness. ... Alignment activities are geared toward improving performance in the **short term**. Adaptability activities are geared toward improving performance in the **long term**. Thus, if a business unit focuses on one of these at the expense of the other, problems and tensions will inevitably arise" (Gibson and Birkinshaw, 2004, p. 209 and p. 212).

Hence, an organizational context should simultaneously favor short-term efficiency and long-term discovery. When trying to resolve the exploration/exploitation dilemma, management has the difficult task of creating the most appropriate short- and long-term focused organizational contexts in order to achieve ambidexterity for innovation.

In line with Gibson and Birkinshaw (2004) and with the literature on innovation management, we consider a firm's organizational context to consist of four dimensions: performance management, formalization, creativity and risk taking. As performance management and formalization tend to focus on short-term goals, these two dimensions were grouped together in a variable called "short-term organizational focus". Conversely, creativity and risk taking are mostly related to long-term goals, and were grouped together in a variable called "long-term organizational focus".

The following section presents each of these four dimensions and explains why they were combined into two aggregate variables. It also outlines support (Toulmin, 1969) for our claim that both short-term organizational focus (H1a) and long-term organizational focus (H1b) have an impact on innovation ambidexterity.

Short-term organizational focus: performance management and formalization

Short-term organizational focus includes both performance-oriented management and formalization. We believe there is a positive link between short-term organizational focus and innovation ambidexterity, a position that is supported by the literature on organization theory (Cardinal, 2001; Deshpande and Zaltman, 1982; Ghoshal and Bartlett, 1994; Gibson and Birkinshaw, 2004; Jansen *et al.*, 2005; Mintzberg, 1979; Snell, 1992).

Organizational contexts favoring performance-oriented management should be based on administrative mechanisms that give employees clear and tangible objectives (Gibson and Birkinshaw, 2004). Performance-oriented management reinforces existing mechanisms and routines through the setting of general guidelines and objectives. Written procedures enable employees to deal with most situations, and standard procedures allow each employee to carry out his/her job (Deshpande and Zaltman, 1982; Jansen, 2005). Such "management by objectives" is often based on a decentralized organization and a collectively shared identity.

However, Snell (1992) observed that management control should not be limited to management by objectives, arguing that it should be comple-mented by a formalization of rules and procedures. Furthermore, Jansen *et al.* (2005) showed that ambidextrous organizations need formalization, that is to say, decision-making based on formal systems, established rules and prescribed procedures (Mintzberg, 1979). Formalization has often been considered part of behavior control (Snell, 1992), where control refers to "any process by which managers direct attention, motivate and encourage organizational members to act in desired ways to meet the firm's objectives" (Cardinal, 2001, p. 22). Formalization and procedures are top-down behavior-control systems that regulate subordinates' actions (Snell, 1992). Standard procedures are best suited for common and foreseeable situations and these procedures should be formalized, that is to say, put in writing (Snell, 1992). Cause-effect knowledge (Ouchi and Maguire, 1975) and "task programmability" (Eisenhardt, 1985) are prerequisite to the use of formal behavior-control systems.

Where formal systems are absent, and as all actions cannot be standardized *a priori*, managers may also have to apply output control (Snell, 1992), that is to say, performance-oriented management. Instead of translating managerial intentions into standard operating procedures, performance-oriented management sets targets and objectives for subor-dinates to pursue. Indeed, there is a theoretical complementarity between formalization and performance-oriented management: *ex ante* behavior-control systems are useful for preventing errors and setting formal rules and procedures; however, too much behavior control may be costly and inefficient in regulating performance (Snell, 1992). Performance-oriented management is reactive and provides *ex post* control (Flamholtz, 1979).

Previous research indicates that formalization and performance man-agement can be grouped together into a single variable, which we have called "short-term organizational focus". The short-term organizational focus can enhance exploitation innovation by improving current products and processes (Jansen *et al.*, 2005). However, high degrees of bureaucratic control inhibit experimentation, creativity and innovation (Aiken and Hage, 1971). As exploitation innovation is essential to pursuing innovation ambidexterity, we postulated that:

H1a: The higher the "short-term organizational focus" (performance management and formalization), the higher the innovation ambidexterity.

Long-term organizational focus: creativity and risk taking

An organizational context focused on short-term performance should be balanced by the creation of a context focused on long-term performance. This requires creativity and risk taking. We believe there is a positive relationship between long-term organizational focus and innovation ambidexterity. This position is supported by the literature on innovation management (Amabile and Conti, 1999; Dewar and Dutton, 1986; Kremen Bolton, 1993; O'Reilly and Tushman, 2004, 2007).

It is widely accepted that creativity is a major component of innovation (e.g. Amabile *et al.*, 1996; Ford, 1996), and organizational creativity is considered a subset of the broader domain of innovation (Woodman *et al.*, 1993). However, the literature contains very few empirical studies of the link between the two concepts. Creativity is fostered by giving autonomy to employees and teams (e.g. Amabile *et al.*, 1996; Baylin, 1985): the freedom to choose which problems to work on and to pursue them independently of directives is seen as a prerequisite of innovation (Baylin, 1985). Giving autonomy to a firm's R&D team and, in general, to the people in charge of innovation is a necessary (though not sufficient) condition for innovation.

Similarly, exploring new possibilities requires risk taking, even though its returns are uncertain and often negative (March, 1991; O'Reilly and Tushman, 2004). Managerial attitudes and practices can influence the nature of innovation (Amabile and Conti, 1999), as pro-change managerial attitudes are needed to support the adoption of radical innovation (Dewar and Dutton, 1986). Managers should encourage risk taking by setting an example and by tolerating failure. In a study of the effects on innovation of the organizational downsizing of the work environment, Amabile and Conti (1999) reported that acceptance of risk taking is the most crucial factor in promoting innovation.

Firms are stimulated to take risks and innovate as a response to decreased performance (Kremen Bolton, 1993). A number of studies have indicated a connection between these two items, as innovation requires a climate in which "calculated risks" are taken (Souder, 1987). Firms should take careful and controlled risks with the objective of improving ultimate performance. In addition, the literature provides evidence for strong links between risk taking and creativity (Amabile and Conti, 1999). A similar observation was made by O'Reilly and Tushman (2007): managers should emphasize long-term orientations and exploration activities through creativity and risk taking. We therefore advanced the following hypothesis:

H1b: The higher the "long-term organizational focus" (creativity and risk taking), the higher the innovation ambidexterity.

The moderating role of competences

Recent research into innovation (Benner and Tushman, 2003; Danneels, 2002; Dougherty and Hardy, 1996; Gilsing and Nooteboom, 2006; O'Reilly and Tushman, 2004; Smith and Tushman, 2005) has used the exploration/exploitation construct because it encompasses aspects linked to competences (Gilsing and Nooteboom, 2006). For these authors, exploration innovation refers to strategies based on new technological or marketing competences (Benner and Tushman, 2003; Danneels, 2002), whereas exploitation innovation covers strategies based on accelerating innovation processes that use existing technological and marketing competences.

Following in the footsteps of Gatignon *et al.* (2002), we looked at the specific effects on innovation of competence exploration and competence exploitation, that is to say, of enhancing existing competences and acquiring new competences. Different notions have been used to describe these two types of competences. For example, Dosi *et al.* (2000) used the terms static and dynamic competences, where static competences are aimed at replication and dynamic competences represent skills for learning and resource reconfiguration. Palacios Marques *et al.* (2006) referred to "distinctive competencies" when talking about assets "that seek to combine the exploitation of organisational procedures and norms with exploration" (p. 91), before distinguishing two dimensions: Schumpeterian competences for radical growth and the development of new abilities, and continuous improvement competences for incremental growth and the strengthening of existing capabilities.

The symbiotic relationship between competences and innovation through new product development or technology management has been extensively studied (e.g. Clark and Fujimoto, 1991; Leonard-Barton, 1992; Tushman and Anderson, 1986; Van de Ven, 1986). However, the link between innovation and competences remains uncertain and/or ambiguous. For example, it is still unclear whether innovation outcomes are driven by competences or whether competences are a type of innovation outcome, or both. In addition, little research has been carried out into "how" firms (through their managers) transform resources and competences to create value (Sirmon *et al.*, 2007).

The introduction of such processes of knowledge and competence creation, absorption, integration and reconfiguration (Verona and Ravasi, 2003) is largely the responsibility of managers. Previous research into the key role of strategic leadership has been mostly conceptual and has not investigated the way leaders create and manage competences (Adner and Helfat, 2003; Eisenhardt and Martin, 2000; Teece *et al.*, 1997; Teece, 2006). Management plays a crucial role in developing innovation ambidexterity, as it develops the objectives, goals, methods, processes and procedures that enhance competence exploitation and it identifies favorable opportunities for new technological or marketing competences, thus favoring exploration innovation (Teece, 2006).

Although the effect of management (through organizational context) on innovation and the impact of competences on innovation have been well documented, we believe that these links are more subtle and that competences have a moderating effect on the relationship between context and ambidexterity. The effect of competences on the link between context and innovation, and thus between context and ambidexterity, has, however, not been tested. It is still unclear whether competences act as a determinant of innovation, or whether they reinforce one or more aspects of the organizational context. While most studies have focused on the impact of competences on innovation, we stress the key role of managers in the determination and creation of a context that is suited to ambidexterity, and in the development of the most suitable competences.

We believe that organizational context and competence management act in conjunction, and that poor combinations can lead to sub-optimal performance with respect to innovation ambidexterity. Hence, it is important to develop the right competences in order to reinforce the beneficial effect of organizational context on innovation. More specifically, an organizational context with a short-term focus, that is to say, a context that favors exploitation, must be combined with competence exploitation. Thus, we hypothesized that ambidexterity increases when the short-term organizational focus is coupled with competence exploitation:

H2a: Competence exploitation moderates the positive relationship between short-term organizational focus and innovation ambidexterity.

Similarly, an organizational context with a long-term focus, that is to say, a context that favors exploration, must be combined with competences related to that aspect of development. Therefore, we hypothesized that innovation ambidexterity increases when the long-term focus is coupled with competence exploration:

H2b: Competence exploration moderates the positive relationship between long-term organizational focus and innovation ambidexterity.

Figure 1 shows the theoretical model on which the present study was based.

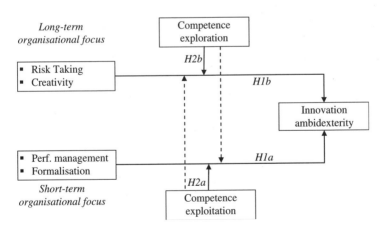

Fig. 1. Theoretical model.

NB: The two dotted lines correspond to complementary analyses (slope tests) that are presented in the discussion.

Methods

Data collection

Questionnaires were sent to the managing directors of the 482 large firms (firms with more than 250 employees, as defined by the OECD) in the Rhône-Alpes region[3] of France. Responses were received from 188 of these firms. In order to filter out firms that are not innovative, the managers were asked the following question "Has your firm developed a new product or service during the last three years?" Firms who gave a negative answer to this question were eliminated from the sample, leaving 119 innovative firms. Removing responses with missing data resulted in a final sample of 108 firms, which corresponds to a response rate of 22%. As this sample was statistically representative in terms of sector distribution in the Rhône-Alpes region (F Test sig. at 99%), our results can be used to make general inferences about firms in the Rhône-Alpes region, but not about French firms in general. The firms in the sample were classified as manufacturing firms (48%), service firms (34%) and others (18%).[4] The "others" category included a very heterogeneous mixture of organizations, ranging from non-merchant services and non-governmental organizations to assistance to elderly people. The sample included firms from many different business sectors.

Very few empirical studies have included both industrial and service firms in their sample (Gatignon *et al.*, 2002; Gibson and Birkinshaw, 2004; McGrath, 2001) and most research has concentrated on manufacturing companies in order to explore innovation, R&D activities and organization (Argyres and Silverman, 2004; He and Wong, 2004; Sidhu *et al.*, 2007). Some studies have focused on one specific industry (e.g. pharmaceuticals: Cardinal, 2001; Gilsing and Nooteboom, 2006; or electronics: Atuahene-Gima, 2005) or on the service sector (e.g. financial services: Jansen *et al.*, 2006). By having a large sample of industrial and service companies we were able to determine whether or not ambidexterity is linked to a firm's business sector. Questionnaires were only sent to firms' head offices and

---

[3] See http://www.panorama.rhone-alpes.cci.fr/4_2_a_entreprises.html (accessed on 20 December 2011).

[4] T-tests showed no significant difference between sectors for any of the considered variables.

participating firms were sent three successive reminders over a one-month period.

We collected most of our data using a single survey instrument and a single informant. Potential concerns resulting from common-method and single-informant biases were addressed using the procedures and statistical tests recommended by Krishnan *et al.* (2006). Hence, we included procedural remedies in order to protect respondent anonymity in the questionnaire, to reduce item ambiguity through survey pretests,[5] to separate scale items for the independent and dependent variables, and to obtain data for the control variables from a secondary source.[6] Statistical remedies included triangulation of survey data with data obtained from the secondary source and from field interviews that were undertaken during an exploratory qualitative study on innovation and management practices in a large domestic appliances group.[7] These procedures allowed us to be confident that neither common method nor single informant bias was a serious problem in our study.

Measurements and questionnaire development

Appendix A shows the measures and their sources. All the items on the questionnaire required seven-point Likert-style responses (from $1 =$ "Strongly agree" to $7 =$ "Strongly disagree"). We ran six confirmatory factor analyses based on the normal-theory maximum-likelihood procedure, grouping measures of theoretically related constructs to ensure acceptable parameter estimate-to-observation ratios. A single-step modification approach was adopted (Kaplan and Wenger, 1993). We also checked the theoretical

---

[5]The questionnaire was pre-tested on 12 R&D managers in order to ensure the validity of the measures. These 12 responses were not integrated in our final data.

[6]For each response, we checked the sector and the size of the firm in the Kompass business directory, in order to obtain missing data and to check the validity of the data.

[7]We used interview notes to validate our creativity and risk taking measures. Two PhD students categorized the interview responses (using 5-point scales), in order to determine the extent to which each of the four creativity items existed in R&D teams. We repeated this procedure for the other multi-item measure (risk taking construct). The correlation between the creativity scale obtained from the survey and the interview notes coded by the independent raters was 0.68 (p < 0.05). The same was done for risk taking (0.70, p < 0.05). No discrepancy was noted regarding variable content, thus allowing us to be quite confident about our scales.

relevance of each new link created in the model (Cox and Wermuth, 1996) and the goodness-of-fit for the six latent constructs. Descriptive statistics are given in Appendix B.

Dependent variable

Innovation ambidexterity has two main dimensions, which were measured using two scales (He and Wong, 2004). Following the addition of a covariance between the two items and using the largest modification index criterion (Jöreskog and Sörbom, 1984), confirmatory factor analyses gave a good model fit for the two variables. For exploitation innovation, "Enhance existing product quality" correlated with "Introduce slightly different products". Theoretically, incremental product innovation is mostly due to quality enhancement. For exploration innovation, "Introduce new product generations" correlated with "Offer totally new products for the market". Again, this link seems logical, as most new products are created in order to generate new markets and, conversely, few new markets are created with old products.

The literature describes several ways of measuring ambidexterity (He and Wong, 2004). The interaction effect (ambidexterity score calculated as the product of the exploitation and exploration innovation scores) was used to search for antecedents of the level of ambidexterity reached by firms (as well as to run simple slope tests to analyze the moderating effects of competences).

Moderating variables

Competence exploitation and competence exploration constructs were based on previous research (Atuahene-Gima, 2005). Appendix A shows a very good fit index. "Reinforce the search for solutions that are close to existing ones" correlated with "Enhance skills that improve productivity of current innovation operations", showing that the implementation of known solutions is linked to skill enhancement (and vice-versa). Firms tend to focus on existing competences to search for solutions in the neighborhood of existing expertise. For competence exploration, two items involved with external research and partnerships are correlated. As firms essentially look for complementary external competences (Teece,

1986), the distinction between technological and market competences is secondary.

Independent variables

Structural relations between dimensions were highlighted by using a second order factorization (Hair *et al.*, 1998) after checking (a) for the theoretical relevance of the construct (Chin, 1998), and (b) that the confirmatory second order factorization model fit better than the confirmatory factor independent model.

Short-term organizational focus. This variable is composed of formalization and performance-oriented management. As would be expected, the two items "There are standard procedures each person has to follow in performing his/her job" and "Written procedures are available to deal with whatever situation arises" are correlated. A second order factorization carried out to construct a single latent variable for short-term focus gave a better model fit index than the independent model (see Appendix A).

Long-term organizational focus. This variable is composed of creativity and risk taking. The two items "Be willing to take risks" and "Consider taking risks as a way to improve performance" are correlated. Statistical analysis confirmed the correlation between these two variables. After improving the model by adding two significant links (see Appendix A), the second order factorization confirmatory model gave a better fit than the independent model.

Control variables

As described in Section 4, below, we controlled for firm size, separating small and large firms (more than 250 employees), and for type of industry.

Results

In order to identify the determinants of ambidexterity intensity, we followed the direction suggested by recent research on innovation (Atuahene-Gima, 2005; Danneels, 2002; Nerkar, 2003) and looked for a positive interaction between the two types of innovation. We also calculated an ambidexterity

Table 1. Determinants of ambidextrous firms.

	Model (a)		Model (b)	
	Coef.	Student t	Coef.	Student t
Constant	1.31	*1.03*	0.84	*1.36*
Industry sector	0.26	*1.39*	0.09	*1.09*
Other sector	0.18	*0.91*	0.02	*0.73*
Services sector	Ref.		Ref.	
mgt_st: Short-term organizational focus	**0.12**	*2.09***	**0.17**	*1.96***
mgt_lt: Long-term organizational focus	**2.98**	*2.96****	**2.91**	*2.52****
comp_exploit: Competence exploitation	**0.13**	*1.91**	**0.18**	*1.97***
comp_explor: Competence exploration	**1.26**	*2.13***	**1.06**	*2.41***
mgt_lt x comp_exploit			**−0.53**	*2.31***
mgt_st x comp_exploit			**0.89**	*2.08***
mgt_lt x comp_explor			**1.02**	*3.66****
mgt_st x comp_explor			**−0.77**	*2.08***
R^2	**0.35**		**0.55**	
Fischer test	4.68		8.48	
Observations	108		108	

Note: Figures in italics are White robust standard errors with: * = significant at 10%; ** = significant at 5%; *** = significant at 1%.

score ("ambi") by multiplying the exploitation innovation score by the exploration innovation score (He and Wong, 2004; Gibson and Birkinshaw, 2004). This multiplicative interaction reflects the fact that exploitation and exploration innovations are non-substitutable and interdependent.

Two models (OLS regressions) were drawn up in order to study the determinants of ambidexterity scores and to test our hypotheses. Model (a) estimates the effects of activity sector, organizational context and competences on ambidexterity scores. Model (b) includes the crossed effects of context and competences. The regression results are given in Table 1.

The two models show there is no significant effect of sector of activity on ambidexterity. More interestingly, the regressions highlighted the fact that both short-term organizational focus and long-term organizational focus increase ambidexterity scores. These results support H1a and H1b. Econometric results allowed us to analyze this effect: long-term organizational focus (risk taking and creativity) is much more efficient in producing ambidexterity than short-term organizational focus (performance-oriented management and formalization). Furthermore, both competence exploitation and short-term organizational focus positively affect ambidexterity.

The most interesting result — that the interactions between context and competence management have significant effects on ambidexterity — appears in model (b). Including the crossed effects of organizational context and competences increased R^2 by 20 points. The results of a Fisher test for restrictions ($F = 7.38$; $p < 0.01$) led us to prefer model (b). Hence, ambidexterity scores are not only affected by organizational context and competences individually, but also by combinations of organizational context and competences. Ignoring these crossed effects produces less efficient estimations of ambidexterity scores. Some combinations (long-term organizational focus plus competence exploration and short-term organizational focus plus competence exploitation) lead to higher ambidexterity scores. Other combinations have negative impacts on innovation ambidexterity. This supports H2a and H2b and confirms that a complementary managerial focus is more efficient for ambidexterity than the development of separate, and potentially inadequate, competences and organizational context.

Discussion

The present research examined the antecedents for innovation ambidexterity. A study of 108 large, innovative firms, carried out using OLS regressions and slope tests, showed that the firms that perform best (in terms of combining exploration and exploitation innovations) focus on risk taking and creativity. In addition, competence exploration and competence exploitation have a strong moderating effect. Taken together, our results highlight the importance of management's ability to orchestrate and integrate contradictory innovation activities (O'Reilly and Tushman, 2007) through an adequate combination of context and competences.

Contributions

Long-term organizational focus (risk taking and creativity) increases innovation ambidexterity more than short-term organizational focus (performance-oriented management and formalization). Our results also indicate that competences have a heterogeneous effect: competence exploration has a greater impact on ambidexterity scores than competence exploitation.

Simple slope tests were conducted to obtain further insight into these relationships. Based on estimated coefficients of model (b) (direct and crossed effects of context and competences), these tests allowed us to graphically represent linear and estimated relations between ambidexterity scores and short-term or long-term organizational focus, according to the levels of competence exploitation and competence exploration. Adopting the method of Aiken and West (1991), we split competences into two groups – a high group (two standard deviations above the mean, solid line) and a low group (two standard deviations below the mean, dashed line), and plotted the estimated relationship between organizational context and ambidexterity (see Figs. 2 and 3).

Figure 2(a) shows that short-term organizational focus has a strong positive effect on ambidexterity scores at higher levels of competence exploitation (simple slope: $b = 1.96$, $t = 3.91$, $p < 0.01$). However, it has a negative effect on lower levels of competence exploitation (simple slope: $b = -1.62$, $t = 2.39$, $p < 0.05$). Conversely, long-term organizational focus has a positive effect on ambidexterity (Fig. 2(b)), whatever the level of competence exploitation (simple slope: $b = 1.84$, $t = 2.12$, $p < 0.05$ for low

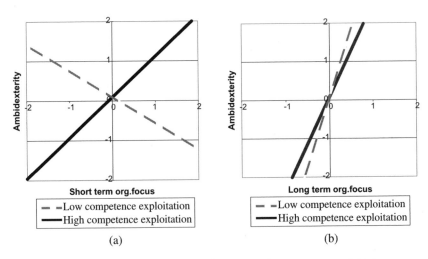

Fig. 2.   Interaction of organizational context and competence exploitation.

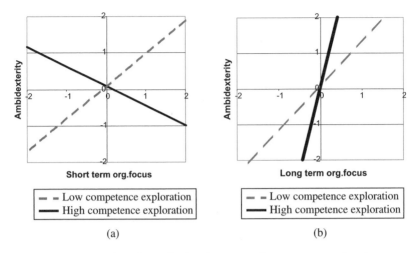

Fig. 3. Interaction of organizational context and competence exploration.

levels of competence exploitation, and simple slope: $b = 1.07$, $t = 2.32$, $p < 0.05$ for high levels).

As can be seen from Fig. 3(a), short-term organizational focus has a negative effect on innovation ambidexterity when levels of competence exploration are high (simple slope: $b = -1.20$, $t = 3.75$, $p < 0.01$). The reverse relationship was found when competence exploration is low (simple slope: $b = 1.53$, $t = 2.69$, $p < 0.01$). Interestingly, as Fig. 3(b) shows, long-term organizational focus always has a strong positive effect on ambidexterity (simple slope: $b = 4.72$, $t = 3.90$, $p < 0.01$ for high levels of competence exploration, and simple slope: $b = 1.10$, $t = 3.78$, $p < 0.01$ for low levels).

Figures 2 and 3 confirm that organizational context positively influences ambidexterity scores when adequate competences are developed. Short-term organizational focus only has a positive impact on ambidexterity when competence exploitation is high. Similarly, the positive effect of long-term organizational focus on ambidexterity is much stronger when competence exploration is high.

Implications for theory

Our analysis of the determinants of innovation ambidexterity contributes to two main research streams: innovation management and organization theory. By providing evidence of the strong impact of organizational context on innovation ambidexterity, our findings emphasize the key role of managers, first highlighted by Barnard (1938). Firms should ensure managers create an appropriate context, as developing supportive short- and long-term organizational focuses increases ambidexterity scores for large firms. However, the most effective way of enhancing ambidexterity is to give long-term aspects, such as creativity and risk taking, higher priority than short-term aspects, such as formalization and performance-oriented management. This result is consistent with the findings of Adler *et al.* (1999) in that effective management appears to be a precondition for consistent organizational and long-term performance. Such investment should focus on enhancing flexibility and innovation to avoid short-term pressures.

Our results also support the view that managers play a dominant role in the development of a firm's competences (O'Reilly and Tushman, 2007). The incentives given by managers to develop either competence exploration or competence exploitation moderate the link between context and ambidexterity. Thus, competence development should be closely linked to the firm's organizational context. Incentives given to employees through the management practices underlying organizational context are not independent from the way management deals with competences. Competence exploration can only be developed in organizational contexts that promote creativity and risk taking, whereas competence exploitation can only be developed in organizational contexts that promote performance and short-term goals. Developing new competences strengthens the positive effect of long-term organizational focus. It is essential for firms to emphasize the development of new competences over immediate output in order to avoid core rigidities (Leonard-Barton, 1992). However, incentives to develop competence exploration weaken the effect of short-term organizational focus on ambidexterity. Concentrating on exploration and the search for variety while simultaneously trying to implement formalization causes inefficiency (Adler *et al.*, 1999). Greater variety is usually not associated (and is incompatible) with continuous processes and routines (Safizadeh *et al.*, 1996).

Our findings on the moderating impact of competence exploitation differ from previous results. Competence exploitation has a very low moderating effect on long-term organizational focus but a strong moderating effect on short-term organizational focus. In fact, the effect of short-term organizational focus becomes negative when incentives for developing competence exploitation are low. This reinforces the observation that, in order to achieve innovation ambidexterity, senior management should develop a strictly coherent organizational context that combines adequate context creation and competences.

More generally speaking, having stressed that the creation of a long-term organizational focus oriented towards risk, creativity and entrepreneurship is more valuable for ambidexterity than concentrating on short-term profit targets, we suggest that theory should develop "holistic measurement systems" to include such critical factors for success as "building new growth platforms" (Hamel, 2009, p. 94). The present research provides a link between the competence-based view and the literature on organizational theory and management practices. This link will facilitate research into whether the creation of an organizational context predetermines the competences that will be developed, or vice-versa. The processes that occur between context and competences still need to be explored.

Limitations and suggestions for future research

The present study has two main limitations that should be addressed through further research. First, we used a single key-informant approach, with the same respondents providing information for both the independent and the dependent variables in the regression analysis. Previous research has shown high correlations between perceived and objective measures of performance (Venkatraman and Ramanujam, 1986), and the near absence of correlation inflation for self-reported data (Crampton and Wagner, 1994). As in other similar studies (Mom *et al.*, 2007; Krishnan *et al.*, 2006), and even though few individuals within a firm are knowledgeable enough to provide information on all innovation characteristics and outcomes, we ensured that the data collected related to the organization as a whole and not just to the individual respondent. We also applied procedural and statistical remedies in order to ensure that neither common-method nor single-informant biases were a serious problem in the study.

Secondly, it was difficult to make comparisons within a single type of activity due to the relatively small size of the sample. In addition, the study is limited to one region, Rhône-Alpes, and the results may not be generally applicable to innovation activities in other parts of France. Consequently, no general inferences can be made from our results. Although a larger sample would have increased the statistical power of our analyses, our sample was large enough to establish significance in the results and to obtain reliable models. Further work using larger datasets and a multi-region comparison approach is needed in order to investigate whether our results remain valid for different activity sectors.

Conclusion

The present study investigated the determinants of innovation ambidexterity, a facet that has not been addressed by previous research, which has concentrated on the link between ambidexterity and performance (He and Wong, 2004) or on the determinants of contextual ambidexterity (Gibson and Birkinshaw, 2004). The fact that several observed variables have significant impacts on the innovation ambidexterity scores of large firms has strong methodological implications: treating ambidexterity as exogenous ignores the fact that ambidexterity scores depend on observed covariates. This may generate biases when analyzing the link between ambidexterity and performance, for example.

By highlighting the need to adopt a managerial approach to innovation, the present study suggests that managers should concentrate on long-term management, rather than on short-term management. Research into how managers can continually explore, develop and reconfigure the competences needed to strengthen the positive effects on innovation ambidexterity of long-term organizational focus is still in its infancy. Further analysis of organizational context and the incentives required to build associated competences may be particularly fruitful for researchers and practitioners.

Appendix

Appendix A.   Confirmatory factor analysis of measures.

Exploitation innovation

$\chi2 = 1.228$ ($p = 0.268$); **RMSEA = 0.03; GFI = 0.996; IFI = 0.998; NNFI = 0.985;** $\alpha = 0.652$

	SRW[a]	CR[b]
Exploitation innovation (He and Wong, 2004)	During the last three years, your firm was able to...	
1. Enhance existing product quality (c1↔c2)[c]	0.425	8.164
2. Introduce slightly different products	0.392	8.353
3. Make production processes more flexible	0.656	4.941
4. Reduce production costs or consumption	0.694	4.235

Exploitation innovation

$\chi2 = 2.918$ ($p = 0.88$); **RMSEA = 0.10; GFI = 0.992; IFI = 0.990; NNFI = 0.936;** $\alpha = 0.754$

	SRW[a]	CR[b]
Exploration innovation (He and Wong, 2004)	During the last three years, your firm was able to...	
1. Introduce new product generations (c1↔c2)[c]	0.702	5.962
2. Offer totally new products for the market	0.875	2.245
3. Enter new technological fields	0.510	8.368
4. Sell to new customers in new markets	0.477	8.535

(*Continued*)

Appendix A. (Continued)

Competence exploitation

$\chi 2 = 1.90$ ($p = 0.168$); **RMSEA = 0.07**; **GFI = 0.996**; **CFI = 0.997**; **IFI = 0.997**; **NNFI = 0.981**; $\alpha = 0.827$

		SRW[a]	CR[b]
Competence exploitation (Atuahene-Gima, 2005)	Systems in the firm encourage employees to...		
	1. Upgrade current knowledge and skills for familiar products or technologies	0.869	3.548
	2. Upgrade skills in product processes in which the firm already possesses experience	0.797	5.475
	3. Reinforce the search for solutions that are close to existing ones (c3↔c4)[c]	0.486	8.706
	4. Enhance skills that improve productivity of current innovation operations	0.674	7.758

Competence exploration

$\chi 2 = 0.456$ ($p = 0.500$); **RMSEA = 0.00**; **GFI = 0.999**; **CFI = 1.000**; **IFI = 1.003**; **NNFI = 1.019**; $\alpha = 0.767$

		SRW[a]	CR[b]
Competence exploration (Atuahene-Gima, 2005)	Systems in the firm encourage employees to...		
	1. Acquire new technologies and skills	0.768	4.566
	2. Adopt new managerial and organizational skills that are important for innovation	0.691	6.170
	3. Locate partners to have access to new markets (c3↔c4)[c]	0.491	8.111
	4. Find partners that provide access to new technological practices	0.639	6.942

[a]Standardized regression weights; [b]Critical ratio of variance; [c]Item x (here c1) is correlated with item y (here c2).

Short-term organizational focus

Second order factorization model:

$\chi2 = 38.204$ ($p = 0.004$); RMSEA = 0.08; GFI = 0.954; CFI = 0.967; IFI = 0.968; NNFI = 0.949; $\alpha = 0.791$[d]

Variable	Scale items	α	SRW[a]	CR[b]
Formalization (Cardinal, 2001; Deshpande and Zaltman, 1982; Jansen, 2005; Snell, 1992)	Please indicate the degree to which you agree with the following propositions related to your firm:	**0.882**		
	1. There are standard procedures each person has to follow in performing his/her job ($c1 \leftrightarrow c2$)[c]		0.695	8,241
	2. Written procedures are available to deal with whatever situation arises		0.771	7,420
	3. There is strict enforcement of written rules and procedures		0.868	2,257
	4. Employees are constantly checked on for rule violations		0.744	7,900
Performance-oriented management (Cardinal, 2001; Gibson and Birkinshaw, 2004; Snell, 1992)	Systems in the firm encourage employees to…	**0.787**		
	1. Reach challenging and aggressive short-term goals		0.748	6.434
	2. Be held accountable for their performance		0.795	5.578
	3. Be rewarded or punished based on rigorous measurement of business performance		0.719	6.923
	4. Use their appraisal feedback to improve their performance		0.517	8.526

(Continued)

Long-term organizational focus
Second order factorization model:

$\chi 2 = 18{,}050$ ($p = 0.321$); **RMSEA = 0.02; GFI = 0.975; CFI = 0.997; IFI = 0.997; NNFI = 0.995;** α **= 0.874**[e]

Variable	Scale items	α	SRW[a]	CR[b]
Creativity (Amabile et al., 1996; Gibson and Birkinshaw, 2004)	Please indicate the degree to which you agree with the following propositions related to your firm:	**0.769**		
	1. It gives everyone sufficient authority to do their job (c1$_{creativity}$ ↔ c1$_{risk}$)		0.524	8.823
	2. It values creativity and new ideas		0.801	6.729
	3. It encourages experimentation on innovation projects		0.894	4.164
	4. It issues creative challenges to their people (c4$_{creativity}$ ↔ c1$_{risk}$)		0.565	8.704
Risk taking (Gibson and Birkinshaw, 2004)	Systems in the firm encourage employees to....	**0.769**		
	1. Be willing to take risks (c1 ↔ c3)[c]		0.698	8.018
	2. Treat failure as a learning opportunity		0.897	4.017
	3. Consider taking risks as a way to improve performance		0.818	6.318
	4. Have access to resources for innovation with no certainty of success		0.622	8.523

[a] Standardized regression weights; [b] Critical ratio of variance; [c] Item x (here c1) is correlated to item y (here c2). [d] Short-term organizational focus confirmatory independent model: $\chi 2 = 46{,}162$ ($p = 0.000$); RMSEA = 0.10; GFI = 0.940; CFI = 0.940; IFI = 0.956; NNFI = 0.935. [e] Long-term organizational focus confirmatory independent model: $\chi 2 = 55{,}947$ ($p = 0.000$); RMSEA = 0.18; GFI = 0.870; CFI = 0.829; IFI = 0.831; NNFI = 0.748.

Appendix B.   Descriptive statistics.

Variables	Mean	Sd.	1	2	3	4	5
Industry	0.48	—					
Services	0.34	—					
Other sectors	0.18	—					
Exploitation Innovation	1.40	0.62					
Exploration Innovation	1.99	0.61					
1. Ambidexterity score	2.61	1.05	1.0000				
2. Short-term organizational focus	0.97	0.28	0.2848	1.0000			
3. Long-term organizational focus	1.71	0.71	0.0877	0.2062	1.0000		
4. Competence exploitation	1.39	0.54	0.3600	0.5159	0.4416	1.0000	
5. Competence exploration	2.99	0.96	0.1034	0.3408	0.6263	0.4751	1.0000

Chapter 11

The Organisation of "Knowledge Bases"

Jonathan Sapsed
CENTRIM, University of Brighton, UK

Introduction

"Knowledge bases" within organisations are usually conceptualised as technical or functional disciplines, such as mechanical engineering, electronic engineering, marketing, accounts, project management and so forth. Typically, management scholars analyse the knowledge bases profile of firms by proxy measures such as the patents or publications generated within these disciplines, where they are available.[1] Similarly, practicing managers often organise their firms with the disciplinary categories in mind. Even where an organisation is designed to mix them up: such as in matrix or cross-functional management, knowledge assets are persistently thought of at the high level of functions.

This chapter argues that there is an inconspicuous sub-level of specialised knowledge base associated with tools, products, project experience and requirements that may hamper the intents of higher level organisation design. The concept of "knowledge bases" is operationalised not as disciplinary fields or sub-fields but at the level of the team. The chapter

---

[1]Exemplary studies of the patent analysis tradition include Granstrand *et al.*, 1997; Patel and Pavitt, 1997; Brusoni *et al.*, 2001. This chapter is based on an article published in the Special Issue in honour of Keith Pavitt of *International Journal of Innovation Management*: "How should 'Knowledge Bases' be Organised in Multi-Technology Corporations?", 2005, **9**(1), 75–102.

shows how individual engineers share or do not share their knowledge with team members and their colleagues outside the team. By considering these dynamics, which are rooted in identity, career aspirations and learning paths, we gain a more complete understanding of knowledge bases and how to organise them.

The chapter analyses two case studies of organisations attempting to manage transitions aimed at improved co-ordination processes. These are similar firms in high-tech, multi-technology, knowledge-intensive businesses. Both are project-based, in the same geographical region and about the same size, yet they have taken their organisations in contrary directions. The first has moved from organisation around functional disciplines to product-based, cross-functional teams, while the second has done the reverse. The chapter reviews the effects of these different organisational solutions on the processes of knowledge integration within the firms, the effects on communities of practice and the ways in which the systems have developed and adapted in response to the reorganisations.

The next section in the chapter reviews the literature on cross-functional teamworking, pointing out the controversy over its purported advantages. It shows that there are tensions generated by cross-functional team structures. The third section addresses these tensions by looking at the received theory on social identification and the more recent work on communities of practice. In the following section we outline the method for the study; an inductive approach based on grounded theory procedures that attempt to guard against tautological research. Next we outline five categories that were common across the two companies: organisational change; knowledge integration; loss effects and problems; deployment of expertise and evolution. We close by offering two conclusions.

Cross-functional Teamworking

It is a commonly found proposition in the management literature that cross-functional teams or matrix-style organisation is associated with better knowledge sharing, and consequently, better performance than pure functional forms (e.g. Eisenhardt and Tabrizi, 1995; Cummings, 2004). But the discussion of functional organisation versus cross-functional organisation is not new. The distinction between functional and project-oriented organisation was well described by Sapolsky in 1972, in a military context:

> "A functionally specialized organization is responsible for a partic-
> ular organizational process or skill, e.g. aeronautical engineering,
> accounting, or typing, irrespective of the purposes to which those
> processes or skills are applied. A project-type organization is
> responsible for a particular organizational purpose, e.g. strategic
> retaliation, conventional warfare, or counterinsurgency, and thus
> ties together all the process and skills necessary to accomplish that
> purpose." (p. 62)

Indeed, Sapolsky (1972) himself referred to "the classical statement"
on the distinction by Luther Gulick in 1937. While the lineage goes
back some time, in recent years cross-functional project teamworking
has emerged as an important imperative for organisations and the subject
of considerable managerial and scholarly attention. Empirical research
suggests that most new product development (NPD) activity uses the cross-
functional form (Griffin, 1997). Gobeli and Larson (1987) present data for
a sample of 1,634 project managers in NPD, construction and new services
and processes where less than 50% of managers used a pure functional
structure, while 85% used some form of cross-functional matrix structure.
As regards performance, Holland *et al.*'s (2000) review shows that inter-
functional communication and transparency was correlated or associated
with successful NPD projects.

Cross-functionality is only one type of diversity that is said to benefit
teamworking outcomes, alongside age, gender, ethnicity, personal background, etc. Roberts (1987) asserts that diversity of technical background,
age and values appears to heighten project team performance, as well as
maintaining tension and challenge in the team. Too much similarity, comfort
and familiarity reduces productivity and tends against the refreshment
of technical knowledge through external contacts. Leonard and Sensiper
(1998) argue that although diversity entails the management of divergent
viewpoints, this "creative abrasion" can generate discussion and thought,
resulting in new ideas. Leonard and Sensiper suggest "... intellectually heterogeneous groups are more innovative than homogeneous ones." (p. 118).

However, research on diverse teams also shows that group members
tend to have lower job satisfaction, higher turnover and higher stress

(Keller, 2001). By contrast to traditional functional silos, in terms of knowledge management there is a problem in co-ordinating a diverse set of areas of expertise (Denison *et al.*, 1996). While various authors argue that for systemic tasks like NPD, cross-functional teams (CFTs) are more effective, Roberts (1987) and Allen (1984) claim functional organisations show the best technical performance. This is contested by Gobeli and Larson's (1987) study, which shows that project managers generally felt that dedicated cross-functional project teams and project matrix-type structures were judged most effective on criteria of technical performance, costs and schedule. More functional configurations were considered ineffective.

Roberts (1987) warns of the erosion of technical skills if a cross-functional project team is maintained over time. Engineers are removed from the disciplinary structure of their functions, and while matrix organisation is a noble ideal, usually one interest dominates. There is often tension and conflict. Members of cross-functional teams, which are typically temporary working groups, often act as champions of their respective functions (Denison *et al.*, 1996). Donnellon (1993) refers to team members withholding their functional knowledge from the CFT as a means of defending functional territory. As a practical solution Donnellon suggests shifting the role of the functional manager away from controlling the resources that are "made available" to CFTs, in favour of a "supplier" role; teams themselves should be responsible for delivery. This generally supports Gobeli and Larson's position above that recommends the balance of responsibility in favour of project team managers.

Teamworking, Identity and Communities of Practice

These tensions could simply be interpreted as the group-serving bias observed in behavioural decision-making research, which is shown to have an even greater effect than self-serving biases (Taylor and Doria, 1981). However, individual and group identity is another notion fraught with problems and factorial issues. Social identification theory suggests that the immediate group is often more salient for the individual than an abstract, secondary organisation, as the immediate group is where interpersonal proximity and task interdependence is greatest (Ashforth and Mael, 1989). The immediate group can be a functional discipline or project team, but typically individuals have multiple, conflicting identities in the organisation. These are usually unresolved and are managed separately — "compartmentalised" — sometimes giving rise to hypocrisy and "selective forgetting" (Ashforth and Mael, 1989, p. 35).

For the ethnomethodology field — the study of sense making in everyday life — the team context is not so much imposed by the external functions of the collected team members, as negotiated and achieved through the individuals' interactions in the team setting (Sharrock, 1974; Housley, 2000). Work on individual and group productivity bears this out. Roberts (1987) observes that in the innovation literature the nature of the immediate work group in terms of composition and supervision matter greatly to productivity among technical professionals, in addition to exogenous factors like the individuals' job maturity.

This somewhat dated debate becomes relevant again with the current interest in "communities of practice", as described by Lave and Wenger (1991) and Brown and Duguid (1991) — "These groups of interdependent participants provide the work context within which members construct both shared identities and the social context that helps those identities to be shared." (Brown and Duguid, 2001, p. 202). These communities naturally emerge around local work practice and so tend to reinforce "balkanisation" around functions or occupation, but also extend to wider, dispersed networks of similar practitioners (van Maanen and Barley, 1984; Constant, 1987). Brown and Duguid's solution is "intercommunal negotiation" of differently practising individuals, challenging and stretching each other's assumptions about ways of working. Cross-functional teamworking is an organisational setting that promotes this kind of intercommunal negotiation.

But the real value of cross-functional teamworking appears to be the channels it opens to the bodies of knowledge that are exogenous to the team. This is confirmed by recent research by Keller (2001), which shows that there is an important mediating variable between cross-functional diversity in a team and performance: external communications. By itself, functional diversity had a strong, negative direct effect on budget performance, and no direct effect on schedules, but the presence of external communications effects improvement to technical quality, schedule and budget performance, but reduces group cohesiveness.

In general, a high frequency of knowledge sharing outside of the group has long been established as positively related to performance, as gatekeeper individuals pick up and import vital signals and understanding (Allen, 1984; Ancona and Caldwell, 1992; Brown and Utterback, 1985). In particular, cross-functional composition in teams is argued to permit access to disciplinary knowledge bases outside (Sapsed *et al.*, 2002).

From this discussion, several threads of research point to a view that cross-functional teamworking may be regarded as an organisational means of promoting the exchange of knowledge and practice across disciplines and communities. The literature suggests that this benefits creative activities such as NPD but there are associated penalties with regard to technical performance and professional career development. The picture that emerges is one of teamworking as organisational design (Galbraith, 1994; Mohrman *et al.*, 1995) to promote the objectives of knowledge sharing, as well as the accustomed objective of efficiency in manufacturing operations (Tranfield *et al.*, 2000).

Method

The empirical research presented here consists of two case studies of companies attempting to design and implement contrary organisational designs to manage essentially the same sorts of problems that arise in project-based, complex task environments. The two case study organisations, LandTraining Simulations and Visual Displays,[2] both operate in high-tech project-based businesses in related sectors and provide differentiated products to many of the same customers. The products and solutions they develop require integrated contributions from several diverse knowledge fields and technical disciplines. Both development facilities are located within a mile of each other in the UK, although they have corporate affiliations in North America (Box 1).

For these similarities the organisations make comparable case studies for comparison. Although one, LandTraining Simulations, is a division of a much larger organisation and the other, Visual Displays, is independent, LandTraining Simulations is quite autonomous in terms of its organisational operations and management. The two face similar structural constraints from country, region and industry, have similarly sized workforces with

---

[2]These names are used instead of the actual companies' for reasons of confidentiality.

LandTraining Simulations

LandTraining Simulations is a provider of customised simulators and training solutions to military and civilian markets. It is based in a cluster of simulation firms in the UK, but is a division of a 5000-employee international business headquartered in North America. Because of volatility in the defence industry and the project-based nature of the business, the division's workforce fluctuates from year-to-year from 60–200 staff. Its products support training of land-based military applications such as for air defence, artillery and tanks, and battle command and control simulation. Civilian applications include simulators to train airline pilots. The products are typically high value, highly customised or one-off units. They are complex products to develop, requiring the integration of various engineering disciplines; software, design, databases, production, electro-mechanical and electronic. In addition, specialist knowledge of the applications is required, such as image generation or user-end knowledge such as the behaviour of artillery in the field.

Increasingly, LandTraining Simulations has had to recruit and build capability in a new and different product area, microcomputer-based training (CBT), which is proving to be an effective and low-cost alternative to high-end customised simulators. In response, LandTraining Simulations has been trying to effect a shift in thinking away from technology and equipment to training needs and solutions.

Visual Displays

Visual Displays is a supplier of high-end screen displays and structures for a wide range of visualisation applications. These include corporate presentation and broadcasting, training devices and a growing range of applications in virtual reality for education and engineering, as well in entertainment. Visual was created in 1984 to take advantage of the trend towards outsourcing of subsystems in simulators. While the firm is developing markets for the newer applications, its core customer

Box 1.

base remains that of simulators in the same way as their neighbour LandTraining, for whom they have supplied screen modules. The firm is organised around three core cross-functional teams that specialise in specific product lines. Although this permits a degree of standardisation, the workflow is project based and involves high degrees of customisation for each client. The production of these display systems requires the integration of knowledge bases in electronics, mechanical engineering, software and structural design as well as specific know-how in optics, projectors and mirrors. Increasingly, Liquid Crystal Displays are being introduced to this product market.

The firm has been growing at a steady rate of around 20% for ten years and is entering a stage of consolidation and maturity, as distinct from its early period as an entrepreneurial start-up. It currently has 170 employees, most of which are at the firm base in the same simulation cluster as LandTraining Simulations. Visual Displays also has sales and marketing branches and a spin-off Virtual Reality company in North America.

Box 1.   (*Continued*)

similar skill sets, and need to cope with the same problems of knowledge integration and uncertain, discontinuous business conditions. What is particularly intriguing for research purposes with these two case studies is that despite the resemblance, each has designed and implemented organisational changes that move in contrary directions. LandTraining Simulations has moved from project-based, cross-functional teams to a predominantly functional organisation, while Visual Displays has done the reverse.

The research was aimed at exploring and understanding the team-working and knowledge dynamics and the effects of the reorganisations. The research process was influenced by the procedures and thinking of grounded theory (Glaser and Strauss, 1967; Strauss and Corbin, 1990). Grounded theory is an inductive approach to research that is concerned with avoiding preconceptions and the tautological confirmation of them. It is useful for research aiming at deep contextual understanding where labelling and analysis is tightly coupled to observed or recorded phenomena. In LandTraining Simulations, the author conducted 15 face-to-face interviews with software team leaders, project managers, managers for systems engineering and purchasing, a systems architect and a director for engineering and software. In Visual Displays, 13 interviews were conducted with product team managers, technical development managers, programme managers, directors of sales and marketing, product strategy, operations and corporate organisation. The interviews had a modal length of one hour each.

Company documentation was also collected and analysed, including organisational diagrams, internal presentations used to support the initiatives and process and procedure documents such as work breakdown structures. The interviews were semi-structured but diversions from the "script" were also explored and recorded as respondents occasionally raised important issues that were unanticipated. The interviews were taped, transcribed and the data was systematically coded according to categories, properties and dimensional scales (Strauss and Corbin, 1990). For example, the following quote from one project manager:

> "... if you're designing a switch box then the electrical guys are designing all the wiring and the circuit, and the mechanical guy [is] designing the box to put it in and where on a particular piece of equipment this box is going to fit, so they work very closely together. And that has been a problem in the past; that the electrical guys go off and do their thing, the mechanical guys go off and do their thing and when you come to actually put this unit together it doesn't fit ... that's improved now, it only happens once and it's improved it, it is just a matter of banging heads together."

was coded as follows:

Category: Team knowledge requirement
Property: Product integration
Dimensional scale: Cross-discipline interaction — no interaction.

All interviews were systematically coded in this way, building up a table of variables for each organisation. Relationships between these variables were then mapped, which allowed the subsuming of many of them, revealing five categories that were common to both organisations: organisational change; effects on knowledge integration; loss effects and problems; deployment of expertise and evolution.

Such grounded theory procedures intrinsically involve subjective interpretation but efforts are made to leave an audit trail and to validate the constructs with others to check for empirical reliability. The results were verified with the practitioners from the firms through interactive workshops and written reports, as well as academic colleagues. Finally, follow-up interviews were conducted approximately one year after the initial interviews in order to check that the results were robust over time and not unduly affected by the "snapshot" approach. This follow-up phase revealed what had subsequently occurred in the firms and resulted in the fifth factor, evolution. The two firms are compared under each of the five key factors below (Table 1).

The Case Studies

Organisational change and the role of boundary objects

The first category relates to the transitions in the two organisations; the motivations for them and the artefacts and tools — so-called boundary objects — that were developed to facilitate the changes.

LandTraining Simulations

LandTraining Simulations' organisation structure was previously oriented around project-based, cross-functional teams, in which engineers worked

Table 1.   Key factors in the case study organisations.

	Organisation design	Knowledge integration	Loss effects	Deployment of expertise	Evolution
Land Training Simulations	From CF project teams to functional groups.	Regular reviewing and integration of project pieces.	Project manager loses control.	Niche experts and generalist systems architects.	Project teams for novel projects.
Visual Displays	From functional groups to CF product teams.	Improved product lines. Inter-team knowledge breakdown.	Engineers losing community and skills breadth.	Generalists deployed on R&D.	Functions co-locating. Middle tier emerging in teams.

LandTraining Simulations

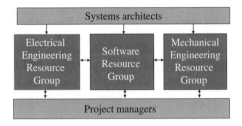

Fig. 1.

for "heavyweight" project managers. This has changed to a functional system organised around technical disciplines called "resource groups", with project managers procuring pieces of work as deliverables from the functional managers. Groups from each discipline are assigned to the project with one engineer designated as the group leader for that project (Fig. 1).

This is the form of organisation Donnellon (1993) argues that effectively relegates functional managers to the position of suppliers of resources, which should tend to encourage their co-operation from a project management viewpoint. The reorganisation was motivated by two concerns. First, management were aware that under the prior system an engineer with a particular skill may have been required on one project and "owned" by another team. The change was intended to make engineering resources more widely accessible and allocated more suitably. Secondly, engineers had been dissatisfied with the old project-based system because they were frequently working in isolation from their technical peers. The transition to functional groups was attempting to re-establish closer ties within the disciplines. The engineers took advantage of a move to a new building with large, open-plan space and set up their workspaces in functional tribal settlements.

To support the changes, representatives of all functions were involved in the creation of graphical process maps, showing linkages between the key players and groups in the new project process. These maps were devised by a cross-functional working group, effectively serving as boundary objects (Star and Griesemer, 1989), artefacts that embody and symbolise negotiated agreement between the different communities (Brown and Duguid, 2001; Carlile, 2002). By contrast, key performance indicators (KPIs) for the measurement of overheads, project completions, overspend, etc. were developed at engineering development meetings and implemented within the functions. While the interfaces between communities are agreed at the boundaries and embodied in the process maps, the KPIs enable measurement within the functional communities.

Visual Displays

Visual Displays' reorganisation was antithetical to LandTraining Simulations'. Visual moved from a functional system into three cross-functional teams that specialise in three product lines: first, wide "panorama"style screens; secondly, wraparound, spherical screens with several projectors blending to generate the image; and thirdly, special customised products with a rear-mounted projector. Each team has between 10 and 20 projects ongoing within the product line. Bids, sales and marketing and R&D functions were located outside of the product teams. Project managers were combined together with electronic, mechanical and commissioning engineers in the multi-disciplinary teams, in order to achieve a greater customer focus and relationship. There was also a desire to promote learning across disciplines, as the firm's corporate organisation director explained, "ideally a display engineer is multi-disciplinary, he is an expert in one technology but knows something about all of them. The idea of the teams was that engineers would pick up skills from the other disciplines."

To compensate for breaking up the functional disciplines, a new management role was introduced, the technical development manager (TDM). TDMs were appointed for electronic design, mechanical design and programme management and were intended to provide leadership for the functional discipline. Although "owned" by an individual team, the idea was that they would lead their functional communities across the organisation (Fig. 2). This is a quasi-matrix device often recommended for project-based organisations (e.g. Hobday, 2000).

Visual Displays' reorganisation was a much more planned and deliberate strategy than LandTraining Simulations'. The perceived need for a more formal organisation design to improve communications came about because of the firm's growth of 30% per annum. The directors wanted to mix up disciplines, which they felt had become large enough to become too entrenched and internally focused. Similarly to LandTraining, this was an effect of the previous building which encouraged "groupishness" through

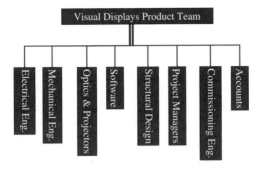

Fig. 2.

its architecture of several small rooms, each of which housed a co-located functional group. The reorganisation preceded a move to a new building, which permitted large, open plan spaces.

There was a 12-month process of design, advocacy and planning during which all disciplines were consulted. The initiative was managed by a cross-functional working group involving strategic retreats, regular presentations on the new organisation structure with consultation on details like job designs. The initiative was supported by internal publicity, including a countdown poster campaign and T-shirts. A definite "D-Day" date was set when people would move desks and take up their new roles.

This long period of consultation served to span boundaries between the disciplinary communities, so that the new organisation design was built on a base of consensual legitimacy. Similarly to the process maps in LandTraining, an important boundary object developed in Visual Displays was a cross-team work breakdown structure (WBS). This was intended to give an operational focus to complement the product focus achieved by the reorganisation. Previously, projects and functions had their own spreadsheets, databases and time-cost reporting. The introduction of the WBS meant that they could now plan and measure against the same codes, and could begin using enterprise management tools. The WBS was based on a product structure, a hierarchical architecture of product sub-assemblies and components, negotiated jointly between engineers of all the disciplines.

The WBS is an effective boundary object, framed at a high enough level to allow discretion over the activities reported within the codes, but allowing for monitoring of overspending. Code categories include, for instance, technical investigation, performance characteristics review, system testing and so on. This is an example of the distinction between the framing and content of complex management problems and solutions, as shown by Fiol (1994). Consensus is achieved with the framing of the problem, the need for accounting and accountability, the cash flow pressures of a project-based organisation, the need for common approaches to project management for better integration, but leaving sufficient scope for the inescapable content discrepancies and divergences within the agreed structure. In both companies, boundary objects played an important role in facilitating the reorganisations through providing informational support and symbolising agreement between the communities.

Effects on knowledge integration

The second category refers to the task of integrating the diverse knowledge bases in the development and installation of products. This involves teamworking through consulting colleagues, reviewing, verifying and final integration both within and between the newly created teams.

LandTraining Simulations

The integration of knowledge resources is stressed as a key capability for turning the ownership of those resources into competitive advantage (Grant, 1991, 1996a, 1996b). For both LandTraining and Visual, the major problems of projects arise with integrating the pieces of the project together. These problems tend to occur late on in the production phase. Integration is complex and all about teamworking. But "teamworking" in this task environment is generally a matter of individuals independently completing their project pieces and validating these with others prior to the pieces being integrated "... most people can work largely in isolation, they are following their schedules that are laid down on the Gantt charts, but they're generally doing fairly individual things ... "[3] or more bluntly "... people don't tend to talk to other people, they just sit and code their chunk." [4]

---

[3] Author's interview with software team leader A, LandTraining Simulations.
[4] Author's interview with software team leader C, LandTraining Simulations.

However, communication becomes critical at the integration stage, as explained by this software team leader:

"... you can still break it down into bits, and they go off and do their bit and then come back and say, 'I have finished'. And it's at that point that you've got to fit all the bits together and hopefully, they talked to each other whilst it has been going on, and then fitting all the bits together is a lot easier ... in the end, if people have been speaking then it all comes together much more smoothly, it wastes a lot less time in trying to iron out problems".[5]

So although the teamworking in the company is not interdependent on a task level in the short term, in the sense that one team member cannot proceed without a colleague's actions, a high degree of communication is important in integrating the quite different knowledge bases together. Problems occur if validation and cross-checking has been insufficient and these problems are exacerbated if engineers are part-time players on a project. However, in general, managers in LandTraining reported a preference for the new functional system shortly after the change was made. They found that engineers were less tied-up than in the prior project-teamworking system.

Visual Displays

Meanwhile, combining technical disciplines in product teams had improved integration processes in Visual Displays. The firm had previously had problems that would only appear at the final stage of installation at the customer's site. Design and production engineers would only learn that their systems were not fitting together when the problem reached crisis point. Following the reorganisation, commissioning engineers' feedback on integration problems is communicated directly to the designers and engineers in the product teams at an early stage. Engineers have a greater sense of the "big picture", understanding the issues and problems of their colleagues in other disciplines.

However, in spite of the improvement in knowledge integration in the product development teams, breakdowns in knowledge transfer continued

---

[5] Author's interview with software team leader B, LandTraining Simulations.

to occur between the teams and the external services and functions. The non-technical bids and business development functions are dependent on the product teams' engineering knowledge, and frequently need to interrupt their workflow. There are similar problems between R&D and the product teams where new product prototypes are passed over to the product teams at a stage they consider too early. These are typical problems that arise in complex organisations where knowledge integration is an inter-team, as much as an intra-team organisational problem (Grant, 1996a, 1996b, 2001; Sapsed *et al.*, 2002).

Loss effects and problems

The third common category was associated with various perceptions of loss and dispossession resulting from the reorganisations.

LandTraining Simulations

One objective of the change to functional organisation was to satisfy engineers' needs for exposure and organisational proximity to their disciplinary community.

> "... one of the problems that the guys found in the project teams and they were always moaning because ... you might have three, four software engineers on a project where there were thirty or forty in the company and they got isolated over in their project group. They were always talking to the 'leccies [electrical engineers] and the clankies [mechanical engineers] and they never got to talk to their colleagues [laughs]. So they always felt a bit sort of isolated from their colleagues and felt they were missing out on the engineering chit-chat that goes on and the cross-fertilisation and in a way I think they felt a lack of technical leadership".[6]

Organisation into functional groups has effectively addressed this desire for regular contact with disciplinary peers. But there is a corresponding denuding of the project manager. Some complained of the loss of their previous pastoral role, where the project manager was responsible for all the

---

[6] Author's interview with project manager A, LandTraining Simulations.

team members' appraisals and personal development. Another frustration is the shift in authority between the project manager and the resource group manager:

> "I've got no one in this company that works for me so I have not only got to manage people who are working for my project, I have also got to manage the management because I am dependent on them as well. I'm dependent on them to release the resources — the resources that I want at the time I want them".[7]

This belies the view that this form of organisation relegates functional managers to mere "supplier" status as described by Donnellon (1993). The experience in LandTraining Simulations suggests commitment to release resources can be difficult to attain and that the balance of power favours the functional manager.

Visual Displays

Visual's shift from functional teams to cross-functional teams brought the equal and opposite effects to LandTraining's reversion to functions. One director commented "I think we've lost some things. I think we've lost technical specialisms. When all the designers worked together, they learned a lot from each other."[8] Lack of regular exposure to technical peers has the effects of eroding the currentness of the individual engineers' skill sets and losing the benefits of disciplinary communities of practice. One product team manager explained:

> "... as a company although we're quite small, we've got quite a cross section of engineering skills, when you look at all three teams. When you look at them [the engineers] individually unfortunately, it tends to narrow them down a bit. That's not just my view ... we're aware that their skill levels are very directed towards their own team, and really couldn't jump straight into another team and start working effectively. That would not happen".[9]

---

[7] Author's interview with project manager A, LandTraining Simulations.
[8] Author's interview with director A, Visual Displays.
[9] Author's interview with technical development manager A, Visual Displays.

Although gaining a sense of the "big picture" for their team's product, the engineers lose the overall viewpoint of the organisation. A corollary of team specialisation on products is a tendency towards balkanisation on product lines rather than functions "... it has almost set up three different companies", one TDM observed. The TDM role of maintaining technical community across the teams has proved difficult to achieve as the pressures of current projects in the product team take priority:

> "... unfortunately you're up against team leaders who control their own teams and they're not going to really want their staff to spend a lot of time doing for example, learning about another product, spending time with another team. If for example, Panorama is stuck for one design engineer, they need one from another team, that is their first port of call that's what they've got to say, 'well, I need another person, can these other teams supply him' and they'll immediately go on the defensive saying 'Oh no, we can't let anyone go' [laughs]. I'm not suggesting that is the case but sometimes maybe it is. You may end up employing some contractor, get round it some other way. So that side of it is not so flexible, [if] we had all the design engineers in one group, it's just a case of moving work around between them, because the team environment was not an issue. It does tend to put up walls, there's no doubt about that. It's got its pluses and its minuses, if you ask my opinion it's got more pluses than minuses".[10]

This shows that in some respects knowledge sharing and teamworking was actually damaged as a result of introducing cross-functional team structure. In both cases, there were significant loss effects as a result of the reorientations of teams.

Deployment of expertise

The fourth category relates to expertise; how it develops and becomes specialised, the implications of this specialisation for the organisation, and how experts and gurus are deployed.

---

[10] Author's interview with technical development manager A, Visual Displays.

LandTraining Simulations

The software and engineering teams in LandTraining contain a diversity of specialised knowledge bases. Individuals within teams tend to develop specific know-how, for instance, in image generation or user interfaces, and are then deployed on tasks in subsequent projects that draw on this same knowledge. Over time they accumulate an expertise and this specialisation is reinforced on successive projects. The downside of this is that this knowledge is uneven across the teams and the organisation. The one or two experts on a key technology or tool are not always available when their expertise is demanded, presenting a major resource-loading problem. This specialism may be in a particular engineering field, for example, all three software teams call upon an engineer with expertise in sound. Specific product knowledge is also rare and valuable. One software manager describes the dilemma associated with one engineer's rare knowledge of the DEC PDP product family[11] as well as the specific application:

> "... this particular guy who's been here a long time, and he has got excellent experience in a number of areas, and the thing is he is a major player on one of the current projects, and if we get this Skyfire [project] we will need him very badly for that one because he used to work on Skyfire many, many years ago and it's an old PDP product. Most of us don't have any knowledge of PDPs now; none of us know really how that product used to work apart from him .... Generally our products now are PC-based, this one's in the days of PDP. So he's currently allocated .... But he is really needed on Skyfire as well, so if we win Skyfire, what the hell do we do? He's allocated up to his eyeballs so we are almost just hoping that he can finish that before we go on Skyfire, and I don't know how the hell you'd ever train up someone to pick up Skyfire. Yes, you might get someone who knows PDP and who knows Assembler and things like that, but they won't know the product".[12]

---

[11]The DEC PDP was a line of minicomputers in the 1960s, which later evolved into micro or supermicro computers in the 1970s and 1980s.

[12]Author's interview with software team leader A, LandTraining Simulations.

From a project-completion viewpoint, it makes more sense to deploy the specialists on tasks rather than the less-experienced:

> "Most engineers are capable of doing all the tasks, it's just how efficient they will do those tasks ... you know that if you can get someone else to do it, but it's going to take twelve weeks, as opposed to someone who can do it in two weeks. You know, because they have got to be trained for eight weeks and then they make loads of mistakes and then that's got to be redone, and they have got to have all the training there and so on. So people are very much in their own little area and I don't think it is a bad thing I think that really does focus people's skills most of the time, and I think it does mean we get a much better product in my view ..."[13]

However, there is also the recognition that this reinforcement of expertise tends to promote a teamworking structure around knowledge specialisms, which undermines the firm's organisational strategy:

> "... What we don't want in the company of course is an I[mage] G[eneration] team and a GUI [Graphical User Interface] team and a core services team. That's not the way the company has been structured, but effectively it is because we have one or two people who do GUIs, some of them do IGs and so on, and we keep those people in those areas of work .... I just think these people are in those specialist areas, so you almost have two levels of teams, in some respects".[14]

This admission illustrates how there are levels of "knowledge base" within an organisational structure. At a high, abstract level there are the technical disciplines (within which patenting activity can be observed and measured). Yet below this is a level of specialisation that relates to particular products, processes and tasks that is not so easily identifiable. Typically, senior management organises at the first level, while project managers, engineering and resource managers find themselves organising at the second. The two

---

[13] Author's interview with software team leader C, LandTraining Simulations.

[14] Author's interview with software team leader C, LandTraining Simulations.

levels may be, and frequently are, in conflict from a knowledge sharing and development perspective. Often, people are assigned to organisational units reflecting their broad profession, but in terms of how they allocate their time and attention they serve the pressing requirements of operations. Their "specialised expertise" is in knowing how to efficiently achieve results in a set of activities with high entry barriers of learning, rather than in a particular subfield of their engineering discipline.

In LandTraining, specialist experts do not appear to be affected by the reorganisation in terms of their everyday activities. However, LandTraining also has a small group of generalist experts. These are the "throbbing heads", gurus who possess rare knowledge bases combining know-how from all the engineering domains that go into producing simulators, albeit uneven. This expertise has accumulated over years of experience in the industry, and is complemented by insights into the idiosyncrasies of the business process, and the dynamics of competition.

LandTraining's management have deployed these experts as "systems architects" focusing their attention largely on the bid stage of the process. This design was attempting to provide an overview to more accurately cost bids and assess the feasibility of prospects. The functional teams could be seen to have a fragmented and "localised" perspective on bids, and the systems architect role was introduced to provide overview, which is seen as critical to bid work. Previously, there was a perceived discontinuity from bid team to project team, which were typically entirely different sets of people. Under the new system, the systems architects work intensively on the bid, defining the engineering solution and cost framework. Following contract award, their involvement tapers off, but is still available as a resource for consultation.

Visual Displays

Visual Displays also has a small number of highly experienced engineers named the "display gurus". One director explains:

> "There are a handful of people in the company that you can identify as a display guru. We can't go to the universities and take graduates who've taken a course in display systems, because of course those courses don't exist, so we've got to breed them ourselves, develop

them and train them. They are very much a multi-disciplinary person — its electronics expertise, mechanical, design, optical, software; it's a mixture of all those things".[15]

But unlike LandTraining Simulations, these experts are deployed as a R&D team, working on a variety of internal projects that address the applications that the market will want in years to come. This is consistent with the Visual organisation design in which the "erudite overview" should be less critical than in LandTraining, because of the compensating influence of the TDMs and the cross-fertilisation in the teams. In practice, the interface between the R&D team, bids and the product teams is problematic, the point at which prototypes are passed on to the more commercially-oriented teams is ambiguous. In addition, the accumulated expertise of the display gurus is not easily accessible to the product engineers since they are organisationally and philosophically separate. R&D engineers nevertheless find themselves distracted from their R&D projects by bid work, in effect enacting the systems architects role in LandTraining. Both organisations find their specialists are deployed more or less on the same tasks as before the changes, while their generalists' time is spread thinly on support activities.

Evolution

This fifth category, evolution, was added following validation research visits one year after the initial fieldwork was conducted. It captures the subsequent adaptation to the new system, which to some extent might also be interpreted as "slippage" into the original state.

LandTraining Simulations

LandTraining's organisational structure has changed significantly since implementation of the changes. The previous section referred to the "teams within teams" that exist within LandTraining Simulations as an effect of knowledge specialisations. Subsequent to the reorganisation, the large software team of 25 people has been formally divided into three small teams, focusing on projects requiring three distinctive software competences,

---

[15] Author's interview with director A, Visual Displays.

as well as some "floaters" who will work in all areas. To some degree then, project-based team structure has re-emerged, which reintroduces the concern among engineers that they will become too embedded in one area of application. One software team leader put it "... I think people are a little bit unsure and unhappy about [it] because not everyone likes the category they're currently working on and the ... thing is 'well, am I going to get stuck in this one?'" [16]

In addition, some cross-functional teamworking has been reintroduced. For projects that involve a high degree of novelty for the firm, project managers have asserted the need for a dedicated team of people drawn on a full-time basis from the resource groups. The resulting organisation is rationalised as CFTs for new, novel projects, functional organisation for familiar, "business as usual" work.

Visual Displays

Similarly, some of the old order is re-emerging in Visual Displays. Physical layout now resembles the previous structure, as team members of the same discipline have all moved their desks together. This is professedly because of the differing preferences for lighting and noise levels between the functions, but may also be interpreted as the tribal instinct returning.

Again similar to LandTraining, another management layer has formed in all three product teams. The original design was attempting to maintain as flat a hierarchy as possible, but the size of the teams was too large for one team leader to handle. In fact, the senior management of Visual is considering another reorganisation to address some of the deficiencies of the current system. These include the inter-team breakdowns of knowledge transfer noted above, e.g. making the product team more responsible for bids work and trying to better integrate product team engineers and R&D engineers working on new product development.

Although the development from the original designs is categorised as evolution, correcting and adapting the system after intervention, it is interesting that both organisations have reverted to previous practice to some extent. This could also be viewed as the attraction to homeostasis, as

---

[16] Author's interview with software team leader A, LandTraining Simulations.

described in Schön's (1971) *Beyond the Stable State*. Certainly, this applies as regards the reaction of the disenfranchised elements; project managers needing to direct a dedicated team for a difficult project; the impulse for engineers to colocate with their peers. These issues are discussed more generally in the conclusions.

Conclusions

The chapter has outlined the recent literature debating the best way of organising technical disciplines in multi-technology corporations. It has shown how this discussion is long-standing and echoes debates in the past. The research presented followed a grounded theory approach to two case studies of firms reorganising in contrary directions. As such, the research is subjective in its interpretation and limited in how the results may be generalised. As regards the first weakness, the author has collected data from multiple sources and attempted to validate the analysis with the practitioners from the firms involved and with academic colleagues to check that it was accurate. As for the second weakness, a follow-up stage was conducted a year after the initial research to mitigate the time-specificity of the reorganisation. However, the population of multi-technology corporations is extremely numerous and diverse and there would be a huge variety of outcomes from a range of reorganisations. The two cases here serve as powerful contrasting illustrations of cross-functional and functional organisational design. Bearing in mind the caveats, we can make the following conclusions.

The antinomy of cross-functional diversity and specialisation

The contrasting experience of the two cases shows how the benefits of specialisation bring the converse disadvantages. While cross-functional teamworking brings some benefits from a product viewpoint, there is a corresponding loss in disciplinary collegiality. Organisation on functional lines tends to the antithetical problems of disempowered project managers and challenges the integrity of projects. This suggests there is no single "best practice" for teamworking organisation in complex task environments. Rather, there appears to be an antinomy, a contradiction of equally valid principles between the advantages and drawbacks of cross-functional teamworking organisation. One seasoned project manager from LandTraining Simulations suggested the organisation design should be influenced by the external conditions prevailing at the time; if engineers are in demand then accommodate them in a favourable structure, whereas in lean times for the firm, deploy them for organisational benefit:

"As long as I've been in the industry, it's never been resolved, there's always this movement, we've always been going backwards and forwards between one way or the other .... I don't think there is an answer; if there is, someone would have had it. We're stuck with it, the fact that we are always changing, people can recalibrate it. And again the priorities change you see, if the job market is tight [for] your project engineers you've got to be a bit more careful as to how you look after engineers, and how you feed their aspirations. If you're in a situation where there's a shortage of people out there, or recessionary times, and also you haven't got much work you've got to do, got financial pressures, then perhaps you give less priority to that, you worry about other issues, just getting the job done, and again it's a lot of external influences that could factor in."[17]

From the other side, a Visual Displays director concurs on the pros and cons of functional versus cross-functional structures:

"We have achieved a good part of what we wanted to achieve, we certainly have removed a lot of the barriers that we had, the internal walls, where problems were thrown over walls, what you do find is, you almost can't win in some respects, you knock down some walls and others emerge in other places. The issue is more one of wherever the walls pop up, trying to squash them down again, it's a constant battle. I don't believe there is any perfect ideal structures, the nature of our business is we're full of matrix structures in our organisation, and it's not just one simple matrix, it's a number of multi-dimensional matrices going on. The challenge is trying to identify where the walls are happening and trying to do things to minimise them."[18]

---

[17] Author's interview with project manager B, LandTraining Simulations.

[18] Author's interview with director A, Visual Displays.

Both firms were quite sensitive to the positive and negative effects of their teamworking designs. Various mechanisms and techniques were employed to mitigate the unfavourable consequences. Boundary spanning activities and objects were used and were important in promoting intercommunal negotiation, such as the process maps, WBS and working groups. These helped to gain agreement and understanding of the new organisations.

Less successful were the attempts to compensate for the loss effects of the new structures, such as the TDMs in Visual. The technical leadership role was not fulfilled as the same individuals were also assigned to specific product teams. This role may be more successful in better-resourced companies without the pressures of project-based workflow. Yet, accounts of large technical organisations show a remarkably similar pattern. One example is Jack Morton's (1971) book on the management of Bell Labs — perhaps the best resourced and most successful technical organisation of the twentieth century.

Morton, writing in 1971 about the previous three decades, shows that the concern over knowledge sharing and the co-ordination of specialisation is not a new one. He recounts the various organisational and spatial bonds that were introduced to couple Bell Labs and Western Electric, as well as AT&T and the operating companies. These bonds, such as relocation of personnel or assigning a common manager to separate units, were designed to balance the isolating effects of earlier separations. Barriers are sometimes desired to avoid domination and creativity in research and it is the job of the manager to adjust the system with bonds or barriers as is appropriate to the current situation. This recalibration, as our project manager above put it, seems to be an endless task; as Morton says, "... the job never ends" (1971, p. 63). We can see, then, that even in large technical organisations the antimony between diversity and specialisation is not easily remedied by organisational devices.

Organisation design and knowledge bases

Organisation design is a popular topic for theoretical literature and prescriptions for practitioners. This chapter outlined some often-cited ideas on designing for teamworking and for complexity. Galbraith, (1972, 1994), for example, stresses the design of complex organisations. Wageman (2001) provides evidence to suggest that team design affects team performance significantly more than any subsequent coaching. The two cases here show some of the limitations of design, as an *ex ante* means of predictable control. In both cases the outcomes were quite different to the intended plan. Both showed some "slippage" to new hybrid forms. Similar to Mintzberg's (1994a, Mintzberg *et al.*, 1996) observations of emergent corporate strategies, it may be that organisation designs are rarely implemented as they are conceived. They evolve and adapt and in a short space of time look quite different to the design. As illustrated by the two cases, they may exhibit self-organising properties as studied by work on complex open systems (see Lewin, 1999).

The cases show how natural "self-organisation" occurs and that received knowledge profiles and prior structures have a continuing influence. Land-Training Simulations' teams are actually more organised around specialised knowledge and skill sets than technical functions, as noted by one of the software team leaders, in spite of the pronounced reorganisation. While reorganisations tend to revolve around knowledge bases at the higher level of professional disciplines and functions, for convenience and efficiency engineers often find themselves deployed according to a lower level of specialisation, related to product knowledge, specific tools or non-codified ways of getting work done. The view of knowledge bases as observed through classes and subclasses of patenting activity would pick up on the first level, but probably not the second. Yet neglecting to attend to this lower level of knowledge base is an important factor in why organisation design tends to have undesired effects, or no effect at all.

Acknowledgements

This research was supported by the UK's Engineering and Physical Sciences Research Council, grants M74092 and GR/R54132/01. I am grateful to Stefano Brusoni, Mike Hobday, Raphie Kaplinsky, Paul Nightingale, Jim Utterback and the anonymous referees for their comments and suggestions. Gratitude is also due to the practitioners in the study who gave their time and insights so generously.

Chapter 12

Supplier Strategies for Integrated Innovation[1]

Thorsten Teichert
University of Hamberg, Germany

Ricarda B. Bouncken
University of Bayreuth, Germany

Introduction

Management of innovation is widely perceived as a prominent source of competitive advantage (Balachandra and Friar, 1997; Griffin, 1997) and crucial strategic issue (Henderson and Clark, 1990; Utterback, 1994) in need of alignment with a firm's overall strategy (Pinto and Prescott, 1988). Among others, Cooper and Kleinschmidt (1995; Cooper, 1984) had described five prominent factors of new product performance: process, strategy, organization, culture, and management commitment.

The investigations on success factors focusing on the single organization fail to address issues prevalent outside of the organization. Studies assume that the innovating company acts in an "empty space" without any constraints, besides those of its own innovation. This seems less plausible in the context of ongoing innovation activities in supply chains. Here, new product concepts have to be aligned with existing interfaces in both directions of the supply chain (up- and downstream) to successfully diffuse into the market.

---

[1] An earlier version of this chapter was published in the *International Journal of Innovation Management*, 2011, **15**(1), 95–120.

The innovation activities of suppliers are particularly confronted by manufacturers' requirements, such as product and process objectives, frame specifications, and target prices. These requirements can range from more informal and flexible suggestions to tight and formal upstream pre-settings. We refer to these as supply chain rigidities. Supply chain innovation rigidities result from a manufacturers' need to manage the integration of several components from different suppliers into a coherent innovation. Rigidities help to co-ordinate this multi-supplier innovation process; for example, innovations performed by one firm can more easily be integrated into the product concept of a manufacturer. Even though rigidities are important, they have not been considered in previous studies.

As supply chain rigidities may constitute a major contingency for innovation, the authors of this study believe the lack of rigidity research results in a significant gap in the literature. The more suppliers face innovation rigidities, the more is it questionable whether suppliers can pursue autonomous strategic planning and reap value from their innovation activities. As such, the question of how suppliers can increase success in an environment of rigidities must be answered. These questions include: What are the strategic options? How do soft factors, or dynamic capabilities, particularly in a planning capability and innovation orientation, influence performance and interact with the strategic approach?

This chapter's intent is to solve some of the questions in this important puzzle. We will analyze the effects of two strategic approaches on suppliers' success and the relationships between strategy and soft factors of innovation management. Our study will compare effects under conditions of high and low innovation rigidities.

For the strategic approach, we draw upon the distinction among "deliberate" and "emergent" strategy formulation (Mintzberg and McHugh, 1985). This integrates the bitter debate of whether strategies are a result of a formal and deliberate planning process or if they emerge as firms incrementally learn and experiment along their path (Brews and Hunt, 1999). Previous studies have disagreed on the superiority of a formal or emergent style of innovation project management (Brown and Eisenhardt, 1995). Given different degrees of supply chain-induced innovation rigidities, it becomes questionable whether innovation can be the object of detailed rationalized and formal planning by a single company, or of a more intuitive ad-hoc planning, which might better adapt to contingencies. As a result, we analyze the effect of rigidities on the strategic approach and aim to deliver answers to the question of whether suppliers' strategies can either be derived from a formal and deliberate planning process or emerge as suppliers incrementally learn and experiment along their path.

As customer requirements and technology change over time, internal dynamic capabilities may need to adjust according to the changes to achieve product market success. It has been determined that more innovative firms which follow soft capabilities (Alegre-Vidal *et al.*, 2004) are more liberal regarding internal conflict in maintaining creativity (Dyer and Song, 1998) and foster organizational structures that are in the intermediate zone between order and disorder (Brown and Eisenhardt, 1997). As such, an internal innovation orientation will be influential in the success of innovative suppliers. Thus, we not only investigate the strategy-performance link, but also investigate an intermediate effect of internal capabilities, namely the suppliers' innovation orientation. We also integrate a second dynamic capability, the planning capability, which acts as a flexible, contingency orientated, and goal orientated planning competence.

The results of this study will be derived by testing a structural equation model. Our model will explain how two strategic approaches can be transformed into dynamic capabilities and into market performance under different degrees of supply chain rigidities. A survey of 241 high-tech SME companies serves for the hypothesis testing. Structural equation modeling is used to reveal direct, as well as indirect, effects. While we aim to observe the direct effects of strategy on market success, we also aim to measure both the strategic planning approach to innovation, as well as the dynamic innovation capabilities, as intermediary variables in our analyses. We will apply a moderator analysis to differentiate the causal effect chain based on environmental settings, i.e. a highly (strong rigidities) and lowly (few rigidities) defined supply chain. We will also test mediator effects through the planning capability.

In summary, this chapter will attempt to bring light into the black-box of performance enhancing innovation strategy and its contingencies in the supply chain. More specifically, we research the relationship between innovation strategy approaches and success under the moderating role of high or low innovation rigidities of the supply chain. To deduce an even more fine-grained picture, we investigate the intermediary effects of capabilities. Thus, our research will contribute to the knowledge of innovation strategies, internal capabilities and their performance effects under different contingencies in a supply chain. From the multi-faceted view and the thorough methodology, we can derive suggestions for effective innovation management in supply chains.

Theory

Innovation rigidities

The assumption that the innovating company acts in an "empty space" without any constraints from its internal innovation is no longer plausible in the context of ongoing innovation activities across firms in alliances, networks and particularly in supply chains. The innovative suppliers, which are generally highly specialized, develop innovative components or modules. Innovations by several suppliers are combined into a coherent product concept of manufacturers. New product concepts and innovation strategies must be aligned with the existing interfaces of the supply chain. The multi-supplier innovation process requires co-ordination enabling innovations performed by several firms to be integrated into the product concept of a manufacturer (Gilbert *et al.*, 2003). Manufacturers in need of having to manage the integration of several components establish innovation rigidities. These can range from more informal and flexible suggestions, to tight and formal upstream presets on suppliers. We refer to these as the innovation rigidities of well-defined supply chains. Rigidities reduce the autonomy of suppliers, but can also improve suppliers' actions and innovations by providing direction, and as such, reducing uncertainty. Suppliers may face different degrees of supply chain rigidities depending on the power of the supplier, the relationship between supply chain partners, the shape of the supply chain, the dominance of consumer needs and of the overall industry structure. In particular, under high innovation rigidities, it is unclear if and how suppliers can improve upon their performance by autonomous strategic planning or by their internal innovation capabilities.

Innovation rigidities and strategic approaches

Innovation strategy can be regarded as a timed string of conditional resource allocation decisions to achieve specific goals (Ramanujam and Mensch, 1985). Commonly, an innovation strategy is understood as a description of a firm's targeted innovation position with regard to its competitive environment, in terms of its new product and market development policies (Dyer and Song, 1998). We refer to strategy as a pattern in a stream of decisions that include a commitment to actions and resources, both intended and realized (Mintzberg, 1978). Strategies can either be derived from a formal and deliberate planning process, or emerge as suppliers incrementally learn and experiment along their path (Fredrickson, 1984; Fredrickson and Iaquinto, 1989). According to the Planning School, strategy is a deliberate and "rational" (Idenburg, 1993, p. 133) process that includes an in-depth analysis of markets and an implementation of the alternatives, as a means and an end (Cohen and Cyert, 1973; Guerard *et al.*, 1990). Ansoff (1991), as the proponent of the Planning School, states that *a priori* formal planning is necessary for achieving performance. Contrarily, for emergent strategy formulation, means and ends are specified simultaneously, or intertwined (Fredrickson, 1984; Fredrickson and Iaquinto, 1989). As the emergent strategy does not concentrate on explicit objectives and formal approaches, it is necessary to react in a flexible way that muddles through by trial and error (Idenburg, 1993).

Given different high supply chain rigidities, it becomes questionable whether innovation can be the object of detailed rationalized and formal planning by a single company or of more intuitive ad-hoc planning, which better applies to contingencies and changes. Furthermore, the fulfillment of *ex ante* defined innovation goals may not be sufficient to ensure long-term success, because customers, as well as supply chain requirements, may change over time.

The stronger the supply chain rigidities a supplier faces are, the less opportunity exists for a single supplier's sovereign strategic planning. Changes induced by directives, or requirements of manufacturers, might interfere with the suppliers' forecasts, goals, and plans. As a result, suppliers might be forced into rapid competency changes. Implementations of the deliberate and formal planning might then become obsolete. External changes might require flexibility and ad-hoc creativity, which are rarely associated with formalized planning. Hence, formal strategic planning cannot provide a secure foundation for formulating a long-term strategy. Furthermore, there are significant risks of sunk costs associated with the planning process. As such, the positive factors of formal planning are likely to be absorbed by the customers' directives, in the case of high supply chain rigidities. Under low supply chain rigidities, however, suppliers will be able to improve upon their success by deliberate planning which enables them to set their own agenda for their companies' future.

High rigidities will often exist in the context of powerful downstream partners, particularly in that of large manufacturers. Manufacturers are in the position to dictate the specifications of the innovations provided by their suppliers. If manufacturers are very powerful and have a high internal innovation capability, then SMEs might only exhibit a workbench character. Generally, with growing dependence, and under high rigidities, particularly frequent changes in manufacturers' demands require higher levels of flexibility in the suppliers. Trials and experiences of an emergent strategy approach might improve suppliers' success under high rigidities. An emergent strategy's power lies in intuition, experimentation, creativity, and autonomous testing associated with trial and error. This is not available under high rigidities that may change quickly and exert strict and formal limitations to autonomous creativity and innovation development. Hence, the freedom the emergent strategy approach requires does not exist in an environment of high supply chain rigidities, which limit the freedom. Thus, an emergent strategy approach would only be advantageous for achieving long-term competitive advantage in settings of low supply chain rigidities, where suppliers can experiment with ideas, technologies, designs, and diverse interfaces of components. Thus, neither of the strategic approaches will increase their market success under high rigidities. However, internal dynamic capabilities may improve market success, even under high rigidities.

Hypothesis 1: Supply chain rigidities moderate the relationship of deliberate and emergent strategies and market successes. Both strategic types only increase market success under low supply chain rigidities.

Innovation rigidities and dynamic capabilities

A broad spectrum of innovation types have been developed and implemented in supply chains. These innovations range from new components and services for existing products, new designs, new uses, and new technological solutions, to completely new products. New products and services developed in supply chains, as such, can cover incremental, radical, and even breakthrough, innovations. Even though uncertainties increase with growing novelty, supply chain partners always have to co-ordinate the innovation task, which is a cross-functional task. As such, the diverse functions of a supplier continuously need to resonate with each other and with the markets for the successful achievement and implementation of innovations. Thus, internal dynamic capabilities are necessary to cope with change and achieve product market success. Simpson *et al.* (2006) propose that innovation capabilities impact a firm's number, rate, and type of innovations. Furthermore, Baker *et al.* (2003) postulate that firms can develop routines and structures for innovation. Following this, we identify two dynamic capabilities important for innovation performance in a supply chain. We argue that (i) a smart and flexible planning capability, and (ii) a sustained internal innovation orientation, act as important dynamic capabilities in supply chain innovation. Both can be proactively designed and provide the basis for long-term innovation success.

The planning capability refers to the planning expertise, i.e. timeliness, plan content, and fulfillment of objectives, as well as their contribution to the overarching business goals. Planning capabilities are based on assumptions about the organizational environment necessary to contribute to market success. The planning capability, as a dynamic capability, enables a firm to react to changes and contingencies. Planning has an inbuilt flexibility. If suppliers have a dynamic planning capability, they continuously can use internal creativity and flexible responses to market and technology changes. Even in environments of high supply chain rigidities, suppliers can use the presets of their manufacturers to adapt to and transform deliberate planning for product development. The dynamic planning capability increases the identification of components and products that apply to customers' expectations, and, as such, increase market success. Thus, suppliers can increase their performance by deliberate planning under conditions of high and low innovation rigidities. Under low supply chain rigidities, suppliers use deliberate planning for the development of successful products to increase their market performance. Having developed internal planning capabilities, suppliers can also improve upon their success in environments of high supply chain rigidities if they accommodate the rigidities of their manufacturers into their strategic planning.

Hypothesis 2: Under high supply chain rigidities, suppliers' planning capability mediates the relationship between deliberate planning and market success. Suppliers achieve success through planning capability, when following deliberate planning.

Innovation orientation can assist a firm's proclivity, openness, and inclination to generate and distribute novel ideas on processes and products within supply chains. Thus, the innovation orientation increases the success of total innovation programs (Manu, 1992). An innovation orientation contains structures, processes, and positive attitudes toward innovation, critically including people and processes, as well as technology-related issues. This embraces an organization's inclination towards the horizontal and vertical exchange of novel ideas. The integral and highly flexible perspective allows for the comparison of the concept with an overarching "entrepreneurial orientation" (Zhou *et al.*, 2005, p. 54), which has been shown to support innovation success across a broad range of environmental settings, in both less and highly uncertain environments (Tushman and Anderson, 1986; Tushman and O'Reilly, 1996).

An innovation orientation is a dynamic capability that empowers many members of the organization. Ideas from different levels of the organization are used for the development of new products. An innovation orientation provides a high degree of flexibility. The high potential of new ideas and the flexibility allows suppliers under conditions of low and high rigidities to develop and improve upon innovations that apply to the market. Accordingly, an innovation orientation is expected to improve market success under high and low supply chain rigidities.

Hypothesis 3a: The innovation orientation increases market success under high and low innovation rigidities.

In settings of low supply chain rigidities, suppliers can develop their own routines and structures for innovation. Formal planning can lay out the organizational structure of an innovation orientation. Suppliers can define, in extension of their formal planning, many organizational devices, e.g. creativity rooms, opportunities for informal vertical and horizontal communication, and teamwork. Additionally, the emergent planning, leaving room for experimentation, open communication, trial and error, and feedback slopes, can create a framework for an innovation orientation. The fundamental assumptions of the emergent approach correspond highly to the innovation orientation, implying a willingness to move beyond old habits and try new ideas at different levels of the organization. Ignoring the effects by innovation rigidities, both deliberate and emergent strategies can serve as a basis for shaping innovation orientation as visionary, and planning may provide complementary guidance.

Under high rigidities, suppliers still find it difficult to develop and operate using their own framework for their innovation orientations. Instead, they depend on presets and directives from their manufacturers, which also might change suddenly. Suppliers need to integrate manufacturers' requirements into their planning and the implementation of structures and processes associated with an innovation orientation. This interferes with the potential benefits of an emergent strategy. We argue that suppliers can only develop their innovation orientation by an emergent strategy if they have the freedom to operate, which will exist in an environment of low rigidities. Instead, the deliberate planning will also, under high rigidities, provide the processes and structures necessary for an innovation orientation.

Hypothesis 3b: Supply chain rigidity moderates the relationship between an emergent strategy and an innovation orientation. The emergent strategy only increases an innovation orientation under low rigidities.

Empirical Study

Sample

Our sample is composed of 241 small and mid-sized companies within the high-tech sector. We contacted 656 executives personally by telephone or by post, asking them to fill out our questionnaire. To ensure that firms are representative of the industry, all contacted suppliers were carefully selected on the basis of an industry database, which provided information about the size of the firm, as well as the products and services offered by the firms. After two rounds of mailings, 242 surveys were returned; 241 of these could be analyzed. Consequently, the response rate was 37%.

We compared firms that returned the completed questionnaire with those that did not according to control variables (firm age, firm size, position of the suppliers in the supply chain). We could not find major differences between respondents and non-respondents. The average firm size was 100–150 employees. The firms operated as second- or third-tier suppliers in either the IT or the airline industry, representing the view of soft- and hardware, respectively. To check the key information quality of our data collection, two researchers made a series of telephone calls to verify the position of the key informants in the companies.

Model

Our model is an extension of the standard shape of LISREL models (Jöreskog and Aish, 1990). We checked the descriptive statistics of each item (see Appendix), as well as their normal distribution. Neither skewness nor kurtosis exceeded values of 1, confirming no significant deviations from a normal distribution. To examine the moderating effect of rigidities, we conducted a multi-group estimation. We follow the method of Byrne (2004) to test moderating effects by multi-group estimations in structural equation modeling. The sign and the statistical significance of the path coefficients and their corresponding *t*-values and Chi-square-differences served to test the hypothesized relationships.

To build the groups, we used a median split of the entire sample to divide the respondents into two subgroups of low or high supply chain rigidity. The model consists of a two-stage causal effect using supply chain rigidity as the key moderating effect. Hypothesis 1 postulates that the direct effects of both strategic types on market success are moderated by different levels of supply chain rigidities. Hence, we expect different effect sizes of these relationships for low and high supply chain rigidity. In Hypothesis 2, we state a moderated mediation: under high supply chain rigidities, suppliers' planning capability mediates the relationship between deliberate planning and market success. Hypothesis 3a demands the analysis of the effect through an innovation orientation on market success in both groups: high and low innovation rigidities. For Hypothesis 3b, again we have to check the moderating effect by innovation rigidity on the relationship between emergent strategy and innovation orientation.

Measures

Multiple indicators are used to measure the latent constructs. The scales used to measure our constructs were inspired by previous studies. In accordance with previous findings, all constructs were measured as reflective indicators.

Table 1. Continuum of deliberate and emergent strategy.

	Deliberate	Emergent
Acquisition of information	Research of market opportunities.	Actions and market opportunities are not planned in advance.
Processing of information	Analysis of the rationales of market growth.	Intuition.
Decision making	Development of different options and subsequent decisions.	Trial and error.

While single constructs might have been formulated as well by formative scales, we did not choose this approach, out of both content and consistency considerations. Most items were measured with 5-point Likert-type scales (1 = I strongly disagree, 5 = I strongly agree).

Strategic approach

We measured the strategic planning approach by dimensions (see Table 1) raised in previous studies (Leontiades and Tezel, 1980; Robinson and Pearce, 1983; Pearce *et al.*, 1987). According to the acquisition of information, the deliberate approach is associated with in-depth research of market changes and risks. In contrast, the emergent approach, in its extreme, does not plan single actions in advance. According to the processing of information, the means–ends relationships and causal effects from market development were analyzed within deliberate strategy formulation. Instead, the emergent strategy builds upon intuition. In reference to evaluation and decision-making, the deliberate strategy formulation pursues the investigation of different options. Opposing at its extreme, the emergent approach is about trial and error.

Innovation orientation

We followed Siguaw *et al.* (2006) in distinguishing specific innovation outputs from a broader innovation orientation. More specifically, we directed an action-oriented instead of structural view, and emphasized the transformation from the strategy into specific action (Bouncken *et al.*,

2007). We measured innovation orientation, analogous to market orientation (Kohli and Jaworski, 1990), by the potential it provides for companies' innovation activities. Our construct of innovation orientation was guided by the idea of the organizations' inclination towards the horizontal and vertical exchange of novel ideas and focused on the internal innovation process. According hereto, innovation is a bottom-up, creative process which requires interdisciplinary exchange and integration within the company for success. Innovation orientation thus aims at overcoming functional barriers and considers how strongly everyone is engaged in innovation behavior. Therefore, we used the following items: the firms' engagement towards (i) the constant search for novel product concepts, (ii) the constant refinement and development of products, (iii) the fast and cross-functional implementation of innovation, and (iv) the horizontal and vertical participation of all personnel in developing novel ideas. These items jointly serve as reflective indicators, as they simultaneously reflect the extent of an innovation orientation.

Planning capability

Planning, as a dynamic capability, was adapted from the study of Bouncken *et al.* (2007). We measured planning capability by four items which describe the degree of planning expertise. All major aspects of planning, as a competence, are covered, i.e. timeliness, plan content, fulfillment of objectives, as well as the contribution to overarching business goals.

Market success

For market success, we are interested in the market performance of products, instead of technical or short-term measures of success. Subjective measures of performance have been widely used and most studies find high convergent validity with objective measures, such as publicly available accounting data, for selected studies (Worren *et al.*, 2002). We measured our construct of market success based on six indicators. Two of them measure overall customer satisfaction: if customers are satisfied with the products and if their expectations are met (Lam *et al.*, 2004). Three other indicators specifically measure the long-term market performance: loyalty of customers, revisiting customers, recommendations of customers leading to additional turnover (Zeithaml *et al.*, 1996). The last item measures the degree of acquired reputation (LeBlanc and Nguyen, 1995). All items simultaneously reflect the market success of a company.

Rigidities

To build the groups, we used a median split of the entire sample into two sub-groups with low and high supply chain rigidity. Prior to the data collection in 2007, we discussed and readjusted our scales on supply chain rigidities in a workshop with 12 academics and 7 supply chain managers. Afterwards, items were specified in a pilot study composed of 17 executives from small and medium sized suppliers in the IT industry. Four items proved to be of importance to differentiate between different settings of supply chain rigidity: determination of the behavior of partners in the supply chain, required fit of product program, technical compatibility and volatility of technologies on the market. These items were integrated into an overall score and a median split was applied for each of the two industry groups. This ensured an equal distribution of both industry branches into both sub-groups. Out of the 117 observations with high supply chain rigidity, 72 came from the IT and 45 from the airline sector, whereas the 124 observations with low supply chain rigidity consisted of 68 IT companies and 56 airline suppliers. Thus, possible industry effects could be balanced.

Measurement validity

We estimated the model postulated in Fig. 1 using AMOS 7. In many studies, measurement invariance between models has been ignored. We, instead, checked the comparability between the two groups by measuring the invariance (Byrne, 2004). After controlling for comparability, we chose a model which constrained measurement weights and intercepts. As compared to the fully unconstrained model, these constraints only lead to a slight decrease in the entire model fit, which was not significant (CMIN 45.459, p-value $= 0.160$). The overall fit measures indicated a good model fit. The normed Chi-square value of 1.32 was much lower than the threshold value of 3.0. Bentler's comparative fit index (CFI), that compares the hypothesized model against an independence model as a baseline model (Arbuckle and Wothke, 1999), is 0.91, which slightly exceeds the required value of 0.90 (Byrne, 2001). The RMSEA of 0.036 (90% — Interval of

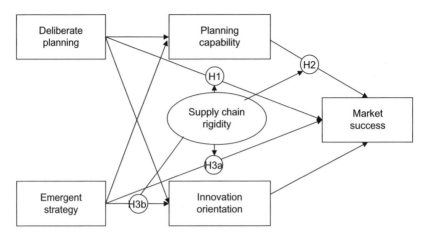

Fig. 1.   Causal effect model with moderator effects of supply chain rigidity.

0.027 to 0.045) is significantly lower than the threshold value of 0.08, which indicates a good fit (Browne and Cudeck, 1993).

For the local fit, we find standardized factor loadings above 0.4. All respective t-values are above 2.0, indicating that none of the items are to be excluded from the model. Therefore, we do not illustrate the t-values in detail in the table in the appendix. A few indicators did not reach the necessary indicator reliability value of 0.4. Only the indicators of the construct "deliberate strategy" consistently had an indicator reliability value higher than the threshold value. As a result, all items were used in our model.

Nearly all constructs fulfilled the necessary condition for convergent validity (see Appendix for details), even though their extracted average variance was moderate. Cronbach's alpha and composite reliability almost always reached the necessary condition of 0.7 (Nunnally and Bernstein, 1994) and 0.6 (Bagozzi and Yi, 1988). Only the dependent latent variable "emergent strategy" had a slightly lower Cronbach's alpha value. All of the constructs reached the necessary level of composite reliability. Thus, the measures demonstrated adequate convergent validity and reliability. Overall, we found good convergent validity and reliability, as well as moderate discriminant validity, in the model.

Results

To examine the influence of supply chain rigidities, we performed a multi-group estimation. We applied a median split on the entire sample

Table 2.   Model fits of the multi-group analyses.

Model	NPAR	Chi^2	DF	Delta Chi^2	RMSEA	AIC	CFI
1 Unconstrained	142	479.429	362		0.037	763.429	0.919
2 Measurement weights and intercepts	105	524.889	399	45.46 df$=37$ p<0.16	0.036	734.889	0.913
3 Structural weights according to hypotheses	102	527.887	402	2.998 df$=3$ p<0.39	0.036	731.887	0.913
4 All structural weights constrained	98	540.46	406	12.573 df$=4$ p<0.01	0.037	736.46	0.907

into a low and high rigidity group. We first allowed (Table 2) a free estimation of all measurement and structural coefficients in both groups ($=$ fully unconstrained model). This model served as the base model for more restrictive models. Enforcing equality into the measurement model ($=$ equal measurement weights and intercepts) resulted in a non-significant difference in Chi-squares (45.46, df$=37$; p 0.16). This indicates that the measurement model is invariant across the two groups, ensuring an identity of constructs within both groups. Following this, we restricted the structural coefficients to be equal where we did not expect different causal paths between situations of low and high rigidities. Again, the difference in Chi-squares was non-significant (2.998, df$=3$; p 0.39). This indicates that the two groups were not different in the other structural coefficients. Finally, we forced the hypothesized structural differences to be zero ($=$ equality of all structural weights). This fully constrained multi-group analysis did not fit as well as the other models, with a significant Chi-square difference (12.573, df$=4$; p 0.01), as compared to our target model. We conclude that our proposed model fits best to the observed empirical data. This provides a strong signal for the relevance of the proposed moderating effects of rigidities.

Having identified the best fitting model, we investigate the obtained parameter estimates for the causal effects (Table 3) and relate this empirical evidence to our proposed hypotheses. Hypothesis 1 postulates that both strategy approaches only directly impact market success in the case of low supply chain rigidities. Results illustrate that both approaches have

Table 3.   Structural parameters and hypotheses.

Effect related to hypothesis	Path	Low rigidity		High rigidity		Confirmation (✓)/ Rejection (x)
		Estimate (S.E.)	t-value	Estimate (S.E.)	t-value	
Causal effects with significant differences under situations of low and high rigidity						
H1	Deliberate Market Strategy → Success	0.196 *(0.088)*	0.026	−0.029 *(0.085)*	0.729	✓
	Emergent Market Strategy → Success	0.211 *(0.113)*	0.061	0.019 *(0.092)*	0.834	✓
H2	Planning Market Capability → Success	0.093 *(0.091)*	0.309	0.439 *(0.144)*	0.002	(✓)
H3b	Emergent Innovation Strategy → Orientation	0.401 *(0.163)*	0.014	0.022 *(0.119)*	0.855	✓
Causal effects with no significant differences under situations of low and high rigidity						
H3a	Innovation Market Orientation → Success	0.215 *(0.065)*	***			✓
No explicit hypothesis, as not the focus	Deliberate Planning Strategy → Capability	0.204 *(0.048)*	***			
	Deliberate Innovation Strategy → Orientation	0.338 *(0.096)*	***			

a significant and positive effect on market success for low rigidities. The emergent strategy (b = 0.211; p = 0.06) and the deliberate strategy (b = 0.196; p = 0.03) effect market success under low rigidities. We find that neither strategy exerts a significant influence on market success in the case of high rigidities (p > 0.8/0.7). Thus, our results are in line with Hypothesis 1, confirming that both strategies (deliberate, as well as emergent) only exert a significant direct effect on market success when supply chain rigidity is low.

In Hypothesis 2, we state a moderated mediation: under high supply chain rigidities, suppliers' planning capability should partially, or fully, mediate the relationship between deliberate planning and market success. The postulated partial, or complete, mediation, was checked using a comparison of our proposed causal effects model against a direct effects only model and against a fully mediated model, each in the group of high rigidities. The first small model only contains the direct paths between planning and market success. The fully mediated effects model exclusively contains the indirect effects of both planning models.

Complete mediation exists when (i) the direct effect of the antecedent ("deliberate planning") on market success is significant in the direct effects only model, and (ii) is not significant in the extended models. To test for partial versus full mediation, we performed a nested model comparison. Whereas the difference in the Chi-square was well above the critical value (Delta Chi^2 = 21.884, df = 2, p = 0.001) when comparing the direct effects model with the partially mediated model, we did not find a statistically significant improvement between the partially and fully mediated model (Delta Chi^2 = 1.193, df = 1, p = 0.275). This only indicates a partial mediation. However, planning capability only exerts a significant direct influence on market success if supply chain rigidity is high (b = 0.42; p = 0.002). The estimate of the direct effect of deliberate planning on market success is insignificant in our full model. Thus, we note a strong tendency towards the confirmation of Hypothesis 2.

Hypothesis 3a stated that the innovation orientation increases market success under high and low innovation rigidities. The results show that the innovation orientation always influences market success positively. As such, Hypothesis 3a is confirmed.

Hypothesis 3b stated that innovation rigidity moderates the relationship between emergent strategy and innovation orientation, where the emergent strategy only increases an innovation orientation under low rigidities. The comparison of both groups reveals insights, as an emergent strategy fails to build the capability of innovation orientation in the case of high supply chain rigidities. However, we find that the emergent strategy has a significant positive effect on innovation orientation under low supply chain rigidity (b = 0.42; p = 0.014). This supports Hypothesis 3b. We also find that emergence is needed for shaping innovation orientation in the case of low supply chain rigidities.

Some of our findings are worthwhile to note, which holds true both in the unconstrained causal effects model, as well as in the chosen model (Table 4): the standardized effects of a deliberate strategy on planning capability, as well as on innovation orientation, are both significant as well as of similar size in settings of both low and high supply chain rigidity. Thus, a deliberate innovation strategy seems to strengthen those dynamic capabilities, under both high and low rigidities. This is plausible, as the achievement of planned company-internal capabilities should be independent of supply

Table 4.   Standardized direct and total effects under low/high rigidity.

	Deliberate strategy	Emergent strategy	Planning capability	Innovation orientation
Standardized Direct Effects				
Planning Capability	0.37/0.38	0	0	0
Innovation Orientation	0.42/0.48	0.38/0.03	0	0
Market Success	0.44/-0.05	0.36/0.03	0.12/0.41	0.39/0.26
Standardized Total Effects				
Planning Capability	0.37/0.38	0	0	0
Innovation Orientation	0.42/0.48	0.38/0.03	0	0
Market Success	0.65/0.23	0.51/0.04	0.12/0.41	0.39/0.27

chain restrictions. As such, we propose that a reasonable deliberate innovation strategy supports the creation of planning capabilities. The emergent strategy, however, does not rely on such a formal planning process, and thus, is unlikely to contribute to an enduring planning capability.

Finally, the total effects of an emergent strategy on market success were found to vanish in settings of high rigidities. A deliberate strategy can still contribute to market success, however, its overall effect becomes highly reduced (standardized total effect: 0.23 as compared to 0.65). This stresses the consequences from different degrees of freedom of suppliers in that while the planning impact on market success may be enhanced by less autonomy, strategic action by itself becomes less relevant. Thus, strategic design is of minor relevance for companies facing high restrictions in their innovative activities, due to their embedding in the overall supply chain.

Discussion

The lack of innovation strategy is long disputed in the literature (Dosi, 1982). The above mentioned contextual factors of the supply chain demand a strategic design and alignment of companies' innovation activities. We stress that innovation performance does not come about coincidentally in an empty space, but instead owes a great deal to the firms' ability to innovate within the entire value chain and to the formulation of strategies. The innovation and performance of suppliers within the supply chains and its antecedents along the supply chain, suppliers' strategy, and the suppliers' internal innovation orientation, have been neglected in the literature so far. This study aimed to explore this complex setting.

This chapter positioned itself in the complex areas of innovation strategy, internal capabilities and performance in supply chains. We clarified how suppliers' innovation strategies and two internal dynamic capabilities ((i) planning capability and (ii) innovation orientation), can cope with manufacturers' rigidities and how this affects performance. Our studies researched a new phenomenon neglected in prior studies: the level of rigidities in supply chains on suppliers. By introducing the concept of innovation rigidities in the supply chain, we stress that the innovation of suppliers is constrained and channeled by manufacturers. For the innovation strategy, we build upon the large body of strategy research and transfer the two dominant strategy approaches, the deliberate and the emergent strategy, into the upcoming research field of supply chain innovation.

Furthermore, we introduced the important concept of dynamic capabilities in the dynamic setting of innovation in the supply chain. We investigated two important classes of dynamic capabilities: the planning capability and the innovation orientation. The planning capability is necessary to cope with the changing and challenging contingencies of innovation supply chains, particularly under high rigidities. Our idea of internal innovation orientation was inspired by the distinction of innovation versus innovativeness and the missing results in this firm-level inclination. As such, long-term proclivity towards innovation was found to exist (Menguc and Auh, 2006). Entrenched by the resource-based view (RBV) and its explanation of a sustained competitive advantage, we followed the quest for an increased consideration of the internal capability-performance link (Teece *et al.*, 1997).

In essence (Fig. 2), the routes to market success were found to strongly depend on the level of rigidities. Under low rigidities, suppliers can follow both strategy approaches to achieve performance. The emergent innovation strategy improves market success through enhanced creativity and experimentation with technologies and designs. As it augments the transfer of ideas and the empowerment of employees, an innovation orientation contributes to market success by following the emergent strategy. The deliberate innovation strategy increases market success as it enables a company to thoroughly plan targets, means, and technologies for innovation. An increased transfer of ideas and empowered employees will help to

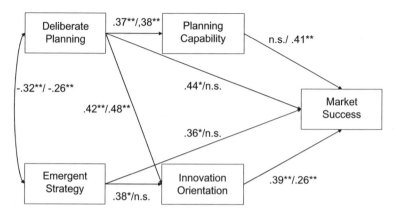

Fig. 2.   Standardized direct effects in subgroups of low/high supply chain rigidity.

develop and implement the deliberate innovation strategy and achieve market success.

Under high innovation rigidities, suppliers should follow a deliberate strategy. Then they have two options by dynamic capabilities. One option is to establish a high innovation orientation. The creative employees and high information exchange will enable suppliers to build up a high flexibility that can react on the requirements of the manufacturer. We argue that the innovation orientation complements both the deliberate planning and rigidities of supply chain innovation. The other option is to pursue the development of a planning capability. Suppliers can cope with the high supply chain rigidities if they developed the art of flexible and contingency-orientated planning. We found that the planning capability mediates the relationship between deliberate planning and market success under high rigidities. Deliberate planning only improves market success under these contingencies through the planning capability. The success by a deliberate strategy indicates that managers should pay more attention to the activities of *ex ante* rational planning, such as road mapping tools, strategic market assessment and thus, the classic tools of strategic planning itself.

An important theoretical contribution of this study is the finding that an internal dynamic capability is enhanced by an adequate strategy. Thus, we improve upon the RBV research, which is often accused of lacking concrete suggestions about strategy formulation. Our results on strategies and performance effects bring life into the theoretic discussion about a sustained competitive advantage. More than that, we can derive different adequacies of innovation strategies according to the contingency factor of supply chain rigidities. We researched long-term market success through internal capabilities and extended the work of scholars who focused on the market orientation–firm performance relationship (Baker and Sinkula, 1999). Upscaling these studies, we investigated contingency conditions — high and low supply chain rigidities.

In summary, our research moves beyond prior results that are somehow related to results on general strategy and planning under high and low uncertainty. High uncertainty is not fully, but in some ways, equivalent to low supply chain rigidities, whereas low uncertainty has similarities to a highly defined supply chain. A lowly defined supply chain brings greater autonomy, but increases uncertainty. On the other hand, a highly defined supply chain decreased autonomy and decreased suppliers' uncertainty. To conclude, an emergent general strategy formulation (Mintzberg, 1978) seems suitable under the condition of lowly defined supply chains (high uncertainty).

As always, there are inherent limitations in the study design, and, thus, in the generalizability of the obtained findings. First, the database consists of a sample drawn from two specific industry sectors which are highly dynamic and innovation-driven. Supply chains in more static conditions might reveal less emphasis on strategic actions by individual suppliers, as such, behavior is likely to interfere with long established routine processes. Further variations in the potential for strategic action should be identified, which may be constrained by overall supplier structures and may vary across different innovation types produced in supply chains. Secondly, and due to the limited access to data sources, we had to rely on subjective success measures and were exposed to a potential common method bias in our data, even though we partially confirmed our obtained measures. Thus, there is need for a cross-validation of the findings with additional data, especially with objective measures of long-term company success.

Conceptually, our findings contribute to the recently intensified discussion about the importance of dynamic capabilities for linking strategic planning with company's actions (Teece *et al.*, 2007). We provide a dedicated view on innovation orientation and planning capability as dynamic capabilities. Both capabilities illustrate exerting strong intermediary effects on market success. It is reasonable to assume that other capabilities might further explain the process which links overarching strategy with the business environment and which ultimately affects long-term outcomes (Zhou *et al.*, 2005). Thus, future research on the organizational success of supplier companies should follow a multi-faceted view proposed by DeSarbo *et al.* (2005) and investigate more thoroughly the interplay between strategic types and internal capabilities, as well as external environmental contingencies on firm performance.

Appendix

Table A1.   Descriptives: correlation matrix including item means and standard deviations.

Item	Mean	Std. Dev.	D1	D2	D3	D4	E1	E2	E3	P1	P2	P3	P4	I1	I2	I3	I4	M1	M2	M3	M4	M5	M6
D1	3.62	1.02	1.000																				
D2	3.33	1.10	0.593**	1.000																			
D3	3.65	1.01	0.515**	0.525**	1.000																		
D4	3.65	0.96	0.606**	0.542**	0.587**	1.000																	
E1	2.88	1.13	-0.19**	-0.17**	-0.22**	-0.22**	1.000																
E2	2.25	1.10	-0.42**	-0.35**	-0.41**	-0.53**	0.326**	1.000															
E3	2.24	1.07	-0.21**	-0.086	-0.139*	-0.27**	0.361**	0.501**	1.000														
P1	4.05	0.94	0.075	0.189**	0.085	0.149*	-0.019	-0.029	0.106	1.000													
P2	4.22	0.86	0.169**	0.233**	0.103	0.123	0.021	-0.058	0.002	0.579**	1.000												
P3	3.81	0.98	0.090	0.206**	0.208**	0.123	0.002	-0.023	0.033	0.334**	0.386**	1.000											
P4	3.76	1.11	0.109	0.223**	0.142*	0.148*	0.022	-0.102	0.077	0.339**	0.335**	0.382**	1.000										
I1	3.80	0.79	0.208**	0.278**	0.208**	0.216**	-0.148*	-0.17**	-0.055	0.006	0.151*	0.101	0.104	1.000									
I2	3.32	0.97	0.276**	0.249**	0.199**	0.191**	-0.22**	-0.150*	0.000	0.038	0.096	0.132*	0.042	0.425**	1.000								
I3	3.39	0.98	0.238**	0.204**	0.184**	0.152*	-0.19**	-0.140*	0.035	0.020	0.098	0.095	0.016	0.350**	0.677**	1.000							
I4	3.76	0.78	0.179**	0.218**	0.178**	0.174**	-0.084	-0.17**	0.035	0.193**	0.287**	0.152*	0.204**	0.421**	0.355**	0.399**	1.000						
M1	3.94	0.76	0.118	0.075	0.056	0.109	-0.008	-0.028	0.013	0.191**	0.238**	0.315**	0.213**	0.252**	0.153*	0.221**	0.273**	1.000					
M2	3.88	0.90	0.165*	0.151*	0.127*	0.158*	0.020	-0.076	-0.039	0.011	0.144*	0.212**	0.139*	0.237**	0.118	0.145*	0.222**	0.373**	1.000				
M3	4.28	0.74	0.154*	0.141*	0.042	0.076	-0.014	0.011	-0.044	0.091	0.209**	0.213**	0.254**	0.145*	0.128*	0.201**	0.253**	0.359**	0.428**	1.000			
M4	4.00	0.79	0.141*	0.178**	0.084	0.105	0.106	0.058	0.080	0.166*	0.218**	0.272**	0.225**	0.090	0.084	0.140*	0.228**	0.352**	0.345**	0.496**	1.000		
M5	3.61	1.05	0.060	0.091	0.117	0.071	0.103	0.010	0.090	0.078	0.244**	0.268**	0.149*	0.169**	0.109	0.156*	0.223**	0.302**	0.355**	0.472**	0.375**	1.000	
M6	4.40	0.68	0.080	0.053	0.155*	0.092	-0.106	-0.100	-0.051	0.084	0.135*	0.229**	0.147*	0.120	0.111	0.149*	0.280**	0.278**	0.315**	0.440**	0.356**	0.410**	1.000

Table A2.   Assessment of fit of internal structure of the hypothesised model.

Construct		Item	Standard factor loadings[a]	Indicator reliability	α	AVE
Deliberate	D1)	Research of market opportunities.	0.771	0.594	0.83	0.56
	D2)	Analysis of rationales of market growth.	0.758	0.574		
	D3)	Development of different options.	0.683	0.467		
	D4)	Evaluation of actions taken.	0.808	0.652		
Emergent	E1)	Actions and market opportunities are not planned in advance.	0.401	0.158	0.69	0.38
	E2)	Intuition.	0.873	0.763		
	E3)	Trial and error.	0.567	0.319		
Planning Capability	P1)	Objectives are always being pursued, as planned, in advance.	0.562	0.316	0.76	0.14
	P2)	Planned time-frame can always be achieved.	0.854	0.73		
	P3)	Planned objectives are always achieved.	0.817	0.667		
	P4)	Planning measures always support goal achievements.	0.526	0.276		
Innovation Orientation	I1)	Constant search for novel product concepts.	0.756	0.571	0.71	0.28
	I2)	Constant refinement and development of products.	0.777	0.603		
	I3)	Fast and cross-functional implementation of innovation.	0.588	0.345		
	I4)	Horizontal and vertical participation of all personnel in developing novel ideas.	0.587	0.345		
Market Success	M1)	Customers' expectations are met.	0.457	0.209	0.78	0.13
	M2)	Loyalty of customers.	0.479	0.229		
	M3)	Enjoying a good reputation.	0.676	0.457		
	M4)	Customers express their satisfaction with the company.	0.568	0.323		
	M5)	Recommendations from our customers.	0.549	0.301		
	M6)	Revisiting of customers.	0.514	0.265		

[a]All factor loadings are significant (t > 2.0 respectively p < 0.05), and therefore are not listed.

Part V

DEVELOPING COMPETENCIES

Chapter 13

Innovation: A Performance Measurement Perspective

Pervaiz K. Ahmed
Monash University, Sunway Campus, Malaysia

Mohamed Zairi
Hamdan Bin Mohammed eUniversity, Dubai, UAE

Introduction: Performance Management in the Modern Business Context

As competition intensifies and business gears itself up for the challenges of the twenty-first century, performance management continues to be in the spotlight. Increased consumerism, business globalisation and new management practices have raised questions about the way in which performance is measured. Clarity on the terms performance measurement, performance measures and performance measurement systems is a prerequisite to establishing what impact, if any, practices have made on bottom-line business results.

In order for companies to achieve goals they have to measure. Measurement is the basis through which it is possible to control, evaluate and improve processes:

> "When you can measure what you are speaking about and express it in numbers, you know something about it. (Otherwise) your knowledge is a meagre and unsatisfactory kind; it may be the beginning of knowledge but you have scarcely in thought advanced

to the stage of science." (Lord Kelvin, 1824 –1904, quoted in Heim and Compton, 1992, p. 1)

This point is also emphasised by the Foundation of Manufacturing Committee of the National Academy of Engineering:

"World Class Manufacturers recognise the importance of metrics in helping to define the goals and performance expectations for the organisation. They adopt or develop appropriate metrics to interpret and describe quantitatively the criteria used to measure the effectiveness of the manufacturing system and its many interrelated components." (Quoted in Heim and Compton, 1992, p. 6)

Performance Measurement

The complex nature of performance measurement has resulted in a plethora of definitions and has prompted the view that it is "a mystery . . . complex, frustrating, difficult, challenging, important, abused and misused" (Sink, 1991). Practitioners, including strategists, accountants, psychologists and human resource managers, have their own definition of performance measurement. Each requires its application either for internal reporting, such as individuals' performance appraisal, or for external reporting, such as financial accounting ratios. The issue is further complicated by the notion that performance measures may be either individual or organisation-wide. Thus, it is hardly surprising that different definitions exist.

One simple definition which largely overcomes the above problems is the systematic assignment of numbers to entities. This has both a universal application and satisfies the requirements of various stakeholder groups. Zairi (1994) also defines the function of measurement as "to develop a method for generating a class of information that will be useful in a wide variety of problems and situations". This functionality is important as many performance measures are capable of information generation, but unless they are useful, they are meaningless.

In the context of individual performance, performance measurement provides the organisation with a "device through which to focus and enunciate accountability" (Sharman, 1993) and "an objective, impersonal basis for performance evaluation" (Sloma, 1980).

Some authors stress the importance of considering performance measurement as "the process of determining how successful organisations or individuals have been in attaining their objectives" (Evangelidis, 1983). This process approach to performance measurement recognises the existence and importance of inputs and outputs in the development of the performance measurement system.

Many authors have defined performance measurement in terms of the attributes of performance: "What is measured is rarely performance itself, but some specific attribute relating to the performance" (Euske, 1984). It is often the desired behavioural attributes which are the focus for measurement and they provide "feedback on activities that motivate behaviour leading to continuous improvement in customer satisfaction, flexibility and productivity" (Lynch and Cross, 1991).

Performance Measures

Performance measures have been defined as the "characteristics of outputs that are identified for purposes of evaluation" (Euske, 1984) while others have defined them as a "tool" to compare actual results with a pre-set target and to measure the extent of any deviation (Fortuin, 1988). It has also been suggested that performance measures "reflect the contribution of each team or process to the organisation's goal" (Turney, 1991).

Juran (1992) applied a TQM-focused definition by stating that it is "a defined amount of some quality feature that permits evaluation of that feature in numbers". Clearly, to measure all the characteristics of an output would be impractical and undesirable. Therefore, it is the "vital signs which quantify how well activities within a process or the outputs of a process achieve a specified goal" that are the measures selected (Hronec, 1993).

Performance measures will have a range of hierarchical levels — corporate, business and functional (Hax and Majluf, 1991) — depending on the output and "customer" being considered. The line manager, process manager, general manager, customer and shareholder will each have different requirements. An integrated set of performance measures will take into account all these factors. At an individual level, the performance measures "should be important causal factors related to managerial and employee behaviour" (Hendricks, 1994). Performance measures, therefore,

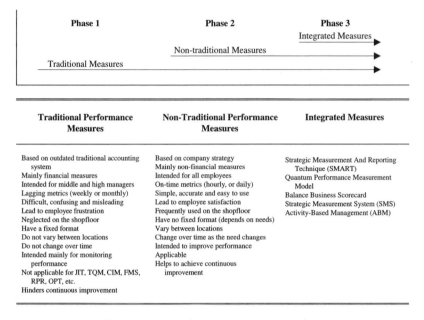

Fig. 1.   Evolution in measurement approaches.

Source: Adapted from Ghalayani and Nobel, 1996.

"communicate how an activity is meeting the needs of internal or external customers" (Turney, 1991) and reflect the contribution of each team or process to the organisation's goals.

The biggest barrier to comparing performance measures is the inconsistency applied to its definition (see Fig. 1). For example, productivity may be a quality measure, a financial performance measure or it may be given a separate classification. This apparent inconsistency can adversely impact on benchmarks and reinforces the need for precision when benchmarking with external organisations.

Authors who have attempted to prescribe performance measures (Table 1) have done so without any indication of the applicability of the measurement frameworks. The measures are, therefore, anecdotal. However difficult it may be, some have achieved success. For instance, the Toyota Motor Company has operated their non-financial measurement system for more than 35 years and is integrated to its continuous improvement commitment (Brancato, 1995). Kelloggs Australia has also introduced a quality-based management system. Although many of the measures are

Table 1. Performance measures.

Fitzgerald *et al.* (1991): Performance service businesses	1 Financial performance measures 2 Quality of service 3 Flexibility 4 Resource utilisation 5 Innovation
Maskell (1991): Performance measures for world-class manufacturing	1 Delivery performance 2 Process time 3 Production flexibility 4 Quality 5 Financial performance 6 Social issues
Lynch and Cross (1991): "The performance pyramid"	1 Market 2 Financial 3 Customer satisfaction 4 Flexibility 5 Productivity 6 Quality 7 Delivery 8 Cycle time 9 Waste
Kaplan and Norton (1992): "The balanced scorecard"	1 Financial perspective 2 Internal business perspective 3 Customer perspective 4 Innovation and learning perspective
Hronec (1993): The vital signs	1 Quality 2 Cost 3 Time

non-financial, they have found them to be more predictive about the future of the company (Brancato, 1995).

Phases of Performance Measurement

Ghalayini and Noble (1996) propose that measurement has undergone phases in development. Three stages can be discerned (Fig. 1).

The first phase, which is deemed to have started in the 1980s, focused heavily on financial measures such as profits, return on investment (ROI) and productivity. Within this system, measures are based on the traditional system of management accounting. Unfortunately, this perspective is handicapped by a number of shortcomings:

(i) *Traditional accounting measures.* Traditional measures are based on a system of accounting which was developed to primarily attribute costs, rather then use, in decision-making.

(ii) *Lagging metrics.* Financial data report on historic events and, therefore, are not useful for operational assessment.

(iii) *Corporate strategy.* Traditional measures do not take into account aspects derived from corporate strategy.

(iv) *Relevance to practice.* Traditional measures quantify performance only in financial terms, yet improvement efforts (such as customer satisfaction and adherence to delivery time) are difficult to translate into strict currency terms.

(v) *Inflexible.* Traditional measures are used in fixed formats across all departments and parts of the business. Often, what is relevant to one section is not relevant to others, thus making the information somewhat redundant in many cases.

(vi) *Expensive.* The collation of an extensive amount of data is often a difficult and expensive process.

(vii) *Continuous improvement.* The setting of standards for performance can often go against the grain of continuous improvement since it can lead to the establishment of norms of output and behaviour, rather than to motivate improvement. For instance, workers may hesitate to improve their performance if they think that the standard for the forthcoming period is to be revised upwards on the basis of current results.

(viii) *Customer requirements and management techniques.* In an environment where customer requirements are of a higher quality, shorter lead time and lower costs have led to empowered decision-making on the shopfloor. Traditional financial reports, which are used by middle managers, do not reflect the organisational reality of more autonomous management approaches.

These problems provided the impetus for the development of non-financial measures. This is exemplified by the second stage of development. The second stage of measurement is characterised by non-financial measures. Characteristically they are:

(i) Measures which relate to manufacturing strategy and are primarily non-financial in nature, such as those pertaining to operational matters which facilitate decision-making for managers and workers.
(ii) Foster improvement rather than just monitor performance.
(iii) Change with the dynamics of the marketplace.

The third stage is characterised by an integrated use of financial and non-financial measures. These integrated systems, by examining performance from multiple angles and the trade-offs openly, attempt to guard against sub-optimisation.

Performance Measurement Systems

A performance measurement system has been defined as a "tool for balancing multiple measures (cost, quality and time) across multiple levels (organisation, processes and people)" (Hronec, 1993). It is a "systematic way of evaluating the inputs, outputs, transformation and productivity in a manufacturing or non-manufacturing operation".

The performance measurement system is an object whose purpose is to measure, via a set of rules and procedures, using some form of yardstick (Ijiri and Jaedicke, 1981). It should also focus on continuous improvement. The data provided by the performance measurement system needs to be "relevant, factual information on core business processes and key activities" (Miller, 1992).

A systems perspective as exemplified by a TQM approach, stresses the need for measurement through the Deming continuous improvement cycle of "plan, do, check, act" (Deming, 1986). Essentially, what gets measured gets done. Feedback is a central theme which runs through most TQM activities, and a performance measurement system provides the vehicle for this process to operate in an objective way. Within benchmarking, for example, identification of the performance gap requires a robust performance measurement system to be effective. Processes within a TQM environment are reviewed across functional barriers and, therefore, the performance measurement system is required "to integrate organisational activities across various managerial levels and functions".

Kaplan (1991) states that an effective performance measurement system "should provide timely, accurate feedback on the efficiency and effectiveness of operations". Within the dynamic marketplace, accurate information ahead of the competition may result in the difference between survival and non-survival. Dixon *et al.* (1990) identify five characteristics of successful measurement systems:

(i) Be mutually supportive and consistent with the business's operating goals, objectives, critical success factors and programmes.
(ii) Convey information through as few and as simple a set of measures as possible.
(iii) Reveal how effectively customers' needs and expectations are satisfied. Focus on measures that customers can see.
(iv) Provide a set of measurements for each organisational component that allows all members of the organisation to understand how their decisions and activities affect the entire business.
(v) Support organisational learning and continuous improvement.

Traditional performance measurement systems have focused on the shareholder and top management with an overview of how the company operated in the previous financial year. They provide an element of consistency in that the common denominator is always impacted on the bottom line, but these measures are retrospective and often produced a long time after the year has ended. According to Kaplan and Norton (1992), however, the real battle is for the hearts and minds of customers rather than the shareholder and top management in the fight for business survival. This dimension is not well represented in the traditional performance measurement system.

Line managers require accurate performance measures on a much more regular basis to enable effective process management. Whether the traditional measures provide shareholders and top management with the information they require is open to debate, as data which is required on tactical performance is used to assess the firm's current level of competitiveness and direct its efforts in attaining a desired competitive position in order to survive and prosper in the long run (Kaplan, 1991).

Performance Measurement and Innovation

A key to maintaining competitive success is the ability to repeatedly and successfully commercialise new products. However, measuring innovation success is riddled with several problems. One of the key problems is due to the multi-dimensionality surrounding innovation outcomes. This is further compounded by the fact that measurement confusion often arises in the hierarchical level of assessment, which varies from one individual product to a portfolio of products to the firm. For instance, for most firms, the issue is one of financial performance and is defined in hard terms, whilst the metric for project success often has time as a primary focus, and so forth.

Moreover, while it is widely accepted that developing new products is important in ensuring success and profitability, to date there has been no common set of performance measures for the innovation function. Proposed measures are often a mixture of input and output measures together with some measures for evaluating the process used (see Fig. 2).

Often, measures are defined at the micro level, identifying success metrics for individual projects. This creates a gap between discrete/unique projects and firm performance at the industry level. Loch *et al.* (1996) propose that this gap has to be closed in delineating three performance measurement levels:

(i) *Firms business performance.* It measures the firm's success in the market.
(ii) *Development output performance.* It measures the development function's contribution to the firm's business objectives.
(iii) *Development process performance.* It measures the quality of development execution (competencies) which drives the performance.

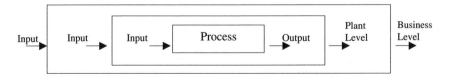

Fig. 2.   Systems-level view of measurement.

As Loch *et al.* point out, it is well to note that while process performance is an important driver of output, it is not directly so for business performance. For instance, development processes are a determinant of costs, speedy product development and quality. However, new products must be taken together with other factors, such as cost position, excellence in marketing strategies and sales to determine business profits and growth. Thus, it may be possible for a process to be capable of excellent delivery in terms of new products to the marketplace, but if the market values other types of performance, say technical performance over innovation, then the company is still likely to fail. Hence, the right performance dimension must be chosen (a point which we return to discuss in the section on strategy and innovation), and only after this can the appropriate definition and selection of process drivers be made.

The problem of defining the correct measure is not a new one. There exists a vast body of literature which deals with the diverse ways in which performance can be measured (Biggadale, 1979; Booz *et al.*, 1982; Bourgeois, 1980; Hitt and Ireland, 1985; Johne and Snelson, 1988; Venkatraman and Ramanujan, 1986). For example, Venkatraman and Ramanujan develop a two-dimensional approach to the measurement of business performance:

(i) *Dimension 1*. It is concerned with the use of financial (profit, sales, growth, turnover and ROI) versus operational criteria (innovativeness, market standing and social responsibility).
(ii) *Dimension 2*. It is concerned with alternate data sources (primary versus secondary). Dess and Robinson (1984) conclude that subjective perceptual measures can be used when accurate objective measures are unavailable. This is better than the alternative of removing performance measurement altogether. Hart (1993) and Pearce *et al.* (1987) provide further support for utilising indirect and proxy measures by suggesting that they can be fruitfully applied in place of direct measures.

New product development is one aspect of company performance and, therefore, what has been written about business performance is just as pertinent to innovation measurement. However, some researchers have examined this issue much more directly.

At the project level, Marquis (1969), in what is considered a classic case study, identified a number of drivers of success. The important ones were defined as:

(i) Understanding user needs.
(ii) Internal communication.
(iii) External communication.

Rothwell *et al.* (1974), in project SHAPPO, added the following:

(i) Attention to marketing.
(ii) Efficiency of development.
(iii) Authority of R&D.

Cooper (1984) and Cooper and Kleinschimdt (1987), in examining how new product success could be measured, highlighted other possible additions:

(i) Project definition.
(ii) Product superiority.
(iii) Synergies with marketing.

Cooper (1984) utilised eight performance measures which, after a factor analysis, yielded three independent dimensions of new product development success. These were:

(i) *Impact*. The impact or importance of the programme on a company's sales and profits.
(ii) *Success rate*. The success rate of the programme, assessing the track record of the company's products.
(iii) *Relative performance*. Capturing the relative performance of the programme in relation to objectives and competitors in terms of profits and success.

Cooper's (1979) study is important for several reasons. First, it highlighted that success along one dimension does not imply success in the other two dimensions. Secondly, it highlighted that different types of strategies need to be considered, and that these necessitate different interpretations and measurements of success. Cooper advocates that companies must first define the type of success they are searching for and then select the most appropriate strategy. Subsequently, Cooper and Kleimschmidt (1987) reinforce the proposition that success is not a simple uni-dimensional concept.

Cordero (1990) identified three measures. These are:

(i) Overall performance:

  (a) Pay-out period.
  (b) The percentage of sales as compared to the industry average.
  (c) The sales of new products developed in the last five years as a percentage of current sales.

(ii) Technical performance:

  (a) Business opportunity, which is the monetary value of the total market created by technical inputs.
  (b) The number of patents.
  (c) The number of publications and citations.

(iii) Commercial performance:

  (a) Cash flow.

Griffin and Page (1993), as part of the PDMA taskforce in 1990, provide a structure to the variety of measures which deal with product development success. After interviewing academics and practitioners, they identified 14 most commonly used performance measures and categorised them into four categories. They also defined measures which are considered to be the "most desirable", but often remain under-used or even unused. The reasons cited for the poor deployment of these measures include poor systems, adverse company culture and lack of accountability.

Strategy and Measurement

Companies pursue innovation for different reasons, and any measurement must be cognizant and aligned to this fact. As Griffin and Page (1996) note, research shows that interactions exist between innovation format and strategy, such that:

(i) The factors which produce project success differ by project strategy.
(ii) Different strategies produce different kinds of success.

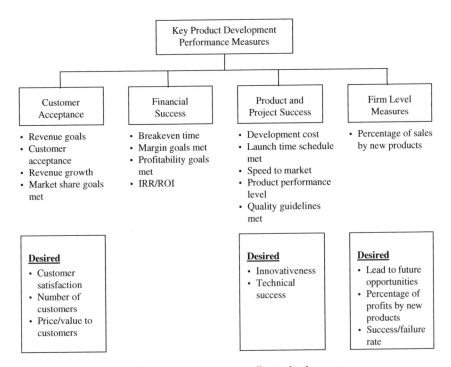

Fig. 3.   Performance measures according to business category.

Source: Griffin and Page, 1996.

(iii) The project strategy mix pursued differs across more and less successful firms.

A good way of picturing the inter-relationship between strategy and innovation is through an extension of the Ansoff product–market matrix. This matrix-type approach was first adapted and introduced by Booz *et al.* (1982). It is a three-by-three matrix with six distinct categories:

(i) *New to the world (NTW).* New products which create an entirely different market.

(ii) *New to the company (NTC).* New products which, for the first time, allow a company to enter an established market.

(iii) *Additions to existing product lines (AEL).* New products which supplement a company's established product lines.

	Newness to the market		
	Low		**High**
High	New to the company		New to the world
Newness to the firm	Product improvement	Add to existing lines	
Low	Cost reductions	Repositionings	

Fig. 4.   Innovation project-strategy framework.
Source: Griffin and Page, 1996.

(iv) *Improvement in/revisions to existing products (IM).* New products which provide improved performance, or greater perceived value, and replace existing products.

(vi) *Repositioning (RP).* Existing products targeted to new markets or market segments.

(vii) *Cost reductions (CR).* New products which provide similar performance at lower cost.

The market/company framework is a useful way to interlink different types of measures to different formats of innovation. Griffin and Page (1996) identify the most useful measure according to project type. These are presented in Fig. 5 below.

Furthermore, since different strategies produce different types of emphasis upon product development, it is unlikely that one set of measures can capture all facets of innovation across different strategies. Miles and Snow (1978) propose a generic typology of strategy on the basis of the speed of the response to changes in the product-market environment. The four categories are:

(i) *Prospectors.* Companies which respond early and are sensitive even to weak signals from the market. They attempt to be "first" with new products, markets and technologies.

Newness to the firm	Newness to the market — Low	Newness to the market	Newness to the market — High
High	**New to the company** Market share Revenue or satisfaction Met profit goal Competitive advantage		**New to the world** Customer acceptance Customer satisfaction Met profit goal or IRR/ROI Competitive advantage
	Product improvements Customer satisfaction Market share or revenue growth Met profit goal Competitive advantage	**Additions to existing lines** Market share Rev./Rev. Growth/Satis./Accept. Met profit goal Competitive advantage	
Low	**Cost reductions** Customer satisfaction Acceptance or revenue Met margin goal Performance or quality	**Product repositionings** Customer acceptance Satisfaction or share Met profit goal Competitive advantage	**Project strategy** Customer measure #1 Second customer measure Financial measure Performance measure

Fig. 5. The most useful success measures by project strategy.

Source: Griffin and Page, 1996.

(ii) *Analysers.* These companies are rarely forerunners, but through a process of carefully monitoring changes in the marketplace, especially competitors, they become fast followers. Often, they can build advantages through cost efficiencies by utilising a variety of market penetration strategies.

(iii) *Defenders.* They attempt to find and protect niche segments in relatively stable market conditions. They attempt to do so by offering higher quality, better service or lower prices. They tend to be insensitive to changes in the environment, which have little impact on their current operations.

(iv) *Reactors.* They respond only when forced to do so by environmental pressures. They tend to be very passive companies.

Research in the strategy field (Slater and Narver, 1993; Lambkin, 1988; McDaniel and Kolari, 1987) has found evidence linking these four strategy types to product development differences. The key differences are:

  (i) Prospectors and analysers place greater emphasis on growth through new product development than defenders and reactors.

 (ii) Prospectors will tend to be pioneers, whilst analysers will tend towards imitation of new products. Analysers focus attention on business processes that allow them to rapidly add product lines to their existing portfolios.

(iii) Defenders are likely to emphasise product line extension strategies than "new" product market development.

(iv) Reactors are likely to be very inconsistent in their approach to innovation and product development.

On the basis of this framework, Griffin and Page (1996) recommend that:

  (i) Prospector firms consider using some combination of:

    (a) The percentage of profits from new products less than "n" years old.

    (b) The degree today's new products lead to future opportunities.

    (c) The percentage of sales from new products less than "n" years old.

 (ii) Analyser firms should consider using some combination of:

    (a) The degree of new product fit to business strategy.

    (b) The development programme ROI.

    (c) The percentage of profits from new products less than "n" years old.

    (d) The success and failure rate.

(iii) Defender firms should consider using:

    (a) The development programme ROI.

    (b) The degree of new product fit to strategy.

(iv) Reactor firms should consider using some combination of:

  (a) The development programme ROI.
  (b) The success rate/failure rate.
  (c) The degree of new products fit to business strategy.
  (d) The subjective appraisal of the overall programme success.

Effective Performance Measurement Systems

Companies often describe their strategy in terms of customer service, innovation and the quality and capabilities of their people but then fail to measure these variables (Eccles, 1991). While strategies are often focused simply on "enablers", in order to drive these there is a need to measure performance. To reiterate, measurement is important for the following reasons (Zairi, 1992):

  (i) Because you cannot manage what you cannot measure.
 (ii) To determine what to pay attention to and improve.
(iii) To provide a scoreboard for people to monitor their own performance levels.
(iv) To give an indication of the cost of poor quality.
 (v) To give a standard for making comparisons.
(vi) To comply with business objectives.

Generally, organisational environments are committed to continuous improvement, but "traditional summary measures of performance are generally harmful and incompatible with improvement measures" (Zairi, 1992). Performance measures need to promote and encourage the right behaviours within an organisation, that is, those behaviours which assist the organisation to achieve its goals. They need to reflect a positive image which encourages involvement and ownership within a non-threatening environment if it is to succeed in the development of a continuous improvement ethos.

The characteristics of good performance management are (Zairi and Letza, 1995):

  (i) Performance is reflected at various levels of organisational systems. It is measured at the strategic, tactical and operational levels.

(ii) Performance measurement is a distributed activity reflecting various levels of ownership and control.
(iii) Performance measurement reflects a blend of measures for individual tasks/activities to manage processes.
(iv) Performance measurement highlights opportunities for improvement in all areas with leverage points.

Often, measurement of soft aspects is neglected. However, as experience appears to suggest, it is often the case that by developing the soft aspects of measurement that the hard measures will naturally follow. Therefore, a holistic approach to measurement is required which includes both hard and soft measures. Kaplan (1991) has suggested that "companies should concentrate on internal performance improvement with the expectation of positive impacts on financial performance".

Traditional performance measures have focused on outputs whereas there is a need to look towards the drivers of outputs — leadership, strategy, communication and so forth. It is from these that benefits will flow from improvement to the drivers or enablers. Although managers understand the concepts and the need for measurement, many organisations fail to develop performance measurement systems to support their development due to:

(i) Failure to operationally define performance.
(ii) Failure to relate performance to the process.
(iii) Failure to define the boundaries of the process.
(iv) Misunderstood or misused measures.
(v) Failure to distinguish between control and improving measures.
(vi) Measuring the wrong things.
(vii) Misunderstanding/misuse of information by managers.
(viii) Fear of distorting performance priorities.
(ix) Fear of exposing poor performance.
(x) Perceived reduction in autonomy.

The needs and reasons for the failure of many performance measurement systems are evident. Clearly an inappropriate performance measurement system can act as a barrier to its implementation (Zairi, 1992).

Grafting new measures on to an existing system, which will reflect this change, is not the answer. Neither is making slight adjustments to an existing system. Enhanced competitiveness depends on starting from scratch and asking: "Given our strategy, what are the most important measures of performance, how do the measures relate to one another, and what measures truly produce long-term financial success in our business?" (Johnson, 1990).

Today's organisations compete on opportunity recognition, learning speed, innovation, cycle time, quality, flexibility, reliability and responsiveness. Financially orientated systems are outdated and too rule-bound for a business environment where competition is often based on how managers think about their business and how they invest their time and resources. A real strategic measurement system is one that is balanced, integrated and designed to highlight the firm's critical inputs, outputs and process variables (Eccles, 1991).

Models of Integrated Performance Measurement

The dynamics of today's marketplace require effective performance measures to assist managers in making decisions and taking actions. This enables organisational survival and prosperity. Effective performance measurement systems utilise traditional financial measures, but supplement them with non-financial measures to give a much fuller picture and a more relevant management information system.

Historically, performance measurement has been designed for the benefit of shareholders and senior management rather than line managers and employees. Furthermore, the standard approach to calculating the measures and defining the terms as prescribed by the accounting bodies has enabled inter-company comparisons and reluctance by many to challenge their effectiveness. Consequently, measures which indicate return on capital, profitability and liquidity have dominated most performance measurement systems.

A more holistic approach to performance measurement asks: what is it that drives the top-line performance measures? Is it the process, people, leadership or resource utilisation? If so, are these performance measures included? Investment in knowledge, process improvement and people development will have a payback and impact on financial performance in future accounting periods, but there is a need for interim performance measures to check progress.

Many performance measurement systems fail to be effective because they are disparate, often measuring activities that are of local or individual interest to a manager rather than a key activity for the business.

Measurement requires medium to long-term commitment from senior management and all staff with potentially little impact on the financial performance measures in the short run. The drivers which underpin the financial performance measures, such as teamwork, process design, communication, tools and techniques, require non-financial performance measures to ensure that progress is being made and corrective actions are taken.

A linkage between strategy, actions and measures is essential and, unless companies adapt their measures and measurement systems to facilitate their introduction, implementation will fail to reap the expected benefits (Dixon *et al.*, 1990). Adoption of the wrong measures and performance measurement can be a potential obstacle. In the discussion which follows, we present a select set of frameworks for integrated measurement.

Strategic measurement and reporting technique (SMART)

SMART is a new approach to measurement developed by Wang Laboratories in 1989 (Dixon *et al.*, 1990). The aims of SMART are to integrate financial and non-financial reporting and to concentrate measurement on satisfying customer needs. SMART also provides a link between manufacturing and the company's strategic goals, together with a commitment to continuously improve the process by promoting constant evolution.

The operation of SMART (Fig. 6) begins with the corporate vision at the top of the pyramid and defines the markets in which the company competes, the services provided and the scope of the products. The vision leads to goals for the marketplace. Detailed financial goals lead to the business operating system objectives of customer satisfaction, flexibility and productivity. These objectives are achieved by cross-functional processes and the removal of functional boundaries. The final level in the pyramid is the departmental level, where the criteria includes quality, delivery, process time and waste.

For each goal, the objective and criterion of at least one measure is used. The implementation of SMART resulted in 4% of the existing measures being discarded. Many were redefined and new measures added (Dixon *et al.*, 1990).

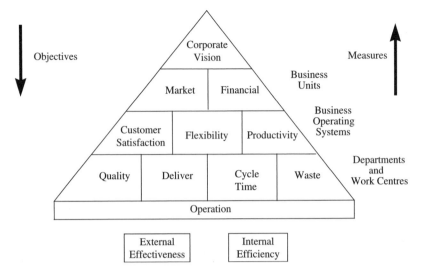

Fig. 6.   The performance pyramid.

Source: Lynch and Cross, 1991.

Quantum performance measurement model

The quantum performance measurement model (Fig. 7) suggests that superior performance is the result of an integrated planning and control system (Bemouski, 1994). Within the quantum performance measurement model, measures are distinguished between process (the activity) and output (the output from the activity). The measures that are used are divided between quality, cost and service (Hronec, 1993).

Balanced business scorecard

Kaplan and Norton (1992) reinforced the view that a balance between financial and non-financial measures is important to modern business:

> "Managers should not have to choose between financial and operational measures... No single measure can provide a clear performance target or focus attention on the critical areas of the business. Managers want a balanced presentation of both financial and operational measures."

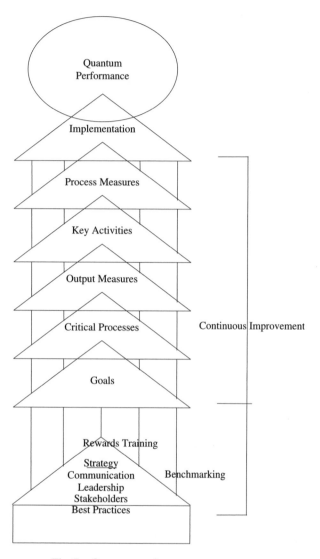

Fig. 7.   Quantum performance measurement.

Source: Hronec, 1993.

Following a year-long research project with 12 companies at the leading edge of performance management, they developed the balanced scorecard which does not dispense with financial measures, but integrates them with complementary operational indicators on "customer satisfaction", "internal processes" and "innovation and improvement" activities as key measures of future financial performance. The scorecard seeks to minimise the amount of information that is presented, but maximise the effectiveness and usefulness of the presentation. This is done by a careful selection of "critical" indicators that really drive the business.

From the "customer" perspective, the scorecard requires the translation of strategic statements at the level of service to specific measures which really matter to the customer, such as quality and delivery time. From the "internal process" perspective, the scorecard focuses upon critical internal operations that are necessary to satisfy customer requirements fully. It also identifies core competencies which are the key to the maintenance of competitive position within the market. The "innovation and improvement" perspective measures the degree to which a business is able to continually improve products and processes to meet the requirements of an increasingly dynamic market.

This balanced approach to performance measurement has a number of significant advantages:

(i) *Strategic focus.* Most importantly, the scorecard focuses on the strategic objectives of the business and measures the degree to which the business is performing satisfactorily to meet these objectives. It also indicates the future direction which should be followed. Apple executives (one of the 12 companies in the study) viewed the scorecard approach as being essential in expanding discussions beyond gross margin, return on equity and market share.

(ii) *Clear and concise.* Most organisations will derive a whole range of indicators for business performance, mainly for individual operating activities. The balanced scorecard, being selective in its choice of indicators, forces senior managers to focus on key measures that are of strategic importance to the business. This provides a crucial balance between short-term and long-term activities.

(iii) *Cross-functional.* The scorecard provides an integrated, or cross-functional, analysis of the business. It can provide information to finance, production, sales, marketing, distribution, administration and so forth on key functional indicators, but may also act as a focus to the entire organisation on what must be done to improve performance.

This integrated approach is crucial to the need to remove perceptions of the business as existing in the form of a series of independent divisions or departments.

Strategic measurement systems (SMS)

Strategic measurement systems was developed to assist management in defining and gaining clarity on their strategies and priorities. It provides managers with data which they may need to support investment proposals, or where R&D backing is required, based on non-financial measures (Vitale *et al.*, 1994). The steps in the development of a SMS are:

 (i) Specify the goal — what are we trying to accomplish?
 (ii) Match the measure to the strategy — what is most important to us? The firm's critical success factors will provide the focus for critical business functions.
(iii) Identify the measures — what would we measure? Feedback will be required from three audiences — customers, investment analysts and industry experts.
(iv) Predict the results — what will change? All aspects of the measure, both positive and negative, need to be considered.
 (v) Build commitment and inspire action — who is on board? Commitment from the top management is required.
(vi) Plan the next step — where do we go from here? This may take the form of setting targets and integration into a formal incentive scheme or communication system.

Thus far, we have reviewed the pertinent theoretical aspects and frameworks of measurement. In the discussion that follows, we present a select group of case studies which serve to highlight the type of innovation measurement and metrics used by companies. The case studies presented highlight the different levels of maturity in measuring innovation, ranging from naïve and ad-hoc systems to comprehensive approaches utilising a variety of measurement methodologies and metrics.

Measurement and Metrics in Practice

Case study one: ICL

Product-based measures

(i) *Cost reduction.* ICL measures its performance in cost reduction by percentage[1] and value-added terms.[2] Regular reviews are held on a periodic basis (monthly) involving customers. The products concerned are examined in relation to the following criteria:

(a) Cost forecasts against targets.
(b) Impact of exchange rates.
(c) Material price changes.
(d) Joint activities to reduce cost by design changes.

In addition, ICL uses value engineering workshops during the early stages of the product development process in order to examine the potential for reducing costs before production starts. The assumption is that at least 80% of product costs should be factored in before the manufacturing phase starts. In previous years, ICL had been setting itself a target of approximately 10% in cost reduction every year. This figure is reliant on two activities:

(i) The ability of the purchasing function to negotiate lower price contracts with suppliers.
(ii) The continuous effort to try and reduce manufacturing costs through innovation, quality improvements and other means.

Process-based measures

(i) *Time to market.* ICL operates in a vulnerable market where, in some categories, product lifetimes could be as little as six months. In line with the company's vision, a process of reducing the introduction times of new circuit boards was started in 1986.[3,4]

---

[1] ICL's cost reduction in percentage terms.
[2] ICL's cost reduction in value-added terms.
[3] Design to manufacture cycle time — manufacturing development build.
[4] Design to manufacture cycle time (printed circuit borads — PCBs) — design release to product general release.

(ii) *Manufacturability assessment.* Manufacturing and design engineers work together in the early stages of new product development. They use design tools based on design for manufacturability (DFM) principles to optimise design so that it will be right the first time. No printed circuit board is allowed to go into production with attributes that would compromise quality or increase manufacturing cycle time.[5-7] The following are some of the benefits achieved from cycle time reduction:

(a) Printed circuit product introduction cycle time reduced to three months.
(b) High data integrity.
(c) Faster and automated take-on of original equipment manufacturer (OEM) design detail (electronic- and data-based).
(d) Common standards between design and manufacturing.
(e) Electronic trading of design and commercial data.
(f) Automated processing of design information for manufacture.

Case study two: Hewlett–Packard

Designer–customer interactions

$$\text{Understanding customer needs} = \frac{\text{Visit to customers}}{\text{Number of designers}}$$

This measure is to promote more interaction between designers and customers by calculating the amount of contact.

Overall effectiveness of product development

(i) Staffing level effectiveness

$$= \frac{\text{Staff initially forecast as needed for a project}}{\text{Staff actually needed by project}} \times 100$$

This measure monitors how closely the projections for the staff needed on a project matched the actual staffing required by the project.

---

[5] Engineering planning cycle time at ICL (PCB assembly planning).
[6] Engineering planning cycle time at ICL (final product assembly planning).
[7] Engineering change cycle time.

Stability of the design

$$= \frac{\text{Number of design changes in a project}}{\text{Total cost of project}} \times 100$$

This measure tracks the number of design changes made. As large projects might need more changes simply because they are larger, this metric, by dividing against the project's costs, adjusts for the size of the project.

Overall effectiveness of the innovation process

Innovation effectiveness

$$= \frac{\text{Number of projects finishing development}}{\text{Number of projects started development}} \times 100$$

Other measures

(i) Progress rate of project

$$= \frac{\text{Months late}}{\text{Total months initially scheduled for project}}$$

(ii) Cost estimation $= \dfrac{\text{Actual cost of phase}}{\text{Projected cost of phase}}$

(iii) Milestone progress rate

$$= \frac{\text{Number of milestones reached during month}}{\text{Number of milestones scheduled that month}} \times 100$$

Case study three: Exxon Chemical

In-process measures

(i) Penetration: Percentage of NPD budget utilising innovation process.
(ii) Percentage of new projects utilising innovation process.
(iii) Focus/Culling: Percentage of NO/GO or hold by stage-gate two.

Results-based measures

(i) Speed of innovation: Elapsed time, stage one through four.
(ii) Performance: Second year EBIT (earning before interest and tax) versus gate four.
(iii) Percentage of revenue from products more than five years old.

Definitions

(i) *Penetration.* The number of projects managed through the innovation process.

(ii) *Focus.* Reflected by early CULLING. Percentage of No Go or hold decisions made during a period of time by the end of stage two (detailed assessment).

(iii) *Speed.* Average period (in months) of average development time for projects approved for commercial launch (stage five) during a specific year.

(iv) *Performance.* NPD/NBD Payout (NBD = new business development). Percentage of actual/projected EBIT ratio in a particular year for projects in their second full year of operation after gate four: "Go Ahead".[8-12]

Case study four: Measurement of R&D at Dupont

Measures developed by the Imaging Systems Department (Research and Development Division) at Dupont are based on a series of key processes:

(i) R&D core processes:

(a) Human development.
(b) Technology planning and development.
(c) Customer-focused innovation.
(d) Product and process design.
(e) Competitive intelligence.
(f) Business team partnership.

(ii) Customer needs groups:

(a) People.
(b) Standard R&D.

---

[8]Fig. 1. Overall number of projects being managed at each stage of the innovation process.
[9]Fig. 2. Number of new projects to stage one.
[10]Fig. 3. Number of GO/NO GO decisions.
[11]Percentage of NO GO or hold decisions made during each year at each stage of the innovation process.
[12]Percentage of sales of products for more than five years — new products as a percentage of revenue.

(c) Occupational Safety and Health Administration (OSHA).

(d) Just in time (JIT) manufacturing.

(e) Process.

(f) Product.

(g) Innovation.

Measures related to the R&D process are referred to as *internal measures* while those related to customer needs are known as *external measures*.

Internal measures

(i) Human development:

    (a) Percentage of courses taken per person.

    (b) Percentage of accomplishment awards.

    (c) Percentage of awards received (externally); organisation's perception of appraisal system.

    (d) Percentage of people actively involved in external professional organisations.

    (e) Percentage of department and local initiatives.

    (f) Percentage of attendance at committee meetings.

    (g) Ratio of courses approved to courses submitted.

    (h) Percentage of degrees earned after employment.

    (i) Percentage of formal university courses.

    (j) Percentage of courses conducted on site.

(ii) Product and process design:

    (a) Yield of vendors.

    (b) Mill cost of formal complaints and raw materials/product type.

    (c) Percentage of clean runs.

    (d) Manufacturing cycle time (receipt of order to shipping).

    (e) Relative product quality — percentage of product line rated first or second by customers.

    (f) Dollar sales of new products in last three years — profits.

    (g) Time spent "fire-fighting" new products and process ("hand holding").

(h) Percentage of machine downtime due to product/process problems of process/product simplifications.

(i) Longevity of product versions.

(j) Effort before versus effort after controlled sale.

(k) Shipping limits of material returned (how much was within specifications versus outside specificatons).

(iii) Business team partnership:

(a) Percentage of people involved in business teams (horizontal integration).

(b) Percentage of new product/process proposals.

(c) Percentage of team awards; survey of business teams — how they treasure R&D participation.

(iv) Technology planning and development:

(a) Percentage of long-term research programmes — need to define timing (active involvement in developing the programmes).

(b) Percentage of patents issued.

(c) Percentage of "core tech" programmes; average time from idea conception (marketing/manufacturing request) to commercialisation.

(d) Percentage of new or modified products and processes delivered.

(e) Percentage of technical publications and presentations external to IMG R&D.

(v) Customer-focused innovation.

The lab programme cycle time:

(a) Percentage of SEED projects applied for.

(b) Percentage of successful SEED projects.

(c) Percentage of milestones achieved on time.

(d) Percentage of patent proposals.

(e) Percentage of new ventures initiated.

(f) Percentage of close customer partnerships.

(g) Percentage of new initiatives started.

(h) Percentage of differentiated products commanding price premium.

(vi) Competitive intelligence:

(a) Percentage of competitive products analysed.

(b) Product technology concepts.

(c) Percentage of patent and literature searches requested (need variable feedback loop).

(d) Comprehensive Competitive Intelligence reports generated/ updated (business).

External key measures

(i) People:

(a) Percentage of people actively participating in external professional societies.

(b) Percentage of external awards received (from groups outside R&D).

(ii) Innovation:

(a) Percentage of successful SEED projects.

(b) Percentage of new ventures initiated.

(iii) Product:

(a) Percentage of raw materials.

(b) Percentage of vendors.

(c) Dollar sales of new products.

(d) Percentage of formal complaints.

(iv) Standard R&D:

(a) Number of patents issued.

(b) Number of publications/presentations outside R&D.

(c) Number of new products/processes.

(d) Time from product/process conception to commercialisation.

(v) OSHA:

(a) Volume of hazardous waste (solid, liquid and gaseous) plantwide.

(vi) Just in time (JIT) manufacturing:

(a) Combined with process and product categories.

(vii) Process:

(a) Yield.

(b) Mill cost.

(c) Manufacturing cycle time (raw materials shipping).

(d) Percentage of clean runs (defect free).

Business level measures: Financials

(i) *Profitability ratios.* These measure the returns generated on sales or investment, often in comparison with industry standards. Examples include:

(a) Profit margin on sales = Net profit after taxes/sales.
(b) Return on total assets = Net profit after taxes/total assets.

(ii) *Activity ratios.* These measure the use of resources and are best used in comparison with industry standards. Examples include:

(a) Fixed asset turnover = Sales/net fixed assets.
(b) Total asset turnover = Sales/total assets.
(c) Average collection period = Receivables/average sales per day.
(d) Inventory turnover = Sales/inventory.

(iii) *Project evaluation and comparison.* These methods help to select competing projects for the utilisation of funds. They are particularly important to commercialisation decisions as new products or processes are often easily conceptualised as the implementation of a project. The following are the two most commonly used techniques:

(a) The payback method calculates and compares the time to pay back initial investments for project alternatives. The more rapid the payback, the more desirable the project. The payback period is the time it takes a company to recover its original investment through net cash flows from the project.
(b) Discounted cash flow finds the present value of the expected net cash flows of an investment, discounted at the cost of capital. Net present value and internal rate of return project evaluation and comparison are types of discounted cash flow analysis. The advantage of these approaches is that they account for both the company's marginal cost of funds and the time profile of expected returns.

Leaning Points from the Case Studies

The case studies presented highlight that while there is a variety of approaches to measuring innovation, the measures can be categorised under three broad headings. These are:

(i) *Process-focused measures.* These are measures which are concerned with speed, cost and quality. They are taken on a regular basis to address aspects of the innovation process which need optimising so that costs are kept to a minimum, time is reduced and quality is enhanced.

(ii) *Product-based measures.* These consist of all the measures concerned with:

  (a) The performance of the product in terms of market share.
  (b) Its worthiness in terms of leading to a competitive advantage — differentiation.
  (c) Its cost in relation to the benefits achieved.
  (d) Its financial worthiness.

(iii) *Business-level measures.* These are primarily financial measures, and present an aggregated picture of the performance of the organisation. Their use to drive innovation has to be guarded carefully because they can lead to a focus on short-term gains, rather than to account for the gains in the long run.

Generally, we can say that:

(i) Process-based and product-based measures are interrelated. Process-based measures are, however, online measures. They often lead to immediate action to deal with the problem and optimise those aspects concerned with the innovation process. Hence bottlenecks do not occur.

(ii) Product-based measures are, however, very often *retrospective* in nature. They can only be compiled once the information is made available, once the project has been complete and the product is performing in the marketplace.

(iii) Being overly concerned with product-based measures early in the innovation process appears to often distract teams from doing the right things (that is, moving the project forward). Imposing these types of measures early on in the process only encourages a mentality of "let's work on less risky projects", "let's play safe". This leads to the achievement of small results without any significant leaps and real impact in the market-place.

(iv) The whole idea of focusing on the innovation process and its improvement is to allow:

  (a) A continuous flow of projects.
  (b) A fast track development process.
  (c) Low cost through improvements and optimising (organisational entitlement) — capability of the process.
  (d) A mixture of large and small projects to reflect a healthy portfolio which incorporates short-term, medium- and long-term business needs.

  It also aims to secure the following:

  (a) Profit improvement.
  (b) Customer satisfaction (market share).
  (c) Consistent growth.
  (d) Competitive supremacy in the business categories concerned.

 (v) The optimisation of the projects *internally* to justify costs and make accurate financial predictions will lead to a "play safe culture" and a product-based culture.
(vi) Optimisation externally is, however, the most recommended route. This necessitates the company to start with its *raison d'être*, the customer, and to align the organisational drivers from then onward.

Final Comments

Performance measures are vital for companies to ensure that they are achieving their goals. Measurement provides an important mechanism to evaluate, control and improve upon existing performance. Measurement creates the basis for comparing performance between different organisations, processes, teams and individuals.

Performance measurements have traditionally focused on financial measures designed to benefit the shareholder rather than the line manager. Innovation managers require data and information which assist them in making business decisions. For example, if the innovation process is beginning to become inefficient, the sooner the manager is made aware of this, the faster the corrective action can be taken. Performance measures are an important means of providing managers with the information they require in order to innovate both effectively and efficiently. Financial information is received much too late by the line manager and will not assist in identifying the cause of the problem. Innovation success is built by having the right approach to measurement, as well as the appropriate metrics to act as vehicles for continuous improvement towards the goal of efficient and effective innovation.

Chapter 14

Learning and Continuous Improvement

John Bessant
University of Exeter, UK

Introduction: The Importance of Learning

Organisations grow through what they know. Knowledge — and the learning processes which generate and deploy such knowledge — lies at the heart of the innovation process and, as such, it represents a key challenge in innovation. Firm-specific knowledge — which may be around a specific technology or understanding of a particular market — represents an important competitive advantage since it has to be accumulated gradually over time. It is often tacit in nature and hard for others to copy and, thus, the strategic advantage conferred is more defensible (Barney, 2001; Prahalad and Hamel, 1994).

But how do organisations go about the process of learning and building sustainable advantage through what they have learned? There is extensive discussion on the mechanisms available to support learning — learning by doing, learning by formal experimentation, learning by collaborating, learning by entering new environments, etc. (Pavitt, 2002). For example, Teece *et al.* (1992) look at the ways in which firms frame and reframe "dynamic capability" while Nonaka (1991) focuses on knowledge capture and sharing routines. Rush *et al.* (1997) and Davies and Hobday (2005) look at ways of capturing learning from projects. Other writers — for example, Senge (1990), Leonard-Barton (1995) and Garvin (1993) — provide different integrated models of proactive learning in organisations,

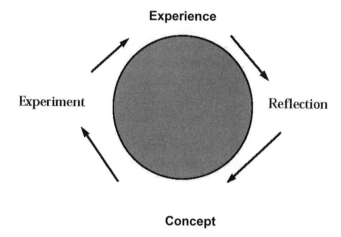

Concept

Fig. 1.   Experiential learning cycle (Kolb, 1975).

indicating the set of capabilities required. Of course, it is not organisations themselves which learn but the individuals within them, and so other studies have focused on the training and development to support and extend the learning capabilities of employees.

It is clear from this that there is no generic solution. Instead, each firm has to work out its own approach; learning capabilities are firm-specific. But it is also clear that there is some commonality of experience — certain classes of approach to the learning problem are used regularly. The examples include benchmarking, collaboration, structured project review and staff development through training.

These approaches can be mapped onto a basic model of the learning process. For example, Fig. 1 shows the well-known experiential learning cycle originally put forward by Kolb (Kolb and Fry, 1975). It views learning as involving a cycle of experiment, experience, reflection and concept development.

Where an individual or firm enters the cycle is not important (though there is evidence for different preferred styles of learning associated with particular entry points). What does matter is that the cycle is completed — and incomplete cycles do not enable learning. Viewed in this way, each of the modes in Table 1 can be linked to one or more stages in the learning cycle; this argues for a multiple approach.

Table 1. Examples of learning mechanisms and their relationship to the learning cycle.

Learning approach	Position on learning cycle	Examples
Benchmarking — learning by comparison	Aids structured reflection	Camp, 1989; Womack *et al.*, 1990.
Collaboration — learning by working with others	Shared experience and experiment	Dodgson, 1993.
Strategic challenge	Structured and challenging reflection	Francis, 1994; Kim, 1998.
Training and development	Introduces new concepts	Pedler *et al.*, 1991.
Project to project learning	Shared experience	Rush *et al.*, 1997; Davies and Hobday, 2005.
Learning from failure	Reflection	Pisano, 1996.

Organisational Routines to Enabling Learning

When talking about learning "capability" in this way, we are really concerned with clusters or patterns of behaviours which have become refined and rehearsed, and which are increasingly and repeatedly used to enable the learning process. In other words, they are "routines" which have been learned and embedded in the organisational culture — the underlying mixture of values and beliefs which drive the "way we do things around here" (Schein, 1984). Winter defines routines as ". . . a relatively complex pattern of behaviour . . . triggered by a relatively small number of initiating signals or choices and functioning as a recognisable unit in a relatively automatic fashion . . ." (Zollo and Winter, 2002). This is not to say that routines are mindless patterns. As Giddens (1984) points out, ". . . the routinised character of most social activity is something that has to be 'worked at' continually by those who sustain it in their day-to-day conduct . . .". It is rather the case that they have become internalised to the point of being unconscious or autonomous.

One such cluster of routines is associated with improving learning at the organisational level by multiplying the number of people actively involved in the process. It is highly relevant to the wider discussion of innovation management capability since it is through these mechanisms that organisations create and deploy knowledge in new or improved products, services and processes. Recent years have seen considerable efforts made to understand and enable high involvement in generating a sustained incremental innovation — activities which are often considered under the generic label "continuous improvement" (CI). This chapter looks at CI in terms of its potential as a strategic capability which firms are increasingly using to help them develop and sustain competencies, and it also suggests that building such capability for incremental innovation may also create possibilities for internal entrepreneurship around more radical innovation challenges.

Continuous Improvement

Continuous improvement (CI) can be defined as "... an organisation wide process of sustained and focused incremental innovation ..." (Bessant, 1994). It is not a new concept — attempts to utilise this approach in a formal way can be traced back to the eighteenth century, when the eighth shogun Yoshimune Tokugawa introduced the suggestion box in Japan. In 1871, Denny's shipyard in Dumbarton, Scotland employed a programme of incentives to encourage suggestions about productivity-improving techniques; they sought to draw out "any change by which work is rendered either superior in quality or more economical in cost". In 1894, the National Cash Register company made considerable efforts to mobilise the "hundred-headed brain" which their staff represented; Eastman Kodak introduced one of the first documented systems of employee involvement in 1989; whilst the Lincoln Electric Company started implementing an "incentive management system" in 1915. NCR's ideas, especially around suggestion schemes, found their way back to Japan where the textile firm of Kanebuchi Boseki introduced them in 1905.

However, it was not until the post-war period that these ideas began to be exploited on a large scale, and they rose to prominence largely as a result of Japanese experience. The idea of employee involvement in improvement programmes was originally introduced to Japan as part of the post-war TWI initiative operated by the US and its allies, but internalisation and the development of a Japanese model — *kaizen* — soon followed (Schroeder and Robinson, 1993).

Kaizen evolved over an extended period and became a keystone of Japanese success in manufacturing. It represents a potent force for improving various aspects of organisational performance. For example, much of its original application was in the domain of quality, where a reputation for poor and shoddy products was turned to one in which world standards, measured in defective parts per million or less, were set. But kaizen has been applied with equal effect in other areas, such as increasing flexibility (through set-up time reduction), increasing plant availability (through total productive maintenance) and cost reduction (in particular, keeping pace with a highly valued Yen) (Bessant, 2003).

The scale of CI activity in large Japanese firms remains impressive. Firms like Toyota (which regularly receives in excess of two million suggestions a year, equivalent to 35 per worker) provide a powerful illustration of the extent to which CI represents a potent mechanism for securing high involvement in regular incremental innovation within Japanese firms. Importantly, participation rates are high, with the majority of the workforce involved, and implementation of their ideas extensive — not least because they represent a stream of small improvements rather than major (and resource-hungry) changes.

During the past 40 years, and driven by concerns around total quality management and "lean production", CI has increasingly been deployed in other countries with similar success. A study of UK experience carried out for the Chartered Institute of Personnel and Development collected evidence to support the contention that in the twenty-first century, "Tayloristic task management gives way to knowledge management; the latter seeking to be cost-efficient by developing an organisation's people assets, unlike the former which views labour as a cost to be minimised" (CIPD, 2001).

Although the task of convincing sceptical managers and shareholders remains difficult, "... more than 30 studies carried out in the UK and US since the early 1990s leave no room to doubt that there is a correlation between people management and business performance, that the relationship is positive, and that it is cumulative: the more and more effective the practices, the better the result ..." (Caulkin, 2001).

Reviews of the regular UK Workplace Employee Relations Survey stress links between the use of more HR practices and a range of positive outcomes, including greater employee involvement, satisfaction and commitment, productivity and better financial performance (Guest *et al.*, 2000).

Company-level studies support this view. Ideas UK is an independent body which offers advice and guidance to firms wishing to establish and sustain employee involvement programmes. It grew out of the UK Suggestion Schemes Association and offers an opportunity for firms to learn about and share experiences with high involvement approaches. Its 2009 annual survey of around 160 organisational members highlighted cost savings of over £100 million with the average implemented idea being worth £1,400, giving a return on investment of around five to one. Participation rates across the workforce are around 28%.

Specific examples include the Siemens Standard Drives (SSD) suggestion scheme which generates ideas which save the company about £750,000 a year. The electrical engineering giant receives about 4,000 ideas per year, of which approximately 75% are implemented. Pharmaceutical company Pfizer's scheme generates savings of around £250,000, and the Chessington World of Adventures ideas scheme saves around £50,000. Much depends on firm size, of course — for example, the BMW Mini plant managed savings of close to £10 million at its plant in Cowley, which they attribute to employee involvement.

Similar data can be found in other countries — for example, a study conducted by the Employee Involvement Association in the USA suggested that companies can expect to save close to £200 annually per employee by implementing a suggestion system. Ideas America report around 6,000 schemes operating. In Germany, specific company savings reported by Zentrums Ideenmanagement include (2010 figures) Deutsche Post DHL €220 million, Siemens €189 million and Volkswagen €94 million. Importantly, the benefits are not confined to large firms — amongst small and medium enterprises (SMEs) were Takata Petri €6.3 million, Herbier Antriebstechnik €3.1 million and Mitsubishi Polyester Film €1.8 million. In a survey of 164 German and Austrian firms representing 1.5 million workers they found around 20% (326,000) of workers were involved and were contributing just under one million ideas (955,701). Of these, two thirds (621,109) were implemented, producing savings of €1.086 billion. The investment needed to generate these was in the order of €109 million, giving an impressive rate of return. Table 2 summarises some key numbers.

Another major survey, involving over 1,000 organisations in a total of seven countries, provides a useful map of the take-up and experience

Table 2. High involvement innovation in German and Austrian companies (Source: Zentrums Ideenmanagement).

Key characteristic	
Ideas/100 workers	62
Participation rate	21%
Implementation rate (of ideas)	69%
Savings per worker (€)	622
Investment per worker (€)	69
Investment to realise each implemented idea (€)	175
Savings per implemented idea (€)	1540
Ideas per worker per year	Ranges from average of 6 to as high as 21

with high involvement innovation in manufacturing. Overall, around 80% of organisations were aware of the concept and its relevance, but its actual implementation, particularly in more developed forms, involved around half of the firms (Boer *et al.*, 1999).

The average number of years which firms had been working with high involvement innovation on a systematic basis was 3.8, supporting the view that this is not a "quick fix", but something to be undertaken as a major strategic commitment. Indeed, those firms which were classified as "CI innovators" — operating well-developed high involvement systems — had been working on this development for an average of nearly seven years. Similar patterns can be found in individual case studies explored in greater detail elsewhere (Gallagher and Austin, 1997).

To this impressive list should be added numerous examples from the public sector where employee engagement schemes have been increasingly used to improve productivity and draw out innovative approaches to public service delivery (Bason, 2011).

CI and Learning/Competence Building

The strength of CI as a learning capability is that it embeds a high frequency learning cycle across much of the organisation. For example, in producing their millions of suggestions every year, the employees of Toshiba, Toyota and others are involved in problem-finding and problem-solving on a daily basis. In the process, they use links to all stages in the learning cycle. The underlying learning behaviours associated with CI have become rehearsed and reinforced to the point where they are now "the way we do things around here". In other words, learning is part of the culture embedded in a cluster of CI routines.

In particular:

(i) CI mobilises more learners across the organisation in a formal sense. Instead of innovation being primarily the province of few specialists, it becomes the responsibility of many.

(ii) It embodies a standardised learning process, usually involving some form of explicit problem-finding and problem-solving and review of methodology, which can be shared and adapted.

(iii) It deals with easily digestible increments of learning which can be absorbed through many frequent, small cycles rather than occasional, disruptive big ones.

(iv) With its emphasis on display and measurement (but also on understanding of those measures by users), it formalises and makes available knowledge which hitherto was in the tacit domain, such as critical process variables. This has close links with the knowledge management model suggested by Nonaka (1991).

(v) Through the involvement of non-specialists, it opens up the possibility for challenges to accepted solutions. Such naïve, but often penetrating, questions can enable "unlearning" to take place.

Typically, CI activities include systematic search, controlled experiment, structured reflection and capture and sharing of learning. In many cases, this is enshrined in a simple problem-solving model such as the Deming wheel of "plan, do, check, act" (PDCA), or variations (Deming, 1986).

There is some empirical support for the view of CI as a mechanism for organisational learning. For example, Sirkin and Stalk (1990), in their description of the turnaround of a US paper mill, identify four learning loops. Leonard-Barton (1991) also explains the successful innovative performance of a US steel mill in terms of learning loops, again based on building a deep understanding of the key process parameters and extending it through a process of experimentation and consolidation. Figuereido (2001) reports similar learning development in his detailed studies of Brazilian steel plants.

Characteristics of Learning Organisations

A number of writers have tried to characterise "learning organisations", and their work suggests that several key components are involved. Table 3 indicates the complementarity between these and effective CI practices.

Table 3. CI practices and learning organisations (based on Garvin, 1993).

Characteristic of learning organisation	CI routines
Training and development emphasis	CI focuses on the formal development of problem-solving skills through tools and techniques. It also emphasises the importance of individual thinking, as well as doing, and seeks to develop this through formal skills training, background personal development, etc.
Establish a formal process	CI revolves around a shared and formalised model of problem-finding and problem-solving. Implementation methodologies for this include Deming's PDCA cycle, six sigma, lean methodologies, etc. Although these "core" approaches are widely used, there is a significant element of adaptation to suit local conditions.
Measurement	Most CI involves some component of measurement — from simple tally charts and data collection through to sophisticated statistical process control techniques. Measurement also focuses attention on getting information about process activities and, in doing so, learning about them and what good performance means. This moves measurement away from being an instrument for control and towards being a tool which people can use to guide improvement, but in doing so it can pose challenges for conventional measurement systems and targets.
Document	Closely associated with measurement is the capture of information resulting from experiments in trying to solve problems. Whether successful or otherwise, there is a high risk of re-inventing the wheel unless information is captured and displayed for others to use. Organisations do not have memories as such, but they do have libraries, databases, procedures, drawings and other storage mechanisms for information and knowledge. The challenge in effective CI is to transfer the experiences of individuals to a form in which it can be more easily shared and communicated to others.

(*Continued*)

Table 3.   (*Continued*)

Characteristic of learning organisation	CI routines
Experiment	Central to successful CI is a climate which allows for extensive experimentation and does not punish failures if those experiments go wrong. This approach of continuing experimentation is essential to improving and developing new processes. Finding out the limits of processes, or possible new ways of managing them, is one of the tasks traditionally carried out in R&D and engineering departments. But mobilising the resource to do this across the whole organisation would take a great deal of effort if it were handled by specialists; CI offers an alternative by giving the responsibility and authority to everyone to undertake experiments.
Challenge	In order to maintain momentum, CI programmes often include not only stretching targets, but continually re-setting them. In his account of how Toyota reduced set-up times on presses, Shingo (1983) describes the relentless re-setting of targets to drive the times down from several hours to, eventually, single minutes. A wide range of CI tools and techniques have been developed to assist this process of systematic challenge, from simple "five why" approaches to complex analysis. Doing this requires a systematic approach to experiment and challenge, as well as a refusal to accept that anything cannot be improved. As one commentator puts it, "... best is the enemy of better ... ". Another motto, reported by Leonard-Barton (1991) and descriptive of this approach, is: "if it ain't being fixed, it's broke!"
Reflect — learn from the past	A common problem in establishing learning cycles within organisations is the absence of time, space and structure for reflection. CI programmes are often characterised by regular meetings, during which progress is reviewed and new problems are identified for work. Again, many of the tools and techniques in CI are designed as structured aids to this process — from simple benchmarking, fishbone and other analytical tools through to more complex aids.

(*Continued*)

Table 3. (*Continued*)

Characteristic of learning organisation	CI routines
Use multiple perspectives	Another powerful mechanism for enhancing and encouraging learning is to bring different perspectives to bear on a problem. This can be done in a number of ways, ranging from bringing different groups together in cross-functional teams to broadening individual experience and outlook through training, rotation, secondment or visiting. It is also here that benchmarking plays an important role: it provides an opportunity to review and explore how other organisations tackle particular issues and problems.
Display	Closely linked to documenting the results of CI is the need to display and communicate them. This serves several purposes: it provides a powerful motivator for the teams or individuals responsible for them, and it also serves to carry over ideas which might find application elsewhere in the organisation.

In summary, it can be argued that CI represents a powerful approach to competence building because it has the potential to develop and embed a continuous learning capability across the organisation. Fulfilling this potential is, however, not easy to achieve and we must now turn our attention to the problems of acquiring and developing CI capability.

Developing CI Capability

Much of the reported experience of implementing CI indicates difficulties, particularly in sustaining the process (Boer *et al.*, 1999; Bessant, 2003). For many firms, CI adoption remains a "fashion" item which they try, find difficult and move on from. However, it is also possible to identify organisations which have succeeded in obtaining *strategic* advantage — where efforts have been made and sustained over decades. (For example, many of the major Japanese firms began their CI activities in the 1950s and have been systematically refining and developing them since.)

Our research suggests that there is a correlation between the extent of what can be termed CI performance — its contribution to reduced costs, improved quality, faster response and so forth — and the extent to which the practice of CI is developed and embedded in the organisation (Bessant, 2003). In particular, we suggest that it is possible to identify a number of key behaviours which have to be learned and reinforced to establish CI capability. These behaviours cluster together and are integrated and built upon to acquire capability in a hierarchical process. (The analogy can be drawn to the process of learning to drive. This involves a progressive acquisition of basic control skills, their integration into increasingly complex suites of behaviour, and gradual development of capability. With time and experience, the capability can be stretched — from simple competence to pass the driving test through to driving different cars, on different roads, under different conditions and so forth. Eventually, a state is reached where driving becomes a near automatic capability, going on in the background whilst conscious attention is given to other tasks.)

The theoretical underpinnings of this approach lie in the concept of "routines". As noted by several authors, the development of firm-specific routines is an important determinant of successful innovative performance (Pentland and Rueter, 1994; Cohen, 1996). While the generic routines can be specified in terms of particular new behaviours which must be learned and reinforced — for example, systematic problem-solving through some form of learning cycle or monitoring and measuring to drive improvement — the particular ways in which different organisations actually achieve this will vary widely. Thus, routines for CI are essentially firm-specific. This is one reason why simply imitating what was done successfully within Japanese firms proved to be such a poor recipe for many UK firms. There is no short cut in the process; CI behaviours have to be learned, reinforced and built upon to develop capability. (Details of the behavioural model and the constituent routines can be found in Bessant, 2003.)

The idea of increasingly skilful practice of the basic CI behaviours, and the notion that improved results (both in terms of business benefits and increased involvement in the CI process) follow from higher levels of such practice, enables us to posit a framework for mapping the evolution of CI capability. (This has much in common with other models such as the Capability Maturity model of software development or the EFQM Business Excellence model (Paulk *et al.*, 1993)). Using this framework, it is possible to position an organisation in terms of the extent to which it has managed to develop and embed CI behaviours. This can be done through observation and examination of artefacts which result from consistent and repeated patterns of behaviour.

A Reference Model for CI Capability

Our analysis of the process of CI development in a wide range of organisations suggests that there is a common pattern of stages of development. (To use the metaphor of the development of CI being a journey, these would represent milestones along the way.) Associated with each is the articulation and acquisition of particular behaviours: as the process develops, so the challenge lies not only in acquiring and embedding behaviours, but in integrating them into a systematic framework. This progress can be represented on a simple two-dimensional "reference model" which maps out stages in the development of both performance and practice (Table 4).

Table 4.   The basic performance and practice dimensions of the model.

Level	Performance	Practice
0 = No CI activity	No impact from CI.	Random problem-solving. No formal efforts or structure. Occasional bursts punctuated by inactivity and non-participation. Dominant mode of problem-solving is by specialists. Short-term benefits.
1 = Trying out the ideas	Minimal and local effects only. Some improvements in morale and motivation. No strategic impact.	CI happens as a result of learning curve effects associated with a particular new product or process, and then fades out again. Or it results from a short-term input — a training intervention, for example — and leads to a small impact around those immediately concerned with it. These effects are often short-lived and very localised.

(Continued)

Table 4.   (*Continued*)

Level	Performance	Practice
2 = Structured and systematic CI	Local level effects. Measurable CI activity, such as the number of participants and ideas produced. Measurable performance effects confined to projects. Little or no "bottom line" impact.	Formal attempts to create and sustain CI. Use of a formal problem-solving process. Use of participation. Training in basic CI tools. Structured idea management system. Recognition system. Often parallel system to operations. Can extend to cross-functional work, but on an ad-hoc basis.
3 = Strategic CI	Policy deployment links local and project level activity to broader strategic goals. Monitoring and measurement drives improvement on these issues which can be measured in terms of the impact on the "bottom line" — for example, cost reductions, quality improvements and time savings.	All of the above, plus the formal deployment of strategic goals. Monitoring and measurement of CI against these goals. In-line system.
4 = Autonomous innovation	Strategic benefits, including those from discontinuous, major innovations and incremental problem-solving.	All of the above, plus responsibility for mechanisms, timing and so forth devolved to problem-solving unit. High levels of experimentation.
5 = The learning organisation	Strategic innovation. Ability to deploy competence base to competitive advantage.	CI as the dominant way of life. Automatic capture and sharing of learning. Everyone is actively involved in the innovation process. Incremental and radical innovation.

Earlier, we saw that competence building is related to learning capability and, thus, the more developed the CI practice, the greater the impact we might expect to see. This is borne out in empirical data where firms which can demonstrate strategic performance advantage can also link this to the extent of the development of CI practice. At low levels of practice development, the emphasis in CI development is primarily on "getting the habit" — articulating and experimenting with CI behaviours and gradually linking them into a structured and systematic framework. In terms of competence development, most activities are concerned with making tacit knowledge explicit — for example, by describing and defining procedures and then improving on them. As the organisation develops higher levels of CI practice, there is a shift towards more experimental forms of learning — from what Melcher *et al.* (1990) call standard-maintaining, to continuously improving systems. At high levels, the kind of autonomous experimentation, sharing and open-ended learning behaviour typified by descriptions of "the learning organisation" becomes the norm.

Learning to Learn

While much of the task in building CI capability is concerned with refining and improving the suite of activities in what is essentially an adaptive learning cycle, it is also clear that at certain stages of CI development, there is a need for what Senge (1990) terms "generative" learning and what Argyris and Schon (1978) call "double loop" learning. That is, the need for reframing the problem and finding new classes of solution. This is particularly associated with moving from one level in the reference model to the next, and is typically the result of the experience of reaching the limits of performance within a particular practice level. For example, "level 2" performance would see regular activity and local level impacts, but no real contribution to strategic goals. The reframing is necessary to develop routines which link the business strategy to the CI activity — through policy deployment, monitoring and measuring behaviours.

Much of this activity is concerned with finding particular problems — "blocks" — and deploying solutions — "enablers" — to deal with them. Over time, it has become clear that many of these "blocks" are commonly experienced. Similarly, many of the "enablers" have widespread applicability (although they will need tailoring to particular circumstances). Table 5 gives some examples; it follows from this that there are real possibilities for learning from others in developing CI capability.

Table 5. Enablers for continuous improvement.

Behavioural routines	Blockages	Enablers
"Getting the CI habit" — Legitimating and embedding basic problem-solving behaviour	Lack of suitable starting point/project to move from concepts into action. No formal process for finding and solving problems. Ideas are not responded to. Lack of skills in problem-solving. Lack of motivation. No structure for CI. Lack of group process skills.	Simple CI activities focused on the workplace — for example, 5S techniques. PDCA or similar structural model plus training in simple idea management system based on rapid response. Training in simple CI tools — brainstorming, fishbone techniques and so forth. Recognition system. Simple vehicles based on groups. Facilitator training.
"Focusing CI" — Getting strategic benefit from CI	No strategic impact of CI. Lack of measurable benefit.	Policy deployment techniques — to focus problem-solving on strategic targets. Hoshin kanri tools. Introduce training in monitoring and measurement. Statistical process control. Process mapping and ownership.
"Spreading the word" — Extending CI beyond the local level		Cross-functional CI teams. Inter-firm development initiatives. Process modelling tools and training.
"Walking the talk"	Lack of co-operation across divisions. Lack of inter-firm CI. Lack of process orientation. Conflict between espoused and practised values. No capture of learning.	Articulation and review. Post-project reviews. Story-board techniques. Encapsulation in procedures.

Extending the scope of high involvement innovation

Much of the discussion of CI has been around "shop-floor" activities and incremental problem-solving. As we have discussed, this represents a powerful high involvement "engine" for innovation, delivering a steady stream of improvements which can contribute to key dimensions of productivity and quality. Importantly, the diffusion of these ideas into services and into public sector operations has been widespread and underlines the generic nature of the opportunity.

Implicit in such models is, however, the potential for higher levels of engagement with innovation. In the reference model, stages above level 3 imply a degree of autonomy and experimentation which is similar to that found in R&D laboratories or entrepreneurial start-up businesses. In principle, high involvement innovation can be extended to engage internal entrepreneurship in which employees identify and work on new business opportunities as major projects which may offer novel growth pathways for the parent organisation.

Analysis of ideas generated in CI schemes suggests that the majority of them are relatively simple "do what we do but better" improvements, and these can be quickly and effectively implemented at the level they are generated, often by the employees who originated them. But there are other ideas which require more resources to generate and implement solutions which have more of a strategic impact. And there are a small number of potentially high-impact ideas which require a significant commitment of resources and time but which offer new departure points — "doing something different". Innovation of this type is usually associated with start-up entrepreneurs who generate a business case for taking their ideas forward and mobilise networks of support to help realise the opportunity. Radical innovation of this kind is usually sourced outside a large organisation but the potential exists for harnessing internal entrepreneurial behaviour to provide a source of renewal and growth.

Studies of "intrapreneurship" indicate the significant potential in mobilising energy, ideas and resources around a new vision, and many organisations attempt to stimulate this kind of culture. For example, 3M attributes much of its success in breakthrough products to well-developed policies and structures to encourage and nurture intrapreneurship (Gundling, 2000). There is growing evidence that suc han approach can be used across a high involvement platform in which employees generate innovation ideas which they can then cluster around and take forward to more significant levels.

Conclusions

Arguably, the development of CI is a critical task for twenty-first century knowledge-based organisations, since it opens up possibilities for high involvement in developing strategic competencies. The embedding of a high frequency cycle of problem-finding, problem-solving, review, sharing and capture of learning is likely to be a critical issue. But it poses major challenges in terms of not only learning new behaviours, but also in forgetting — "unlearning" — many old ones which have traditionally excluded the majority of the workforce from participation in the problem-solving activities that characterise the true learning organisation.

Chapter 15

Creating Value by Generative Interaction[1]

Michael M. Hopkins, Joe Tidd and Paul Nightingale
SPRU, University of Sussex, UK

Introduction

The two related concepts of open innovation and user-centric innovation are currently popular in the management and policy literature on technology and innovation. However, despite the large volume of empirical work, many of the prescriptions being proposed are fairly general, rather than specific to particular contexts and contingencies. The proponents of open innovation tend to offer universal, and often universally positive, prescriptions (Trott and Hartmann, 2009) compared to research on user-led innovation, which suggests that the specific mechanisms and outcomes of open innovation models are very sensitive to context and contingency (Flowers and Henwood, 2008). This is not surprising since the open or closed nature of innovation is historically contingent and does not entail a simple shift from closed to open as often suggested in the literature (Mowery, 2009). Work that is based on Pavitt's (1984) paper and the taxonomy he proposes, shows that patterns of innovation differ fundamentally — by sector, firm and strategy.

There is a need to examine the mechanisms that help to generate successful open innovation (Enkel *et al.*, 2009). In this chapter, we contribute to a shift in the debate from potentially misleading general prescriptions,

---

[1] An earlier version of this chapter was published in *R&D Management*, 2011, **41**(1), 44–60.

and provide some empirical insights into the precise mechanisms and potential limitations of open, user-centric innovation in one particular industrial context — technology and engineering consultancies (TECs). Research in a tradition that goes back to Woodward (1958) shows that complex technologies developed in projects typically involve interactions with distributed external actors and users (Hobday, 1998; Chandler, 1990, p. 68), which makes project success context dependent (Blindenbach-Driessen and van den Ende, 2006). In this chapter, we unpick some of the mechanisms that generate or restrict innovation, with a particular focus on types of client relationships and interactions.

First we review the literatures on open and user-centric innovation, and innovation by project-based organizations. Next we discuss our method, which includes a large web-based survey to identify broad issues and patterns of interaction, and in-depth project-level studies of TECs to reveal the micro- and meso-mechanisms of open, user-centric innovation. We go on to describe the business context of TECs, and then we identify the mechanisms that support *generative interaction* and generate mutual benefits for the actors, particularly benefits that extend beyond the project to affect future cycles of activity. We also identify a dark side of user-centric innovation, which shows that interactions with users can limit innovation (degenerative interaction). Finally, we offer some suggestions about the implications of our findings for technology and innovation management and policy, and highlight some avenues for further research.

Open, User-centric Innovation in Project-based Organizations

The original idea of open innovation was that firms should (also) exploit external sources and resources to innovate, a notion that is difficult to contest. However, wider dissemination of this thesis (Chesbrough, 2003) shows that it is difficult to research and implement (Chesbrough *et al.*, 2006), to the point that it has now become "all things to all people", lacking explanatory or predictive power (Tidd and Bessant, 2009). The empirical evidence on the utility of open innovation is limited, and practical prescriptions overly general (Trott and Hartmann, 2009). Individual case studies are frequently not generalizable, while studies based on the various

Community Innovation Surveys (Laursen and Salter, 2006; Poot *et al.*, 2009) provide only simple counts of external sources and partnerships. Thus, they may suffer from survivor bias and also reveal little about the mechanisms of and limitations to open innovation.

The phenomenon of open innovation is not new (Mowery, 2009) and innovation that exploits external networks through a process of recursive learning and testing is a classic organizational response to the complexity or uncertainty of technology and markets (Freeman, 1991). Thus, the well-established innovation networks literature potentially can contribute much to the debate on open innovation. Innovation networks are more than an aggregation of bilateral collaborative relationships or dyads (Belussi and Arcangeli, 1998) as embedded social context and position relative to other actors have major impacts on innovative activity. Variations in the degree and type of such interaction typically produces a dynamic, inherently unstable and unpredictable set of relationships, which make network-based innovation fundamentally different from the trial-and-error process found within individual firms (Bidault and Fischer, 1994).

Networks shape the flow and the sharing of information, and generate power and control imbalances among actors (Gulati, 1998). This means that the position an organization occupies in a network is strategically important and reflects its power and influence. Sources of power include resources (technology, expertise, economic strength), processes (decision making) and legitimacy (trust) (Hardy and Philips, 1998). Hakansson and Waluszewski (2003) identify types of interactions influenced by network position:

- *product interactions* — where products and groups of products and services interact, are adapted and evolve;
- *process interactions* — where the interdependencies between product and process and between different processes and production facilities interact and are utilized;
- *social interaction within organizations* — where business units within the same organization have social interactions, that comprise knowledge of, and an ability to work with, each other;
- *social interactions between organizations* — external business relationships, which can impede or provide opportunities for innovation.

More recent research has examined the potential for firms explicitly to design or selectively to participate in innovation networks, within a strategic path-creating rather than passive path-dependent process. Doz *et al.*'s (2000) study of 53 research networks identifies two distinct dynamics of formation and growth: emergent networks and engineered networks. The *emergent* network develops as a result of environmental interdependence and common interests. The formation and development of the *engineered* network requires a triggering entity (Doz *et al.*, 2000), which is usually the activity of a nodal firm to recruit network members regardless of their environmental interdependence or similar interests. These different types of network present different opportunities for learning, the development of proprietary standards, locking customers and other related companies into position, ensuring technological compatibility, etc. which gives core positioned firms an advantage over firms on the periphery (Hooi-Soh and Roberts, 2003).

User–producer interactions are particularly important in these networks (Freeman, 1991). User-led innovation results in better-specified open innovation is based on a longer research tradition (von Hippel, 1976; Rothwell *et al.*, 1974) and has greater potential in terms of technology and innovation management (Flowers and Henwood, 2008; NESTA, 2008). Users are characterized variously as "consumers" whose needs must be understood, as "tough customers" (Rothwell and Gardiner, 1983) with exacting demands and as "lead users" (von Hippel, 1986) that promote product modifications and are often able to predict future demand. In user-centric innovation the boundary between consumer and producer, and between "innovators" and "adopters", tends to become blurred as innovation develops and becomes more complex (Hobday *et al.*, 2000).

The scope of user-led innovation has broadened from its original narrow focus on identifying and internalizing specialist knowledge from users (von Hippel, 1976, 1977) that was difficult to capture via market research (Rothwell *et al.*, 1974; Maidique and Zirger, 1985). As Rothwell describes it, tough customers mean good design (Rothwell and Gardiner, 1983) and very demanding customers, such as the military seeking to develop stealth aircraft, provide a powerful "pull" for radical innovation (Rich and Janos, 1994). Users have come to mean external developer communities (von Hippel, 2005) and even wider communities of interest such as open-source software communities (von Hippel and von Krogh, 2006; Osterloh and Rota, 2007).

Lead users are particularly important for the development of complex products; in so-called "vanguard projects" (Davies and Brady, 2000), they may open up the need for new requirements ahead of what is generally available in the market. Sophisticated users in business-to-business markets, such as scientific instruments, capital equipment and information technology (IT) systems, co-develop innovation and act as early adopters. The results in the lead user literature are open to a potential problem of survivor bias, and the practical difficulties related to peripheral firms identifying lead users *ex ante* when success is defined *ex post* and contingent on network position. Helpfully, a recent review identified a number of characteristics of lead users (Morrison *et al.*, 2004): (i) they *recognize requirements early*; (ii) they *expect a high level of benefits* due to their market position and complementary assets; (iii) they *identify and develop their own innovations and applications*; and (iv) they see themselves and are perceived by their peers *to be pioneering and innovative*.

Firms developing innovative complex products and services can benefit from using lead users to both co-develop products and provide feedback that will help to predict the success of the particular innovation (Tidd and Bodley, 2002). A study by Callahan and Lasry (2004) of 55 telecommunications infrastructure projects found that the importance of customer input increased with technological newness. It showed also that there had been a shift from customer surveys and focus groups to co-development, because "conventional marketing techniques [had] proved to be of limited utility, were often ignored, and in hindsight were sometimes strikingly inaccurate" (Callahan and Lasry, 2004). Whyte *et al.* (2008) and Hales and Tidd (2009) provide similar results respectively for semiconductor capital goods and architecture practices.

Such findings are particularly important for project-based organizations (PBO) (Hobday *et al.*, 2000), which inherently are more open and user-centric than conventional organizations. Such organizational forms are used to realize specific, one-off projects (e.g. the construction of a major facility such as an airport or a hospital) or to manage the design and fabrication of complex product systems (CoPS) such as aero engines, flight simulators or communications networks (Hobday, 1998; Whitley, 2006).

Project organizations combine many different elements into an integrated whole, often involving different types of firms, long timescales and high levels of technological risk (Davies *et al.*, 2007). Their organizational efficiency comes from economies of system, rather than economies of scale (Nightingale *et al.*, 2000) because this organizational form enables the creation and re-creation of new organizational structures to fit the demands of each new project and client, and is able more easily than functional organizations to integrate diverse types of knowledge (Hobday *et al.*, 2000a). However, PBOs have an inherent weakness in their ability to co-ordinate resources across projects and to capture innovation and learning (Hobday *et al.*, 2000a). Nevertheless, PBOs are associated with major innovations in project management and organization, in areas such as project financing, regulation and risk-sharing, and in sectors as diverse as pharmaceuticals and civil engineering. Although this type of innovation may appear to be very different from the core innovation process associated with conventional new product development, the underlying process is still one of careful understanding and meeting of user needs. It is important to have user involvement throughout development, and to integrate their different perspectives.

Based on the existing research, when and whether PBOs benefit from open, user-centric innovation is unclear. Selection bias, especially in case studies of exceptionally successful firms or projects, can be misleading in finding the experience to be positive. Research suggests that the dynamics of networks is an important influence on the success or failure of projects. In particular, Lane and Maxfield (1996) suggest successful innovative collaborations result from situations where two organizations with different perspectives and capabilities share commitment to a common direction, interact in a recurring manner and value and monitor and nurture their relationship. Such *generative relationships* can "induce changes in the way participants see their world and act in it and ... give rise to new entities, like agents, artifacts, even institutions" (Lane and Maxfield, 1996, p. 216). Importantly, Lane and Maxfield (1996, p. 221) emphasize that the precise nature of the benefits deriving from generative relationships cannot be anticipated, in part because "relationships generate relationships". The positive results of generative relationships may extend to future projects with the same or other clients, based on a reputation effect. Swan and Scarbrough

(2005) refer to generative interactions rather than relationships, to describe situations involving successful innovation in which knowledge integration is facilitated by network co-ordination. They also refer to degenerative interactions which occur when this co-ordination fails and the knowledge is not integrated.

While these comparative case studies (Lane and Maxfield, 1996; Swan and Scarbrough, 2005) focus on bilateral relationships, in this chapter we extend the concept to the multiple meso-level interactions that occur in the wider business environment. We refer to the sum of these relationships in the ecology (i.e. a particular market in a particular geographic system) as either *generative interactions* or *degenerative interactions*. We combine the insights from work on relationships and their potential for providing feedback effects, with whether these feedback effects are beneficial or deleterious. From a methodological perspective, it is important to emphasize that generative interactions may be localized, to the extent that they are identifiable only at the department or division level in an organization (Lane and Maxfield, 1996). In other words, they may not be apparent at firm level, and are a feature of the environments of only some employees with particular business activities and links. In this chapter we examine the experience of firms engaged in open, user-centric innovation in different industry environments, and identify how different interaction dynamics influence innovation. We focus on TECs, which are precisely the sort of firms where relationships with users are likely to influence both the opportunity for innovation, and the potential to create and capture value.

Method

The research on which this chapter is based was conducted as part of the MINE (Managing Innovation in the New Economy) research programme. A major part of the programme involved a large web-based survey designed to capture the broad range of innovation dynamics in different industry sectors. Cluster analysis enabled the identification of seven stable and statistically different groups of a minimum of 100 firms that use innovation to create and capture value in similar ways. The survey instrument is available at www.minesurvey.polymtl.ca and detailed statistical results are reported elsewhere (Miller *et al.*, 2008; Miller and Floricel, 2007). Based on the innovation dynamics across clusters that were identified, we conducted a series of case studies to investigate innovation within each cluster. In this chapter we focus on the dynamics of one cluster, "systems engineering and consultancy", represented in this chapter by the TECs. We use the case studies to build a theory of how innovation occurs within a group of firms that are part of a cluster; however, we do not test the generalizability of this theory to other sub-groupings (Eisenhardt and Graebner, 2007; Pratt, 2009). The other groups within the cluster include IT consultancies and management consultancies and subsequent research could attempt to generalize our theory to these groups.

We conducted an inductive study to capture the meso- and micro-level mechanisms involved in innovation, based on broad ranging interviews with firms. The interviews included questions on value creation and capture, corporate and innovation strategies, and external influences on innovation.

Theory building does not require random sampling (Pratt, 2009) and sampling for this study was undertaken specifically to support the identification of key modes of innovation in TECs. Because context is important, firms were selected on the basis of their international coverage and experience in the market. The interviews thus provided information of experience in a variety of contexts. Efforts were also made to ensure different industrial sectors were discussed in each firm. In part, this was designed to provide reassurance to interviewees that the information they were providing was not being revealed to competitors. The firms participating in the study were selected from a directory of UK engineering firms (Fullerlove, 2005), which ensured the inclusion of well-known and less-familiar and more and less successful firms in the sample. The final selection of seven firms was on the basis of early agreement to participate in the project and agreement to provide access to data (see Table 1). Note that the unit of analysis is not the individual firm because we would expect to find interactions at the level of business units (Lane and Maxfield, 1996). It is the business unit-level interactions that we asked interviewees about, based on their personal experience. Five of the business units in the sample are focused on particular sectors, but are units within much larger firms (multi-disciplinary, multi-sector consultancies). The other three (see Table 1) are focused on particular industries. TEC participation was based

Table 1.   Characteristics of participating firms.

TEC firms	Age (years)	Group structure	Employees (2006)	Group revenues (2006)	Profit margins (2006)
A	20+	Single sector consultancy	>100	>£10M	14%
B	100+	Single sector consultancy	>1,000	>£100M	6%
C	100+	Multi-disciplinary consultancy	>5,000	>£100M	3%
D	30+	Multi-disciplinary consultancy	>5,000	~£500M	4%
E	100+	Conglomerate offering diverse services, including engineering	>1,000	>£1,000M	5%
F	50+	Multi-disciplinary consultancy	>10,000	>£1,000M	8%
G	50+	Multi-disciplinary consultancy	>25,000	>£5,000M	3%

Source: Company annual reports.

on our agreement that they would remain anonymous. Here we reveal only the most necessary detail and information about the firms.

We conducted 23 semi-structured interviews in eight TEC business units across the seven firms. The business units were engaged in the following sectors: automotive, energy, water, healthcare, industrial processes (x2), public amenities and transport infrastructure. Interviewees included directors and project managers. We tried to identify individuals engaged in innovation and company learning strategies. We interviewed more than one person in each organization, people at different levels and people with different expert knowledge, on the same topic, and discussed historical and recent events, to help to avoid bias and retrospective sense-making in qualitative research (Eisenhardt and Graebner, 2007).

Interviews lasted between 45 and 150 minutes, and were transcribed verbatim. Most of the interviews were conducted on site, which enabled access to key corporate reports and other literature (e.g. publications for clients). Interviewees were encouraged to direct the researchers to secondary sources to triangulate their claims (e.g. in policy reports, trade journals and engineering journals). In addition to questions about innovation, relationships and value creation, we asked participants to identify project examples, which led to identification of additional interviewees and documentation.

Interview transcripts and secondary materials were coded using an open coding system (Strauss and Corbin, 1998) and synthesized into detailed cases based on a standard interview template. The first objective was to identify the micro- and meso-level mechanisms associated with value creation and value capture. This approach was based on that proposed by Swan (2007), and involved recursive cycles between theory and data (Eisenhardt and Graebner, 2007) in order to re-code the data and identify the dynamics among micro- and meso-level mechanisms based on groupings of interviewee quotes. Replication logic was used (Yin, 2009; Eisenhardt and Graebner, 2007) to underpin the core theory presented here and to ensure that our findings were not related to an idiosyncratic case.

Empirical Context: An Introduction to TECs

TECs provide services to support the design, development, maintenance and renewal of most of the physical infrastructures in modern economies (e.g. buildings, transport, utilities) over their entire life cycles. They provide a very wide range of technical services ranging from conceptual design, project development, environmental assessment, site selection, investment and acquisition appraisal and warranty management to decommissioning and rehabilitation.[2]

Examples of large multi-disciplinary consulting firms include employee-owned firms, such as Mott MacDonald, and publicly listed companies such as Atkins Plc. However there are numerous small firms that focus on fewer or even single markets. TECs operate in many distinct economic sectors, nationally and internationally, providing facilities and systems (e.g. water/energy utilities, industrial and commercial assets, transport infrastructure, hospitals, schools), in which many activities are similar. The top ten clients for UK civil engineers in 2005 tendered for contracts individually worth between £286 million and £1.9 billion. These include UK government departments (Transport, Health, Defence) and private sector firms (Asda, National Grid Transco, Land Securities, News Corporation).[3]

---

[2]Other services typically undertaken by the case study firms include asset integrity management, marketing and strategic advice, commercial agreements, operational engineering, commissioning client assets, planning permissions, project management, development of regulations, engineering specifications, feasibility studies, inspection and analysis, site supervision, tender adjudication, interface co-ordination, lifetime studies and testing and inspection.

[3]Anon "Top 10s", *Construction News*, 19 January 2006, 16.

The ecosystem surrounding an infrastructure project is composed of a web of specialized consultants and contractors, typically connected to a central systems integrator. TECs play important roles within this network in helping to define problems and identify solutions. The number of contractual roles open to TECs appears to be increasing. For example, TECs can work with clients on design, or work in consortia with other contractors to provide integrated "design and build" packages which are handed over to the client when the project has reached completion. Private finance initiatives (PFI) allow consortia to design, build, own and run the asset, whereby they deliver to the client not the power station, for example, but electricity at a pre-arranged price per kilowatt hour. Therefore the role of TECs can vary. They can provide services in the form of designing a facility, or may be involved in designing the competition on the basis of which contracts are awarded for the construction of the facility; they may provide technical advice to the client or to the financiers of projects.

As we illustrate in the following section, TECs capture value by building experience and accumulating knowledge through partnerships with operators, strategy consultants and vendors. This builds reputation, technological and project management capabilities, network connections and leads to further assignments. We suggest that the main drivers of innovation in this category are selecting experienced consultants to jointly envision new solutions with clients, structuring the governance of projects for distributed problem-solving between clients and specialized consulting and engineering firms, and developing project management competencies that enable firms to cope with critical changes. TECs tend to access external knowledge systematically and, therefore, operate in a classic open innovation system. The extract below from an interview with an engineer in the transport TEC refers to the development of data-capture methods from work sites, which exploit university research and lead to new safety standards and their wider application in the professional community:

"I know certainly with this work on [Tube Train Line] there is quite a good link with [University X]…they are actually instrumenting some of the sites that we are working on with monitoring instrumentation and their knowledge…they've gained, is then sent back to us so that we can actually see exactly what is going on during a certain remedial process or whatever, and it is that type of stuff that then gets published and is then slowly filtered through and becomes sort of more recognised and it's when then, fine write an updated standard that stuff then raises the level and really that's the cycle".

The managing director of industrial process A TEC described the development of a novel system developed for an application in the highly regulated nuclear sector:

"you get all the expertise from [Client nuclear plant], from [a Blue Chip engineering firm], from [Name of Engineering Procurement Contractor] from [name of another Nuclear Client] all of these experts and the nuclear inspectorate ... and we claimed the credit but the truth is it's an industry developed design .... So you can feel a lot more confident with it because I've had all the ... experts of the industry crawling all over it and changing it."

These two extracts illustrate how knowledge accumulation occurs through networks, and links with universities, other contractors, suppliers and regulators. Much of the knowledge is formalized into decision methodologies that help retain past learning and experience, including professional guidelines and building regulations.

Micro- and Meso-level Mechanisms Contributing to Open, User-centric Innovation

In this section, we show that TECs typically engage in bespoke projects that rely on working closely with clients to specify the design brief. These projects are often critical to the client's business and the cost of failure is high. The case studies show that these units' use of innovation to add value for their clients is often limited (see quotes in Fig. 2). We find that although TECs often engage in open, user-centric innovation, differences in their network relationships influence the rate and direction of innovation (e.g. from award-winning bridges and tunnels to incremental advances such as new ways of applying pre-existing data-capture techniques on site). Since outcomes influence the accumulation of technological capabilities and reputation, they in turn affect future performance. Over time, these approaches can yield very different outcomes as we illustrate below.

Dynamics of generative interaction

Getting to a position where TECs, their clients and other stakeholders, such as contractors and suppliers, can innovate together is a multi-stage process, which under certain conditions can produce a positive feedback cycle or *generative interaction*, which has benefits for both TECs and their clients (see Fig. 1, boxes 1–14).

In the previous section we described how during generative interaction TECs use both external knowledge networks and more conventional internal capability- and reputation-building. Together, these (internal) micro- and (external) meso-level mechanisms account for the generative development of stocks of expertise, which flows through the project network among TECs, their clients and their partners. The most prominent mechanisms in the case studies[4] are depicted in Figs. 1 and 2. The case studies also identified other mechanisms that enhance competitiveness. These include internal organizational processes, such as knowledge-management programmes (developed by each of the multi-disciplinary TECs studied), and emergent capabilities based on the scale and scope of operations. An example here is the ability to offer clients a one-stop-shop covering all the project's design needs (mentioned explicitly by three TECs). This chapter focuses on the mechanisms that feed into the generative interactions associated with innovation, rather than the distinct dynamics associated with successful competition (despite its economic importance).

Figure 1 presents a series of quotes from interviews about mechanisms that are inter-related and occur across a range of client–TEC interactions. These were selected on the basis of replication logic (i.e. they emerged repeatedly in the cases studied). These interactions span project cycles, clients and other stakeholders; Fig. 1, thus, does not represent a single

---

[4]We cannot exclude the possibility that in other TEC firms, beyond our cases, these mechanisms and probably many others, feed generative interaction. Figure 1 should be interpreted as a set of empirically derived propositions, whose sufficiency and generalizability should be tested in future studies.

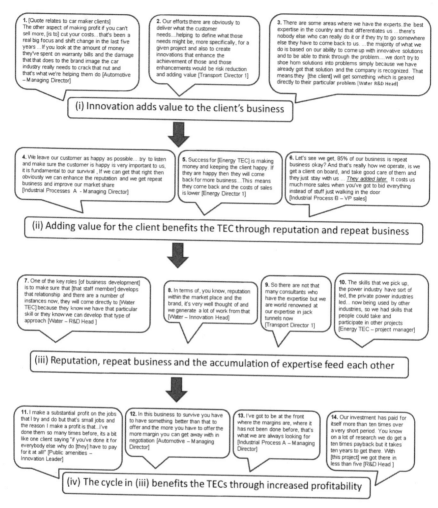

Fig. 1. A chain of mechanisms that support generative interaction.

project cycle. These mechanisms form the core of generative interaction as conceptualized in this chapter.

Figure 1 begins with Proposition (i) that innovation delivers added value to the client's business. Value is generated for clients in a number of ways. For example, through *enhanced prestige* (e.g. being associated with a conspicuous construction, such as London's 30 St. Mary Axe, popularly known as "the Gherkin", or the Burj Al Arab Hotel known as "the

Sail", in Dubai); through *improved functionality* of assets (e.g. improving the acoustics in a concert hall, reducing hospital infection rates); *cost savings* (e.g. designs that use pre-fabricated components to enable faster build times (e.g. railway station platforms, railway embankment renewals); or *less disruption* (e.g. using tunnel jacking and ground freezing to slide a pre-fabricated road tunnel under operational railway lines in Boston's "big dig") or *improved safety* (e.g. using movement monitoring systems to reduce the risk of collapses during excavations). This list is based on information gleaned from the interviews with TECs (e.g. see quotes 1 and 2 in Fig. 1) and a review of some leading UK engineering publications. However, it should be regarded as illustrative rather than exhaustive.

Proposition (ii) in Fig. 1 states that when TECs generate client-added value this may have ongoing benefits for the TEC. The mechanisms through which this is achieved include better chances of repeat business and enhanced reputation (boxes 3–6). This may improve the competitiveness of TECs in tenders. A project manager described this as:

> "we were in a competitive situation on the [Nuclear plant] project which made a big difference … I suppose [to] how much profit at the end of the day, how much profit we can make. When you are in a competitive situation it's, you know, you get beaten up a lot more commercially at the start. But I am sure that one of the things that went in our favour was our track record at the [name of prior client] project because all of the people within the nuclear industry they know each other and they are interconnected and I am sure they talk to each other. So I am sure the [previous] project helped us actually win the [Nuclear plant] project."

Generating repeat business or increasing reputation and enhancing competitiveness are important in lowering the cost of sales by spreading the fixed costs involved in running a TEC and bidding for contracts (see quotes 5 and 6). However, as the next quote shows, although powerful, reputation in a particular technical field is not a panacea:

> "if people aren't aware of us and they advertise for designers … it can be difficult for us to actually win you know because it's an open

market and money comes into it but actually more than 50% of the
work we do, we get from people phoning us up and asking us to
do it and luckily they'll do just about anything to get us to do it ...
[but] we just lost a design competition for one in [place name] and
I haven't had any feedback yet unfortunately ... what we would say
is why, why is the practice that's got by far and away the more
expertise ... why have we lost this competition?" [Public amenities
TEC, innovation leader.]

This extract and quotes 7–10 lead on to Proposition (iii) in Fig. 1, namely,
that there is a reinforcing dynamic between reputation, repeat business and
accumulation of expertise, all of which feed into one another. Finally,
quotes 11–14 under Proposition (iv) in Fig. 1 suggests that this cycle
generates greater profit margins for TECs. This could be due to reductions
in the costs of sales, but might be due also to innovation and the scarcity of a
particular resource (see quotes 3 and 9), which allow premium pricing. This
supports research that suggests that firms use "magnet" projects to enhance
their reputation in design or problem solving, in order to attract customers
(Dodgson *et al.*, 2005).

Interviewees spoke about the benefits from reputation and client
relations including the ability to influence the client and other stakeholders,
such as contractors, in project decision making. The "soft" skills and status
of the TEC project manager can also be important in influencing clients'
receptiveness to innovative solutions. This, in turn, may allow the TEC to
work in ways that create value for their clients. The following extract from
an interview with a transport director and a leading engineer illustrates these
points:

"... so understanding of customers' needs and identifying solutions
that will satisfy them is a particular strength. It's obviously
grounded in technical expertise, but it's also dependent on advocacy,
mentoring, learning from experience and conveying that understanding to the customers through precedent and reputation ... I
mean our competitors obviously do that to a certain extent as well."
[Transport director 1.]

If the TEC staff can indeed convey the benefits of an innovative approach and actually deliver added value, then the cycle is complete and should generate benefits for TEC and client (see Fig. 1), opening the way to future cycles and more generative interaction.

Two important caveats must be stressed. The first is that innovation is not a necessary pre-condition to drive the cycle illustrated in Proposition (iii). TECs can grow organically through an accumulation of reputation/repeat business/expertise without being particularly innovative. However, in contributing to the creation of added value for the client, innovation is an important driver of generative interactions and the potentially beneficial outcome of these interactions. Also, as our interviewees pointed out, it may be difficult to innovate within a client project. Figure 2 puts forward two propositions which, in our view, represent a key challenge to the promotion of generative interaction in engineering projects. Proposition (v) is that TECs often do not have the resources required for independent innovation (although there are some modes of innovation they do manage alone — see

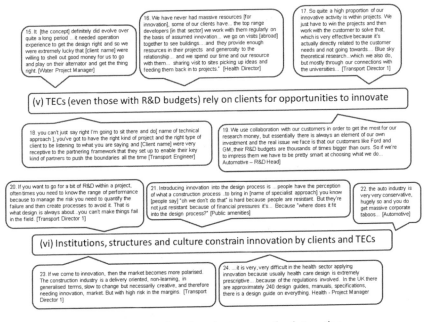

Fig. 2.   Overcoming obstacles to generative interaction.

footnote [5]). It is notable that while water TEC and automotive TEC both had R&D facilities, unlike the other TECs, even these TECs were still reliant on external funding or other resources to take forward innovation (quotes 15 and 19). Proposition (vi), supported by quotes 21–24, is that both clients and contractors (including TECs) are strongly constrained by the existing institutions, inter- and intra-organizational structures, culture and power (Nelson, 2008; Burnes, 2004; Bijker, 1995). Often, these constraints are quite justifiable, not least because of the different perspectives of project stakeholders, as we explore in more detail below.

In projects, the TEC has to innovate with the client, and other contractors in the project's innovation network also have to be brought into agreement. This is important because generative interaction can only occur when the gap between the project participants undertaking design and its implementation is bridged. This applies particularly to civil engineering projects because design consulting and engineering procurement consulting are very distinct types of business.[6] The TECs in our sample emphasized this requirement for harmonization. The transport, public amenities, health and industrial process B TECs all referred to the importance of such methods as "open-book accounting", which allow contractors and clients to work together within a mutually shared understanding of each other's incentive structures. Such approaches were one way in which innovation could be introduced into a project:

---

[5]The focus of this chapter is generative and degenerative interaction; discussion of innovation by TECs would go beyond this. However, we should emphasize that innovation in TECs does occur outside of externally funded projects. For example, the larger TECs in our sample [Firms D, E and G] had developed software programmes and/or knowledge management systems that helped them to work more efficiently.

[6]The public amenities TEC project manager and an engineer in the transport TEC described the key differences as being that designers invested in few physical assets and expected smaller fees on which they earned higher margins, while engineering procurement consultants (EPC) have to invest large amounts in equipment, and take on a bigger financial risk during the building phase of projects, for which they earned a smaller margin of the total project budget. Although this might be quite a large sum, the risks were also higher. TECs occasionally participate in risk/reward sharing with EPC, but profit margins can be quickly eroded if there are mistakes (e.g. penalties for the delays: the cases of the Wembley football stadium in the UK, and the collapse of the UK London tube maintenance company, Metronet, are examples of failures in risky projects producing very adverse impacts on the firms involved).

"…commercial risk, health and safety, technical risk…there are lots of different types of risk but the way to manage this area is to actually get the parties together in a different procurement way and have a workshop on risk where everybody in a non-confrontational way…can raise it, it gets owned, examined and proportioned and then you can show that the risk of being conventional is actually higher in all sorts of ways. All those factors where the risk hits you can demonstrate and then you can move forward to introduce…which is effectively innovation". [Transport TEC director 1.]

The health TEC had found an alternative way to introduce innovation and facilitate generative interactions. They chose to forgo joining the consortia bidding for larger but higher risk contracts to design and build hospitals. Instead they favoured taking and adapting the traditional role of the client's technical advisor (who helps the client to develop the tender documentation and run the competition). The health TEC project manager explained that "you sacrifice a much bigger fee for the right to be more innovative in the business…technical advisor role isn't new but the way we approach it…is quite new". The benefit comes from persuading the client to put out a more detailed tender than is usual. The advantage of this (in addition to a higher fee for the health TEC) is that: "If the brief is very well defined and the design is well defined then…not only is the programme time shortened, but the cost of bidding is a lot less". The health TEC claimed that by showing clients how to create space in the bidding process for innovative designs, they were attracting a new stream of stimulating international work and also introducing clients to the one-stop-shop for additional design features provided by their multi-disciplinary consultancy. The health project manager concluded "all this can be looked at outside of if you like the red hot competitive bidding stage … it's [a] more rational integrated holistic engaging approach with the client so that you get buy in."

These routes to more influence over the project, adopted by the Health and the Transport TEC may be critical since innovative projects are often perceived to be more risky, especially in the context of large capital intensive projects.

In summary, when TECs, clients and other stakeholders are able to overcome the constraints depicted in Fig. 2, then a positive feedback loop of generative interaction will develop in which open user-centric innovation leads to added value for clients and repeat business, better client relationships, accumulation of technical expertise and enhanced reputation for the TEC. These mechanisms enable TECs to work with clients prepared to sign off on innovative solutions. This cycle produces benefits for the TEC in the form of increased profit margins (beyond reduced cost of sales), based on the ability to put a premium price on work that requires particular skills, or because prior experience and innovative methods enable more efficient and/or more cost-effective work than is being offered by the competition.[7]

Dynamics of degenerative interaction

We have shown how a generative interaction feedback loop can be inhibited or interrupted. We will now describe how the interactions between TEC and client can deteriorate into degenerative interactions through a different feedback loop (see Fig. 3). These negative interactions are related to the client's attempts to reduce costs through tender-based competition to push down prices, or through contracts that push the risk onto the contractors. Proposition (vii) at the centre of Fig. 3 is that clients' efforts to protect themselves may produce degenerative interactions in a business environment. For example, in the UK, government procurement of civil engineering services is a business environment that frequently produces degenerative interactions.

Quotes 26 and 29–31 in Fig. 3 suggest that they may arise as a result of competitive tendering among TECs. In the previous section, we described how TECs win work to design assets, or provide consulting services to the client directly or work in a consortium to serve the client. While competition is often important to maintain a healthy industry (Tidd and Bessant, 2009), our interviews show that staff in several TECs consider that tenders are often badly managed. Competitive tendering processes referred to explicitly by interviewees include "lump sum" contracts (services for a fixed fee) and PFI

---

[7] Others have suggested that innovative projects may benefit TECs by enhancing staff retention and recruitment as customers with interesting projects and enthusiastic staff are keen to work in an innovative and successful TEC (Salter and Gann, 2003).

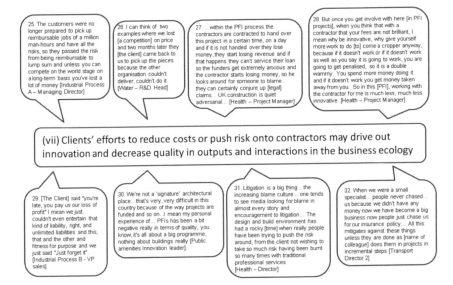

Fig. 3. Mechanisms that feed degenerative interaction.

(and related public/private partnerships (PPP)), which they saw as contributing to a deterioration of their business environment. One suggested that:

> "the problem [is] it's a very expensive business to bid to do PPP projects … if you fail you know you've spent an awful lot of money which could be on these big projects millions of pounds and then fail to win it." Health TEC director echoed this: "we work on a reduced fee until we win the job. Now if you don't win the job then you make a loss."

The interviewees' opinions were divided about the merits and downsides of tender-based competition to drive innovation. However, interviewees from three of the largest TECs suggested that fixed fee and PFI competitions were generally avoided and an advisory role was preferred (see health TEC in *Dynamics of generative interaction*, above). Since two of these firms have a good reputation for innovation, this would seem an undesirable consequence of this form of competition. Indeed, one TEC noted that some regions had taken steps to try to reduce the negative consequences of price competition: "Federal acquisition in the [United] States prohibits the use of fee competition. Fee competition if you want [something] that is divisive to innovation is very strong. It pushes prices down, your risks right up ... and the [designer's] fee right down." [Transport — director 2.]

The outputs from PFI projects were seen as being poor quality: "PFI has been a bit negative really in terms of quality" (Public amenities — innovation leader). Similarly, the vice president of sales in industrial process B TEC noted that quality was adversely affected in fixed fee projects:

"[In the past] there was far more lump sum bidding [in the UK] ... a client would come out with ... work and they'd say ... 'Give me your price to do the full engineering and construction management on a fixed price,' okay, and of course they, they picked the lowest price and then what they get is ... a contractor they're working with who all the time is snapping at their legs trying to get change orders to get the prices so they can make some money, but on the top of that they're giving as crumby a product as possible because they're trying to get their costs down, okay? And so what happens is these jobs regularly went extremely pear-shaped, I mean running very late, way over budget, major punch-up ending up in claims and this consumes huge amount of time in both the client and the contractor resolving large claims, okay?"

However, the transport, health and industrial process A and B TECs emphasized that clients tried to pass on the risks to their suppliers: "The customers are no longer prepared to pick up reimbursable jobs of a million man-hours and have all the risks." [Industrial process A TEC — managing director.]

A consequence of this client behaviour is that it leads to an increasingly adversarial environment in which litigation is more common, which has a negative impact on innovation (quotes 27–29 in Fig. 3).

A director of one TEC (unspecified due to the association with litigation) succinctly described how the client would not get an innovative solution by pushing the risk onto the TEC:

"The procurement of services in our business is changing ... they [the client] are then looking at it from the point of view of minimizing their risk and transferring risk on to their suppliers. They want us to take different sorts of risk than we would have done in the past. They are transferring risks that we are not best able to deal with ... they are trying to persuade us to take risks that our insurers don't want us to take ... therefore what happens at the end of the day we have now come into a situation with another key government customer ... [where the TEC said] if we are going to be sued for this [if it goes wrong] then here is our solution [the client said] 'oh we didn't mean that' ... you [the client] cannot transfer this risk to us [the TEC] and expect us to come up with an innovative or the best idea ... Insurance costs [for TECs] in the market place are going sky high. One way to ensure we get good insurance quotes is that we have a risk management structure that demonstrates to the insurance community how we manage risks. You then find it starts to impact on some of the things you would do."

He went on to describe another situation where liability had implications for future innovative solutions:

"We were sued for some work overseas where at the time some concrete mixes we used were more risky but they were a good idea at the time and in the past would not have been sued for advising on this particular approach because a government would not have chases us .... We got chased in hindsight for something that was natural practice in the world community and we ended up shelling out money from our insurance policies. What that then makes us do is we are now not only saying how do we control risk today we are trying to guess which way the insurance market is going in the future so that makes us even more conservative if we are not careful ..."

Of course the greatest loss to the TEC in these circumstances is the inability to interest the client in an innovative solution, which in turn limits the ability to provide the best solutions in terms of added value.

Discussion and Conclusion

In the study reported here, we set out to characterize the dynamics of innovation in TECs, and through an inductive process, to build on a line of theory conceived by Lane and Maxfield (1996) and extended by Swan and Scarbrough (2005). Our contribution adds to the literature on generative and degenerative interactions between TECs and other organizations in the same business ecology. Based on a series of empirically supported, testable propositions we extended the scope of the term generative interaction, and argued that it occurs through a series of inter-related mechanisms that allow TECs to establish and build on a trajectory of innovative projects through a process as follows: (i) innovation adds value to the client's business; (ii) adding value for the client benefits the TEC through reputation and repeat business; (iii) reputation, repeat business and the accumulation of expertise feed into each other; (iv) this cycle benefits TECs by contributing to increased profitability in this business ecology (although equally they may suffer from degenerative interactions elsewhere). However, (v) TECs are dependent on clients to be able to innovate during projects, particularly as they do not typically have access to the resources they need for physical testing. Therefore, although computer simulations allow a degree of "off-line" learning, TECs generally lack the sort of protected space for sufficient "off-line" R&D that Nelson (2008) observes in other contexts (see, e.g quote 20 in Fig. 2). Furthermore, (vi) clients, and indeed TECs and other project contractors, are often resistant or unable to support the introduction of innovations to allow such testing for institutional or cultural reasons. Yet, some staff in TECs, in certain situations, are able to overcome progress through multiple cycles of the type outlined in Fig. 1, thus enjoying generative interaction in that business ecology.

It is important to stress that the process of generative interaction is dependent on context.[8] In many situations, the scope for generative interaction is limited and innovation networks are ineffective and lead only to technically adequate designs and services, or even have a negative influence. The negative effects may produce a downward spiral in the relationships among participants, which we term degenerative interaction. Based on our findings, we would suggest that clients' efforts to reduce costs or push the risk onto contractors may extinguish innovation and result in poor quality outputs and interactions in that business ecology.

---

[8]e.g. the water TEC suggested that its clients in the UK water utilities had R&D budgets related to regulatory requirements. This suggests that the regulatory context influences the process of generative interaction.

Generative and degenerative interactions are the products of firm-specific competencies and also the experience and characteristics of the TEC, the client, and their environment. In line with Lane and Maxfield (1996), we find these interactions to be context specific and unlikely to be identified by firm-level analysis of large TEC firms. The interactions we observed are those of individuals or teams in particular markets and were only observed through examination at that level (e.g. private finance initiatives in the UK). Generative interactions involve both the meso- and micro-levels, spanning teams of specialized individuals in the firm and the communities of clients, competitors, contractors, suppliers and regulators with whom they interact.

Although the cases in this study relate only to TECs, we find little support for the notion that open, user-centric innovation is sufficient for sustainable competitive advantage. Instead, we find that traditional internal knowledge routines and capabilities, such as developing technical niches and cross-disciplinary working, in combination with external knowledge networks and partnerships, can promote *generative interactions*. These can generate self-reinforcing cycles that build up expertise and a client base in specific contexts. The obvious implication of this is that open forms of innovation are not a substitute for building internal capabilities, but rather act as valuable complementary capabilities, similar to the concept of complementary assets highlighted by Teece (1986).

Generative interaction is a useful concept to explain the success of some firms, in some markets, in open, user-centric innovation. However, we cannot generalize about other business environments or geographic regions at this stage.

Our results suggest that open and user innovation need to be tested in different sectoral contexts and cannot be seen as a general solution for firms seeking to innovate. In addition to focusing on firm level strategies and mechanism for open innovation, we need to understand the effects of the interactions with the business context and ecology. Understanding the relative contributions of internal capabilities and external networks, and how they combine to create and capture value during innovation is likely to involve different mechanisms in different sectors. Understanding these mechanisms and their interactions could contribute to more precise prescriptions for open innovation and the avoidance of negative consequences.

Bibliography

Abernathy, W.J. and Clark, K.B. (1985) Innovation: mapping the winds of creative destruction. *Research Policy*, **14**(1), 3–22.

Abernathy, W.J. and Utterback, J. (1978) Patterns of industrial innovation. *Technology Review*, **80**, 40–47.

Acs, Z. and Audretsch, D.B. (1988) Innovation in large and small firms: an empirical analysis. *American Economic Review*, **78**, 678–690.

Acs, Z. and Audretsch, D.B. (1990) *Innovation and Small Firms*. Cambridge, MA: MIT Press.

Adler, P.S. (1989) When knowledge is the critical resource, knowledge management is the critical task. *IEEE Transactions on Engineering Management*, **36**(2), 87–95.

Adler, P.S., Goldoftas, B. and Levine, D.I. (1999) Flexibility versus efficiency? A case study of model changeovers in the Toyota production system. *Organization Science*, **10**, 43–68.

Adner, R. and Helfat, C.E. (2003) Corporate effects and dynamic managerial capabilities. *Strategic Management Journal*, **24**, 1011–1025.

Aiken, L.S. and West, S.G. (1991) *Multiple Regression: Testing and Interpreting Interactions*. Newbury Park, CA: Sage Publications.

Aiken, M. and Hage, J. (1971) The organic organization and innovation. *Sociology*, **5**, 63–82.

Albert, M.B., Avery, D., McAllister, P. and Narin, F. (1991) Direct validation of citation counts as indicators of industrially important patents. *Research Policy*, **20**, 251–259.

Alegre-Vidal, J., Lapiedra-Alcami, R. and Chiva-Gomez, R. (2004) Linking operations strategy and product innovation: an empirical study of Spanish ceramic tile producers. *Research Policy*, **33**(5), 829–839.

Allen, T.J. (1984) *Managing the Flow of Technology: Technology Transfer and the Dissemination of Technological Information within the R&D Organization*. Cambridge, MA: MIT Press.

Altman, E.I. (1971) *Corporate Bankruptcy in America*. Idaho Falls, ID: Lexington Books.

Altman, E.I. (1983) *Corporate Financial Distress*. New York, NY: John Wiley and Sons.

Alvesson, M. (2000) Social identity in knowledge-intensive companies. *Journal of Management Studies*, **37**(8), 1101–1123.

Amabile, T.M. and Conti, R. (1999) Changes in the work environment for creativity during downsizing. *Academy of Management Journal*, **42**, 630–640.

Amabile, T.M., Conti, R., Coon, H., Lazenby, J. and Herron, M. (1996) Assessing the work environment for creativity. *Academy of Management Journal*, **39**, 1154–1184.

Ambrosini, V., Bowman, C. and Collier, N. (2009) Dynamic capabilities: an exploration of how firms renew their resource base. *British Journal of Management*, **20**, 9–24.

Ambrosini, V. and Bowman, C. (2009) What are dynamic capabilities and are they a useful construct in strategic management? *International Journal of Management Reviews*, **11**(1), 29–49.

Amidon, D. (1998) The evolving community of knowledge practice: the Ken awakening. *International Journal of Technology Management*, **16**(1/2/3), 45–63.

Amit, R. and Schoemaker, P.J.H. (1993) Strategic assets and organisational rent. *Strategic Management Journal*, **14**, 33–46.

Ancona, D. and Caldwell, D. (1992) Bridging the boundary: external activity and performance in organizational teams. *Administrative Science Quarterly*, **37**, 634–665.

Anderson, P. and Tushman, M.L. (1990) Technological discontinuities and dominant designs: a cyclical model of technological change. *Administrative Science Quarterly*, **35**, 604–633.

Anderson, R.C., Narin, F. and McAllister, P.R. (1978) Publication ratings versus peer ratings of universities. *Journal of the American Society for Information Science*, **29**, 91–103. Reprinted in B.C. Griffith, ed. (1980), *Key Papers in Information Science*. White Plains, NY: Knowledge Industry Publications, Inc.

Angle, H. and Van de Ven, A. (1989) Managing the innovation journey. In A. Van de Ven, H. Angle and M. Poole (eds.), *Research on the Management of Innovation*. New York, NY: Harper and Row.

Ansoff, H.I. (1991) Critique of Mintzberg, Henry the Design School — Reconsidering the basic premises of strategic management. *Strategic Management Journal*, **12**(6), 449–461.

Arbuckle, J.L. and Wothke, W. (1999) *Amos 4.0 User's Guide*. Chicago, IL: SPSS Inc. and SmallWaters Corporation.

Archibugi, D. (1992) Patenting as an indicator of technological innovation: a review. *Science and Public Policy*, **19**(6), 357–368.

Argenti, J. (1976) *Corporate Collapse*. New York, NY: McGraw-Hill.

Argyres, N.S. and Silverman, B.S. (2004) R&D, organization structure, and the development of corporate technological knowledge. *Strategic Management Journal*, **25**, 929–958.

Argyris, C. and Schon, D.A. (1978) *Organisational Learning: A Theory of Action Perspective*. Menlo Park, CA: Addison-Wesley.

Arnold, J. and Moizer, P. (1984) A survey of the methods used by UK investment analysts. *Accounting and Business Research*, Summer.

Arrow, K.J. (1962) The economic implications of learning by doing. *Review of Economic Studies*, **29**(3), 155–173.

Arundel, A., van de Paal, G. and Soete, L. (1995) Innovation strategies of Europe's largest industrial firms (PACE report). MERIT, University of Limbourg, Maastricht.

Ashforth, B.E. and Mael, F. (1989) Social identity theory and the organisation. *Academy of Management Review*, **14**(1), 20–39.

Atuahene-Gima, K. (2005) Resolving the capacity-rigidity paradox in new product innovation. *Journal of Marketing*, **69**, 61–83.

Augsdorfer, P. (1996) *Forbidden Fruit*. Aldershot: Avebury.

Bacon, F. (1620) *The New Organon and Related Writing*.

Badham, R., Couchman, P. and McLoughlin, I. (1997) Implementing vulnerable socio-technical change projects. In I. McLoughlin and M. Harris (eds.), *Innovation, Organizational Change and Technology*. London: Thomson.

Bagozzi, R.P. and Yi, Y. (1988) On the evaluation of structural equation models. *Journal of the Academy of Marketing Science*, **16**(1), 74–94.

Baker, T., Miner, A.S. and Eesley, D.T. (2003) Improvising firms: bricolage, account giving and improvisational competencies in the founding process. *Research Policy*, **32**(2), 255–276.

Baker, W.E. and Sinkula, J.M. (1999) The synergistic effect of market orientation and learning orientation on organizational performance. *Journal of the Academy of Marketing Science*, **27**(4), 411–427.

Balachandra, R. and Friar, J.H. (1997) Factors for success in R&D projects and new product innovation: a contextual framework. *IEEE Transactions on Engineering Management*, **44**(3), 276–287.

Barley, S. (1986) Technology as an occasion for restructuring: evidence from observation of CT scanners and the social order of radiology departments. *Administrative Science Quarterly*, **31**, 78–108.

Barnard, C. (1938) *The Functions of the Executive*. Harvard: Harvard University Press.

Barnes, B. (1977) *Interests and the Growth of Knowledge*. London: Routledge and Kegan Paul (Routledge Direct Editions).

Barney, J.B. (1991) Firm resources and sustained competitive advantage. *Journal of Management*, **17**(1), 99–120.

Barney, J.B. (2001) Is the resource-based "View" a useful perspective for strategic management research? Yes. *Academy of Management Review*, **26**(1), 41–56.

Barney, J.B. (2002) *Gaining and Sustaining Competitive Advantage*, 2nd edition. Upper Saddle River, NJ: Prentice Hall.

Barreto, I. (2010) Dynamic capabilities: a review of past research and an agenda for the future. *Journal of Management*, **36**, 256–280.

Barton, J. (1993) Adapting the intellectual property system to new technologies. In M.B. Wallerstein, M.E. Mogee and R.A. Schoen (eds.), *Global Dimensions of Intellectual Property Rights in Science and Technology*. Washington, DC: National Academy of Sciences Press.

Bason, C. (2011) *Leading Public Sector Innovation*. London: Policy Press.

Baumard, P. (1999) *Tacit Knowledge in Organizations*. London: Sage Publications.

Baxter, W.T. (1984) *Inflation Accounting*. Deddington: Philip Allan.

Baylin, L. (1985) Autonomy in the industrial R&D lab. *Human Resource Management*, **24**, 129–146.

Becker, M. (2001) Managing dispersed knowledge: organizational problems, managerial strategies and their effectiveness. *Journal of Management Studies*, **38**(7), 1037–1051.

Bellon, B. and Whittington, G. (1996) *Competing through Innovation*. Dublin: Oak Tree Press.

Belussi, F. and Arcangeli, F. (1998) A typology of networks: flexible and evolutionary firms. *Research Policy*, **27**, 415–428.

Bemouski, K. (1994) Baldrige award recipients share their experience. *Quality Progress*, February, 35–40.

Benner, M.J. and Tushman, M.L. (2003) Exploitation, exploration, and process management: the productivity dilemma revisited. *Academy of Management Review*, **28**, 238–256.

Berkhout, G., Hartmann, D. and Trott, P. (2010) Connecting technological capabilities with market needs using a cyclic innovation model. *R&D Management*, **40**(5), 474–490.

Bertin, G. and Wyatt, S. (1988) *Multi-Nationals and Industrial Property*. Hemel Hempstead: Harvester-Wheatsheaf.

Bessant, J. (1994) Rediscovering continuous improvement. *Technovation*, **14**(1), 17–29.

Bessant, J. (2003) *High Involvement Innovation*. Chichester: John Wiley and Sons.

Bessant, J. and Tidd, J. (2011) *Innovation and Entrepreneurship*, 2nd edition. Chichester: John Wiley and Sons.

Bidault, F. and Fischer, W.A. (1994) Technology transactions: networks over markets. *R&D Management*, **24**(4), 373–386.

Biggadale, E.R. (1979) *Corporate Diversification: Entry Strategy and Performance*. Cambridge, MA: Harvard University Press.

Bijker, W.E. (1995) *Of Bicycles, Bakerlites and Bulbs: Towards a Theory of Sociotechnical Change*. Cambridge, MA: MIT Press.

Blackler, F. (1995) Knowledge, knowledge work and organizations: an overview and interpretation. *Organization Studies*, **16**(6), 1021–1046.

Blackler, F., Crump, N. and McDonald, S. (2000) Organizational processes in complex network activities. *Organization*, **7**(2), 277–300.

Blindenbach-Driessen, F. and van den Ende, J. (2006). Innovation in project-based firms: the context-dependency of success factors. *Research Policy*, **35**, 545–561.

Blum, M. (2004) *Product Development as Dynamic Capability*. In Institut für Industrielle, Universität der Bundeswehr München, Germany, 178.

Blundell, R., Griffith, R. and Van Reenen (1993) Knowledge stocks, persistent innovation and market dominance. Paper given to SPES discussion group, Brussels, September.

Boer, H., Berger, A., Chapman, R. and Gertsen, F. (1999) *CI Changes: From Suggestion Box to the Learning Organisation*. Aldershot: Ashgate.

Bogner, W., Thomas, H. and McGee, J. (1999) Competence and competitive advantage: towards a dynamic model. *British Journal of Management*, **10**, 275–290.

Boisot, M.H. (1995) Is your firm a creative destroyer? Competitive learning and knowledge flows in the technological strategies of firms. *Research Policy*, **24**, 489–506.

Booz, Allen and Hamilton (1982) *New Product Development for the 1980s*. New York, NY: Booz, Allen and Hamilton, Inc.

Bouncken, R.B., Koch, M. and Teichert, T. (2007) Innovation strategy explored: innovation orientation's strategy preconditions and market performance outcomes. *Zeitschrift für Betriebswirtschaft*, Special Issue **2/2007**, 71–95.

Bourgeois, L.J. (1980) Performance and consensus. *Strategic Management Journal*, **1**(3), 227–248.

Bowen, K. (1994) *The Perpetual Enterprise Machine: Seven Keys to Corporate Renewal through Successful Product and Process Development*. New York, NY: Oxford University Press.

Brancato, C. (1995) New corporate performance measures. *The Conference Board Report*, 118-95-RR.

Breu, K. and Hemingway, C. (2002) The power of communities of practice for subverting organisational change. Paper presented at 3rd European Conference on Organizational Knowledge, Learning and Capabilities, Athens, Greece, April 5–6.

Brews, P.J. and Hunt, M.R. (1999) Learning to plan and planning to learn: resolving the planning school/learning school debate. *Strategic Management Journal*, **20**(10), 889–913.

Broad, W.J. (1997) Study finds public science is pillar of industry. *The New York Times, Science Times*, Tuesday, 13 May.

Brown, J. and Utterback, J. (1985) Uncertainty and technical communication patterns. *Management Science*, **31**(3), 301–311.

Brown, J.S. and Duguid, P. (1991) Organization learning and communities of practice: towards a unified view of working, learning and innovation. *Organization Science*, **2**(1), 40–57.

Brown, J.S. and Duguid, P. (1998) Organizing knowledge. *California Management Review*, **40**(3), 90–111.

Brown, J.S. and Duguid, P. (2001) Knowledge and organization: a social practice perspective. *Organization Science*, **12**(2), 198–213.

Brown, S. (1998) Manufacturing seniority, strategy and innovation. *Technovation*, **18**(3), 111–132.

Brown, S.L. and Eisenhardt, K.M. (1995) Product development: past research, present findings, and future directions. *Academy of Management Review*, **20**(2), 343–378.

Brown, S.L. and Eisenhardt, K.M. (1997) The art of continuous change: Linking complexity theory and time-paced evolution in relentlessly shifting organizations. *Administrative Science Quarterly*, **42**(1), 1–34.

Browne, M. and Cudeck, R. (1993) Alternative ways of assessing model fit. In K.L. Bollen (ed.), *Testing Structural Equation Models*. Newbury Park, CA: Sage Publications.

Bruni, D.S. and Verona, G. (2009) Dynamic marketing capabilities in science-based firms: an exploratory investigation of the pharmaceutical industry. *British Journal of Management*, **20**, 101–117.

Brusoni, S., Prencipe, A. and Pavitt, K. (2001) Knowledge specialisation, organisational coupling, and the boundaries of the firm: why do firms know more than they make? *Administrative Science Quarterly*, **46**, 597–621.

Bryman, A. (2000) Telling technological tales. *Organization*, **7**(3), 455–475.

Buderi, R., Carey, J., Gross, N. and Lowry-Miller, K. (1992) Global innovation: who's in the lead? *Business Week Patent Scoreboard*, 3 August 1993.

Budworth, D.W. (1993) Intangible assets and their renewal. Foundation for Performance Measurement, UK National Meeting, London, October.

Burgelman, R.A. (1983) A model of the interaction of strategic behavior, corporate context, and the concept of strategy. *Academy of Management Review*, **8**, 61–71.

Burnes, B. (2004) *Managing Change: A Strategic Approach to Organisational Dynamics*, 4th edition. Harlow: Pearson Education Prentice Hall.

Business Week (1993) The global patent race picks up. 9 August.

Buzzell, R.D. and Gale (1987) *The PIMS Principle*. New York, NY: Free Press.

Byrne, B.M. (2001) *Structural Equation Modeling with AMOS — Basic Concepts, Applications, and Programming*. Mahwah, New Jersey: Lawrence Erlbaum Associates.

Byrne, B.M. (2004) Testing for multigroup invariance using AMOS Graphics: a road less travelled. *Structural Equation Modeling: A Multidisciplinary Journal*, **11**, 272–300.

Callahan, J. and Lasry, E. (2004) The importance of customer input in the development of very new products. *R&D Management*, **34**(2), 107–117.

Calvert, J., Ibarra, C., Patel, P. and Pavitt, K. (1996) Innovation outputs in European industry: results from the CIS. EIMS Publication Number 34, European Commission — DG XIII, Luxembourg.

Camp, R. (1989) *Benchmarking — The Search for Industry Best Practices that Lead to Superior Performance*. Milwaukee, WI: Quality Press.

Cantwell, J. (1992) The internationalisation of technological activity and its implications for competitiveness. In O. Granstrand, L. Hakanson and S. Sjolander (eds.), *Technology Management and International Business: Internationalisation of R&D and Technology*. Chichester: John Wiley and Sons.

Cantwell, J. (1995) The globalisation of technology: what remains of the product cycle model. *Cambridge Journal of Economics*, **19**, 155–174.

Cantwell, J., Gambardella, A. and Granstrand, O. (2004) *The Economics and Management of Technological Diversification*. London: Routledge.

Cardinal, L.B. (2001). Technological innovation in the pharmaceutical industry: the use of organizational control in managing research and development. *Organization Science*, **12**, 19–37.

Carlile, P.R. (2002) A pragmatic view of knowledge and boundaries: boundary objects in new product development. *Organization Science*, **13**(4), 442–455.

Carpenter, M.P., Narin, F. and Woolf, P. (1981) Citation rates to technologically important patents. *World Patent Information*, **4**, 160–163.

Caulkin, S. (2001) *Performance through People*. London: Chartered Institute of Personnel and Development.

Cepeda, G. and Vera, D. (2007) Dynamic capabilities and operational capabilities: a knowledge management perspective. *Journal of Business Research*, **60**, 426–437.

Cesaratto, S. and Mangano, S. (1993) Technological profiles and economic performance in the Italian manufacturing sector. *Economics of Innovation and New Technology*, **2**, 237–256.

Chan, S.H., Martin, J.D. and Kensinger, J.W. (1990) Corporate research and development expenditures and share value. *Journal of Financial Economics*, **26**(2), 255–276.

Chandler, A.D. (1990) *Scale and Scope: The Dynamics of Industrial Capitalism*. Cambridge, MA: Belknap Press.

Chandler, L.V. (1962) *Strategy and Structure: Chapters in the History of American Industrial Enterprise*. Cambridge: MIT Press.

Chaney, R., Devinney, T. and Winer, R. (1991) The impact of new product introductions on the market value of firms. *Journal of Business*, **64**(4), 573–610.

Cheng, Y.T. and Van de Ven, A.H. (1996) Learning the innovation journey: order out of chaos? *Organization Science*, **7**, 593–614.

Chesbrough, H.W. (2003) *Open Innovation: The New Imperative for Creating and Profiting from Technology*. Boston, MA: Harvard Business School Publishing.

Chesbrough, H.W., Vanhaverbeke, W. and West, J. (2006) *Open Innovation: Researching a New Paradigm*. Oxford: Oxford University Press.

Chiesa, V. and Manzini, R. (1997) Competence-based diversification. *Long Range Planning*, **30**(2), 209–217.

Chin, W.W. (1998) Issues and opinion on structural equation modeling. *MIS Quarterly*, **22**, 7–17.

Christensen, C. (1997) *The Innovator's Dilemma*. Boston, MA: Harvard Business School Press.

Christensen, C.M. and Overdorf, M. (2000) Meeting the challenge of disruptive change. *Harvard Business Review*, **78**, 66–76.

Chusil, M.J. (1978) How much to spend on R&D. *PIMS Newsletter*, No. 13.

Ciborra, C. and Patriotta, G. (1998) Groupware and teamwork in R&D: limits to learning and innovation. *R&D Management*, **28**(1), 43–52.

CIMA (1993) *Performance Measurement in the Manufacturing Sector*. Chartered Institute of Management Accountants.

CIPD (2001) *Raising UK Productivity: Why People Management Matters*. London: Chartered Institute of Personnel and Development.

Clark, D.N. (2000) Implementation issues in core competence strategy making. *Strategic Change*, **9**(2), 115–127.

Clark, K.B. and Fujimoto (1991) *Product Development Performance*. Boston, MA: Harvard University Press.

Clark, P. (2000) *Organizations in Action: Competition Between Contexts*. London: Routledge.

Clark, P.A. and Staunton, N. (1989) *Innovation in Technology and Organization*. London: Routledge.

Clinton, W.L. and Gore, Jr., A. (1993) *Technology for America's Economic Growth: A New Direction to Build Economic Strength*. Office of the President of the United States.

Cohen, K.J. and Cyert, R.M. (1973) Strategy — Formulation, Implementation, and Monitoring. *Journal of Business*, **46**(3), 349–367.

Cohen, M.D. (1996) Individual learning and organizational routine. In M.D. Cohen and L.S. Sproull (eds.), *Organisational Learning*. London: Sage Publications.

Cohen, W. and Levin, R. (1989) Empirical studies of innovation and market structure. In R. Schmalensee and R. Willig (eds.), *The Handbook of Industrial Organisation*, Vol. 1. Oxford: Elsevier.

Cohen, W. and Levinthal, D. (1990) Absorptive capacity: a new perspective on learning and innovation. *Administrative Science Quarterly*, **35**, 128–152.

Collis, D.J. (1994) How valuable are organizational capabilities? *Strategic Management Journal*, **15**, 143–152.

Collis, D.J. and Montgomery, C. (1998) Creating corporate advantage. *Harvard Business Review*, **76**(3), 71–83.

Constant, E.W. (1987) The social locus of technological practice: community, system or organisation. In W. Bijker, T. Hughes and T. Pinch (eds.), *The Social Construction of Technological Systems: New Directions in the Sociology and History of Technology*. Cambridge, MA: MIT Press.

Contu, A. and Willmott, H. (2000) Comment on Wenger and Yanow. Knowing in practice: a "delicate flower" in the organizational learning field. *Organization*, **7**(2), 269–276.

Cook, S. and Brown, J. (1999) Bridging epistemologies: the generative dance between organizational knowledge and organizational knowing. *Organization Science*, **10**(4), 381–400.

Coombs, R., Narandren, P. and Richards, A. (1994) An innovation output indicator for the UK economy. Report to the ESRC. Manchester, UMIST.

Coombs, R., Narandren, P. and Richards, A. (1996) A literature-based innovation output indicator. *Research Policy*, **25**, 403–413.

Coombs, R., Saviotti, P. and Walsh, V. (1992) *Technological Change and Company Strategies*. London: Academic Press.

Cooper, R.G. (1994) Third-generation new product processes. *Journal of Product Innovation Management*, **11**(1), 3–14.

Cooper, R.G. (1984) New Product Strategies: what distinguishes the top performers? *Journal Product Innovation Management*, **1**(3), 151–164.

Cooper, R.G. and Kleinschmidt, E.J. (1987) New products: what separates winners from losers. *Journal of Product Innovation Management*, **4**, 169–187.

Cooper, R.G. and Kleinschmidt, E.J. (1995) Benchmarking the firm's critical success factors in new product development. *Journal of Product Innovation Management*, **12**, 374–391.

Cordero, R. (1990) The measurement of innovation performance in the firm: an overview. *Research Policy*, **19**, 180–192.

Cox, D.R. and Wermuth, N. (1996) *Multivariate Dependencies-Models, Analysis and Interpretation*. London: Chapman and Hall.

Coy, P. and Carey, J. (1993) The global patent race picks up speed. *Business Week Patent Scoreboard*, 16 August.

Coyne, K.P. (1986) Sustainable competitive advantage — what it is and what it isn't. *Business Horizons*, January/February, Indiana University.

Crampton, S.M. and Wagner, J.A. (1994) Percept-percept inflation in micro-organizational research: an investigation of prevalence and effect. *Journal of Applied Psychology*, **79**, 67–76.

Crepon, B. and Mairesse, J. (1993) Innovation and productivity — the contribution of SESI's innovation survey to econometric analysis. Paper given to SPES discussion group, Brussels, September.

Cummings, J.N. (2004) Work groups, structural diversity, and knowledge sharing in a global organization. *Management Science*, **50**(3), 352–364.

Danneels, E. (2002) The dynamics of product innovation and firm competences. *Strategic Management Journal*, **23**, 1095–1121.

Danneels, E. (2007) The process of technological competence leveraging. *Strategic Management Journal*, **28**(5), 511–533.

Danneels, E. (2008) Organizational antecedents of second-order competences. *Strategic Management Journal*, **29**, 519–543.

Dasgupta, P. and Stiglitz, J. (1980) Industrial structure and the nature of innovative activity. *Economic Journal*, **90**, 266–293.

Davenport, T. (1992) *Process Innovation: Re-engineering Work through Information Technology*. Boston, MA: Harvard University Press.

Davies, A. and Brady, T. (2000) Organisational capabilities and learning in complex product systems: towards repeatable solutions. *Research Policy*, **29**(7–8), 931–953.

Davies, A. and Hobday, M. (2005) *The Business of Projects: Managing Innovation in Complex Products and Systems*, Cambridge: Cambridge University Press.

Davies, A., Brady, T. and Hobday, M. (2007) Charting a path toward integrated solutions. *Sloan Management Review*, **47**(3), 39–48.

Davies, M., Paterson, R. and Wilson, A. (1991) *UK GAAP*. Middlesex: Longman.

DeFillippi, R. and Arthur, M. (1998) Paradox in project based enterprise: the case of filmmaking. *California Management Review*, **40**(2), 125–139.

Day, G.S. (1994) The capabilities of market-driven organizations. *The Journal of Marketing*, **58**(4), 37–52.

Day, G. and Schoemaker, P.J.H. (2000) Avoiding the pitfalls of emerging technologies, *California Management Review. Winter Issue*, **42**(2), 8–33.

de Gues, A. (1996) *The Living Company*. Boston, MA: Harvard Business School Press.

De Wit, R. and Meyer, R. (2005) *Strategy: Process, Content, Context*, 3rd edition. London: Thomson.

Deming, W.E. (1986) *Out of the Crisis*. Cambridge, MA: MIT Press.

Deng, Z. and Lev, B. (1998) The valuation of acquired R&D. Working Paper.

Deng, Z., Lev, B. and Narin, F. (1998) Science and technology indicators as predictors of stock performance. Draft paper.

Denison, D.R., Hart, S.L. and Kahn, J.A. (1996) From chimneys to crossfunctional teams: developing and validating a diagnostic model. *Academy of Management Journal*, **39**(4), 1005–1023.

DeSarbo, W.S., Di Benedetto, C.A., Song, M. and Sinha, I. (2005) Revisiting the Miles and Snow strategic framework: uncovering interrelationships between strategy types, capabilities, environmental uncertainty, and firm performance. *Strategic Management Journal*, **27**(3), 467–488.

Deshpande, R. and Zaltman, G. (1982) Factors affecting the use of market research information: a path analysis. *Journal of Marketing Research*, **19**, 14–31.

Dess, G.G. and Robinson, R.B. (1984) Measuring organisational performance in the absence of objective measures. *Strategic Management Journal*, **5**(3), 265–273.

Devinney, T.M. (1993) How well do patents measure new product activity? *Economics Letters*, **41**, 447–450.

Dewar, R.D. and Dutton, J.E. (1986) The adoption of radical and incremental innovations: an empirical analysis. *Management Science*, **32**, 1422–1433.

Dierickx, I. and Cool, K. (1989) Asset stock accumulation and sustainability of competitive advantage. *Management Science*, **35**, 1504–1514.

Dixon, J.R., Nanni, A.J. and Vollmann, T. (1990) *The New Performance Challenge: Measuring Operations for World-Class Competition*. London: Irwin.

Dodgson, M. (1993) *Technological Collaboration in Industry*. London: Routledge.

Dodgson, M. and Rothwell, R. (1995) *The Handbook of Industrial Innovation*. London: Edward Elgar.

Dodgson, M., Gann, D. and Salter, A. (2005) *Think, Play, Do: Technology, Innovation and Organization*. Oxford: Oxford University Press.

Duncan, R. (1976) The ambidextrous organization: designing dual structures for innovation. In Killman, R. H., L. R. Pondy, and D. Sleven (eds.), *The Management of Organization*. New York, NY: North Holland.

Donnellon, A. (1993) Cross-functional teams in product development: accommodating the structure to the process. *Journal of Product Innovation Management*, **10**, 377–392.

Dosi, G. (1982) Technological paradigms and technological trajectories. *Research Policy*, **11**, 147–162.

Dosi, G., Teece, D.J. and Winter, S. (2000) *The Nature and Dynamics of Organizational Capabilities*. Oxford, Oxford University Press.

Dougherty, D. (1992) Interpretive barriers to successful product innovation in large firms. *Organization Science*, **3**, 179–202.

Dougherty, D. (2001) Reimagining the differentiation and integration of work for sustained product innovation. *Organization Science*, **12**(5), 612–631.

Dougherty, D. and Hardy, C. (1996) Sustained product innovation in large, mature organizations: overcoming innovation-to-organization problems. *Academy of Management Journal*, **39**, 1120–1153.

Doz, Y.L., Olk, P.M. and Ring, P.S. (2000) Formation processes of R&D consortia: which path to take? Where does it lead? *Strategic Management Journal*, **21**, 239–266.

Dutta, S., Narasimhan, O. and Rajiv, S. (1999) Success in high-technology markets: Is market capability critical? *Market Science*, **18**, 547–568.

Dutta, S., Zbaracki, M.J. and Bergen, M. (2003) Pricing process as a capability: a resource-based perspective. *Strategic Management Journal*, **24**, 615–630.

Dyer, B. and Song, X.M. (1998) Innovation strategy and sanctioned conflict: a new edge in innovation? *Journal of Product Innovation Management*, **15**(6), 505–519.

Eccles, R. (1991) The performance measurement manifesto. *Harvard Business Review*, January/February.

Edwards, K.L. and Gordon, T.J. (1984) Characterisation of innovations introduced on the US market in 1982. Report to the US Small Business Administration, Connecticut, Futures Group.

Eisenhardt, K. and Graebner, M. (2007) Building theory from cases: opportunities and challenges. *Academy of Management Journal*, **14**(4), 532–550.

Eisenhardt, K.M. (1985) Control: organizational and economic approaches. *Management Science*, **31**, 134–149.

Eisenhardt, K.M. and Martin, J.A. (2000) Dynamic capabilities: what are they? *Strategic Management Journal*, **21**(10/11), 1105–1121.

Eisenhardt, K.M. and Tabrizi, B. (1995) Accelerating adaptive processes: product innovation in the global computer industry. *Administrative Science Quarterly*, **40**(1), 84–110.

Ellis, P., Hepburn, G. and Oppenheim, C. (1978) Studies on patent citation networks. *Journal of Documentation*, **34**(1), 12–20.

Ellonen, H.K., Jantunen, A. and Kuivalainen, O. (2011) The role of dynamic capabilities in developing innovation-related capabilities. *International Journal of Innovation Management*, **15**(3), 459–478.

Ellonen, H.K., Wikström, P. and Jantunen, A. (2009) Linking dynamic capability portfolios and innovation outcomes. *Technovation*, **29**, 753–762.

Enkel, E., Gassmann, O. and Chesbrough, H. (2009) Open Innovation: exploring the phenomenon. *R&D Management*, **39**(4), 311–316.

Eriksson, P. and Kovalainen, A. (2008) *Qualitative Methods in Business Research*. London: Sage Publications.

EU (1996) *Panorama of European Industry*. Eurostat, Statistical Office of the European Community.

EU (1997) *Competitiveness Report*. White paper, European Union. Euske, K.J. (1984) *Management Control: Planning, Control, Measurement and Evaluation*. Reading, MA: Addison-Wesley.

Evangelidis, K. (1983) Performance measured performance gained, *The Treasurer*, February, 45–47.

Feinman, S. and Fuentevilla, W. (1976) *Indicators of International Trends in Technological Innovation*. Washington, DC: National Science Foundation.

Fernández, E., Montes, J.M. and Vázquez, C.J. (2000) Typology and strategic analysis of intangible resources: a resource-based approach. *Technovation*, **20**, 81–92.

Figueiredo, L. (2001) Latin America transformed — globalization and modernity. *Journal of International Development*, **13**(2), 289–290.

Fiol, C.M. (1994) Consensus, diversity, and learning in organizations. *Organization Science*, **5**(3), 403–420.

Fitzgerald, L., Brignall, T.J., Johnston, R. and Silvestro, R. (1991) Product costing in service organisations. *Management Accounting Research*, **2**(4), 227–248.

Flamholtz, E.G. (1979) Organizational control systems as a managerial tool. *California Management Review*, **22**, 50–59.

Fleck, J. (1997) Contingent knowledge and technology development. *Technology Analysis and Strategic Management*, **9**(4), 383–397.

Flowers, S. and Henwood, F. (2008) *International Journal of Innovation Management*, Special Issue on User Innovation, **12**(3).

Forcadell, F.J. (2007) The Corporate Growth of the Firm: a resource-based approach. *Journal of American Academy of Business*, **11**(2), 151.

Ford, C. (1996) A theory of individual creative action in multiple social domains. *Academy of Management Review*, **21**, 1112–1142.

Fortuin, L. (1988) Performance indicators: why, where and how? *European Journal of Operations Management*, **34**, 1–9.

Fox, S. (2000) Practice, Foucault and actor-network theory. *Journal of Management Studies*, **37**(6), 853–868.

Francis, D. (1994) *Step by Step Competitive Strategy*. London: Routledge.

Franko, L.G. (1989) Global corporate competition: who's winning, who's losing, and the R&D factor as one reason why. *Strategic Management Journal*, **10**, 449–474.

Fredrickson, J.W. (1984) The comprehensiveness of strategic decision-processes — extension, observations, future-directions. *Academy of Management Journal*, **27**(3), 445–466.

Fredrickson, J.W. and Iaquinto, A.L. (1989) Inertia and creeping rationality in strategic decision-processes. *Academy of Management Journal*, **32**(3), 516–542.

Freeman, C. (1971) The role of small firms in innovation in the United Kingdom since 1945. Committee of inquiry on small firms, Report No. 6, HMSO, London.

Freeman, C. (1982) *The Economics of Industrial Innovation*. London: Pinter.

Freeman, C. (1991) Networks of innovators: a synthesis of research issues. *Research Policy*, **20**, 499–514.

Furrer, O., Thomas, H. and Goussevskaia, A. (2008) The structure and evolution of the strategic management field: a content analysis of 26 years of strategic management research. *International Journal of Management Reviews*, **10**(1), 1–23.

Galbreath, J. (2005) Which resources matter the most to firm success? An exploratory study of resource-based theory. *Technovation*, **25**, 979–987.

Galbraith, J.R. (1972) *Designing Complex Organizations*. Reading, MA: Addison-Wesley.

Galbraith, J.R. (1994) *Competing with Flexible Lateral Organizations*. Reading, MA: Addison-Wesley.

Gallagher, M. and Austin, S. (1997) *Continuous Improvement Casebook*. London: Kogan Page.

Gambardella, A. and Torrisi, S. (1998) Does technological convergence imply convergence in markets? Evidence from the electronics industry. *Research Policy*, **27**, 445–463.

Garfield, E. (1955) Citation indexes for science. *Science*, **122**, 108–111.

Garfield, E. (1986) Do Nobel Prize winners write citation classics? *Current Comments*, **23**, 182.

Garvin, D. (1993) Building a learning organisation. *Harvard Business Review*, July/August, 78–91.

Gatignon, H., Tushman, M.L., Smith, W. and Anderson, P. (2002) A structural approach to assessing innovation: construct development of innovation locus, type, and characteristics. *Management Science*, **48**, 1103–1122.

Geroski, P. (1991) Innovation and the sectoral sources of UK productivity growth. *Economic Journal*, **101**, 1438–1451.

Geroski, P. (1994) *Market Structure, Corporate Performance and Innovative Activity*. Oxford: Oxford University Press.

Geroski, P. and Pomroy, R. (1990) Innovation, and the evolution of market structure. *Journal of Industrial Economics*, **28**, 299–314.

Geroski, P., Machin, S. and van Reenen, J. (1993) The profitability of innovating firms. *RAD Journal of Economics*, **24**, 198–211.

Ghalayini, A.M. and Noble, J.S. (1996) The changing basis of performance measurement. *International Journal of Operations and Production Management*, **16**(8), 63–80.

Gherardi, S. and Nicolini, D. (2002) Learning in a constellation of interconnected practices: canon or dissonance. *Journal of Management Studies*, **39**(4), 419–436.

Gherardi, S., Nicolini, D. and Odella, F. (1998) Towards a social understanding of how people learn in organizations: the notion of situated curriculum. *Management Learning*, **29**(3), 273–297.

Ghoshal, S. and Bartlett, C.A. (1994) Linking organizational context and managerial action: The dimensions of quality of management. *Strategic Management Journal*, **15**, 91–112.

Gibson, C.B. and Birkinshaw, J. (2004) The antecedents, consequences and mediating role of organizational ambidexterity. *Academy of Management Journal*, **47**, 209–226.

Giddens, A. (1984) *The Constitution of Society*. Berkeley, CA: University of California Press.

Gilsing, V. and Nooteboom, B. (2006) Exploration and exploitation in innovation systems: the case of pharmaceutical biotechnology. *Research Policy*, **35**, 1–23.

Glaser, B.G. and Strauss, A.L. (1967) *The Discovery of Grounded Theory: Strategies for Qualitative Research*. New York, NY: Aldine de Gruyter.

Gobeli, D.H. and Larson, E.W. (1987) Relative effectiveness of different project structures. *Project Management Journal*, **XVIII**(2), 81–85.

Golden, B.R. (1992) Research notes: the past is the past — or is it? The use of retrospective accounts as indicators of past strategy. *Academy of Management Journal*, **35**, 848–860.

Goold, M., Campbell, A. and Alexander, A. (1994) *Corporate-level Strategy: Creating Value in the Multibusiness Company*. New York, NY: John Wiley and Sons.

Gouldner, A. (1970) *The Coming Crisis of Western Sociology*. London: Heinemann.

Granstrand, O., Patel, P. and Pavitt, K. (1997) Multi-technology corporations: why they have "distributed" rather than "distinctive core" competencies. *California Management Review*, **39**, 8–25.

Grant, R.M. (1991) The resource-based theory of competitive advantage: implications for strategy formulation. *California Management Review*, **33**, 114–135.

Grant, R.M. (1996a) Towards a knowledge based theory of the firm. *Strategic Management Journal*, **17**(Winter Special Issue), 109–122.

Grant, R.M. (1996b) Prospering in dynamically-competitive environments: organizational capability as knowledge integration. *Organization Science*, **7**(4), 375–387.

Grant, R.M. (1997) The knowledge-based view of the firm: implications for strategy formulation. *Long Range Planning*, June, 451–463.

Grant, R.M. (2001) Knowledge and organization. In I. Nonaka and D.J. Teece (eds.), *Managing Industrial Knowledge: Creation, Transfer and Utilization*. London: Sage Publications.

Griffin, A. (1997) PDMA research on new product development practices: updating trends and benchmarking best practices. *Journal of Product Innovation Management*, **14**(6), 429–458.

Griffin, A. and Page, A.L. (1993) An interim report on measuring product development success and failure. *Journal of Product Innovation Management*, **10**, 291–308.

Griffin, A. and Page, A.L. (1996) PDMA success measurement project: recommended measures for product development success and failure. *Journal of Product Innovation Management*, **13**, 478–496.

Griliches, Z. (1981) Market value, R&D and patents. *Economics Letters*, **7**, 183–187.

Griliches, Z. (1984) Market value, R&D, and patents. In Z. Griliches and A. Pakes (eds.), *Patents, R&D and Productivity*. Chicago: University of Chicago Press.

Griliches, Z. (1990) Patent statistics as economic indicators: a survey. *Journal of Economic Literature*, **28**(4), 1661–1797.

Griliches, Z., Hall, B.H. and Pakes, A. (1991) R&D, patents and market value revisited. *Economics of Innovation and New Technology Journal*, **1**(3), 183–202.

Guerard, J.B., Bean, A.S. and Stone, B.K. (1990) Goal-setting for effective corporate-planning. *Management Science*, **36**(3), 359–367.

Guest, D., Michie, J., Sheehan, M. and Conway, N. (2000) *Employment Relations, HRM and Business Performance: An Analysis of the 1998 Workplace Employee Relations Survey*. London: CIPD.

Gulati, R. (1998) Alliances and networks. *Strategic Management Journal*, **19**, 293–317.

Gulick, L.H. (1937) Notes on the theory of organization. In L. Gulick and L. Urwick (eds.), *Papers on the Science of Administration*. New York, NY: Institute of Public Administration, 3–35.

Gundling, E. (2000) *The 3M Way to Innovation: Balancing People and Profit*. New York, NY: Kodansha International.

Hair, J.F., Anderson, R.E., Tatham, R.L. and Black, W.C. (1998) *Multivariate Data Analysis with Readings.* Upper Saddle River, NJ: Prentice-Hall.

Hakansson, H. and Waluszewski, A. (2003) *Managing Technological Development.* London: Routledge.

Hales, M. and Tidd, J. (2009) Routines and representations at work in new product development. *Industrial and Corporate Change,* **18**(4), 551–574.

Hall, B. (1993a) The stock market value of R&D investment during the 1980s. *American Economic Review,* **83**, 259–264.

Hall, B. (1993b) Industrial research during the 1980s: did the rate of return fall? *Brookings Papers on Economic Activity,* 289–343.

Hall, B., Griliches, Z. and Hausman, J. (1986) Patents and R&D: is there a lag? *International Economic Review,* **27**(2), 265–283.

Hall, B., Mairesse, J. and Mohnen, P. (2010) Measuring the returns to R&D. In B.H. Hall and N. Rosenberg (eds.), *Handbook of the Economics of Innovation,* Chapter 24. Netherlands: Elsevier.

Hall, B.H., Jaffe, A. and Trajtenberg, M. (1998) *Market Value and Patent Citations: A First Look.* Paper Prepared for the Conference on Intangibles and Capital Markets, New York University.

Hall, R. (1992) The strategic analysis of intangible resources. *Strategic Management Journal,* **13**, 135–144.

Hall, R. (1993c) A framework linking intangible resources and capabilities to sustainable competitive advantage. *Strategic Management Journal,* **14**, 607–618.

Hamel, G. (2000) *Leading the Revolution.* Boston, MA: Harvard Business School Press.

Hamel, G. (2009) Moon shots for management. *Harvard Business Review,* February, 91–98.

Harhoff, D., Narin, F., Scherer, F.M. and Vopel, K. (1998) Citation frequency and the value of patented inventions. *The Review of Economics and Statistics,* **81**(3), 511–515.

Hardy, C. and Phillips, N. (1998) Strategies of engagement: lessons from the critical examination of collaboration and conflict in an interorganizational domain. *Organization Science,* **9**(2), 217–230.

Harris, M. (1997) Power, knowledge and social process in technology analysis: the case of CAD/CAM. *Journal of Information Technology,* **12**, 61–71.

Hax, A.C. and Majluf, N.S. (1991) *The Strategy Concept* and *Process: A Pragmatic Appraoch.* Prentice-Hall International Inc.

Hayes, N. and Walsham, G. (2000) Safe enclaves, political enclaves and knowledge working. In C. Pritchard, R. Hull, M. Chumer and H. Willmott (eds.), *Managing Knowledge: Critical Investigations of Work and Learning.* London: MacMillan.

He, Z.-L. and Wong, P.K. (2004) Exploration vs. exploitation: an empirical test of the ambidexterity hypothesis. *Organization Science,* **15**, 481–494.

Heim, J.A. and Compton, W.D. (1992) *Manufacturing Systems: Foundations of World-class Practice.* Washington, DC: National Academy of Engineering.

Helfat, C.E. and Peteraf, M.A. (2003) The dynamic resource-based view: capability lifecycles. *Strategic Management Journal,* **24**, 997–1010.

Helfat, C.E. and Raubitschek, R.S. (2000). Product sequencing: co-evolution of knowledge, capabilities and products. *Strategic Management Journal,* **21**, 961–979.

Helfat, C.E., Finkelstein, S., Mitchell, W., Peteraf, M.A., Singh, H., Teece, D.J. and Winter, S.G. (2007) *Dynamic Capabilities: Understanding Strategic Change in Organisations*. Malden: Blackwell Publishing.

Henderson, R.M. and Clark, K.B. (1990) Architectural innovation: the reconfiguration of existing product technologies and the failure of established firms. *Administrative Science Quarterly*, **35**(1), 9–30.

Hendricks, J.A. (1994) Performance measures for JIT manufacture. *Industrial Engineering*, January, 26–29.

Herstatt, C., and von Hippel, E. (1992) From experience: developing new product concepts via the lead user method: a case study in a "low-tech" field. *Journal of Product Innovation Management*, **9**(3), 213–221.

Hildreth, P., Kimble, C. and Wright, P. (2000) Communities of practice in the distributed international environment. *Journal of Knowledge Management*, **4**(1), 27–38.

Hislop, D. (1999) The Movex project: knowledge management at Brightco. In H. Scarbrough and J. Swan (eds.), *Case Studies in Knowledge Management*,. London: IPD.

Hislop, D., Newell, S., Scarbrough, H. and Swan, J. (1997) Innovation and networks: linking diffusion and implementation. *International Journal of Innovation Management*, **1**(4), 427–448.

Hitt, M.A. and Ireland, R.D. (1985) Corporate distinctive competence, strategy, industry and performance. *Strategic Management Journal*, **3**(3), 273–293.

Hobday, M. (1998) Product complexity, innovation and industrial organization. *Research Policy*, **26**(6), 689–710.

Hobday, M. (2000) The project-based organisation: an ideal form for managing complex products and systems? *Research Policy*, **29**, 871–893.

Hobday, M., Rush, H. and Tidd, J. (2000a) Innovation in complex product systems. *Research Policy*, **29**, 793–804.

Holland, S., Gaston, K. and Gomes, J. (2000b) Critical success factors for cross functional teamwork in new product development. *International Journal of Management Reviews*, **2**(3), 231–259.

Hooi-Soh, P. and Roberts, E.B. (2003) Networks of innovators: a longitudinal perspective. *Research Policy*, **32**, 1569–1588.

Housley, W. (2000) Category work and knowledgeability within multidisciplinary team meetings. *Text*, **20**(1), 83–107.

Hronec, S.M. (1993) *Vital Signs: Using Quality, Time and Cost Performance Measurements*. New York, NY: Amacom.

Idenburg, P.J. (1993) Four styles of strategy-development. *Long Range Planning*, **26**(6), 132–137.

Ijiri, Y. and Jaedicke, R. (1981) Reliability and objectivity of accounting measurements. In R.O. Mason and E. Burton Swanson (eds.), *Measurement for Management Decision*. Boston, MA: Addison-Wesley.

Iles, P. (1994) Developing learning environments: challenges for theory, research and practice. *Journal of European Industrial Training*, **18**(3), 3–9.

Jacobsson, S. and Oskarsson, C. (1995) Educational statistics as an indicator of technological activity. *Research Policy*, **24**, 127–136.

Jacobsson, S., Oskarsson, C. and Joakim, P. (1996) Indicators of technological activities. *Research Policy*, **25**, 573–585.

Jaffe, A., Trajtenberg, M. and Henderson, R. (1993) Geographic localisation of knowledge spillovers as evidenced by patent citations. *Quarterly Journal of Economics*, **108**(3), 577–598.

Jaffe, A.B. (1986) Technological opportunity and spillovers of R&D: evidence from firms patents, profits and market values. *The American Economic Review*, **76**, 948–999.

Jaffe, A.B. (1989) Characterising the "technological position" of firms, with application to quantifying technological opportunity and research spillovers. *Research Policy*, **18**, 87–97.

Jansen, J.J.P. (2005) *A Multiple-Level Study of Absorptive Capacity, Exploratory and Exploitative Innovation and Performance*. Unpublished doctoral dissertation, RSM Erasmus University, Rotterdam, Netherlands.

Jansen, J.J.P., Van den Bosch, F.A.J. and Volberda, H.W. (2005) Exploratory innovation, exploitative innovation, and ambidexterity: the impact of environmental and organizational antecedents. *Schmalenbach Business Review*, **57**, 351–363.

Jansen, J.J.P., Van den Bosch, F.A.J. and Volberda, H.W. (2006) Exploratory innovation, exploitative innovation, and performance: effects of organizational antecedents and environmental moderators. *Management Science*, **52**, 1661–1674.

Jelinek, M. and Litterer, J. (1994) Organizing for technology and innovation. In W. Souder and J. Sherman (eds.), *Managing New Technology Development*. New York, NY: McGraw Hill.

Jensen, E. (1987) Research expenditures and the discovery of new drugs. *Journal of Industrial Economics*, **XXXVI**(1), 83–96.

Johne, A.F. and Snelson, P. (1988) Marketing's role in successful product development. *Journal of Marketing Management*, **3**(3), 256–268.

Johnson, H. (1990) *Relevance Regained: Total Quality Management and The Role of Management Accounting*. New York, NY: Academic Press.

Jöreskog, K.G. and Aish, A.M. (1990) A panel model for political efficacy and responsiveness: an application of LISREL 7 with weighted least squares. *Quality and Quantity*, **24**(4), 405–426.

Jöreskog, K.G. and Sörbom, D. (1984) *LISREL-VI: Analysis of Linear Structural Relationships by the Method of Maximum Likelihood*. Mooresville: Scientific Software Inc.

Juran, J.M. (1992) *Juran on Quality by Design*. New York, NY: Free Press.

Kaplan, D. and Wenger, R.N. (1993) Asymptotic independence and separability in covariance structure models: implications for specification error, power, and model modification. *Multivariate Behavioral Research*, **28**, 467–482.

Kaplan, R.S. (1991) New systems for measurement and control. *The Engineering Economist*, **36**(93), 201–218.

Kaplan, R.S. and Norton, D.P. (1992) The balanced scorecard — measures that drive performance. *Harvard Business Review*, January/February, 71–79.

Katkalo, V.S., Pitelis, C.N. and Teece, D.J. (2010). Introduction: On the nature and scope of dynamic capabilities. *Industrial and Corporate Change*, **19**(4), 1175–1185.

Kay, J. (1993) *The Foundations of Corporate Success*. Oxford: Oxford University Press.

Keller, R.T. (2001) Cross-functional project groups in research and new product development: diversity, communications, job stress, and outcomes. *Academy of Management Journal*, **44**(3), 547–555.

Keupp, M.M., Palmié, M. and Gassmann, O. (2012) The strategic management of innovation: a systematic review and paths for future research. *International Journal of Management Reviews*, **14**(1).

Khanna, T. and Palepu, K. (1997) Why focused strategies may be wrong for emerging markets. *Harvard Business Review*, **75**(4), 41–51.

Kim, L. (1998) Crisis construction and organizational learning: capability building in catching-up at Hyundai Motor. *Organization Science*, **9**(4), 506–521.

Kleinknecht, A. (1987) Measuring R&D in small firms: how much are we missing? *The Journal of Industrial Economics*, **36**(2), 253–256.

Kleinknecht, A. and Bain, D. (1993) *New Concepts in Output Measurement*. London: St. Martin's Press.

Kleinknecht, A. and Reijnen, J.O.N. (1993) Towards literature-based innovation output indicators. *Structural Change and Economic Dynamics*, **4**(1), 199–207.

Kleinman, H. (1975) Indicators of the output of new technological products from industry. Report to the National Science Foundation, National Technical Information Service, Department of Commerce, Washington.

Klomp, L. and Van Leeuwen, G. (2001) Linking innovation and firm performance: a new approach. *International Journal of the Economics of Business*, **8**(3), 343–364.

Kogut, B. and Zander, U. (1992) Knowledge of the firm, combinative capabilities, and the replication of technology. *Organization Science*, **3**(3), 383–397.

Kohli, A.K. and Jaworski, B. (1990) Market orientation: the construct, research propositions, and managerial implications. *Journal of Marketing*, **54**(April), 1–18.

Kolb, D. and Fry, R. (1975) Towards a theory of applied experiential learning. In C. Cooper (ed.), *Theories of Group Processes*. Chichester: John Wiley and Sons.

Kremen Bolton, M.K. (1993) Organizational innovation and substandard performance: when is necessity the mother of innovation? *Organization Science*, **4**, 57–65.

Krishnan, R., Martin, X. and Noorderhaven, N.G. (2006) When does trust matter to alliance performance? *Academy of Management Journal*, **49**(5), 894–917.

Laamanen, T. and Wallin, J. (2009) Cognitive dynamics of capability development paths. *Journal of Management Studies*, **46**, 950–981.

Lam, S.Y., Shankar, V., Krishna Erramilli, M. and Murthy, B. (2004) Customer value, satisfaction, loyalty, and switching costs: an illustration from a business-to-business service context. *Journal of the Academy of Marketing Science*, **32**(3), 293–311.

Lambkin, M. (1988) Order of entry and performance in new markets. *Strategic Management Journal*, **9**, 127–140.

Lane, D. and Maxfield, R. (1996) Strategy under complexity: fostering generative relationships. *Long Range Planning*, **29**(2), 215–231.

Langley, A. (1999) Strategies for theorizing from process data. *Academy of Management Review*, **24**, 691–710.

Laursen, K. and Salter, A. (2006) Open for innovation: the role of openness in explaining innovation performance among UK manufacturing firms. *Strategic Management Journal*, **27**(2), 131–150.

Lave, J.C. and Wenger, E. (1991) *Situated Learning: Legitimate Peripheral Participation*. Cambridge: Cambridge University Press.

Lavie, D. (2006) Capability reconfiguring: an analysis of incumbent responses to technological change. *Academy of Management Review*, **31**, 153–174.

Lazega, E. (1992) *Micropolitics of Knowledge: Communication and Indirect Control in Workgroups*. New York, NY: De Gruyter.

LeBlanc, G. and Nguyen, N. (1995) Cues used by customers evaluating corporate image in service firms. An empirical study in financial institutions. *International Journal of Service Industry Management*, **7**(2), 44–56.

Leifer, R. (2000) *Radical Innovation*. Boston, MA: Harvard Business School Press.

Leonard, D. and Sensiper, S. (1998) The role of tacit knowledge in group innovation. *California Management Review*, **40**(3), 112–132.

Leonard-Barton, D. (1991) Core capabilities and core rigidities: a paradox in managing new product development. *Strategic Management Journal*, **13**, 111–125.

Leonard-Barton, D. (1992) The organisation as learning laboratory. *Sloan Management Review*, Fall.

Leonard-Barton, D. (1995) *Wellsprings of Knowledge: Building and Sustaining the Sources of Innovation*. Boston, MA: Harvard Business School Press.

Leontiades, M. and Tezel, A. (1980) Planning perceptions and planning results. *Strategic Management Journal*, **1**(1), 65–75.

Levin, R., Cohen, W. and Mowery, D. (1985) R&D, appropriability, opportunity, and market structure: new evidence on the Schumpeterian hypothesis. *American Economic Review*, **75**, 20–24.

Levin, R.C., Klevorick, A., Nelson, R. and Winter, S. (1987) Appropriating the returns from industrial research and development. *Brookings Papers on Economic Activity*, **3**, 783–831.

Levinthal, D.A. and March, J.G. (1993) The myopia of learning. *Strategic Management Journal*, **14**, 95–112.

Levitt, B. and March, J.G. (1988) Organisational learning. *Annual Review of Sociology*, **14**, 319–340.

Lewin, A.Y. (1999) Application of complexity theory to organization science. *Organization Science*, **10**(3), 215.

Lichtenthaler, E. (2005) Corporate diversification: identifying new businesses systematically in the diversified firm. *Technovation*, **25**(7), 419–440.

Liedtka, J. (1999) Linking competitive advantage with communities of practice. *Journal of Management Enquiry*, **8**(1), 5–16.

Ljungquist, U. (2007) Core competency beyond identification: presentation of a model. *Management Decision*, **45**(3), 393–402.

Loch, C., Stein, L. and Terweisch (1996) Measuring development performance in the electronics industry. *Journal of Product Innovation Management*, **13**, 3–20.

Lockett, A., Thompson, S. and Morgenstern, U. (2009) The development of the resource-based view of the firm: a critical appraisal. *International Journal of Management Reviews*, **11**(1), 9–28.

Loof, H. and Heshmati, A. (2002) Knowledge capital and performance heterogeneity: a firm-level innovation study. *International Journal of Production Economics*, **76**(1), 61–85.

Luchs, B. (1990) Quality as a strategic weapon: measuring relative quality, value and market differentiation. *European Business Journal*, **2**(4), 34–47.

Lynch, R.L. and Cross, K.F. (1991) *Measure Up! Yardsticks for Continuous Improvements*. Oxford: Blackwell Publishing.

Maidique, M. and Zirger, B. (1985) The new product learning cycle. *Research Policy*, **14**(6), 299–309.

Mairesse, J. and Grilliches, Z. (1984) Comparing productivity growth: an exploration of French and U.S. industrial and firm data. *European Economic Review*, **21**(1–2), 89–11.

Mairesse, J. and Cueno, P. (1985) Recherche-développement et performances des enterprises: une etude econometrique sur donnees individuelles. *Revue Economique*, **36**, 1001–1042.

Mairesse, J. and Hall, B. (1996) Estimating the productivity of research and development in French and United States manufacturing firms: an exploration of simultaneity issues with GMM method. In K. Wagner and B. van Ark (ed.), *International Productivity Differences*. Amsterdam: Elsevier.

Mairesse, J. and Mohnen, P. (2010) Using innovation surveys for econometric analysis, UNU-MERIT working paper 2010–23, Maastricht. http://www.merit.unu.edu/publications/wp.php?year_id=2010.

Mairesse, J. and Sassenou, M. (1991) R&D and productivity: a survey of econometric studies at the firm level. *OECD STI Review*, **8**, 9–44.

Mansfield, E. (1984) R&D and Innovation: some empirical findings. In Z. Griliches and A. Pakes (eds.), *Patents, R&D and Productivity*. Chicago: University of Chicago Press.

Mansfield, E. (1990) *Managerial Economics*. London: WW Norton Company.

Manu, F.A. (1992) Innovation orientation, environment and performance: a comparison of U.S. and European Markets. *Journal of International Business Studies*, **29**(2), 239–247.

March, J. (1998) Introduction: a chronicle of speculations about organizational decision making. In J. March (ed.), *Decisions and Organisations*. Oxford: Blackwell Publishing.

March, J.G. (1991) Exploration and exploitation in organizational learning. *Organization Science*, **2**, 71–87.

Marquis, J.G. (1969) The anatomy of successful innovations. *Innovation*, **1**, 28–37.

Maskell, B. (1991) *Performance Measurement for World Class Manufacturing: A Model for American Companies*. Cambridge, MA: Productivity Press.

McCabe, D. (1996) The best laid schemes of TQM: strategy, politics and power. *New Technology, Work and Employment*, **11**(1), 28–38.

McDaniel, S.W. and Kolari, J.W. (1987) Marketing strategy implications of the Miles and Snow strategic typology. *Journal of Marketing*, **51**, 19–30.

McDermott, R. (1999) Why information technology inspired but cannot deliver knowledge management. *California Management Review*, **41**(1), 103–117.

McGrath, R.G. (2001) Exploratory learning, innovative capacity and managerial oversight. *Academy of Management Journal*, **44**, 118–131.

McLoughlin, I. (1999) *Creative Technological Change: The Shaping of Technology and Organizations*. London: Routledge.

Melcher, A., Acar, W. and DuMont, P. (1990) Standard maintaining and continuous improvement systems: experiences and comparisons. *Interfaces*, **20**(3), 24–40.

Menguc, B. and Auh, S. (2006) Creating a firm-level dynamic capability through capitalizing on market orientation and innovativeness. *Journal of the Academy of Marketing Science*, **34**(1), 63–73.

Miles, R.E. and Snow, C.C. (1978) *Organisational Strategy, Structure and Porcess*. New York, NY: McGraw-Hill.

Miller, J. (1992) Designing and implementing anew cost management system. *Journal of Cost Management*, Winter, 41–53.

Miller, R. and Floricel, S. (2007) Games of innovation: a new theoretical perspective. *International Journal of Innovation Management*, Special Issue **11**(1), 1–36.

Miller, R., Olleros, X. and Molinié, L. (2008) Innovation games: a new approach to the competitive challenge. *Long Range Planning*, **41**, 378–94.

Millett, S.M. and Honton, E.J. (1991) *A Manager's Guide to Technology Forecasting and Strategy Analysis Methods*. Columbus, OH: Battelle Press.

Mintzberg, H. and McHugh, A. (1985) Strategy formation in an adhocracy. *Administrative Science Quarterly*, **30**(2), 160–197.

Mintzberg, H. (1978) Patterns in Strategy Formation. *Management Science*, **24**(9), 934–948.

Mintzberg, H. (1979) *The Structuring of Organizations*. Englewood Cliffs: Prentice-Hall.

Mintzberg, H. (1994) Rethinking strategic planning. *Long Range Planning*, **27**(3), 12–30.

Mintzberg, H., Pascale, R.T., Goold, M. and Rumelt, R.P. (1996) The "Honda effect" revisited. *California Management Review*, **38**(4), 78–117.

Mitsuru, K. (1999) Strategic innovation in large companies through strategic community management: an NTT multimedia revolution case study. *European Journal of Innovation Management*, **2**(3), 95–108.

Mole, V., Griffiths, D., Boisot, M. and Lemmon, T. (1996) Spinning a good yarn: the identification of core comptencies at Courtaulds. *International Journal of Technology Management, Special Issue on the Fifth International Forum on Technology Management*, **11**(3/4), 425–440.

Mohrman, S.A., Mohrman, Jr., A.M. and Cohen, S.G. (1995) Organizing knowledge work systems. In M.M. Beyerlein, D.A. Johnson and S.T. Beyerlein (eds.), *Advances in Interdisciplinary Studies of Work Teams Vol. 2: Knowledge Work in Teams*. Greenwich, CT: JAI Press, Inc.

Mom, T.J.M., Van Den Bosch, F.A.J. and Volberda, H.W. (2007) Investigating managers' exploration and exploitation activities: the influence of top-down, bottom-up, and horizontal knowledge inflows. *Journal of Management Studies*, **44**, 910–931.

Morgan, N.A., Zou, S., Vorhies, D.W. and Katsikeas, C.S. (2003) Experiential and informational knowledge, architectural marketing capabilities, and the adaptive performance of export ventures: a cross-national study. *Decision Sciences*, **34**, 287–321.

Morrison, P.D., Roberts, J.H. and Midgley, D.F. (2004) The nature of lead users and measurement of leading edge status. *Research Policy*, **33**, 351–362.

Morton, J.A. (1971) *Organizing for Innovation: A Systems Approach to Technical Management*. New York, NY: McGraw-Hill.

Mowery, D. and Rosenberg, N. (1989) *Technology and the Pursuit of Economic Growth*. Cambridge.

Mowery, D.C. (2009) Plus ca change: industrial R&D in the third industrial revolution. *Industrial and Corporate Change,* **18**(1), 1–50.

Narayanan, V.K., Colwell, K. and Douglas, F.L. (2009) Building organizational and scientific platforms in the pharmaceutical industry: a process perspective on the development of dynamic capabilities. *British Journal of Management*, **20**, 25–40.

Narin, F. (1969) *Principal Investigator. TRACES — Technology in Retrospect and Critical Events in Sciences.* IIT Research Institute. Prepared for NSF under Contract NSF C-535. Vol. 2.

Narin, F. (1976) Evaluative bibliometrics: the use of publication and citation analysis in the evaluation of scientific activity. Contract NSF C-627, National Science Foundation. 31 March, Monograph: 456 p. NTIS Accession #PB252339/AS.

Narin, F. (1991) Globalisation of research, scholarly information and patents — ten-year trends. In *Proceedings of the North American Serials Interest Group (NASIG) Sixth Annual Conference*, 14–17 June.

Narin, F., Noma, E. and Perry, R. (1987) Patents as indicators of corporate technological strength. *Research Policy*, **16**, 143–155.

National Endowment for Science, Technology and the Arts (NESTA) (2008) *The New Inventors: How Users are Changing the Rules of Innovation*. London: NESTA.

Nelson, R. (1991) Why do firms differ and how does it matter? *Strategic Management Journal*, **12**, 61–74.

Nelson, R. and Winter, S. (1982) *An Evolutionary Theory of Economic Change*. Cambridge, MA: Harvard University Press.

Nelson, R.R. (2008) What enables rapid economic progress: what are the needed institutions? *Research Policy*, **37**, 1–11.

Nerkar, A. (2003) Old is gold? The value of temporal exploration in the creation of new knowledge. *Management Science*, **49**, 211–229.

Newell, S., Scarbrough, H., Swan, J. and Hislop, D. (2000) Intranets and knowledge management: de-centred technologies and the limits of technological discourse. In C. Pritchard, R. Hull, M. Chumer and H. Willmott (eds.), *Managing Knowledge: Critical Investigations of Work and Learning*. London: Macmillan.

Newey, L.R. and Zahra, S.A. (2009) The evolving firm: how dynamic and operating capabilities interact to enable entrepreneurship. *British Journal of Management*, **20**, 81–100.

Nightingale, P. (2000) The product-process-organisation relationship in complex development projects. *Research Policy*, **29**(7–8), 913–930.

Nonaka, I. (1991) The knowledge-creating company. *Harvard Business Review*, November/December.

Nonaka, I. (1994) A dynamic theory of organisational knowledge creation. *Organisation Science*, **5**(1), 14–37.

Nooteboom, B. (1996) Globalisation, learning and strategy. Paper delivered at EMOT Workshop, Durham University, 28–30 June.

Nunnally, J.C. and Bernstein, I.H. (1994) *Psychometric Theory*, 3rd edition. New York, NY: McGraw-Hill.

O'Reilly, C.A. and Tushman, M.L. (2004) The ambidextrous organization. *Harvard Business Review*, **82**, 74–81.

O'Reilly, C.A. and Tushman, M.L. (2007) *Ambidexterity as a Dynamic Capability: Resolving the Innovator's Dilemma*. Research Paper N°1963, Stanford.

OECD (1996) *Innovation, Patents and Technological Strategies*. Paris: OECD.

OECD (1992) *OECD Proposed Guidelines for Collecting and Interpreting Technological Innovation Data — Oslo Manual*. OECD/GD(92)26, Paris.

OECD (2009) *Innovation in Firms. A Microeconomic Perspective*. Paris: OECD.

Orlikowski, W. (1992) The duality of technology: rethinking the concept of technology in organizations. *Organization Science*, **3**(3), 398–427.

Orr, J. (1990) Sharing knowledge, celebrating identity: war stories and community memory in a service culture. In D. Middleton and D. Edwards (eds.), *Collective Remembering: Memory in a Society*. London: Sage Publications.

Oskarsson, C. (1993) Diversification and growth in US, Japanese and European multi-technology corporations. Mimeo, Department of Industrial Management and Economics, Chalmers University of Technology, Gothenburg.

Osterloh, M., and Rota, S.G. (2007) Open Source Software Development — Just Another Case of Collective Invention? *Research Policy*, **36**(2), 157–171.

Ouchi, W.G. and Maguire, M.A. (1975) Organization control: two functions. *Administrative Science Quarterly*, **20**, 559–569.

Pakes, A. and Griliches, Z. (1984) Patents and R&D at the firm level: a first look. In Z. Griliches (ed.), *R&D, Patents and Productivity*. Chicago, IL: University of Chicago Press.

Pakes, A. (1985) On patents, R&D and the stock market rate of return. *Journal of Political Economy*, **93**, 390–409.

Palacios Marques, D., Garrigos Simon, F.J. and Devece Caranana, C. (2006) The effect of innovation on intellectual capital: an empirical evaluation in the biotechnology and telecommunications industries. *International Journal of Innovation Management*, **10**(1), 89–112.

Pan, S. and Scarbrough, H. (1999) Knowledge management in practice: an exploratory case study. *Technology Analysis and Strategic Management*, **11**(3), 359–374.

Pandza, K. and Thorpe, R. (2009) Creative search and strategic sense-making: missing dimensions in the concept of dynamic capabilities. *British Journal of Management*, **20**, 118–131.

Partington, D. (2000) Building grounded theories of management action. *British Journal of Management*, **11**, 91–102.

Patel, P. (1995) Localised production of technology for global markets. *Cambridge Journal of Economics*, **19**, 141–154.

Patel, P. (1996) Are large firms internationalising the generation of technology? Some new evidence. *IEEE Transactions on Engineering Management*, **43**, 41–47.

Patel, P. (2011) *Performance Characteristics of Large Firms at the Forefront of Globalization of Technology*. SPRU electronic working paper series (SEWPS), University of Sussex, UK. www.sussex.ac.uk/spru/research/sewps.

Patel, P. and Pavitt, K. (1991) Large firms in the production of the world's technology: an important case of "non-globalisation". *Journal of International Business Studies*, **22**, 1–21.

Patel, P. and Pavitt, K. (1992) The innovative performance of the world's largest firms: some new evidence. *Economics of Innovation and New Technology*, **2**, 91–102.

Patel, P. and Pavitt, K. (1997) The technological competencies of the world's largest firms: complex and path-dependent, but not much variety. *Research Policy*, **26**, 141–156.

Patel, P. and Vega, M. (1998) Technology strategies of large European firms. Draft final report for "Strategic Analysis for European S&T Policy Intelligence" project funded by EC Targetted Socio-Economic Research Programme. Brighton, February 1998.

Patel, P. and Vega, M. (1999) Patterns of internationalisation of corporate technology: location versus home country advantages. *Research Policy*, **28**, 144–155. Patent and Trademark Office (1976) Technology assessment and forecast. US Department of Commerce. Sixth report, June.

Patent and Trademark Office (1995) *Manual of Patent Examining Procedures.* Section 904.02, 6th edition. US Department of Commerce.

Patton, M.Q. (2002) *Qualitative Research and Evaluation Methods.* Thousand Oaks: Sage Publications.

Paulk, M., Curtis, Chrissis and Bush (1993) *Capability Maturity Model for Software.* Pittsburgh, PA: Software Engineering Institute, Carnegie-Mellon University.

Pavitt, K. (1984) Sectoral patterns of technical change: towards a taxonomy and a theory. *Research Policy*, **13**, 343–373.

Pavitt, K. (1988) Uses and abuses of patent statistics. In A.F.J. Van Raen (ed.), *Handbook of Quantitative Studies of Science and Technology.* Amsterdam: North-Holland.

Pavitt, K. (1990) What we know about the strategic management of technology. *California Management Review*, **32**, 17–26.

Pavitt, K. (2000) *Technology, Management and Systems of Innovation.* London: Edward Elgar.

Pavitt, K. (2002) Innovating routines in the business firm: what corporate tasks should they be accomplishing? *Industrial and Corporate Change*, **14**(1), 147–133.

Pavitt, K. and Patel, P. (1988) The international distribution and determinants of technological activities. *Oxford Review of Economic Policy*, **4**(4), 35–55.

Pavitt, K., Robson, M. and Townsend, J. (1987) The size distribution of innovating firms in the UK: 1945–1983. *Journal of Industrial Economics*, **35**, 297–316.

Pavitt, K., Robson, M. and Townsend, J. (1989) Technological accumulation, diversification and organisation in UK companies, 1945–1983. *Management Science*, **35**(1), 3–26.

Pavlou, P.A. and Sawy, O.A.E. (2011) Understanding the elusive black box of dynamic capabilities. *Decision Sciences*, **42**(1).

Pawson, R. (2001) The promise of a realist synthesis. Working Paper, Evidence Network, Queen Mary College, London.

Pearce, J.A., Robbins, D.K. and Robinson, R.B. (1987) The impact of grand strategy and planning formality on financial performance. *Strategic Management Journal*, **8**(2), 125–134.

Pedler, M., Boydell, T. and Burgoyne, J. (1991) *The Learning Company: A Strategy for Sustainable Development.* Maidenhead: McGraw-Hill.

Penrose, E.T. (1968) *The Theory of the Growth of the Firm.* London: Basil Blackwell.

Pentland, B. and Rueter, H. (1994) Organisational routines as grammars of action. *Administrative Science Quarterly*, **39**, 484–510.

Peters, T. and Waterman (1982) *In Search of Excellence.* New York, NY: Harper and Row.

Pike, R., Meerjanssen, J. and Chadwick, L. (1993) The appraisal of ordinary shares by investment analysts in the UK and Germany. *Accounting and Business Research*, **23**(92), 489–499.

Pinto, J.K. and Prescott, J.E. (1988) Variations in critical success factors over the stages in the Project Life-Cycle. *Journal of Management*, **14**(1), 5–18.

Pisano, G.P. (1996) *The Development Factory: Unlocking the Potential of Process Innovation.* Boston, MA: Harvard Business School Press.

Poot, T., Faems, D. and Vanhaverbeke, W. (2009) Toward a dynamic perspective on open innovation: a longitudinal assessment of the adoption of internal and external innovation strategies in the Netherlands. *International Journal of Innovation Management*, **13**(2), 177–200.

Porter, M.E. (1983) The technological dimension of competitive strategy. In R.S. Rosenbloom (ed.), *Research on Technological Innovation, Management* and *Policy*, Volume 1. Greenwich, CT: JAI Press, Inc.

Porter, M.E. (1985) *Competitive Advantage: Creating and Sustaining Superior Performance*. The Free Press.

Porter, M.E. (1991) Towards a Dynamic Theory of Strategy. *Strategic Management Journal*, **12**(Winter Special Issue), 95–117.

Praest, M. (1998) Changing technological capabilities in high-tech firms: a study of the telecomunication industry. *The Journal of High Technology Management Research*, **9**(2), 175–193.

Prahalad, C.K. and Hamel, G. (1990) The core competence of the corporation. *Harvard Business Review*, May/June, **68**, 79–91.

Prahalad, C.K. and Hamel, G. (1994) *Competing for the Future*. Boston, MA: Harvard University Press.

Prahalad, C.K. and Hamel, G. (1996) Keynote address at the strategic management society conference, Phoenix, 10–13 November.

Pratt, M. (2009) From the editors: for the lack of a boilerplate — tips on writing up (and reviewing) qualitative research. *Academy of Management Journal*, **52**(5), 856–862.

Prencipe, A. (1997) Technological competencies and product's evolutionary dynamics: a case study from the aero-engine industry. *Research Policy*, **25**, 1261–1276.

Price, D.J. de Solla (1969) Measuring the size of science, *Proceedings of the Israel Academy of Science and Humanities*, **4**(6), 98–111.

Raelin, J. (1997) A model of work based learning. *Organization Science*, **8**(6), 563–578.

Ramanujam, V. and Mensch, G.O. (1985) Improving the strategy-innovation link. *Journal of Product Innovation Management*, **2**(4), 213–223.

Rappaport, A. (1986) *Creating Shareholder Value: The New Standard for Business Performance*. London: Macmillan.

Rich, B. and Janos (1994) *Skunk Works*. London: Warner Books.

Roberts, E.B. (1987) Introduction: managing technological innovation — a search for generalizations. In E.B. Roberts (ed.), *Generating Technological Innovation*. Oxford: Oxford University Press.

Robinson, R.B. and Pearce, J.A. (1983) The impact of formalized strategic-planning on financial performance in small organizations. *Strategic Management Journal*, **4**(3), 197–207.

Rogers, E.M. (1984) *Diffusion of Innovations*. New York, NY: Free Press.

Rosenberg, N. (1982) *Inside the Black Box: Technology and Economics*. Cambridge: Cambridge University Press.

Rosenberg, N. and Birdzell, Jr., L.E. (1991) Science, technology and the Western miracle. *Scientific American*, **263**(5), 42–54.

Rothwell, R. and Gardiner, P. (1984) Invention and re-innovation — the case of the Hovercraft. SPRU Working Paper, University of Sussex.

Rothwell, R. (1992) Successful industrial innovation: critical success factors for the 1990s. *R&D Management*, **22**(3), 221–239.

Rothwell, R. and Gardiner, P. (1983) Tough customers, good design. *Design Studies*, **4**(3), 161–169.

Rothwell, R., Freeman, C., Horlsey, A., Jervis, V.T.P., Robertson, A.B. and Townsend, J. (1974) SAPPHO updated — project SAPPHO phase II. *Research Policy*, **3**, 258–291.

Roussel, P.A., Saad, K.N. and Erickson, T.J. (1991) *Third Generation R&D: Managing the Link to Corporate Strategy*. Cambridge, MA: Harvard Business School Press.

Rumelt, R.P., Schendel, D. and Teece, D.J. (1991) Strategic management and economics. *Strategic Management Journal*, **12**, 5–29.

Rush, H., Brady, T. and Hobday, M. (1997) *Learning Between Projects in Complex Systems*. Centre for the Study of Complex Systems.

Safizadeh, M.H., Ritzman, L.P., Sharma, D. and Wood, C. (1996) An empirical analysis of the product-process matrix. *Management Science*, **42**, 1576–1591.

Salter, A. and Gann, D. (2003) Sources of ideas for innovation in engineering design. *Research Policy* **32**(8), 1309–1324.

Samuelson, P. (1993) A case study on computer programs. In J. Wallerstein, M. Mogee and R. Schoen (eds.), *Global Dimensions of Intellectual Property Rights in Science and Technology*. Washington, DC: National Academy Press.

Santarelli, E. and Piergiovanni, R. (1996) Analysing literature-based innovation output indicators: the Italian experience. *Research Policy*, **25**, 689–711.

Sapolsky, H.M. (1972) *The Polaris System Development: Bureaucratic and Programmatic Success in Government*. Cambridge, MA: Harvard University Press.

Sapsed, J., Bessant, J., Partington, D., Tranfield, D. and Young, M. (2002) Teamworking and knowledge management: a review of converging themes. *International Journal of Management Reviews*, **4**(1), 71–85.

Scarbrough, H. and Corbett, M. (1992) *Technology and Organization: Power, Meaning and Design*. London: Routledge.

Schankerman, M. and Pakes, A. (1986) Estimates of the value of patent rights in European countries during the post-1950 period. *Economic Journal*, **96**, 1052–1076.

Schein, E. (1984) Coming to a new awareness of organisational culture. *Sloan Management Review*, Winter, 3–16.

Scherer, F.M. (1965) Firm size, market structure, opportunity and the output of patented inventions. *American Economic Review*, **55**, 1097–1125.

Scherer, F.M. and Ravenscraft, D. (1982) *Applied Economics*. Boston, MA: Brookings Institution Press.

Scholes, P. (1974) *The Concise Oxford Dictionary of Music*. London: Oxford University Press.

Schön, D. (1971) *Beyond the Stable State*. New York, NY: Random House.

Schroeder, M. and Robinson, A. (1993) Training, continuous improvement and human relations: the US TWI programs and Japanese management style. *California Management Review*, **35**(2), 35–57.

Schumpeter, J. (1984) *The Theory of Economic Development*. Cambridge, MA: Harvard University Press.

Sciteb/CBI (1991) *R&D Short-termism? Enhancing the R&D Performance of the UK Team*. ORBIC.

Senge, P. (1990) *The Fifth Discipline: The Art and Practice of the Learning Organisation.* New York, NY: Doubleday.

Seppänen, M. (2009) Empirical classification of resources in a business model concept. *Intangible Capital*, **5**(2), 102–124.

Sharman, P. (1993) The role of measurement in activity-based management. *CMA Magazine*, September, 25–29.

Sharrock, W.W. (1974) On owning knowledge. In R. Turner (ed.), *Ethnomethodology: Selected Readings.* Harmondsworth: Penguin.

Shingo, S. (1983) *A Revolution in Manufacturing: The SMED System.* Cambridge, MA: Productivity Press.

Sidhu, J.S., Volberda, H.W. and Commandeur, H.R. (2007) The multifaceted nature of exploration and exploitation. *Organization Science*, **18**, 20–38.

Siguaw, J.A., Simpson, P.M. and Enz, C.A. (2006) Conceptualizing innovation orientation: a framework for study and integration of innovation research. *Journal of Product Innovation Management*, **23**, 556–574.

Silberston, A. (1989) *Technology and Economic Progress.* London: Macmillan.

Simpson, P.M., Siguaw, J.A. and Enz, C.A. (2006) Innovation orientation outcomes: the good and the bad. *Journal of Business Research*, **59**(10–11), 1133–1141.

Sink, D.S. (1991) The role of measurement in achieving world-class quality and productivity management. *Industrial Engineering*, June, 23–28.

Sirkin, H. and Stalk, G. (1990) Fix the process, not the problem. *Harvard Business Review*, July/August, 26–33.

Sirmon, D.G., Hitt, M.A. and Ireland, R.D. (2007) Managing firm resources in dynamic environments to create value: looking inside the black box. *Academy of Management Review*, **32**, 273–292.

Slater, S.F. and Narver, J.C. (1993) Product-market strategy and performance: an analysis of the Miles and Snow typology types. *European Journal of Marketing*, **27**(1), 33–51.

Sloma, R.S. (1980) *How to Measure Management Performance.* London: Macmillan.

Smith, K. (1992) Technological innovation indicators: experience and prospects. *Science and Public Policy*, **19**(6), 383–392.

Smith, K. (2005) Measuring innovation. In J. Fagerberg, D. Mowery and R. Nelson (eds.), *The Oxford Handbook of Innovation.* Oxford: Oxford University Press.

Smith, W.K. and Tushman, M.L. (2005) Managing strategic contradictions: a top management model for managing innovations streams. *Organization Science*, **16**, 522–536.

Snell, S.A. (1992) Control theory in strategic human resource management: the mediating effect of administrative information. *Academy of Management Journal*, **35**, 292–327.

Soete, L. (1979) Firm size and inventive activity: the evidence reconsidered. *European Economic Review*, **12**, 319–340.

Song, M., Nason, R.W. and Di Benedetto, C.A. (2008) Distinctive market and information technology capabilities and strategic types: a cross-national investigation. *Journal of International Market*, **16**, 4–38.

Souder, W.E. (1987) *Managing New Product Innovations.* Idaho Falls, ID: Lexington Books.

Stacey, R.D. (1993) *Strategic Management and Organisational Dynamics.* London: Pitman Publishing.

Star, S.L. and Griesemer, J.R. (1989) Institutional ecology, "translations" and boundary objects: amateurs and professionals in Berkeley's Museum of Vertebrate Zoology, 1907–39. *Social Studies of Science*, **19**, 387–420.

Starbuck, W. and Milliken, F (1988) Challenger: fine tuning the odds until something breaks. *Journal of Management Studies*, **25**(4), 319–340.

Steward, F. (1994) Innovation strategies of UK pharmaceutical companies. Paper presented at the International Conference on Management of Technology, March, Miami.

Stewart, T.A. (1994) Your company's most valuable asset: intellectual capital. *Fortune*, 3 October, 68–74.

Stoneman, P. (1990) The adoption of new technology — theory and evidence. ESRC dissemination conference. London, 4 December.

Storey, J. and Barnett, E. (2000) Knowledge management initiatives: learning from failure. *Journal of Knowledge Management*, **4**(2), 145–156.

Strauss, A. and Corbin, J. (1990) *Basics of Qualitative Research: Grounded Theory Procedures and Techniques*. Newbury Park, CA: Sage Publications.

Strauss, A. and Corbin, J. (1998) *Basics of Qualitative Research.* London: Sage Publications.

Swan, J. and Scarbrough, H. (2005) The politics of networked innovation. *Human Relations*, **58**(7), 913–943.

Swan, J. and Scarbrough, H. (2001) Editorial: knowledge management: concepts and controversies. *Journal of Management Studies*, **38**(7), 913–921.

Swan, J. (2007) Modes of organizing biomedical innovation in the UK and US and the role of integrative and relational capabilities. *Research Policy*, **36**, 529–547.

Swan, J., Newell, S., Scarbrough, H. and Hislop, D. (1999) Knowledge management and innovation: networks and networking. *Journal of Knowledge Management*, **3**(4), 262–275.

Taffler, R.J. (1982) Forecasting company failure in the UK using discriminant analysis and financial ratio data. *Journal of the Royal Statistical Society, Series A*, **145**(3), 342–358.

Taffler, R.J. (1991) Z-scores: an approach to the recession. *Accountancy*, **108**(1175), 95–101.

Taylor, D.M. and Doria, J.R. (1981) Self-serving and group-serving bias in attribution. *Journal of Social Psychology*, **113**, 201–211.

Teece, D. (1986) Profiting from technological innovation: implications for integration, collaboration, licensing and public policy. *Research Policy*, **13**, 343–373.

Teece, D.J. and Pisano, G. (1994) The dynamic capabilities of firms: an introduction. *Industrial and Corporate Change*, **3**, 537–556.

Teece, D.J. (2000) Strategies for managing knowledge assets: the role of firm structure and industrial context. *Long Range Planning*, **33**(1), 35–54.

Teece, D.J. (2006) *Explicating Dynamic Capabilities: The Nature and Microfoundations of (long run) Enterprise Performance*. Working Paper, University of California, Berkeley.

Teece, D.J. (2007) Explicating dynamic capabilities: the nature and microfoundations of (sustainable) enterprise performance. *Strategic Management Journal*, **28**(13), 1319–1350.

Teece, D.J., Pisano, G. and Shuen, A. (1997) Dynamic capabilities and strategic management. *Strategic Management Journal*, **18**(7), 509–533.

Teece, D.J., Pisano, G. and Schuen, A. (1992) Dynamic capabilities and strategic management. Working Paper, University of California, Berkeley.

Tether, B.S., Smith, I.J. and Thwaites, A.T. (1997) Smaller enterprises and innovation in the UK: the SPRU innovations database revisited. *Research Policy*, **26**, 19–32.

Tidd, J. and Bessant, J. (2005) *Managing Innovation: Integrating Technological, Market and Organisational Change*, 3rd edition. Chichester: John Wiley and Sons.

Tidd, J. and Bessant, J. (2009) *Managing Innovation: Integrating Technological, Market and Organisational Change*, 4th edition. Chichester: John Wiley and Sons.

Tidd, J. and Bodley, K. (2002) The effect of project novelty on the new product development process. *R&D Management*, **32**(2), 127–138.

Tidd, J. and Trewhella, M. (1997) Organisational and technological antecedents for knowledge acquisition and learning. *R&D Management*, **27**(4), 359–375.

Tidd, J., Driver, C. and Saunders, P. (1996) Linking technological, market and financial indicators of innovation. *Economics of Innovation and New Technology*, **4**, 155–172.

Tirpak, T.M., Miller, R. Schwartz, L. and Kashdan, D. (2006) R&D structure in a changing world. *Research-Technology Management*, **49**(5), September–October, 19–26.

Toulmin, S. (1969) *The Uses of Argument*. Cambridge: Cambridge University Press.

Townsend, J., Henwood, F., Thomas, G., Pavitt, K. and Wyatt, S. (1981) Innovation in Britain since 1945. SPRU Occasional Paper No. 16, Science Policy Research Unit, Sussex University.

Trajtenberg, M. (1990) A penny for your quotes: patent citations and the value of innovations. *Rank Journal of Economics*, **21**, 11.

Tranfield, D. and Smith, S. (1998) The strategic regeneration of manufacturing by changing routines. *International Journal of Operations and Production Management*, **18**(2), 114–129.

Tranfield, D., Smith, S., Foster, M. and Parry, I. (2000) Strategies for managing the team-working agenda: developing a methodology for team-based organization. *International Journal of Production Economics*, **65**, 33–42.

Tranfield, D., Young, M., Partington, D., Bessant, J. and Sapsed, J.D. (2003) Knowledge management routines for innovation projects: developing an hierarchical model. *International Journal of Innovation Management*, **7**(1), 27–50.

Trott, P. and Hartmann, D. (2009) Why open innovation is old wine in new bottles. *International Journal of Innovation Management*, **13**(4), 715–736.

Trott, P., Maddocks, T. and Wheeler, C. (2009) Core competencies for diversifying: case study of a small business. *Strategic Change*, **18**, 27–43.

Tseng, C.H. (2005) Navigating the international arena with technology capability and market responsiveness: a contingency model exploring the performance satisfaction of small and medium-sized enterprises. *Journal of Applied Management and Entrepreneurship*, **10**, 75–96.

Tsoukas, H. and Vladimirou, E. (2000) On organizational knowledge and its management: an ethnographic investigation. Paper presented at knowledge management: concepts and controversies, University of Warwick, 10–11 February.

Tsoukas, H. (1996) The firm as a distributed knowledge system: a constructionist approach. *Strategic Management Journal*, **17**(Winter Special Issue), 11–25.

Turney, J. (1991) What drives the engines of innovation? *New Scientist*, **40**.

Turney, P.B.B. (1993) Beyond TQM with work-force activity, Management Accounting, September, 28–31.

Tushman, M.L. and Anderson, P. (1986) Technological discontinuities and organizational environments. *Administrative Science Quarterly*, **31**, 439–465.

Tushman, M.L. and O'Reilly, C. (1996) Ambidextrous organizations: managing evolutionary and revolutionary change. *California Management Review*, **38**(4), 8–30.

Utterback, J. (1994) *Mastering the Dynamics of Innovation*. Boston, MA: Harvard School Press.

Van de Ven, A.H. (1986) Central problems in the management of innovation. *Management Science*, **32**, 590–607.

Van de Ven, A.H., Angle, H. and Poole, M.S. (1989) *Research on the Management of Innovation*. New York, NY: Harper and Row.

Van de Ven, A.H. and Poole, M.S. (2005) Alternative approaches for studying organizational change. *Organization Studies*, **26**, 1377–1404.

van Maanen, J. and Barley, S.R. (1984) Occupational communities: culture and control in organizations. In B.M. Staw and L.L. Cummings (eds.), *Research in Organizational Behaviour*. Greenwich, CT: JAI Press, Inc.

Venkatraman, N. and Ramanujan, V. (1986) Measurement of business performance in strategy research: a comparison of approaches. *Academy of Management Review*, **11**, 801–814.

Verburg, R.M., Ortt, J.R. and Dicke, W.M. (2006) *Managing Technology and Innovation: An Introduction*. London; New York, NY: Routledge.

Verona, G. and Ravasi, D. (2003) Unbundling dynamic capabilities: an exploratory study of continuous product innovation. *Industrial and Corporate Change*, **12**, 577–606.

Vitale, J., Mavinac, P. and Hauser, G. (1994) New process-financial scorecard: a strategic measurement system. *Planning Review*, July/August, 22–31.

Volberda, H.W. (1996) Toward the flexible form: how to remain vital in hypercompetitive environments. *Organization Science*, **7**, 359–374.

von Hippel, E. (1976) The dominant role of users in the scientific instrument innovation process. *Research Policy*, **5**, 212–239.

von Hippel, E. (1977) The dominant role of the user in semiconductor and electronic subassembly process innovation. *IEEE Transactions in Engineering Management*, **24**, 60–71.

von Hippel, E. (1986) Lead users: a source of novel product concepts. *Management Science*, **32**, 791–805.

von Hippel, E. (1988) *The Sources of Innovation*. Oxford: Oxford University Press.

von Hippel, E. (2005) *Democratizing Innovation*. Cambridge, MA: MIT Press.

von Hippel, E. and von Krogh, G. (2006) Free revealing and the private-collective model for innovation incentives. *R&D Management*, **36**(3), 295–306.

Wageman, R. (2001) How leaders foster self-managing team effectiveness: design choices versus hands-on coaching. *Organization Science*, **12**(5), 559–577.

Walker, W.B. (1979) *Industrial Innovation and International Trading Performance*. New York, NY: JAI Press, Inc.

Wang, C.L. and Ahmed, P.K. (2007) Dynamic capabilities: a review and research agenda. *International Journal of Management Reviews*, **9**(1), 31–51.

Ward, A. (2000) Getting strategic value from constellations of communities. *Strategy and Leadership*, **28**(2), 4–9.

Wernerfelt, B.A. (1984) A resource-based view of the firm. *Strategic Management Journal*, **5**, 171–180.

Whitley, R. (2006) Project-based firms: new organizational form or variations on a theme? *Industrial and Corporate Change*, **15**(1), 77–99.

Whyte, J., Ewenstein, B., Hales, M. and Tidd, J. (2008) How to visualize knowledge in project-based work. *Long Range Planning*, **41**(1), 74–92.

Winter, S.G. (2003) Understanding dynamic capabilities. *Strategic Management Journal*, **24**, 991–995.

Womack, J.P., Jones, D.T. and Roos, D. (1990) *The Machine that Changed the World*. New York, NY: Rawson Associates.

Woodman, R.W., Sawyer, J.E. and Griffin, R.W. (1993) Toward a theory of organizational creativity. *Academy of Management Review*, **18**, 293–321.

Woodward, J. (1958) *Management and Technology*. London: HMSO.

Worcester Polytechnic Institute (1988) Analysis of highly cited patents: are they important? Report prepared for the US Patent Office, 16 December.

Worren, N., Moore, K. and Cardona, P. (2002) Modularity, strategic flexibility, and firm performance: a study of the home appliance industry. *Strategic Management Journal*, **23**(12), 1123–1140.

Yin, R.K. (2009) *Case Study Research. Design and Methods*, 4th edition. Thousand Oaks, CA: Sage Publications.

Zahra, S.A., Sapienza, H.J. and Davidsson, P. (2006) Entrepreneurship and dynamic capabilities: a review, model and research agenda. *Journal of Management Studies*, **43**(4), 917–955.

Zairi, M. (1992) *TQM-based Performance Measurement: Practical Guidelines*. Letchworth: Technical Communications Publishing.

Zairi, M. (1994) *Measuring Performance for Business Results*. London: Chapman and Hall.

Zairi, M. and Letza, S. (1995) Performance measurement: a challenge for total quality and the accounting professions. *Asia-Pacific Journal of Quality Management*, **3**(2), 26–41.

Zeithaml, V.A., Berry, L.L. and Parasuraman, A. (1996) The behavioral consequences of service quality. *Journal of Marketing*, **60**(2), 31–46.

Zhao, J. (2009) Diversified business groups and corporate restructuring in China. *Management Research News*, **32**(9), 874–887.

Zhou, K.Z., Kin, C., Tse, Y. and Tse, D.K. (2005) The effects of strategic orientations on technology- and market-based breakthrough innovations. *Journal of Marketing*, **69**(April), 42–60.

Zollo, M. and Winter, S.G. (2002) Deliberate learning and the evolution of dynamic capabilities. *Organization Science*, **13**(3), 339–351

Index